GW00482526

Suzuki GSX1400
Service and Repair Manual

by Matthew Coombs

Models covered

(4758-272)

GSX1400K2. 1402cc. 2002
GSX1400K3. 1402cc. 2003
GSX1400K4. 1402cc. 2004
GSX1400K5. 1402cc. 2005
GSX1400K6. 1402cc. 2006
GSX1400K7. 1402cc. 2007

© Haynes Publishing 2008

ABCDE
FGHIJ
KLMNO
PQRST

A book in the Haynes Service and Repair Manual Series

ISBN: 978 1 84425 758 4

British Library Cataloguing in Publication Data
A catalogue record for this book is available from the British Library.

Printed in the USA

Haynes Publishing
Sparkford, Yeovil, Somerset BA22 7JJ, England

Haynes North America, Inc
861 Lawrence Drive, Newbury Park, California 91320, USA

Haynes Publishing Nordiska AB
Box 1504, 751 45 Uppsala, Sweden

Contents

LIVING WITH YOUR SUZUKI GSX1400

Introduction

Pre-ride checks

MAINTENANCE

Routine maintenance and servicing

Contents

REPAIRS AND OVERHAUL

Engine, transmission and associated systems

Chassis components

Electrical system

Wiring diagrams

REFERENCE

Index

Suzuki
Every Which Way

by Julian Ryder

From Textile Machinery to Motorcycles

Suzuki were the second of Japan's Big Four motorcycle manufacturers to enter the business, and like Honda they started by bolting small two-stroke motors to bicycles. Unlike Honda, they had manufactured other products before turning to transportation in the aftermath of World War II. In fact Suzuki has been in business since the first decade of the 20th-Century when Michio Suzuki manufactured textile machinery.

The desperate need for transport in post-war Japan saw Suzuki make their first motorised bicycle in 1952, and the fact that by 1954 the company had changed its name to Suzuki Motor Company shows how quickly the sideline took over the whole company's activities. In their first full manufacturing year, Suzuki made nearly 4500 bikes and rapidly expanded into the world markets with a range of two-strokes.

Suzuki didn't make a four-stroke until 1977 when the GS750 double-overhead-cam across-the-frame four arrived. This was several years after Honda and Kawasaki had established the air-cooled four as the industry standard, but no motorcycle epitomises the era of what came to be known as the Universal Japanese motorcycle better than the GS. So well engineered were the original fours that you can clearly see their genes in the GS500 twins that are still going strong in the mid-1990s. Suzuki's ability to prolong the life of their products this way means that they are often thought of as a conservative company. This is hardly fair if you look at some of their landmark designs, most of which have been commercial as well as critical successes.

Two-stroke Success

Early racing efforts were bolstered by the arrival of Ernst Degner who defected from the East German MZ team at the Swedish GP of 1961, bringing with him the rotary-valve secrets of design genius Walter Kaaden. The new Suzuki 50 cc racer won its first GP on the Isle of Man the following year and winning the title easily. Only Honda

and Ralph Bryans interrupted Suzuki's run of 50 cc titles from 1962 to 1968.

The arrival of the twin-cylinder 125 racer in 1963 enabled Hugh Anderson to win both 50 and 125 world titles. You may not think 50 cc racing would be exciting - until you learn that the final incarnation of the thing had 14 gears and could do well over 100 mph on fast circuits. Before pulling out of GPs in 1967 the 50 cc racer won six of the eight world titles chalked up by Suzuki during the 1960s as well as providing Mitsuo Itoh with the distinction of being the only Japanese rider to win an Isle of Man TT. Mr Itoh still works for Suzuki, he's in charge of their racing program.

Europe got the benefit of Suzuki's two-stroke expertise in a succession of air-cooled twins, the six-speed 250 cc Super Six being the most memorable, but the arrival in 1968 of the first of a series of 500 cc twins which were good looking, robust and versatile marked the start of mainstream success.

So confident were Suzuki of their two-stroke expertise that they even applied

it to the burgeoning Superbike sector. The GT750 water-cooled triple arrived in 1972. It was big, fast and comfortable although the handling and stopping power did draw some comment. Whatever the drawbacks of the road bike, the engine was immensely successful in Superbike and Formula 750 racing. The roadster has its devotees, though, and is now a sought-after bike on the classic Japanese scene. Do not refer to it as the Water Buffalo in such company. Joking aside, the later disc-braked versions were quite civilised, but the audacious idea of using a big two-stroke motor in what was essentially a touring bike was a surprising success until the fuel crisis of the mid-'70s effectively killed off big strokers.

The same could be said of Suzuki's only real lemon, the RE5. This is still the only mass-produced bike to use the rotary (or Wankel) engine but never sold well. Fuel consumption in the mid-teens allied to frightening complexity and excess weight meant the RE5 was a non-starter in the sales race.

The T500 two-stroke twin

Development of the Four-stroke range

When Suzuki got round to building a four-stroke they did a very good job of it. The GS fours were built in 550, 650, 750, 850, 1000 and 1100 cc sizes in sports, custom, roadster and even shaft-driven touring forms over many years. The GS1000 was in on the start of Superbike racing in the early 1970s and the GS850 shaft-driven tourer was around nearly 15 years later. The fours spawned a line of 400, 425, 450 and 500 cc GS twins that were essentially the middle half of the four with all their reliability. If there was ever a criticism of the GS models it was that with the exception of the GS1000S of 1980, colloquially known as the ice-cream van, the range was visually uninspiring.

They nearly made the same mistake when they launched the four-valve-head GSX750 in 1979. Fortunately, the original twin-shock version was soon replaced by the 'E'-model with Full-Floater rear suspension and a full set of all the gadgets the Japanese industry was then keen on and has since forgotten about, like 16-inch front wheels and anti-dive forks. The air-cooled GSX was like the GS built in 550, 750 and 1100 cc versions with a variety of half, full and touring fairings, but the GSX that is best remembered is the Katana that first appeared in 1981. The power was provided by an 1000 or 1100 cc GSX motor, but wrapped around it was the most outrageous styling package to come out of Japan. Designed by Hans Muth of Target Design, the Katana looked like nothing seen before or since. At the time there was as much anti feeling as praise, but now it is rightly regarded as a classic, a true milestone in motorcycle design. The factory have even started making 250 and 400 cc fours for the home market with the same styling as the 1981 bike.

Just to remind us that they'd still been building two-strokes for the likes of Barry Sheene, in 1986 Suzuki marketed a road-going version of their RG500 square-four racer which had put an end to the era of the four-stroke in 500 GPs when it appeared in 1974. In 1976 Suzuki not only won their first 500 title with Sheene, they sold RG500s over the counter and won every GP with them - with the exception of the Isle of Man TT which the works riders boycotted. Ten years on, the RG500 Gamma gave road riders the nearest experience they'd ever get to riding a GP bike. The fearsome beast could top 140 mph and only weighed 340 lb - the other alleged GP replicas were pussy cats compared to the Gamma's man-eating tiger.

The RG only lasted a few years and is already firmly in the category of collector's item; its four-stroke equivalent, the GSX-R, is still with us and looks like being so for many years. You have to look back to 1985 and its launch to realise just what a revolutionary step the GSX-R750 was: quite simply it was the first race replica.

One of the later GT750 'kettle' models with front disc brakes

Suzuki's GT250X7 was an instant hit in the popular 250 cc 'learner' sector

The GS400 was the first in a line of four-stroke twins

The GS750 led the way for a series of four cylinder models

Not a bike dressed up to look like a race bike, but a genuine racer with lights on, a bike that could be taken straight to the track and win.

The first GSX-R, the 750, had a completely new motor cooled by oil rather than water and an aluminium cradle frame. It was sparse, a little twitchy and very, very fast. This time Suzuki got the looks right, blue and white bodywork based on the factory's racing colours and endurance-racer lookalike twin headlights. And then came the 1100 - the big GSX-R got progressively more brutal as it chased the Yamaha EXUP for the heavyweight championship.

And alongside all these mould-breaking designs, Suzuki were also making the best looking custom bikes to come out of Japan, the Intruders; the first race replica trail bike, the DR350; the sharpest 250 Supersports, the RGV250; and a bargain-basement 600, the Bandit. The Bandit proved so popular they went on to build 1200 and 750 cc versions of it. I suppose that's predictable, a range of four-stroke fours just like the GS and GSXs. It's just like the company really, sometimes predictable, admittedly - but never boring.

Big is Beautiful

There was a time, somewhere around 1980, when all motorcycles looked like the Suzuki GSX1400. The great American journalist, Ducati hero and Daytona winner Cook Neilson is generally credited with inventing the term Universal Japanese Motorcycle to describe what the Big Four were producing: air-cooled, across-the-frame fours in conventional duplex loop steel frames. Honda made the CB, Kawasaki the Z and Suzuki the GS ranges. Yamaha hadn't quite got a handle on four-strokes then. The companies' paths diverged when liquid cooling became the norm in the early 1980s, although the in-line four layout remained the most economical way to build a performance engine, or any other engine come to that.

The GSX1400 harks back to those days in more than one way, while hiding some very 21st-century technology. In Japan, this class of bike is often referred to as naked sports, there was even a racing class called NK-1 for these big, unfaired muscle bikes, all part of an attempt to wean us off those expensive supersports machines that need updating every year. The Japanese factories have tried to do this before but the UK market refuses to end its love affair with race replicas. You occasionally hear people talking about the retro bike boom of twenty years ago, but it never happened. What there was both in Japan and Europe was a Kawasaki Zephyr boom. No other factory managed to achieve anywhere near the sales figures that Kawasaki got? Big trail bikes? Europe was knee-deep in Yamaha Ténérés for a few years but again no-one else sold anywhere near the same volume.

The big GSX was Suzuki's attempt to exploit a new niche market. It's difficult to call it retro

Later four-stroke models, like this GSX1100, were fitted with 16v engines

The GSX1400K3

when the bike has very racy three-spoke wheels and fuel injection, but there are styling cues from all over recent history: gold six-pot calipers are very 1990s, the twin-shock swinging arm with its piggy-back reservoir units goes back another decade. The circular, chromed headlamp and twin clocks, also in chrome housings, plus the very spindly looking forks are also very 1980s. Thankfully for many riders who use their bikes for things other than track days the tank range of nearly 200 miles, big seat and passenger carrying ability are also throwbacks to days gone. Unfortunately, all-up weight of well over 200kg also harks back to the behemoths of the past.

Surprisingly for a bike of this type, it isn't a parts bin special. Sure the oil and air-cooled motor has the DNA of the first GSX-Rs and the later Bandit, also intended as a budget alternative to the cutting edge sportsters of the time, but the 1400 doesn't share any

major engine castings with its ancestors. That was obviously an expensive and therefore risky way to go with a bike that was intended for the European market only – the GSX1400 has never been sold in the USA. However, Suzuki's faith was justified and the bike has been in continuous production since 2002 with the only modification of any note being the change from a four-into-two exhaust layout to four-into-one for the 2005 model. That sort of model longevity simplifies things for everyone and keeps costs down from manufacturer through to the end user. It also helps keep second-hand values buoyant.

There is no doubt about it, Suzuki got it right and most owners don't tend to think about their GSX1400 as a retro bike, they prefer the description 'muscle bike'. It's difficult to argue. The fuel injection is good enough to make gear changing all but redundant and – crucially – it's got enough attitude to look the

part. Forget the GSX-R and the Bandit, take another look at those oblong caps over the ends of the camshafts on the cylinder head. What do they remind you of? How about the original GSX1100 from the early 1980s? Now that was a muscle bike.

Acknowledgements

Our thanks are due to V & J Motorcycles of Yeovil who supplied the machine featured in the illustrations throughout this manual. We would also like to thank NGK Spark Plugs (UK) Ltd for supplying the colour spark plug condition photographs, the Avon Rubber Company for supplying information on tyre fitting and Draper Tools Ltd for some of the workshop tools shown.

Thanks are also due to Julian Ryder who wrote the introduction 'Every Which Way', and to Suzuki (GB) Ltd who supplied model photographs.

About this manual

The aim of this manual is to help you get the best value from your motorcycle. It can do so in several ways. It can help you decide what work must be done, even if you choose to have it done by a dealer; it provides information and procedures for routine maintenance and servicing; and it offers diagnostic and repair procedures to follow when trouble occurs.

We hope you use the manual to tackle the work yourself. For many simpler jobs, doing it yourself may be quicker than arranging an appointment to get the motorcycle into a dealer and making the trips to leave it and pick it up. More importantly, a lot of money can be saved by avoiding the expense the shop must pass on to you to cover its labour and overhead costs. An added benefit is the sense of satisfaction and accomplishment that you feel after doing the job yourself.

References to the left or right side of the motorcycle assume you are sitting on the seat, facing forward.

We take great pride in the accuracy of information given in this manual, but motorcycle manufacturers make alterations and design changes during the production run of a particular motorcycle of which they do not inform us. No liability can be accepted by the authors or publishers for loss, damage or injury caused by any errors in, or omissions from, the information given.

Illegal copying

The GSX1400K5

Bike spec

Dimensions, weights and capacities

Wheelbase	1520 mm
Overall length	2160 mm
Overall height	1140 mm
Overall width	810 mm
Seat height	790 mm
Ground clearance	130 mm
Dry weight	
K2 and K3	228 kg
K4	229 kg
K5, K6 and K7	226 kg
Fuel tank capacity	22 litres

Engine

Type	Liquid cooled, in-line 4-cylinder
Capacity	1402 cc
Bore	81.0 mm
Stroke	68.0 mm
Compression ratio	9.5:1
Camshafts	DOHC, chain driven
Valves	4 valves per cylinder
Fuel system	Fuel injection
Clutch	Wet multi-plate, hydraulically operated
Transmission	6 speed constant mesh
Final drive	
Chain	RK GB50GSVZ3 (116 links)
Sprockets	18 tooth front, 41 tooth rear

Chassis

Type	Twin cradle, tubular steel
Rake	26°
Trail	105 mm
Front suspension	
Type	40 mm Telescopic forks
Travel	130 mm
Adjustments	Spring pre-load, compression and rebound damping
Rear suspension	
Type	Twin shock
Wheel travel	123 mm
Adjustments	Spring pre-load, compression and rebound damping
Tyre sizes	
Front	120/70 ZR 17 58W
Rear	190/50 ZR 17 73W
Brakes	
Front	Twin 320 mm discs with opposed six-piston calipers
Rear	Single 260 mm disc with opposed two-piston caliper

Model development

GSX1400K2

The K2 model was introduced in September 2001 and falls very obviously into the 'naked retro muscle bike' category.

The engine is an air/oil-cooled in-line four-cylinder with double overhead camshafts driven by chain off the middle of the crankshaft. Drive is transmitted to the six-speed gearbox via a wet multi-plate clutch with back-torque limiter, and to the rear wheel by chain and sprockets.

The double cradle frame is made from tubular steel and has a detachable section on the right-hand side to ease removal of the engine. The front suspension uses conventional telescopic forks with three-way adjustment. The rear suspension uses twin remote reservoir shock absorbers with three-way adjustment, and an aluminium swingarm.

The front brake system has twin discs with six piston calipers, while the rear system has a single disc and a two-piston caliper.

The engine is fed by a fuel injection system that uses Mikuni throttle bodies and a Mitsubishi management system, and the exhaust system is four-into two on K2, K3 and K4 models, and four-into-one on K5, K6 and K7 models.

Colours are blue and white, blue, and silver.

GSX1400K3

Detail changes in 2003 (K3 model) include re-wiring the headlight and changing the switches to conform to the new 'always-on' legislation, and the use of taper roller bearings in the steering head instead of caged ball bearings.

GSX1400K4

In 2004 (K4 model) the engine control module (ECM) was changed, and colours were blue/white, red/black, and black.

GSX1400K5

In 2005 (K5 model) a new four-into-two-into-one exhaust system was fitted, and an immobiliser system was introduced. Colours are blue/white, red/blue, and black.

GSX1400K6 and K7

There were no changes to the K6 and K7 models.

Professional mechanics are trained in safe working procedures. However enthusiastic you may be about getting on with the job at hand, take the time to ensure that your safety is not put at risk. A moment's lack of attention can result in an accident, as can failure to observe simple precautions.

There will always be new ways of having accidents, and the following is not a comprehensive list of all dangers; it is intended rather to make you aware of the risks and to encourage a safe approach to all work you carry out on your bike.

Asbestos

● Certain friction, insulating, sealing and other products - such as brake pads, clutch linings, gaskets, etc. - contain asbestos. Extreme care must be taken to avoid inhalation of dust from such products since it is hazardous to health. If in doubt, assume that they do contain asbestos.

Fire

● Remember at all times that petrol is highly flammable. Never smoke or have any kind of naked flame around, when working on the vehicle. But the risk does not end there - a spark caused by an electrical short-circuit, by two metal surfaces contacting each other, by careless use of tools, or even by static electricity built up in your body under certain conditions, can ignite petrol vapour, which in a confined space is highly explosive. Never use petrol as a cleaning solvent. Use an approved safety solvent.

● Always disconnect the battery earth terminal before working on any part of the fuel or electrical system, and never risk spilling fuel on to a hot engine or exhaust.

● It is recommended that a fire extinguisher of a type suitable for fuel and electrical fires is kept handy in the garage or workplace at all times. Never try to extinguish a fuel or electrical fire with water.

Fumes

● Certain fumes are highly toxic and can quickly cause unconsciousness and even death if inhaled to any extent. Petrol vapour comes into this category, as do the vapours from certain solvents such as trichloro-ethylene. Any draining or pouring of such volatile fluids should be done in a well ventilated area.

● When using cleaning fluids and solvents, read the instructions carefully. Never use materials from unmarked containers - they may give off poisonous vapours.

● Never run the engine of a motor vehicle in an enclosed space such as a garage. Exhaust fumes contain carbon monoxide which is extremely poisonous; if you need to run the engine, always do so in the open air or at least have the rear of the vehicle outside the workplace.

The battery

● Never cause a spark, or allow a naked light near the vehicle's battery. It will normally be giving off a certain amount of hydrogen gas, which is highly explosive.

● Always disconnect the battery ground (earth) terminal before working on the fuel or electrical systems (except where noted).

Electricity

● When using an electric power tool, inspection light etc., always ensure that the appliance is correctly connected to its plug and that, where necessary, it is properly grounded (earthed). Do not use such appliances in damp conditions and, again, beware of creating a spark or applying excessive heat in the vicinity of fuel or fuel vapour. Also ensure that the appliances meet national safety standards.

● A severe electric shock can result from touching certain parts of the electrical system, such as the spark plug wires (HT leads), when the engine is running or being cranked, particularly if components are damp or the insulation is defective. Where an electronic ignition system is used, the secondary (HT) voltage is much higher and could prove fatal.

Remember...

✗ **Don't** start the engine without first ascertaining that the transmission is in neutral.

✗ **Don't** suddenly remove the pressure cap from a hot cooling system - cover it with a cloth and release the pressure gradually first, or you may get scalded by escaping coolant.

✗ **Don't** attempt to drain oil until you are sure it has cooled sufficiently to avoid scalding you.

✗ **Don't** grasp any part of the engine or exhaust system without first ascertaining that it is cool enough not to burn you.

✗ **Don't** allow brake fluid or antifreeze to contact the machine's paintwork or plastic components.

✗ **Don't** siphon toxic liquids such as fuel, hydraulic fluid or antifreeze by mouth, or allow them to remain on your skin.

✗ **Don't** inhale dust - it may be injurious to health (see Asbestos heading).

✗ **Don't** allow any spilled oil or grease to remain on the floor - wipe it up right away, before someone slips on it.

✗ **Don't** use ill-fitting spanners or other tools which may slip and cause injury.

✗ **Don't** lift a heavy component which may be beyond your capability - get assistance.

✗ **Don't** rush to finish a job or take unverified short cuts.

✗ **Don't** allow children or animals in or around an unattended vehicle.

✗ **Don't** inflate a tyre above the recommended pressure. Apart from overstressing the carcass, in extreme cases the tyre may blow off forcibly.

✔ **Do** ensure that the machine is supported securely at all times. This is especially important when the machine is blocked up to aid wheel or fork removal.

✔ **Do** take care when attempting to loosen a stubborn nut or bolt. It is generally better to pull on a spanner, rather than push, so that if you slip, you fall away from the machine rather than onto it.

✔ **Do** wear eye protection when using power tools such as drill, sander, bench grinder etc.

✔ **Do** use a barrier cream on your hands prior to undertaking dirty jobs - it will protect your skin from infection as well as making the dirt easier to remove afterwards; but make sure your hands aren't left slippery. Note that long-term contact with used engine oil can be a health hazard.

✔ **Do** keep loose clothing (cuffs, ties etc. and long hair) well out of the way of moving mechanical parts.

✔ **Do** remove rings, wristwatch etc., before working on the vehicle - especially the electrical system.

✔ **Do** keep your work area tidy - it is only too easy to fall over articles left lying around.

✔ **Do** exercise caution when compressing springs for removal or installation. Ensure that the tension is applied and released in a controlled manner, using suitable tools which preclude the possibility of the spring escaping violently.

✔ **Do** ensure that any lifting tackle used has a safe working load rating adequate for the job.

✔ **Do** get someone to check periodically that all is well, when working alone on the vehicle.

✔ **Do** carry out work in a logical sequence and check that everything is correctly assembled and tightened afterwards.

✔ **Do** remember that your vehicle's safety affects that of yourself and others. If in doubt on any point, get professional advice.

● If in spite of following these precautions, you are unfortunate enough to injure yourself, seek medical attention as soon as possible.

UK market models

Code	Year	Initial frame No.
K2	2002	JS1BN111200100001
K3	2003	JS1BN111200101509
K4	2004	JS1BN111200102981
K5	2005	not available
K6	2006	JS1BN111200104213
K7	2007	JS1BN111200104876

General Europe market models

Code	Year	Initial frame No.
K2	2002	JS1BN111100100001
K3	2003	JS1BN111100107358
K4	2004	JS1BN111100110570
K5	2005	not available
K6	2006	JS1BN111100114965
K7	2007	JS1BN111100117193

Australia market models

Code	Year	Initial frame No.
K2	2002	JS1BN111300100001
K3	2003	JS1BN111300100331
K4	2004	JS1BN121300100001
K5	2005	not available
K6	2006	JS1BN121300100461
K7	2007	JS1BN121300100943

Frame and engine numbers

The frame serial number is stamped into the right-hand side of the steering head and is repeated on the VIN plate on the left-hand frame downtube. The engine number is stamped into the back of the crankcase. Both of these numbers should be recorded and kept in a safe place so they can be furnished to law enforcement officials in the event of a theft.

The frame serial number and engine serial number should also be kept in a handy place (such as with your driving licence) so they are always available when purchasing or ordering parts for your machine.

Identifying model codes

The procedures in this manual identify the bikes by model code, e.g. K5. The model code corresponds to the production year (which may not necessarily be the same as the year of first registration). The codes can be established from the frame number.

Buying spare parts

Once you have found all the identification numbers, record them for reference when buying parts. Since the manufacturers change specifications, parts and vendors (companies that manufacture various components on the machine), providing the ID numbers is the only way to be reasonably sure that you are buying the correct parts.

Whenever possible, take the worn part to the dealer so direct comparison with the new component can be made. Along the trail from the manufacturer to the parts shelf, there are numerous places that the part can end up with the wrong number or be listed incorrectly.

The two places to purchase new parts for your motorcycle – the franchised or main dealer and the parts/accessories store – differ in the type of parts they carry. While dealers can obtain every single genuine part for your motorcycle, the accessory store is usually limited to normal high wear items such as chains and sprockets, brake pads, spark plugs and cables, and to tune-up parts and various engine gaskets, etc. Rarely will an accessory outlet have major suspension components, camshafts, transmission gears, or engine cases.

Used parts can be obtained from breakers yards for roughly half the price of new ones, but you can't always be sure of what you're getting. Once again, take your worn part to the breaker for direct comparison, or when ordering by mail order make sure that you can return it if you are not happy.

Whether buying new, used or rebuilt parts, the best course is to deal directly with someone who specialises in your particular make.

The frame number is on the right-hand side of the steering head

The VIN plate is on the left-hand frame downtube

The engine number is stamped into the back of the crankcase

Engine oil level

Before you start

✔ Put the bike on the centrestand on level ground.
✔ Start the engine and allow it to reach normal operating temperature.
Caution: Do not run the engine in an enclosed space such as a garage or workshop.
✔ Stop the engine and allow the motorcycle to stand undisturbed for a few minutes to allow the oil level to stabilise.

Bike care

● If you have to add oil frequently, you should check whether you have any oil leaks. If there is no sign of oil leakage from the joints and gaskets the engine could be burning oil (see *Fault Finding*).

The correct oil

● Modern, high-revving engines place great demands on their oil. It is very important that the correct oil for your bike is used.
● Always top up with a good quality motorcycle oil of the specified type and viscosity and do not overfill the engine.

Oil type	API grade SF/SG or SH/SJ with JASO MA
Oil viscosity	SAE 10W/40

1 Wipe the oil level window in the clutch cover so that it is clean.

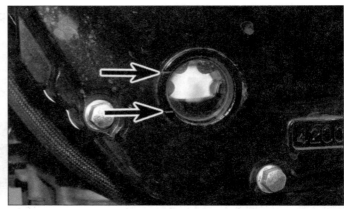

2 With the motorcycle held upright, the oil level should lie between the upper and lower level lines (arrowed).

3 If the level is on or below the lower line, remove the filler cap from the top of the clutch cover.

4 Top the engine up with the recommended grade and type of oil, to bring the level almost up to the upper line on the window. Do not overfill. Refit the filler cap.

Clutch fluid level

> ⚠️ **Warning: Clutch hydraulic fluid can harm your eyes and damage painted surfaces, so use extreme caution when handling and pouring it and cover surrounding surfaces with rag. Do not use fluid from an opened container as it is hygroscopic (absorbs moisture from the air).**

Before you start

✔ Support the motorcycle on the centrestand when checking the fluid level.
✔ The clutch fluid reservoir is on the left-hand handlebar – position the handlebars so the reservoir is as level as possible.
✔ If topping up is necessary, make sure you have the correct hydraulic fluid. DOT 4 is recommended.
✔ Wrap a rag around the reservoir to ensure that any spillage does not come into contact with painted surfaces.

Bike care

● If the fluid reservoir requires repeated topping-up there is a leak somewhere in the system, which must be investigated immediately.
● Check for signs of fluid leakage from the hydraulic hose and release system components – if found, rectify immediately (see Chapter 2).
● Check the operation of the clutch before taking the machine on the road; if there is evidence of air in the system (spongy feel to lever, difficulty selecting gears and clutch drag), it must be bled (see Chapter 2).

1 The clutch fluid level is visible through the window in the reservoir body – it must be above the LOWER level line (arrowed).

2 If the level is on or below the LOWER level line, undo the reservoir cover screws, then remove the cover, the diaphragm plate and the diaphragm.

3 Top up with new clean DOT 4 brake fluid until the level is just below the top of the window. Do not overfill the reservoir, and take care to avoid spills (see **Warning** above).

4 Wipe any moisture out of the diaphragm using an absorbent lint-free cloth.

5 Ensure that the diaphragm is correctly seated before fitting the plate and cover. Tighten the cover screws.

Suspension, steering and drive chain

Suspension and steering

● Check that the front and rear suspension operates smoothly without binding.
● Check that the suspension is adjusted as required.
● Check that the steering moves smoothly from lock-to-lock.

Drive chain

● Check that the drive chain slack isn't excessive, and adjust if necessary (see Chapter 1).
● If the chain looks dry, lubricate it (see Chapter 1).

Brake fluid levels

> ⚠ **Warning:** *Brake hydraulic fluid can harm your eyes and damage painted surfaces, so use extreme caution when handling and pouring it and cover surrounding surfaces with rag. Do not use fluid that has been standing open for some time, as it absorbs moisture from the air which can cause a dangerous loss of braking effectiveness.*

Before you start

✔ Support the motorcycle on the centrestand when checking the fluid level.

✔ The front master cylinder reservoir is on the right-hand handlebar – position the handlebars so the reservoir is as level as possible.

✔ The rear master cylinder reservoir is located behind the right-hand side panel – the panel has a cut-out through which the fluid level is visible, but remove the panel if required to improve the view (see Chapter 7).

✔ If topping up is necessary, make sure you have the correct hydraulic fluid. DOT 4 is recommended.

✔ Wrap a rag around the reservoir being worked on to ensure that any spillage does not come into contact with painted surfaces.

Bike care

● The fluid level in the front and rear brake master cylinder reservoirs will drop slightly as the brake pads wear down.

● If any fluid reservoir requires repeated topping-up this is an indication of an hydraulic leak somewhere in the system, which should be investigated immediately.

● Check for signs of fluid leakage from the hydraulic hoses and components – if found, rectify immediately.

● Check the operation of both brakes before taking the machine on the road; if there is evidence of air in the system (spongy feel to lever or pedal), it must be bled as described in Chapter 6.

FRONT BRAKE

1 The front brake fluid level is visible through the window in the reservoir body – it must be above the LOWER level line (arrowed).

2 If the level is on or below the LOWER level line, undo the reservoir cover screws, then remove the cover, the diaphragm plate and the diaphragm.

3 Top up with new clean DOT 4 brake fluid until the level is just below the top of the window. Do not overfill the reservoir, and take care to avoid spills (see **Warning** above).

4 Wipe any moisture out of the diaphragm using an absorbent lint-free cloth.

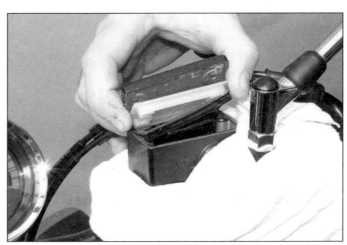

5 Ensure that the diaphragm is correctly seated before fitting the plate and cover. Tighten the cover screws.

REAR BRAKE

1 The rear brake fluid level is visible through the translucent body of the reservoir – the fluid level must be between the UPPER and LOWER level lines (arrowed).

2 If the level is on or below the LOWER level line, remove the right-hand side panel (see Chapter 7). Undo the reservoir cover screws and remove the cover and diaphragm.

3 Top up with new clean DOT 4 brake fluid, until the level is just below the UPPER level line. Do not overfill the reservoir, and take care to avoid spills (see **Warning** above).

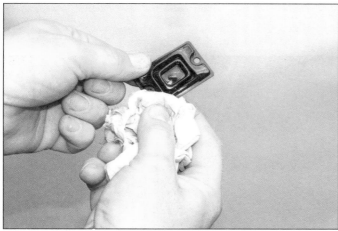

4 Wipe any moisture out of the diaphragm using an absorbent lint-free cloth.

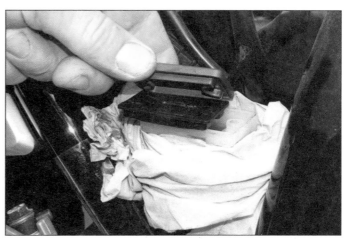

5 Ensure that the diaphragm is correctly seated before fitting the cover. Tighten the cover screws. Install the side panel (see Chapter 7).

Legal and safety checks

Lighting and signalling
● Take a minute to check that the headlight, tail light, brake light, instrument lights and turn signals all work correctly.
● Check that the horn sounds when the button is pushed.
● A working speedometer graduated in mph is a statutory requirement in the UK.

Safety
● Check that the throttle grip rotates smoothly and snaps shut when released, in all steering positions. Also check for the correct amount of freeplay (see Chapter 1).
● Check that the steering moves freely from lock-to-lock.
● Check that the brake lever and pedal, clutch lever and gearchange lever operate smoothly. Lubricate them at the specified intervals or when necessary (see Chapter 1).
● Check that the engine shuts off when the kill switch is operated. Check the starter interlock circuit works correctly (see Chapter 1).
● Check that the stand return springs hold the stands securely up when retracted.

Fuel
● This may seem obvious, but check that you have enough fuel to complete your journey. If you notice signs of fuel leakage – rectify the cause immediately.
● Ensure you use the correct grade unleaded fuel – see Chapter 4 Specifications.

Tyres

The correct pressures

● The tyres must be checked when cold, not immediately after riding. Note that low tyre pressures may cause the tyre to slip on the rim or come off. High tyre pressures will cause abnormal tread wear and unsafe handling.

● Tyre pressure changes as air temperature and atmospheric pressure changes – hence the need for a daily check. A daily check will also bring a slow puncture to your attention.

● Use an accurate pressure gauge. Many garage forecourt gauges are wildly inaccurate. If you buy your own, spend as much as you can justify on a quality gauge.

● Proper air pressure will increase tyre life and provide maximum stability and ride comfort.

Tyre care

● Check the tyres carefully for cuts, tears, embedded nails or other sharp objects and excessive wear. Operation of the motorcycle with excessively worn tyres is extremely hazardous, as traction and handling are directly affected.

● Check the condition of the tyre valve and ensure the dust cap is in place.

● Pick out any stones or nails which may have become embedded in the tyre tread. If left, they will eventually penetrate through the casing and cause a puncture.

● If tyre damage is apparent, or unexplained loss of pressure is experienced, seek the advice of a tyre fitting specialist without delay.

Tyre tread depth

● At the time of writing UK law requires that tread depth must be at least 1 mm over 3/4 of the tread breadth all the way around the tyre, with no bald patches. Many riders, however, consider 2 mm tread depth minimum to be a safer limit. The manufacturer's recommended minimum tread depth is given below.

● Many tyres now incorporate wear indicators in the tread. Identify the triangular pointer or 'TWI' mark on the tyre sidewall to locate the indicator bar and renew the tyre if the tread has worn down to the bar.

Tyre pressures (cold)	Front	Rear
Rider only	36 psi (2.5 Bar)	36 psi (2.5 Bar)
Rider and passenger	36 psi (2.5 Bar)	42 psi (2.9 Bar)

Minimum tyre tread depths	
Front	1.6 mm
Rear	2.0 mm

1 Remove the cap from the valve – if there isn't one there, fit a new one.

2 Check the tyre pressures when the tyres are cold and keep them properly inflated. Fit the cap on completion.

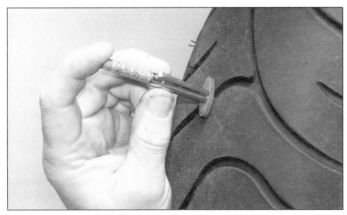

3 Measure tread depth at the centre of the tyre using a tread depth gauge.

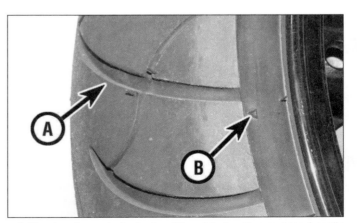

4 Tyre tread wear indicator bar (A) and its location marking (usually either an arrow, a triangle or the letters TWI) on the sidewall (B).

Chapter 1
Routine maintenance and Servicing

Contents

Degrees of difficulty

Easy, suitable for novice with little experience	**Fairly easy,** suitable for beginner with some experience	**Fairly difficult,** suitable for competent DIY mechanic	**Difficult,** suitable for experienced DIY mechanic	**Very difficult,** suitable for expert DIY or professional

Engine

Engine idle speed
    Normal idle (engine hot) . . . . 1100 ± 100 rpm
    Fast idle (engine cold) . . . . 1600 ± 100 rpm
Spark plugs
    Type
        Standard . . . . NGK CR8EK or Nippondenso U24ETR
        For extended high speed riding . . . . NGK CR9EK or Nippondenso U27ETR
        For cold climate (below 5°C) . . . . NGK CR7EK or Nippondenso U22ETR
    Electrode gap . . . . 0.7 to 0.8 mm
Throttle body synchronisation – max. difference between bodies . . . . . 20 mm Hg
Valve clearances (COLD engine)
    Intake valves . . . . 0.10 to 0.20 mm
    Exhaust valves . . . . 0.20 to 0.30 mm

Frame and cycle parts

Brake pad lining minimum thickness . . . . 1 mm
Drive chain
    Freeplay (on sidestand) . . . . 20 to 30 mm
    Stretch limit (21 pin length – see text) . . . . 319.4 mm
Gearchange lever height . . . . 30 to 40 mm
Rear brake pedal height . . . . 35 to 45 mm
Throttle freeplay . . . . 2 to 4 mm
Tyre pressures (cold) and tread depth . . . . see *Pre-ride checks*

Lubricants and fluids

Drive chain lubricant . . . . Aerosol chain lubricant suitable for O-ring chains or heavy motor oil (such as gear oil)
Engine oil type . . . . API grade SF/SG or SH/SJ with JASO MA 4-stroke motorcycle oil
Engine oil viscosity . . . . SAE 10W40
Engine oil capacity
    Oil change . . . . 4.2 litres
    Oil and filter change . . . . 4.8 litres
    Following engine overhaul – dry engine, new filter . . . . 5.7 litres
Brake and clutch fluid . . . . DOT 4
Steering head bearings . . . . Lithium-based multi-purpose grease
Swingarm pivot bearings . . . . Multi-purpose grease
Suspension linkage bearings . . . . Lithium-based multi-purpose grease
Bearing seal lips . . . . Lithium-based multi-purpose grease
Gearchange lever/rear brake pedal/footrest pivots . . . . Lithium-based multi-purpose grease
Front brake lever and clutch lever pivots . . . . Lithium-based multi-purpose grease
Throttle cables . . . . Aerosol cable lubricant
Stand pivots and spring hooks . . . . Lithium-based multi-purpose grease
Throttle grip . . . . Multi-purpose grease or dry film lubricant

Torque settings

Brake hose banjo bolts . . . . 23 Nm
Engine oil drain plug . . . . 23 Nm
Fork clamp bolts . . . . 23 Nm
Handlebar clamp bolts . . . . 23 Nm
Rear axle nut . . . . 100 Nm
Spark plugs . . . . 11 Nm
Steering stem nut . . . . 65 Nm
Timing rotor cover bolts . . . . 11 Nm
Torque arm nuts
    Front . . . . 28 Nm
    Rear . . . . 34 Nm

Pre-ride

- [ ] See 'Pre-ride checks' at the beginning of this manual.

After the initial 600 miles (1000 km)

Note: *This check is usually performed by a Suzuki dealer after the first 600 miles (1000 km) from new. Thereafter, maintenance is carried out according to the following intervals of the schedule.*

Every 600 miles (1000 km) or 1 month

- [ ] Check, adjust, clean and lubricate the drive chain (Section 1)

Every 3500 miles (5500 km) or 6 months

Carry out all the items under the Pre-ride checks and the 600 mile (1000 km) check, plus the following:

- [ ] Check for drive chain and sprocket wear and chain stretch (Section 1)
- [ ] Clean the air filter element (Section 2)
- [ ] Check the spark plugs (Section 3)
- [ ] Check the fuel system hoses and components (Section 4)
- [ ] Change the engine oil (Section 5)
- [ ] Check and adjust the engine idle speed (Section 6)
- [ ] Check throttle cable operation and freeplay (Section 7)
- [ ] Check the clutch (Section 8)
- [ ] Check the cooling system (Section 9)
- [ ] Check the brake system (Section 10)
- [ ] Check the brake pads for wear (Section 10)
- [ ] Check the tyre and wheel condition, and the tyre tread depth (Section 11 and Pre-ride checks)
- [ ] Check the tightness of all nuts and bolts (Section 12)
- [ ] Check and lubricate all pivots and cables (Section 13)

Every 7000 miles (11,000 km) or 12 months

Carry out all the items under the 3500 mile (5500 km) check, plus the following:

- [ ] Replace the spark plugs with new ones (Section 3)
- [ ] Check throttle valve synchronisation (Section 14)
- [ ] Check the PAIR system (Section 15)
- [ ] Check the steering head bearing freeplay (Section 16)
- [ ] Check the front and rear suspension (Section 17)

Every 10,500 miles (16,500 km) or 18 months

Carry out all the items under the 3500 mile (5500 km) check, plus the following:

- [ ] Replace the air filter element with a new one (Section 2)
- [ ] Change the engine oil and fit a new oil filter (Section 5)

Every 14,000 miles (22,000 km) or 2 years

Carry out all the items under the 7000 mile (11,000 km) check, plus the following:

- [ ] Check the valve clearances (Section 18)

Every 2 years

- [ ] Change the brake fluid (Section 10)
- [ ] Change the clutch fluid (Section 8)

Every 4 years

- [ ] Fit new fuel system hoses (Section 4)
- [ ] Fit a new clutch hose (Section 8)
- [ ] Fit new brake hoses (Section 10)

Non-scheduled maintenance

Note: *These items are not part of a mileage or time maintenance schedule, but are necessary to ensure trouble-free running of the motorcycle.*

- [ ] Replace the fuel filter with a new one (Section 4)
- [ ] Replace the clutch master cylinder and release cylinder seals with new ones (Section 8)
- [ ] Replace the brake master cylinder and caliper seals with new ones (Section 10)
- [ ] Check the wheel bearings (Section 11)
- [ ] Re-grease the steering head bearings (Section 16)
- [ ] Change the front fork oil (Section 17)
- [ ] Re-grease the swingarm bearings (Section 17)
- [ ] Check the sidestand, centrestand and starter interlock (safety) circuit (Section 19)
- [ ] Check the battery (Section 20)

Component locations on the right-hand side

1 Shock compression damping
  adjuster
2 Shock pre-load adjuster
3 Rear brake light switch
4 Throttle cable adjusters
5 Front brake fluid reservoir

6 Fork preload and rebound damping
  adjuster
7 Fork compression damping
  adjuster
8 Engine oil filter
9 Engine oil drain plug

10 Engine oil inspection window
11 Engine oil filler cap
12 Rear brake fluid reservoir
13 Rear brake pedal height adjuster
14 Shock compression damping adjuster
15 Drive chain adjuster

Component locations on the left-hand side

1 Steering head bearing adjuster
2 Fork preload and rebound damping
  adjuster
3 Clutch fluid reservoir
4 Spark plugs

5 Engine idle speed adjuster
6 Fuel filter
7 Air filter element
8 Battery
9 Shock preload adjuster

10 Shock compression damping adjuster
11 Drive chain adjuster
12 Shock rebound damping adjuster
13 Oil pressure take-off point
14 Fork compression damping adjuster

Introduction

1 This Chapter is designed to help the home mechanic maintain his/her motorcycle for safety, economy, long life and peak performance.

2 Deciding where to start or plug into the routine maintenance schedule depends on several factors. If the warranty period on your motorcycle has just expired, and if it has been maintained according to the warranty standards, you may want to pick up routine maintenance as it coincides with the next mileage or calendar interval. If you have owned the machine for some time but have never performed any maintenance on it, then you may want to start at the nearest interval and include some additional procedures to ensure that nothing important is overlooked. If you have just had a major engine overhaul, then you may want to start the maintenance routine from the beginning. If you have a used machine and have no knowledge of its history or maintenance record, you may desire to combine all the checks into one large service initially and then settle into the maintenance schedule prescribed.

3 Before beginning any maintenance or repair, the machine should be cleaned thoroughly. Cleaning will help ensure that dirt does not contaminate the engine and will allow you to detect wear and damage that could otherwise easily go unnoticed.

4 Certain maintenance information is sometimes printed on decals attached to the motorcycle. If the information on the decals differs from that included here, use the information on the decal.

Every 600 miles (1000 km)

1 Drive chain and sprockets

Check, adjust, clean and lubricate the drive chain

Check chain slack

1 A neglected drive chain won't last long and will quickly damage the sprockets. Routine chain adjustment and lubrication isn't difficult and will ensure maximum chain and sprocket life.

2 To check the chain, place the bike on its sidestand and shift the transmission into neutral. Make sure the ignition switch is OFF.

3 Push up on the bottom run of the chain midway between the two sprockets and measure the amount of slack, then compare your measurement to that listed in this Chapter's Specifications **(see illustration)**. As the chain stretches with wear adjustment will be necessary (see below). Since the chain will rarely wear evenly, roll the bike forward so that another section of chain can be checked (having an assistant to do this makes the task a lot easier); do this several times to check the entire length of chain, and mark the tightest spot.

Caution: Riding the bike with excess slack in the chain could lead to damage.

4 In some cases where lubrication has been neglected, corrosion and galling may cause the links to bind and kink, which effectively shortens the chain's length and makes it tight **(see illustration)**. Thoroughly clean and work free any such links, then highlight them with a marker pen or paint. After the bike has been ridden repeat the measurement for slack in the highlighted area. If the chain has kinked again and is still tight, replace it with a new one. A rusty, kinked or worn chain will damage the sprockets and can damage transmission bearings. If in any doubt as to the condition of a chain, it is far better to fit a new one than risk damage to other components and possibly yourself.

5 Check the entire length of the chain for damaged rollers, loose links and pins, and missing O-rings, and replace it with a new one if necessary. **Note:** *Never fit a new chain onto old sprockets, and never use the old chain if you fit new sprockets – replace the chain and sprockets as a set.* See Steps 12 to 18 for sprocket checks and chain stretch checks.

Adjust chain slack

6 Move the bike so that the chain is positioned with the tightest point at the centre of its bottom run, then put it on the sidestand.

7 Slacken the rear axle nut **(see illustration)**. Slacken the nuts on the torque arm bolts **(see illustrations)**.

8 Slacken the locknut on each adjuster bolt, then turn the adjuster bolt on each side evenly until the amount of freeplay specified at the beginning of the Chapter is obtained

1.3 Push up on the chain and measure the slack

1.4 Neglect has caused the links in this chain to kink

1.7a Slacken the axle nut (arrowed) . . .

1.7b . . . the nut (arrowed) securing the torque arm to the caliper . . . .

1.7c . . . and to the swingarm

1.8a Loosen the adjuster locknut . . .

1.8b . . . then turn the adjuster bolt as required

at the centre of the bottom run of the chain **(see illustration)**. If you are tightening the chain turn the bolts out (anti-clockwise). If you are slackening the chain turn the bolts in (clockwise) then push the wheel forwards so the adjustment markers contact the bolt heads. Following adjustment, check that the rear edge of each marker is in the same position in relation to the index lines on the swingarm **(see illustrations)**. It is important the same index lines on each side align with the rear edge of the marker; if not, the rear wheel will be out of alignment with the front. If there is a discrepancy in the marker positions, adjust one of them so that its position is exactly the same as the other. Check the chain freeplay again as described above and readjust if necessary.

9 Tighten the axle nut to the torque setting specified at the beginning of the Chapter **(see illustration 1.7a)**. Recheck the adjustment as above, then check that the wheel runs freely. Make sure that the adjuster bolt heads are set against the alignment markers, turning them out slightly if necessary, then tighten the locknuts **(see illustration 1.8a)**. Tighten the torque arm nuts to the specified torque **(see illustrations 1.7b and c)**.

Clean and lubricate the chain

10 If required, wash the chain in paraffin (kerosene) or a suitable non-flammable or high flash-point solvent that will not damage the O-rings, using a soft brush to work any dirt out if necessary. Wipe the cleaner off the chain and allow it to dry, using compressed air if available. If the chain is excessively dirty remove it from the machine and allow it to soak in the paraffin or solvent (see Chapter 6). *Caution: Don't use petrol (gasoline), an unsuitable solvent (such as trichloroethylene) or other cleaning fluids which might damage the internal sealing properties of the chain. Don't use high-pressure water to clean the chain. The entire process shouldn't take longer than ten minutes, otherwise the*

O-rings could be damaged.

11 The best time to lubricate the chain is after the motorcycle has been ridden. When the chain is warm, the lubricant will penetrate the joints between the sideplates better than when cold. **Note:** *Suzuki specifies a heavy motor oil (such as gear oil) or an aerosol chain lube that it is suitable for O-ring or X-ring (sealed) chains; do not use any other chain lubricants – the solvents could damage the chain's sealing rings. Apply the oil to the area where the sideplates overlap – not the middle of the rollers* **(see illustration)**.

> **HAYNES HiNT** *Apply the lubricant to the top of the lower chain run, so centrifugal force will work the oil into the chain when the bike is moving. After applying the lubricant, let it soak in a few minutes before wiping off any excess.*

1.8c The rear edge of the marker must align with same marks on both sides

1.11 Apply lubricant to the overlap between the chain sideplates

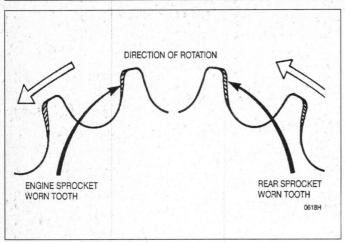

1.13 Check the sprockets in the areas indicated to see if they are worn excessively

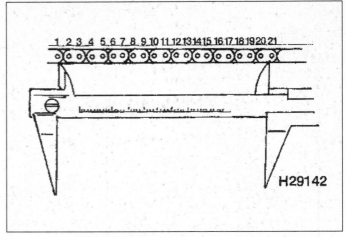

1.17 Measure the distance between the 1st and 21st pins to determine chain stretch

 Warning: Take care not to get any lubricant on the tyres or brake system components. If any of the lubricant inadvertently contacts them, clean it off thoroughly using a suitable solvent or dedicated brake cleaner before riding the machine.

Check the drive chain stretch and sprocket wear

12 Check the entire length of the chain for damaged rollers, loose links and pins, and missing O-rings. Fit a new chain if damage is found. **Note:** *Never install a new chain on old sprockets, and never use the old chain if you install new sprockets – replace the chain and sprockets as a set.*

13 Remove the front sprocket cover (see Chapter 6). Check the teeth on the front sprocket and the rear sprocket for wear **(see illustration)**. If the sprocket teeth are worn excessively, replace the chain and both sprockets with a new set.

14 Inspect the drive chain slider on the front of the swingarm for excessive wear and damage and replace it with a new one if necessary.

15 Measure the amount of chain stretch as follows:

16 Slacken the rear axle nut **(see illustration 1.7a)**. Slacken the nuts on the torque arm bolts **(see illustrations 1.7b and c)**.

17 Slacken the adjuster bolt locknuts, then turn the adjuster bolts out evenly until the chain is tight, but not taut **(see illustrations 1.8a and b)**. Measure along the bottom run the length of 21 pins (from the centre of the 1st pin to the centre of the 21st pin) and compare the result to the stretch limit specified at the beginning of the Chapter **(see illustration)**. Rotate the rear wheel so that several sections of the chain can be measured, then calculate the average. If the chain stretch measurement exceeds the service limit the chain must be replaced with a new one (see Chapter 6). **Note:** *Never fit a new chain onto*

old sprockets, and never use the old chain if you fit new sprockets – replace the chain and sprockets as a set.

18 If the chain is good, reset the adjusters so that there is the correct amount of freeplay (see Steps 8 and 9).

2 Air filter

Caution: If the machine is continually ridden in dusty conditions, the filter should be cleaned more frequently.

Check and cleaning

1 Remove the fuel tank (see Chapter 4). Unclip and remove the storage tray **(see illustration)**.

2 Unscrew the fuel tank bracket bolts and remove the bracket **(see illustration)**.

2.1 Remove the storage tray

2.2 Unscrew the bolts (arrowed) and remove the bracket

2.3a Undo the screws . . .

2.3b . . . and lift out the air filter

3 Undo the air filter screws and withdraw the filter from the housing **(see illustrations)**.
4 Tap the filter on a hard surface to dislodge any dirt. If available use compressed air to clean the filter element, holding the filter with its open end down and directing the air from the outside to the middle (i.e. in the opposite direction to normal air flow) **(see illustration)**.

If the element is damaged or extremely dirty, fit a new one.
5 Make sure the inside of the filter housing is clean. Excessive oil in the housing is an indication of high crankcase pressure caused by too much oil in the engine or worn piston rings or cylinders.
6 Release the clip and remove the plug from

the drain hose on the bottom of the filter housing and allow any fluid to drain, then refit the cap and secure it with the clip **(see illustration)**.
7 Install the filter with the arrow to the front and tighten the screws **(see illustration)**.
8 Fit the tank bracket and tighten its bolts **(see illustration)**.

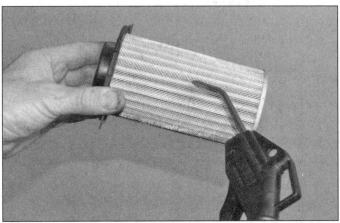

2.4 Clean the filter element using compressed air if available

2.6 Filter housing drain plug (arrowed)

2.7 Make sure the filter is the correct round with the arrow to the front

2.8 Fit the tank bracket

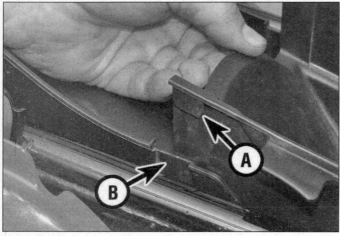

2.9 Make sure the tab (A) locates over the rim (B) on each side

3.3 The cylinder ID should be on each lead

3.4 Pull the cap off the spark plug

3.5 Unscrew and remove the spark plug

9 Refit the storage tray, making sure it locates correctly **(see illustration)**. Install the tank (see Chapter 4).

Renewal

10 Remove the old air filter as described above and install a new one.

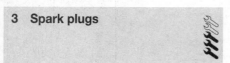
3 Spark plugs

Check and adjustment

Special tool: A wire gauge is necessary for this job.

1 Make sure your spark plug socket is the correct size before attempting to remove the plugs – a suitable one is supplied in the motorcycle's tool kit which is stored under the seat. Make sure the ignition is switched OFF.
2 To access the spark plugs, remove the fuel tank (see Chapter 4).
3 Check that the cylinder location is marked

on each spark plug lead and mark them accordingly if not **(see illustration)**.
4 Clean the area around the spark plug channel seal to prevent any dirt falling in, then pull the cap off each spark plug **(see illustration)**.
5 Using either the plug socket supplied in the bike's toolkit or a deep socket type wrench, unscrew each plug from the cylinder head **(see illustration)**. Lay each plug out in relation to its cylinder; if any plug shows up a problem it will then be easy to identify the troublesome cylinder.
6 Look for excessive deposits and evidence of a cracked or chipped insulator around the centre electrode. Compare your spark plugs to the colour spark plug reading chart at the end of this manual. Check the threads, the washer and the ceramic insulator body for cracks and other damage. If in doubt concerning the condition of the plugs, install new ones – the expense is minimal.
7 Inspect the electrodes for wear. Both the centre and side electrodes should have

square edges and the side electrodes should be of uniform thickness. If the electrodes are not excessively worn, and if the deposits can be easily removed with a wire brush, the plugs can be re-gapped and re-used.
8 Before installing the plugs, make sure they are the correct type and heat range and check the gap between the side (earth) electrodes and the centre electrode **(see illustration)**.

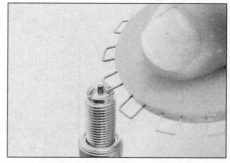

3.8a Using a wire gauge to measure the spark plug electrode gap

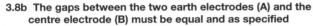

3.8b The gaps between the two earth electrodes (A) and the centre electrode (B) must be equal and as specified

3.8c Adjust the electrode gap by bending the side electrodes only

Compare the gap to that specified and adjust as necessary **(see illustration)**. If the gap must be adjusted, bend the side electrodes only and be very careful not to chip or crack the insulator nose **(see illustration)**. Make sure the sealing washer is in place on the plug before installing it.

9 Fit the plug into the end of the tool, then use the tool to insert the plug **(see illustration)**. Since the cylinder head is made of aluminium, which is soft and easily damaged, thread the plug as far as possible into the head turning the tool by hand **(see illustration)**. Once the plug is finger-tight, the job can be finished with a spanner on the tool supplied or a socket drive **(see illustration 3.5)**. If a torque wrench can be applied, tighten the spark plugs to the torque setting specified at the beginning of the Chapter. Otherwise, tighten them according the instructions on the box – generally if new plugs are being used tighten them by 1/2 a turn after the washer has seated, and if the old plugs are being reused tighten them by

1/8 to 1/4 turn after they have seated. Do not over-tighten them.

> **HAYNES HINT** *You can slip a short length of hose over the end of the plug to use as a tool to thread it into place. The hose will grip the plug well enough to turn it, but will start to slip if the plug begins to cross-thread in the hole – this will prevent damaged threads.*

10 Fit the spark plug caps, making sure they are pressed fully onto the plugs **(see illustration 3.4)**. Make sure the seals are seated correctly around the rims of the channels.

11 Install the fuel tank (see Chapter 4).

> **HAYNES HINT** *Stripped plug threads in the cylinder head can be repaired with a thread insert – see 'Tools and Workshop Tips' in the Reference section.*

Renewal

12 Remove the old spark plugs as described above and install new ones.

4 Fuel system

> ⚠ *Warning: Petrol (gasoline) is extremely flammable, so take extra precautions when you work on any part of the fuel system. Don't smoke or allow open flames or bare light bulbs near the work area, and don't work in a garage where a natural gas-type appliance is present. If you spill any fuel on your skin, rinse it off immediately with soap and water. When you perform any kind of work on the fuel system, wear safety glasses and have a fire extinguisher suitable for a Class B type fire (flammable liquids) on hand.*

3.9a Fit the plug into the tool . . .

3.9b . . . and thread it into the head by hand

4.1a Check the tank and its hoses . . .

4.1b . . . the vacuum hoses . . .

Check the fuel system hoses and components

1 Raise and support the fuel tank (see Chapter 4) and check the tank, the fuel delivery and return hoses, the fuel tank drain and breather hoses, the intake air pressure sensor vacuum hoses, the crankcase breather hose, the air filter drain hose and the PAIR system hoses (see Section 15), for signs of leaks, deterioration or damage **(see illustrations)**. In particular check that there are no leaks from the fuel hose or hose unions. Replace any hose that is cracked or deteriorated with a new one (Steps 6 to 8).

2 If the joint between the fuel pump mounting plate and the tank is leaking, ensure the mounting bolts are tightened to the specified torque setting (see Chapter 4); if the leak persists, remove the pump and fit a new O-ring (see Chapter 4).

3 Inspect the joints between the fuel rail, the injectors and the throttle bodies **(see illustration)**. If there are any leaks, remove the fuel rail and fit new seals and O-rings to the injectors (see Chapter 4).

Filter renewal

4 Cleaning or renewal of the fuel strainer and filter is advised after a particularly high mileage has been covered, although no interval is specified by Suzuki. It is also necessary if fuel starvation is suspected.

5 The filter and strainer are both part of the fuel pump assembly, but are available separately. Remove the pump from the fuel tank, then disassemble it as required to remove the filter and/or strainer (see Chapter 4).

Hose renewal

⚠ *Warning: Petrol (gasoline) is extremely flammable, so take extra precautions when you work on any part of the fuel system. Don't smoke or allow open flames or bare light bulbs near the work area, and don't work in a garage where a natural gas-type appliance is present. If you spill any fuel on your skin, rinse it off immediately with soap and water. When you perform any kind of work on the fuel system, wear safety glasses and have a fire extinguisher suitable for a Class B type fire (flammable liquids) on hand.*

6 The fuel delivery and return hoses, intake air pressure sensor vacuum hoses and PAIR system hoses should be replaced with new ones at the specified interval regardless of their apparent condition.

7 Remove the fuel tank (see Chapter 4). Refer to Chapter 4 and disconnect the hoses from the fuel tank, throttle bodies and the PAIR control valve, noting the routing of each one and how it is secured. **Note:** *It is advisable to make a sketch of the hoses before removing them to ensure they are correctly installed.*

8 Where appropriate, secure each new hose to its unions using new clips. Run the engine and check that the fuel system is working correctly and there are no leaks before taking the machine out on the road.

4.1c . . . the crankcase breather hose (arrowed) and all others

4.3 Check the fuel rail and injector joints (arrowed)

5.3 Unscrew the oil filler cap . . .

5.4a . . . then unscrew the drain plug . . .

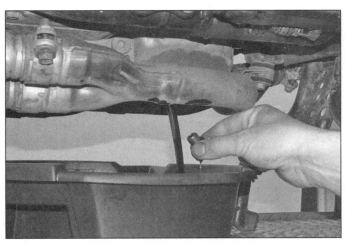

5.4b . . . and allow the oil to drain

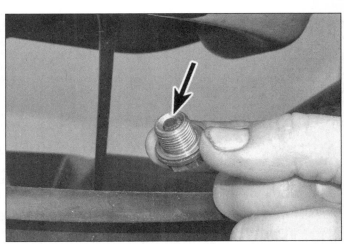

5.4c Clean the magnetic tip (arrowed) . . .

5 Engine oil and filter

Oil change

 Warning: Be careful when draining the oil, as the exhaust pipes, the engine, and the oil itself can cause severe burns.

5.4d . . . and cut the old washer off

1 Regular oil and filter changes are the single most important maintenance procedure you can perform on a motorcycle. The oil not only lubricates the internal parts of the engine, transmission and clutch, but it also acts as a coolant, a cleaner, a sealant, and a protector. Because of these demands, the oil takes a terrific amount of abuse and should be drained and the engine refilled with new oil of the correct type and grade at the specified service interval. The oil filter should be changed with every third oil change.

2 Before changing the oil, warm up the engine so the oil will drain easily.

3 Support the bike on the centrestand on level ground, and position a drain tray below the engine. Unscrew the oil filler cap from the clutch cover to vent the crankcase and to act as a reminder that there is no oil in the engine **(see illustration)**.

4 Next, unscrew the oil drain plug from the sump on the bottom of the engine and allow the oil to flow into the drain tray **(see illustrations)**. Note the magnet inside the plug and clean off any metal swarf **(see illustration)**. Check the condition of the sealing washer on the drain plug and fit a new one if it is damaged or worn – you will probably need to cut the old one off **(see illustration)**. It is good practice to fit a new washer whenever the drain plug is removed.

 HAYNES HiNT *To help determine whether any abnormal or excessive engine wear is occurring, place a strainer between the engine and the drain tray so that any debris in the oil is filtered out and can be examined. If there are flakes or chips of metal in the oil or on the drain plug magnet, then something is drastically wrong internally and the engine will have to be disassembled for inspection and repair. If there are pieces of fibre-like material in the oil, the clutch is wearing excessively and should be checked.*

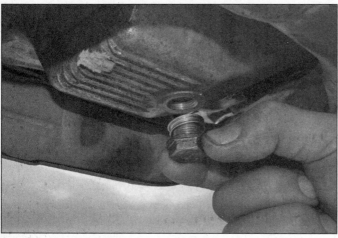

5.5 Fit a new sealing washer and tighten the plug to the specified torque

5.9a Unscrew the filter . . .

5.9b . . . and drain it into the tray

5 When the oil has completely drained, fit the plug into the sump, preferably using a new sealing washer, and tighten it to the torque setting specified at the beginning of this Chapter (see illustration). Avoid overtightening, as damage to the sump will result.

6 Refill the engine with the correct amount and type of oil (see Specifications). With the motorcycle upright on level ground, the oil level should lie between the upper and lower level lines on the inspection window (see *Pre-ride checks*). Install the filler cap. Start the engine and let it run for two or three minutes (make sure that the oil pressure warning light extinguishes after a few seconds). Shut it off, wait a few

minutes, then recheck the oil level. If necessary, add more oil to bring the level almost up to the upper line on the window. Check that there are no leaks from around the drain plug.

7 The oil drained from the engine should be disposed of properly. Check with your local refuse disposal company, disposal facility or environmental agency to see whether they will accept the used oil for recycling. Don't pour used oil into drains or onto the ground.

Oil and oil filter change

Special tool: A filter removing tool is necessary for this job.

⚠️ *Warning: Be careful when draining the oil, as the exhaust pipes, the engine, and the oil itself can cause severe burns.*

8 Drain the engine oil as described in Steps 2 to 5.

9 Now place the drain tray below the oil filter, which is on the front of the engine. Clean the crankcase around the filter, then unscrew the filter using a filter adapter (Suzuki service tool (Pt. No. 09915-40610) or an aftermarket alternative) or strap wrench and tip any residual oil into the drain tray (see illustrations).

10 Smear clean engine oil onto the seal of the new filter, then screw it onto the engine by hand until the seal just seats (see

illustrations). Using a filter adapter (DO NOT use a strap or chain type removing tool), tighten the filter a further two whole turns (see illustration). **Note:** *Although Suzuki specify two whole turns, the filter can become very tight before this, and tightening it further would possibly have damaged the seal or the filter. It is best to use your own judgement should the filter become very tight – the most important consideration is that the filter does not leak. Check the filter for any torque setting marked on it and apply that if possible.*

11 Wipe any oil off the exhaust pipes to prevent smoking when the engine is started and refill the engine with oil as described in Step 6.

6 Idle speed

1 When the engine is at normal operating temperature, i.e. after a short run, check the idle speed registered on the tachometer against the figure for normal idle speed given at the beginning of this Chapter.

2 If adjustment is required, locate the idle speed adjuster which is a knurled screw on the left-hand end of the throttle bodies (see

5.10a Smear the seal with clean oil . . .

5.10b . . . then thread the filter onto the engine . . .

5.10c . . . and tighten it as described

illustration). With the engine idling and in neutral, turn the adjuster until the specified idle speed is obtained. Turn the screw clockwise to increase idle speed, and anti-clockwise to decrease it. **Note:** *The fast idle mechanism is actuated automatically by the STV servo when the engine is cold and should cancel when engine oil temperature, ambient temperature and lapsed time parameters are reached. If the idle speed cannot be adjusted correctly, check for a possible fault in the oil temperature sensor or sensor wiring, or in the throttle position (TP) sensor (see Chapter 4, Section 10). Details on the fast idle system are given in Chapter 4, Section 15.*

3 Snap the throttle open and shut a few times, then recheck the idle speed. If necessary, repeat the adjustment procedure.

4 If a smooth, steady idle can't be achieved, the throttle valves may need synchronising (see Section 14).

7 Throttle cables

1 Make sure the throttle twistgrip rotates easily from fully closed to fully open with the front wheel turned at various angles. The twistgrip should return automatically from fully open to fully closed when released.

2 If the throttle sticks, this is probably due to a cable fault. Remove the cables (see Chapter 4) and lubricate them (see Section 13). If the inner cables still do not run smoothly in the outer cables, replace them with new ones.

3 With the cables removed, check that the twistgrip turns smoothly around the handlebar – dirt combined with a lack of lubrication can cause the action to be stiff. Remove the handlebar end-weight and the twistgrip, then clean and lightly grease the twistgrip pulley and the inside of the twistgrip housing if necessary (see Chapter 5, Section 5). Install the lubricated or new cables, making sure they are correctly routed (see Chapter 4). If this fails to improve the operation of the throttle, the fault could lie in the throttle bodies. Remove the fuel tank and check the action of the throttle pulley (see Chapter 4).

4 With the throttle operating smoothly, check for a small amount of freeplay in the cables, measured in terms of the amount of twistgrip rotation before the throttle opens, and compare the amount to that listed in this Chapter's Specifications **(see illustration)**. If it is incorrect, adjust the cables as follows.

5 Pull the rubber boots off the cable adjusters **(see illustration)**. Loosen the locknut on the throttle closing cable (the lower cable) adjuster and turn the adjuster fully in. Now loosen the locknut on the throttle opening cable (the upper cable) and turn the adjuster until the specified amount of freeplay is obtained, then retighten the locknut. Hold the twistgrip in the fully closed position and turn the decelerator cable adjuster out until resistance can just be felt in the cable – at this point all the freeplay has been taken up. Tighten the locknut.

6 If the adjusters have reached their limit, or if major adjustment is required, raise or remove the fuel tank and adjust the cables at the throttle body end. Loosen the locknut on the throttle closing cable (the rear cable) adjuster and turn the adjuster until all freeplay has been taken up in the cable **(see illustration)**. Now loosen the locknut on the throttle opening cable (the front cable) and turn the adjuster until the specified amount of freeplay is obtained, then retighten the locknut. Hold the twistgrip in the fully closed position and slowly turn the closing cable adjuster to obtain 1 mm deflection in the inner cable, then tighten the locknut.

7 If the cables cannot be adjusted as specified, install new ones (see Chapter 4).

6.2 Idle speed adjuster (arrowed)

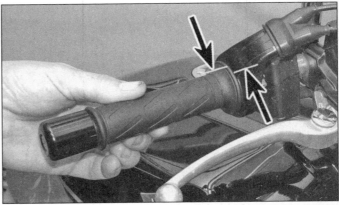

7.4 Throttle cable freeplay is measured in terms of twistgrip rotation

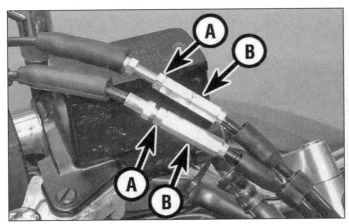

7.5 Throttle cable adjuster locknuts (A) and adjusters (B) – handlebar end

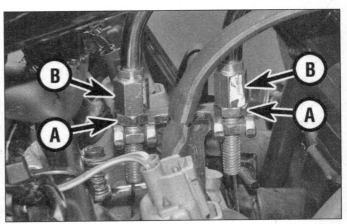

7.6 Throttle cable adjuster locknuts (A) and adjusters (B) – throttle body end

8.6a Adjusting clutch lever span

8.6b Align the required setting on the dial with the arrow on the lever

⚠ **Warning: Turn the handlebars all the way through their travel with the engine idling. Idle speed should not change. If it does, the cables may be routed incorrectly. Correct this condition before riding the bike.**
8 Check that the throttle twistgrip operates smoothly and snaps shut quickly when released.

8 Clutch

Check

1 All models are fitted with an hydraulic clutch, for which there is no method of adjustment.
2 Check the fluid level in the reservoir (see *Pre-ride checks*).
3 Inspect the hydraulic hose and its connections for signs of fluid leakage, and flex the hose to check for cracking, deterioration and wear. Also check around the release mechanism components (master cylinder on the handlebar and release cylinder on the left-hand side of the engine) for damage and leakage.
4 Change the clutch fluid every two years (Step 7) and replace the hose with a new one either if damaged or deteriorated, or every four years irrespective of condition (Steps 8 and 9). The master and release cylinder seals should be changed every few years, or if leakage from them is evident (Steps 10 and 11).
5 Check the operation of the clutch. If there is evidence of air in the system (spongy feel to the lever, difficulty in engaging gear, drag when in gear), bleed the clutch (see Chapter 2). If the lever feels stiff or sticky, overhaul the release mechanism (see Chapter 2).
6 The clutch lever has a span adjuster that alters the distance of the lever from the handlebar. Pull the lever away from the handlebar and turn the adjuster dial until the setting that best suits the rider is obtained

(see illustration). Each setting is identified by a number on the adjuster dial, which must align with the arrow on the lever, at which point a projection on the lever bracket locates in a cut-out in the adjuster (see illustration).

Clutch fluid change

7 The clutch fluid should be changed at the specified interval or whenever a master or release cylinder overhaul is carried out. Refer to Chapter 2 for details. Ensure that all the old fluid is be pumped from the hydraulic system and that the level in the fluid reservoir is checked and the clutch tested before riding the motorcycle.

Clutch hose

8 The hose will deteriorate with age and should be replaced with a new one regardless of its apparent condition (see Chapter 2).
9 Always use new sealing washers when fitting a new hose. Refill the system with new clutch fluid and bleed the system as described in Chapter 2.

Master and release cylinder seals

10 Clutch system seals will deteriorate over a period of time and lose their effectiveness, leading to sticky operation of the clutch master cylinder or the piston in the release cylinder,

9.1a Check the hoses and their unions on the engine . . .

or fluid loss. Although seal replacement is not subject to a specific time or mileage interval, it is advised after a high mileage has been covered and particularly if fluid leakage or a sticking or vague action is apparent.
11 A rebuild kit for the master cylinder is available (cup, seal, piston, spring, circlip, washer and rubber boot are included), and a seal and spring are available for the release cylinder (see Chapter 2).

9 Oil cooling system

⚠ **Warning: The engine must be cool before beginning this procedure.**
1 Check the oil cooler, hoses and hose unions for evidence of leaks (see illustrations). Examine each hose along its entire length. Look for deformation, abrasions and other damage. Replace any damaged components with new ones (see Chapter 3). If there is evidence of leakage at a hose union, detach the hose and replace the union O-ring with a new one (see Chapter 3).
2 Check the oil cooler fins for mud, dirt and insects, which may impede the flow of air through the cooler. If the fins are dirty, remove

9.1b . . . and on the cooler as described

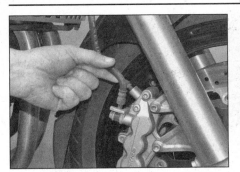

10.3 Flex the brake hoses and check for cracks, bulges and leaking fluid

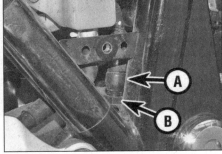

10.5 Brake light switch (A) and adjuster nut (B)

10.6 Adjusting front brake lever span

the cooler (see Chapter 3) and clean it using water or low pressure compressed air directed through the fins from the back. If the fins are bent or distorted, straighten them carefully with a screwdriver. Where there is substantial damage to the surface area, replace the cooler with a new one (see Chapter 3).

3 If oil temperature rises above normal (i.e. the engine is running too hot) the fan on the back of the cooler should come on automatically to draw extra air through the cooler and reduce the temperature. The fan should switch off automatically once the temperature has reduced to a normal level. If it does not, refer to Chapter 3 and check the fan, the fan switch and fan circuit carefully.

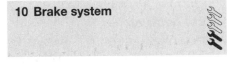

10 Brake system

Brake system check

1 A routine general check of the brake system will ensure that any problems are discovered and remedied before the rider's safety is jeopardised.

2 Check the brake lever and pedal for loose fixings, improper or rough action, excessive play, bends, and other damage. Replace any damaged parts with new ones (see Chapter 5). Clean and lubricate the lever and pedal pivots if their action is stiff or rough (see Section 13).

3 Make sure all brake fasteners are tight. Check the brake pads for wear (see below) and make sure the fluid level in each reservoir is correct (see *Pre-ride checks*). Look for leaks at the hose connections and check for cracks in the hoses **(see illustration)**. If the lever or pedal is spongy, bleed the brakes (see Chapter 6).

4 Make sure the brake light operates when the front brake lever is pulled in. The front brake light switch is not adjustable. If it fails to operate properly, check it (see Chapter 8).

5 Make sure the brake light is activated just before the rear brake takes effect. The switch is mounted behind the right-hand side panel. If adjustment is necessary, remove the panel (see Chapter 7). Hold the switch and turn the adjuster nut on the switch body **(see illustration)**. If the brake light comes on too late, turn the ring clockwise to raise the switch. If the brake light comes on too soon or is permanently on, turn the ring anti-clockwise to lower the switch. If the switch doesn't

operate the brake light, check the bulbs, the switch and the circuit (see Chapter 8).

6 The front brake lever has a span adjuster which alters the distance of the lever from the handlebar. Pull the lever away from the handlebar and turn the adjuster dial until the setting which best suits the rider is obtained **(see illustration)**. Each setting is identified by a number on the dial which aligns with the arrow on the lever bracket, at which point a projection on the lever bracket locates in a cut-out in the adjuster **(see illustration 8.6b)**.

7 Check the position of the rear brake pedal. The distance between the top edge of the brake pedal and the top of the rider's footrest should be in the range specified at the beginning of this Chapter **(see illustration)**. To adjust the pedal height, loosen the locknut on the top of the master cylinder pushrod clevis, then turn the pushrod using the hex at the top until the pedal is at the correct height **(see illustration)**. Tighten the locknut securely and check the adjustment of the brake light switch (see Step 5).

Brake pad wear check

8 Each brake pad has grooves in the friction material that should be plainly visible from the most obvious vantage point, but note that an

10.7a Measure the height of the brake pedal

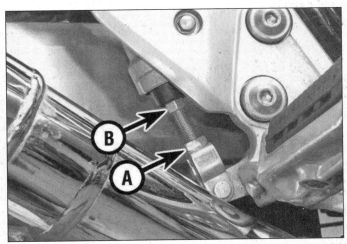

10.7b To adjust it slacken the locknut (A) and turn the pushrod (B)

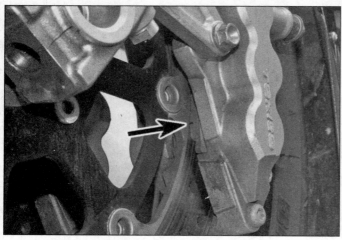

10.8a Front brake pad wear indicator (arrowed)

10.8b Rear brake pad wear indicator (arrowed)

accumulation of road dirt and brake dust could make them difficult to see **(see illustrations)**. If the material has worn down to the bottom of the groove(s) they must be replaced with new ones.

9 If the groove(s) can't be seen, then the amount of friction material remaining should be, and it will be obvious when the pads need replacing (1 mm of friction material is the minimum) – if necessary remove the pad spring, displace the caliper itself, or use a mirror for the best viewpoint (see Chapter 6). **Note:** *Some after-market pads may use different indicators to those on the original equipment.*

10 If the pads are dirty or if you are in doubt as to the amount of friction material remaining, remove them for inspection and measure the thickness of the material (see Chapter 6).

11 If the pads are excessively worn, check the brake discs (see Chapter 6). If the pads appear to be wearing unevenly, remove the caliper and check the operation of the pistons (see Chapter 6).

12 Refer to Chapter 6 for details of pad removal and installation.

Brake fluid change

13 The brake fluid should be changed at the prescribed interval or whenever a master cylinder or caliper overhaul is carried out. Refer to Chapter 6, Section 11 for details. Ensure that all the old fluid is be pumped from the hydraulic system and that the level in the fluid reservoir is checked and the brakes tested before riding the motorcycle.

Brake hoses

14 The hoses will deteriorate with age and should be replaced with new ones regardless of their apparent condition (see Chapter 6).

15 Always use new sealing washers when fitting new hoses. Refill the system with new brake fluid and bleed the system as described in Chapter 6.

Brake caliper and master cylinder seals

16 Brake system seals will deteriorate over a period of time and lose their effectiveness, leading to sticky operation of the brake master cylinders or the pistons in the brake calipers, or fluid loss. Although seal replacement is not subject to a specific time or mileage interval, it is advised after a high mileage has been covered and particularly if fluid leakage or a sticking caliper action is apparent.

17 Replace all the seals in each caliper as a set – a rebuild kit for each caliper is available; master cylinder seals are supplied as a kit along with a new piston and spring (see Chapter 6).

11 Wheels and tyres

Wheels

1 Cast wheels are virtually maintenance free, but they should be kept clean and checked periodically for cracks and other damage. Also check the wheel runout and alignment (see Chapter 6). Never attempt to repair damaged cast wheels; they must be replaced

11.1 Check that the wheel balance weights are firmly attached

with new ones. Check that the wheel balance weights are fixed firmly to the wheel rim **(see illustration)**. If you suspect that a weight has fallen off, have the wheel rebalanced by a motorcycle tyre specialist.

Tyres

2 Check the tyre condition and tread depth thoroughly – see *Pre-ride checks*. Check the valve rubber for signs of damage or deterioration and have it renewed if necessary by a tyre fitting specialist. Also, make sure the valve stem cap is in place and tight.

Wheel bearings

3 Wheel bearings will wear over a considerable mileage and should be checked periodically to avoid handling problems.

4 Support the motorcycle upright using an auxiliary stand so that the wheel being examined is off the ground. Check for any play in the bearings by pushing and pulling the wheel against the hub **(see illustration)**. Also rotate the wheel and check that it turns smoothly and without any grating noises.

5 If any play is detected in the hub, or if the wheel does not rotate smoothly (and this is not due to brake or transmission drag), remove the wheel and check the bearings for wear or damage (see Chapter 6).

11.4 Check for play in the wheel bearings

12 Nuts and bolts

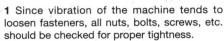

1 Since vibration of the machine tends to loosen fasteners, all nuts, bolts, screws, etc. should be checked for proper tightness.
2 Pay particular attention to the following, referring to the relevant Chapter:

Spark plugs
Engine oil drain plug
Lever and pedal bolts
Footrest and stand bolts/nuts
Engine mounting bolts/nuts
Frame section bolts/nuts
Shock absorber bolts/nuts; swingarm pivot bolt/nut
Handlebar clamp and holder bolts/nuts
Front fork clamp bolts (top and bottom yoke) and fork top bolts
Steering stem nut
Front axle nut and axle clamp bolts
Rear axle nut
Front and rear sprocket nuts
Brake caliper and master cylinder mounting bolts, brake caliper body bolts, rear brake torque arm bolts/nuts
Brake hose banjo bolts and caliper bleed valves
Brake disc bolts
Exhaust system bolts/nuts

3 If a torque wrench is available, use it along with the torque settings given at the beginning of this and other Chapters.

13 General lubrication

Pivot points

1 Since the components of a motorcycle are exposed to the elements, those with pivots should be checked and lubricated periodically to ensure safe and trouble-free operation.

2 The clutch and brake lever pivots, footrest pivots, brake pedal and gearchange lever pivots and linkage, and stand pivots and spring ends should be lubricated frequently. In order for the lubricant to be applied where it will do the most good, the component should be removed (see Chapter 5). The lubricant recommended by Suzuki for each application is listed at the beginning of the Chapter. If chain or cable lubricant is being used, it can be applied to the pivot joint gaps and will usually work its way into the areas where friction occurs, so less disassembly of the component is needed (however it is always better to do so and clean off all corrosion, dirt and old lubricant first). If motor oil or light grease is being used, apply it sparingly as it may attract dirt (which could cause the controls to bind or wear at an accelerated rate).

Throttle cables

3 To lubricate the throttle cables, disconnect the cable at its upper end (see Chapter 4), then lubricate it with a pressure adapter and aerosol cable lubricant **(see illustrations)**.

14 Throttle valve synchronisation

Special tool: A set of vacuum gauges is necessary for this job.

⚠️ **Warning: Petrol (gasoline) is extremely flammable, so take extra precautions when you work on any part of the fuel system. Don't smoke or allow open flames or bare light bulbs near the work area, and don't work in a garage where a natural gas-type appliance is present. If you spill any fuel on your skin, rinse it off immediately with soap and water. When you perform any kind of work on the fuel system, wear safety glasses and have a fire extinguisher suitable for a Class B type fire (flammable liquids) on hand.**

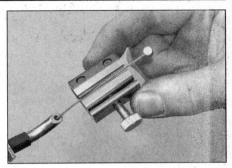

13.3a Fit the cable into the adapter . . .

⚠️ **Warning: Take great care not to burn your hand on the hot engine unit when accessing the gauge take-off points on the throttle bodies. Do not allow exhaust gases to build up in the work area; either perform the check outside or use an exhaust gas extraction system.**

1 Throttle valves that are out of synchronisation will result in increased fuel consumption, increased engine temperature, less than ideal throttle response and higher vibration levels. Synchronisation is the process of adjusting the throttle valves so they each pass the same amount of fuel/air mixture to their respective cylinders. This is done by measuring the vacuum produced in each intake tract as the piston descends on its induction stroke and adjusting the throttle valves accordingly.
2 To synchronise the throttle valves you will need a set of vacuum gauges or calibrated tubes to measure engine vacuum. The equipment used should be suitable for a four cylinder engine and come complete with the necessary hoses to fit the take off points on the throttle bodies. **Note:** *Because of the nature of the synchronisation procedure and the need for special instruments, most owners leave the task to a Suzuki dealer.*
3 Start the engine and let it run until it reaches normal operating temperature, then shut it off.
4 Raise and support the fuel tank (see Chapter 4). Visually identify the synchronisation

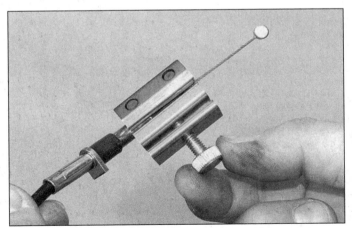

13.3b . . . and tighten the screw to seal it in . . .

13.3c . . . then apply the lubricant using the nozzle provided inserted in the hole in the adapter

14.4a Throttle valve synchronising screw (arrowed) for Nos. 1 and 2

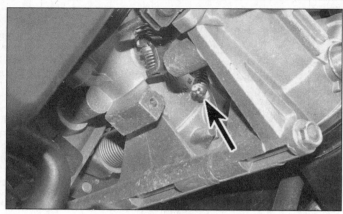

14.4b Throttle valve synchronising screw (arrowed) for Nos. 3 and 4

screws situated in the main throttle valve linkage running along the front of the throttle bodies – there is one screw between Nos. 1 and 2 throttle bodies for synchronising those two together and it is accessed from the underside, one between Nos. 3 and 4 for synchronising those two, again accessed from the underside, and one in the middle to synchronise each throttle body pair to

the other, and this is accessed from the top and is the front one of the two synchronising screws in the middle of the throttle bodies **(see illustrations)**. The other synchronisation screws are in the secondary throttle valve linkage running along the back of the throttle bodies and are for synchronising the secondary throttle valves, and these should be left alone – do not confuse the two.

5 Disconnect each IAP sensor vacuum hose from its take-off stub on each throttle body, leaving the PAIR vacuum hose connected to its stub on the No. 3 throttle body **(see illustrations)**. Connect the vacuum gauge hoses to the take-off stubs. Make sure they are a good fit because any air leaks will result in false readings. Disconnect the IAP sensor wiring connector **(see illustration)**.

14.4c Throttle valve synchronising screw (arrowed, but hidden by hose) for each pair

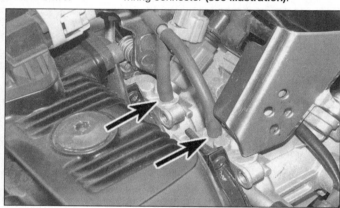

14.5a IAP sensor vacuum hoses (arrowed) on throttle bodies 1 and 2

14.5b IAP sensor vacuum hoses (arrowed) on throttle bodies 3 and 4

14.5c Disconnect the wiring connector from the IAP sensor

14.7 Synchronising the throttle valves

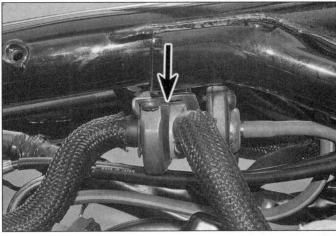

15.1a PAIR control valve (arrowed) and hoses . . .

6 Start the engine and if necessary adjust the idle speed to the level specified at the beginning of this Chapter using the idle speed adjuster screw **(see illustration 6.2)**. If using vacuum gauges fitted with damping adjustment, set this so that the needle flutter is just eliminated but so that they can still respond to small changes in pressure.

7 The vacuum readings for the cylinders should be the same. If the vacuum readings differ, adjust the throttle bodies by turning the synchronising screws until the readings are the same **(see illustration)**. Note that unless you have a very expensive set of digital gauges there is always likely to be some margin of error in the readings that cannot be eliminated – a maximum difference of 20 mmHg between readings is considered acceptable. Do not press hard on the screws whilst adjusting them, otherwise a false reading will be obtained. First synchronise the No. 1 body to No. 2 using the left-hand synchronising screw until the readings are the same **(see illustration 14.4a)**. Then synchronise No. 3 body to No. 4 using

the right-hand screw **(see illustration 14.4b)**. Finally synchronise Nos. 1 and 2 bodies to Nos. 3 and 4 using the centre screw **(see illustration 14.4c)**. Ensure the idle speed remains at the specified level throughout the procedure and adjust it if necessary as required.

8 When all gauges read the same, open and close the throttle twistgrip quickly to settle the linkage, and recheck the gauge readings, readjusting if necessary.

9 When the adjustment is complete, turn the engine OFF. Disconnect the vacuum gauge hoses and refit the IAP vacuum hoses (see Step 5). Reconnect the IAP sensor wiring connector.

10 Lower the fuel tank (see Chapter 4). Start the engine and re-check the idle speed.

15 PAIR (pulse air injection) system

1 To reduce the amount of unburned hydrocarbons released in the exhaust gases, a

pulse air injection (PAIR) system is fitted. The system consists of the control valve (mounted on the frame tubes above the valve cover), the reed valves (incorporated in the valve cover), and the hoses **(see illustrations)**. The control valve is actuated by a vacuum sourced from the No. 3 throttle body **(see illustration)**.

2 When the vacuum is low the PAIR control valve is open allowing filtered air to be drawn through it, the reed valves and cylinder head passages and into the exhaust ports. The air mixes with the exhaust gases, causing any unburned particles of the fuel in the mixture to be burnt in the exhaust port/pipes. This process changes a considerable amount of hydrocarbons and carbon monoxide into relatively harmless carbon dioxide and water. When the vacuum is high the valve closes, cutting off the air supply – this prevents exhaust popping when the throttle is closed with high engine revs. The reed valves are fitted to prevent the flow of exhaust gases back into the control valve and air filter housing.

15.1b . . . and reed valve housing (arrowed) – there is one on each side

15.1c PAIR control valve vacuum hose (arrowed)

16.4 Checking for play in the steering head bearings

16.6a Loosen the fork clamp bolt (arrowed) on each side . . .

3 The system is not adjustable and requires little maintenance, only to ensure that the hoses are in good condition and are securely connected at each end, and that there is no build-up of carbon fouling the reed valves – remove the fuel tank to access and inspect the components (see Chapter 4). Replace any hoses that are cracked, split or generally deteriorated with new ones. The reed valves can be checked for any build-up of carbon by unscrewing the cover bolts – if any is found, clean up the valves and their housings.

4 Refer to Chapter 4 for further details, and for checks on the system if it is believed to be faulty.

16 Steering head bearings

Freeplay check and adjustment

1 Steering head bearings can become dented, rough or loose during normal use of the machine. In extreme cases, worn or loose steering head bearings can cause steering wobble – a condition that is potentially dangerous.

Check

2 Support the motorcycle on its centrestand, then raise the front wheel off the ground by placing a support under the engine.

3 Point the front wheel straight ahead and slowly turn the handlebars from lock to lock. Any indents or roughness in the bearing races will be felt and if the bearings are too tight the bars will not move smoothly and freely. If the bearings are damaged they should be replaced with new ones (see Chapter 5). If the bearings are too tight, adjust them as described below.

4 Next, grasp the forks and try to move them forwards and backwards **(see illustration)**. Any looseness in the steering head bearings will be felt as front to back movement of the forks. **Note:** *Freeplay in the fork due to worn*

fork bushes can be misinterpreted as steering head bearing play. If play is felt in the steering head bearings, adjust them as follows.

Adjustment

5 Although not essential, it is wise to remove the fuel tank avoid the possibility of damage should a tool slip while adjustment is being made (see Chapter 4). Depending on the tools you have available you may also need to displace the handlebars (see Chapter 5).

6 Loosen the fork clamp bolts in the top yoke and the steering stem nut **(see illustrations)**.

7 Using a slim C-spanner or a suitable drift located in one of the notches in the adjuster

nut, loosen the nut slightly, then tighten it until all front to back freeplay in the bearings is removed, yet the steering is able to move freely from lock to lock **(see illustrations)**. The object is to set the adjuster nut so that the bearings are under a very light loading, just enough to remove any front to back freeplay but not so much as to make the steering tight – see Steps 3 and 4 to check.

Caution: Take great care not to overtighten the adjuster nut – excessive pressure will cause premature failure of the bearings.

8 If a spring balance is available the loading on the head bearings can be checked accurately. Ensure the motorcycle is supported with its

16.6b . . . and the steering stem nut (arrowed)

16.7a Steering head bearing adjuster nut (arrowed)

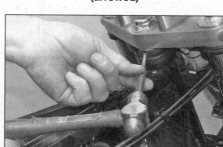

16.7b Using a drift located in one of the notches to adjust the bearings

16.7c Using a C-spanner to adjust the bearings

16.8 Checking the bearing loading with a spring balance

17.2 Check the action of the front suspension as described

front off the ground, then attach one end of the balance to the end of a handlebar grip and set the front wheel in the straight-ahead position. Now pull on the balance, making sure it is at right angles to the bar **(see illustration)**. If the bearing is adjusted correctly, the steering should start to turn when between 200 and 500 grams register on the balance scale. Connect the balance to the other handlebar and check the loading again – the result should be the same.

9 With the bearings correctly adjusted, tighten the steering stem nut and the fork clamp bolts in the top yoke, in that order, to the torque settings specified at the beginning of this Chapter **(see illustrations 16.6b and a)**.

10 Check the bearing adjustment as described above and re-adjust if necessary. Install the removed or displaced components in the reverse order of removal.

Lubrication

11 Over a considerable time the grease in the bearings will be dispersed or will harden allowing the ingress of dirt and water.

12 The steering head should be disassembled periodically and the bearings cleaned and re-greased (see Chapter 5, Section 10).

17 Suspension

1 The suspension components must be maintained in top operating condition to ensure rider safety. Loose, worn or damaged suspension parts decrease the motorcycle's stability and control.

Front suspension check

2 While standing alongside the motorcycle, apply the front brake and push on the handlebars to compress the forks several times **(see illustration)**. They should move up-and-down smoothly without binding. If binding is felt, the forks should be disassembled and inspected (see Chapter 5).

3 Inspect the fork inner tubes for scratches, corrosion and pitting which will cause

premature seal failure – if the damage is excessive, new tubes should be installed (see Chapter 5).

4 Inspect the area above the dust seal for signs of oil leaks, then carefully lever off the dust seal using a flat-bladed screwdriver and inspect the area around the fork seal **(see illustration)**. If leaks are evident, the seals must be re-placed with new ones (see Chapter 5).

5 The forks are adjustable for spring pre-load, rebound damping and compression damping and it is essential that both fork legs are adjusted equally (see Chapter 5).

6 Check the tightness of all suspension nuts and bolts to be sure none have worked loose, referring to the torque settings specified at the beginning of Chapter 5.

Rear suspension check

7 Inspect the rear shock absorbers, particularly on the rod, for fluid leaks, scratches, corrosion and pitting **(see illustration)**. If leaks are found, a new pair of shocks must be installed (see Chapter 5).

17.4 Check for oil leaks around the seals and for pitting on the inner tubes

17.7 Check for leakage and corrosion on the rod

17.9 Checking for play in the swingarm bearings

17.10 Checking for play in the shock mountings and suspension linkage

8 With the aid of an assistant to support the bike, compress the rear suspension several times. It should move up and down freely without binding. If binding is felt, the worn or faulty component must be identified and renewed. The problem could be caused by the shock absorbers or the swingarm bearings.

9 Support the motorcycle on its centrestand. Grasp the swingarm and rock it from side to side – there should be no discernible movement at the rear **(see illustration)**. If there's a little movement or a clicking can be heard, check the tightness of all the rear suspension mounting bolts and nuts, referring to the torque settings specified at the beginning of Chapter 5, and re-check for movement.

10 Grasp the top of the rear wheel and pull it upwards – there should be no discernible freeplay before the shock absorbers begin to compress **(see illustration)**. Any freeplay indicates worn bearings in the swingarm or worn shock absorber mountings. The worn components must be replaced with new ones (see Chapter 5).

11 To make a more accurate assessment of the swingarm bearings, remove the rear wheel (see Chapter 6) and the shock absorbers (see Chapter 5). Grasp the rear of the swingarm with one hand and place your other hand at the junction of the swingarm and the frame. Try to move the rear of the swingarm from side-to-side. Any wear in the bearings will be felt as movement between the swingarm and the frame at the front. If there is any wear, the swingarm will be felt to move forwards and backwards at the front (not from side-to-side). Next, move the swingarm up and down through its full travel. It should move freely, without any binding or rough spots. If the swingarm bearings are worn or if the swingarm does not move freely, new bearings must be fitted (see Chapter 5).

Front fork oil change

12 Although there is no set interval for changing the fork oil, note that the oil will degrade over a period of time and lose its damping qualities. Refer to Chapter 5, Sections 6 and 7 for details of front fork removal, oil draining and refilling. The forks do not need to be completely disassembled to change the oil.

Rear suspension bearing lubrication

13 Although there is no set interval for regreasing the swingarm bearings and shock absorber mounts, over a considerable mileage the grease in the bearings will be washed out or will harden allowing the ingress of dirt and water.

14 The shock absorbers and the swingarm should be removed periodically and the bearings and bushes cleaned and re-greased as necessary (see Chapter 5, Sections 11 and 13).

18 Valve clearances

Special tool: A set of feeler gauges is necessary for this job.

Check

1 The engine must be completely cold when measuring the valve clearances.

2 Remove the spark plugs (see Section 3) and the valve cover (see Chapter 2). The cylinders are numbered 1 to 4 from left to right, viewed as normally seated on the bike.

3 Make a chart or sketch of all valve positions so that a note of each clearance can be made against the relevant valve.

4 Unscrew the timing rotor cover bolts, noting the sealing washer fitted with the top bolt and remove the cover **(see illustration)**. Discard the gasket as new one must be fitted on reassembly. To check the valve clearances the engine must be turned so the valve being checked is closed. To turn the engine use a socket or spanner on the timing rotor – use the large hex cast into the rotor itself, do not use the timing rotor bolt **(see illustration)**. Turn the engine in a clockwise direction only.

18.4a Unscrew the bolts (arrowed) and remove the cover

18.4b Turn the crankshaft in a clockwise direction using a spanner on the hex

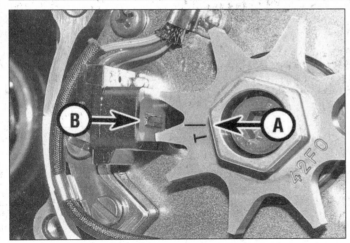

18.5a Align the scribe line (A) with the sensor (B) . . .

18.5b . . . and make sure the lines and cam lobes are positioned as described . . .

18.5c . . . with the scribed line aligned with the cylinder head

18.6 Checking the valve clearance with a feeler gauge

5 Turn the engine clockwise until the line on the timing rotor aligns with the sensing tip on the crankshaft position (CKP) sensor, and the lines on the right-hand end of each camshaft are flush with the cylinder head top surface and pointing away from each other **(see illustrations)**.

6 Check the clearances on Nos. 2 and 4 intake valves and Nos. 3 and 4 exhaust valves as follows. Insert a feeler gauge of the same thickness as the correct valve clearance (see Specifications at the beginning of this Chapter) between the camshaft lobe and the cam follower of each valve in turn **(see illustration)**. The gauge should be a firm sliding fit – you should feel a slight drag when the you pull the gauge out. If not, use the feeler gauges to obtain the exact clearance. Record the measured clearances on your chart. **Note:** *The intake and exhaust valve clearances are different.*

7 Now turn the engine clockwise through 360° so that the line on the timing rotor again aligns with the sensing tip on the CKP sensor, and the lines on the right-hand end of each camshaft are flush with the cylinder head top surface but pointing towards each other.

8 Check the clearances on Nos. 1 and 3 intake valves and Nos. 1 and 2 exhaust valves as described in Step 6. Record the measured clearances on your chart.

Adjustment

9 When all clearances have been measured and recorded, identify whether the clearance on any valve falls outside that specified. If it does, the shim between the follower and the valve must be replaced with one of a thickness which will restore the correct clearance.

10 Changing the shims requires removal of the camshafts (see Chapter 2). Place rags over the spark plug holes and the cam chain tunnel

to prevent a shim dropping into the engine on removal.

11 With the camshafts removed, lift out the cam follower of the valve in question using a magnet or suction tool (such as a valve lapping tool) **(see illustration)**. Retrieve the shim from

18.11a Lift out the cam follower . . .

18.11b . . . and retrieve the shim from inside the follower . . .

18.11c . . . or from the top of the valve

18.12 Measuring the shim thickness with a micrometer

either the inside of the follower or pick it out of the top of the valve using a magnet, a small screwdriver with a dab of grease on it (the shim will stick to the grease), or a suitable pair of pliers **(see illustrations)**. Do not allow the shim to fall into the engine.

12 The shim size should be marked on its upper face – a shim marked 170 is 1.70 mm thick – but the shim should be measured with a micrometer to check that it has not worn **(see illustration)**. If the shim has worn undersize, this must be taken into account and the valve clearance adjusted accordingly.

13 Using the appropriate shim selection chart, find where the measured valve clearance and existing shim thickness values intersect and read off the shim size required **(see illustrations)**.

14 New shims are available in 0.05 mm increments from 1.200 to 2.200 mm and can be obtained from a Suzuki dealer. If the required replacement shim is greater than 2.20 mm (the largest available), the valve is probably not seating correctly due to a build-up of carbon deposits or valve damage. Remove the valve for checking (see Chapter 2).

15 When replacing a shim, lubricate it with engine oil or molybdenum disulphide oil (a 50/50 mixture of molybdenum disulphide grease and engine oil) and fit it into its recess in the top of the valve with the size marking facing up **(see illustration 18.11c)**. Check that the shim is correctly seated, then lubricate the follower with engine oil or molybdenum disulphide oil and fit it onto the valve **(see illustration)**. Repeat the process for any other valves as required, then install the camshaft(s) (see Chapter 2).

16 Rotate the crankshaft several turns to seat the new shim(s), then check the clearances again.

17 Apply a suitable sealant (Suzuki Bond

PRESENT SHIM SIZE (mm)

MEASURED TAPPET CLEARANCE (mm)	1.20	1.25	1.30	1.35	1.40	1.45	1.50	1.55	1.60	1.65	1.70	1.75	1.80	1.85	1.90	1.95	2.00	2.05	2.10	2.15	2.20
0.00-0.04			1.20	1.25	1.30	1.35	1.40	1.45	1.50	1.55	1.60	1.65	1.70	1.75	1.80	1.85	1.90	1.95	2.00	2.05	2.10
0.05-0.09		1.20	1.25	1.30	1.35	1.40	1.45	1.50	1.55	1.60	1.65	1.70	1.75	1.80	1.85	1.90	1.95	2.00	2.05	2.10	2.15
0.10-0.20	SPECIFIED CLEARANCE/NO ADJUSTMENT REQUIRED																				
0.21-0.25	1.30	1.35	1.40	1.45	1.50	1.55	1.60	1.65	1.70	1.75	1.80	1.85	1.90	1.95	2.00	2.05	2.10	2.15	2.20		
0.26-0.30	1.35	1.40	1.45	1.50	1.55	1.60	1.65	1.70	1.75	1.80	1.85	1.90	1.95	2.00	2.05	2.10	2.15	2.20			
0.31-0.35	1.40	1.45	1.50	1.55	1.60	1.65	1.70	1.75	1.80	1.85	1.90	1.95	2.00	2.05	2.10	2.15	2.20				
0.36-0.40	1.45	1.50	1.55	1.60	1.65	1.70	1.75	1.80	1.85	1.90	1.95	2.00	2.05	2.10	2.15	2.20					
0.41-0.45	1.50	1.55	1.60	1.65	1.70	1.75	1.80	1.85	1.90	1.95	2.00	2.05	2.10	2.15	2.20						
0.46-0.50	1.55	1.60	1.65	1.70	1.75	1.80	1.85	1.90	1.95	2.00	2.05	2.10	2.15	2.20							
0.51-0.55	1.60	1.65	1.70	1.75	1.80	1.85	1.90	1.95	2.00	2.05	2.10	2.15	2.20								
0.56-0.60	1.65	1.70	1.75	1.80	1.85	1.90	1.95	2.00	2.05	2.10	2.15	2.20									
0.61-0.65	1.70	1.75	1.80	1.85	1.90	1.95	2.00	2.05	2.10	2.15	2.20										
0.66-0.70	1.75	1.80	1.85	1.90	1.95	2.00	2.05	2.10	2.15	2.20											
0.71-0.75	1.80	1.85	1.90	1.95	2.00	2.05	2.10	2.15	2.20												
0.76-0.80	1.85	1.90	1.95	2.00	2.05	2.10	2.15	2.20													
0.81-0.85	1.90	1.95	2.00	2.05	2.10	2.15	2.20														
0.86-0.90	1.95	2.00	2.05	2.10	2.15	2.20															
0.91-0.95	2.00	2.05	2.10	2.15	2.20																
0.96-1.00	2.05	2.10	2.15	2.20																	
1.01-1.05	2.10	2.15	2.20																		
1.06-1.10	2.15	2.20																			
1.11-1.15	2.20																				

H31236

18.13a Shim selection chart – intake valves

PRESENT SHIM SIZE (mm)

MEASURED TAPPET CLEARANCE (mm)	1.20	1.25	1.30	1.35	1.40	1.45	1.50	1.55	1.60	1.65	1.70	1.75	1.80	1.85	1.90	1.95	2.00	2.05	2.10	2.15	2.20
0.05-0.09				1.20	1.25	1.30	1.35	1.40	1.45	1.50	1.55	1.60	1.65	1.70	1.75	1.80	1.85	1.90	1.95	2.00	2.05
0.10-0.14			1.20	1.25	1.30	1.35	1.40	1.45	1.50	1.55	1.60	1.65	1.70	1.75	1.80	1.85	1.90	1.95	2.00	2.05	2.10
0.15-0.19		1.20	1.25	1.30	1.35	1.40	1.45	1.50	1.55	1.60	1.65	1.70	1.75	1.80	1.85	1.90	1.95	2.00	2.05	2.10	2.15
0.20-0.30	SPECIFIED CLEARANCE/NO ADJUSTMENT REQUIRED																				
0.31-0.35	1.30	1.35	1.40	1.45	1.50	1.55	1.60	1.65	1.70	1.75	1.80	1.85	1.90	1.95	2.00	2.05	2.10	2.15	2.20		
0.36-0.40	1.35	1.40	1.45	1.50	1.55	1.60	1.65	1.70	1.75	1.80	1.85	1.90	1.95	2.00	2.05	2.10	2.15	2.20			
0.41-0.45	1.40	1.45	1.50	1.55	1.60	1.65	1.70	1.75	1.80	1.85	1.90	1.95	2.00	2.05	2.10	2.15	2.20				
0.46-0.50	1.45	1.50	1.55	1.60	1.65	1.70	1.75	1.80	1.85	1.90	1.95	2.00	2.05	2.10	2.15	2.20					
0.51-0.55	1.50	1.55	1.60	1.65	1.70	1.75	1.80	1.85	1.90	1.95	2.00	2.05	2.10	2.15	2.20						
0.56-0.60	1.55	1.60	1.65	1.70	1.75	1.80	1.85	1.90	1.95	2.00	2.05	2.10	2.15	2.20							
0.61-0.65	1.60	1.65	1.70	1.75	1.80	1.85	1.90	1.95	2.00	2.05	2.10	2.15	2.20								
0.66-0.70	1.65	1.70	1.75	1.80	1.85	1.90	1.95	2.00	2.05	2.10	2.15	2.20									
0.71-0.75	1.70	1.75	1.80	1.85	1.90	1.95	2.00	2.05	2.10	2.15	2.20										
0.76-0.80	1.75	1.80	1.85	1.90	1.95	2.00	2.05	2.10	2.15	2.20											
0.81-0.85	1.80	1.85	1.90	1.95	2.00	2.05	2.10	2.15	2.20												
0.86-0.90	1.85	1.90	1.95	2.00	2.05	2.10	2.15	2.20													
0.91-0.95	1.90	1.95	2.00	2.05	2.10	2.15	2.20														
0.96-1.00	1.95	2.00	2.05	2.10	2.15	2.20															
1.01-1.05	2.00	2.05	2.10	2.15	2.20																
1.06-1.10	2.05	2.10	2.15	2.20																	
1.11-1.15	2.10	2.15	2.20																		
1.16-1.20	2.15	2.20																			
1.21-1.25	2.20																				

H31237

18.13b Shim selection chart – exhaust valves

18.15 Fit the shim (arrowed), then fit the follower over the valve

18.17a Apply some sealant to the grommet (arrowed) and crankcase joints . . .

18.17b . . . then fit the cover using a new gasket

1207B or equivalent) to the CKP sensor wiring grommet and to the crankcase joints **(see illustration)**. Install the timing rotor cover using a new gasket and tighten the bolts to the torque setting specified at the beginning of the chapter, not forgetting the sealing washer with the top bolt **(see illustration)**.

18 Install the valve cover (see Chapter 2) and the spark plugs (see Section 3).

19 Sidestand, centrestand and starter interlock circuit

1 Check the stand springs for damage and distortion **(see illustrations)**. The springs must be capable of retracting the stand fully and holding it retracted when the motorcycle is in use. If a spring is sagged or broken it must be replaced with a new one.

2 Lubricate the stand pivots and spring ends regularly (see Section 13).

3 Check each stand and its mount for bends and cracks, and that the bolts and nut are tightened to the correct torque settings (see Chapter 6). If necessary a stand can often be repaired by welding.

4 Check the operation of the starter interlock circuit by shifting the transmission into neutral, retracting the stand, pulling the clutch lever in and starting the engine. Select a gear. Extend the sidestand. The engine should stop as the sidestand is extended.

5 If the sidestand is down, it should be possible to start the engine if the transmission is in neutral and the clutch lever is pulled in. The engine can be started in gear with the clutch lever pulled in, but only if the sidestand is retracted. If the circuit does not operate as described, check the sidestand switch, relay and diodes, the gear position sensor and

the clutch switch (see Chapter 4 for the gear position switch and Chapter 8 for the rest).

20 Battery

1 All models are fitted with a sealed MF (maintenance free) battery. **Note:** *Do not attempt to remove the battery caps to check the electrolyte level or battery specific gravity. Removal will damage the caps, resulting in electrolyte leakage and battery damage.* All that should be done is to check that the terminals are clean and tight and that the casing is not damaged or leaking. See Chapter 8 for further details.

2 If the machine is not in regular use, remove the battery and give it a refresher charge every month to six weeks (see Chapter 8).

19.1a Sidestand springs (arrowed)

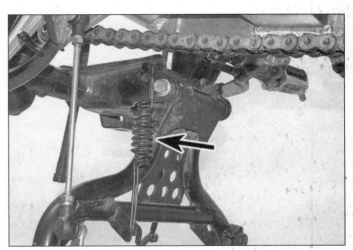

19.1b Centrestand springs (arrowed)

Chapter 2
Engine, clutch and transmission

Contents

Degrees of difficulty

Easy, suitable for novice with little experience	**Fairly easy,** suitable for beginner with some experience	**Fairly difficult,** suitable for competent DIY mechanic	**Difficult,** suitable for experienced DIY mechanic	**Very difficult,** suitable for expert DIY or professional

Specifications

General

Type	Four-stroke in-line four
Capacity	1402 cc
Bore	81.0 mm
Stroke	68.0 mm
Compression ratio	9.5 to 1
Clutch	Wet multi-plate
Transmission	Six-speed constant mesh
Lubrication	Wet sump
Final drive	Chain and sprockets

Cylinder compression

Standard	168 psi (11.8 Bar)*
Minimum	125 psi (8.8 Bar)*
Maximum difference between cylinders	28 psi (2 Bar)*

*Note: *If all cylinders record less than 156 psi or 11 Bar (even if they are above the minimum), or if the difference between any two cylinders is greater than the maximum listed above, or if any one cylinder is less than the minimum, the engine should be overhauled.*

Lubrication system

Oil pressure (with engine warm) . . . .   43 to 85 psi (3.0 to 6.0 Bar) at 3000 rpm, oil at 60°C

Camshafts

Intake lobe height
    Standard . . . .   35.28 to 35.33 mm
    Service limit (min) . . . .   34.98 mm
Exhaust lobe height
    Standard . . . .   34.18 to 34.22 mm
    Service limit (min) . . . .   33.88 mm
Journal diameter . . . .   23.959 to 23.980 mm
Journal holder diameter . . . .   24.012 to 24.025 mm
Journal oil clearance
    Standard . . . .   0.032 to 0.066 mm
    Service limit (max) . . . .   0.15 mm
Runout (max) . . . .   0.10 mm

Cylinder head

Warpage (max) . . . .   0.20 mm

Valves, guides and springs

Valve clearances . . . .   see Chapter 1
Intake valve
    Head diameter . . . .   28.5 mm
    Stem diameter . . . .   4.475 to 4.490 mm
    Guide bore diameter . . . .   4.500 to 4.512 mm
    Stem-to-guide clearance . . . .   0.010 to 0.037 mm
    Side clearance, wobble (max) – see text . . . .   0.35 mm
    Margin thickness (min) . . . .   0.5 mm
    Seat width . . . .   0.9 to 1.1 mm
    Head runout (max) . . . .   0.03 mm
    Stem runout (max) . . . .   0.05 mm
Exhaust valve
    Head diameter . . . .   25.0 mm
    Stem diameter . . . .   4.455 to 4.470 mm
    Guide bore diameter . . . .   4.500 to 4.512 mm
    Stem-to-guide clearance . . . .   0.030 to 0.057 mm
    Side clearance, wobble (max) – see text . . . .   0.35 mm
    Margin thickness (min) . . . .   0.5 mm
    Seat width . . . .   0.9 to 1.1 mm
    Head runout (max) . . . .   0.03 mm
    Stem runout (max) . . . .   0.05 mm
Valve spring free length (intake and exhaust)
    Inner spring . . . .   38.6 mm
    Outer spring . . . .   40.6 mm

Cylinders

Bore standard dimension . . . .   81.000 to 81.015 mm
Warpage of gasket face (max) . . . .   0.20 mm

Pistons

Piston diameter (measured 15 mm up from skirt, at 90° to piston pin axis)
    Standard . . . .   80.980 to 80.995 mm
    Service limit (min) . . . .   80.880 mm
Piston-to-bore clearance
    Standard . . . .   0.015 to 0.025 mm
    Service limit (max) . . . .   0.120 mm
Piston pin diameter
    Standard . . . .   17.996 to 18.000 mm
    Service limit (min) . . . .   17.980 mm
Piston pin bore diameter in piston
    Standard . . . .   18.002 to 18.008 mm
    Service limit (max) . . . .   18.030 mm

Piston rings

Ring end gap (free)
  Top ring
    Standard . . . . 9.5 mm (approx.)
    Service limit (min) . . . . 7.6 mm
  2nd ring
    Standard . . . . 11.0 mm (approx.)
    Service limit (min) . . . . 8.8 mm
Ring end gap (installed)
  Top ring
    Standard . . . . 0.08 to 0.20 mm
    Service limit (max) . . . . 0.50 mm
  2nd ring
    Standard . . . . 0.18 to 0.30 mm
    Service limit (max) . . . . 0.50 mm
Ring thickness
  Top ring . . . . 1.175 to 1.190 mm
  2nd ring . . . . 0.970 to 0.990 mm
Ring groove width in piston
  Top ring . . . . 1.21 to 1.23 mm
  2nd ring . . . . 1.01 to 1.03 mm
  Oil ring . . . . 2.01 to 2.03 mm
Ring-to-groove clearance
  Top ring (max) . . . . 0.18 mm
  2nd ring (max) . . . . 0.15 mm

Clutch

Friction plate
  Quantity 10
  Thickness
    Standard . . . . 3.22 to 3.38 mm
    Service limit (min) . . . . 2.92 mm
  Tab width
    Standard . . . . 13.7 to 13.8 mm
    Service limit (min) . . . . 12.9 mm
Plain plate
  Quantity 9
  Warpage (max) . . . . 0.1 mm
Spring free length
  Standard . . . . 28.96 mm
  Service limit (min) . . . . 27.6 mm

Clutch release mechanism

Clutch fluid . . . . DOT 4
Master cylinder bore diameter . . . . 14.000 to 14.043 mm
Master cylinder piston diameter . . . . 13.957 to 13.984 mm
Release cylinder bore diameter . . . . 35.700 to 35.762 mm
Release cylinder piston diameter . . . . 35.650 to 35.675 mm

Connecting rods

Small-end internal diameter
  Standard . . . . 18.010 to 18.018 mm
  Service limit (max) . . . . 18.040 mm
Big-end side clearance
  Standard . . . . 0.1 to 0.2 mm
  Service limit (max) . . . . 0.3 mm
Big-end width . . . . 20.95 to 21.00 mm
Crankpin width . . . . 21.10 to 21.15 mm
Big-end ID
  Code 1 . . . . 41.000 to 41.008 mm
  Code 2 . . . . 41.008 to 41.016 mm
Crankpin OD
  Code 1 . . . . 37.992 to 38.000 mm
  Code 2 . . . . 37.984 to 37.992 mm
  Code 3 . . . . 37.976 to 37.984 mm
Big-end oil clearance
  Standard . . . . 0.032 to 0.056 mm
  Service limit (max) . . . . 0.08 mm

Crankshaft and bearings

Main bearing journal OD
    Code A . . . .   39.992 to 40.000 mm
    Code B . . . .   39.984 to 39.992 mm
    Code C. . . . .   39.976 to 39.984 mm
Main bearing housing ID
    Code A . . . .   43.000 to 43.008 mm
    Code B . . . .   43.008 to 43.016 mm
Main bearing oil clearance
    Standard. . . . .   0.016 to 0.040 mm
    Service limit (max) . . . .   0.080 mm
Runout (max) . . . .   0.05 mm
Thrust bearing clearance . . . .   0.055 to 0.110 mm
Thrust bearing thickness
    Right-hand side (inner bearing) . . . .   2.425 to 2.450 mm
    Left-hand side (outer bearing) . . . .   Selective fit (see text)

Transmission

Gear ratios (no. of teeth)
    Primary reduction . . . .   1.509 to 1 (73/47)
    Final reduction . . . .   2.277 to 1 (41/18)
    1st gear. . . . .   2.916 to 1 (35/12)
    2nd gear . . . .   1.937 to 1 (31/16)
    3rd gear . . . .   1.526 to 1 (29/19)
    4th gear . . . .   1.285 to 1 (27/21)
    5th gear . . . .   1.136 to 1 (25/22)
    6th gear . . . .   1.000 to 1 (24/24)

Selector drum and forks

Selector fork-to-gear groove clearance
    Standard. . . . .   0.1 to 0.3 mm
    Service limit (max) . . . .   0.5 mm
Selector fork end thickness . . . .   4.8 to 4.9 mm
Selector fork groove width in gears . . . .   5.0 to 5.1 mm

Torque settings

Balancer weight cover bolts. . . . .   10 Nm
Balancer weight shaft holder mounting bolt . . . .   10 Nm
Balancer weight shaft holder pinch bolt. . . . .   10 Nm
Cam chain tensioner cap bolt . . . .   35 Nm
Cam chain tensioner mounting bolts . . . .   10 Nm
Cam chain top guide bolts . . . .   10 Nm
Camshaft holder bolts . . . .   10 Nm
Camshaft sprocket bolts . . . .   25 Nm
Clutch centre nut . . . .   90 Nm
Clutch cover bolts . . . .   11 Nm
Clutch hose banjo bolts . . . .   23 Nm
Clutch master cylinder clamp bolts . . . .   10 Nm
Clutch release cylinder bleed valve . . . .   8 Nm
Clutch spring bolts. . . . .   10 Nm
Clutch spring bolt holders . . . .   23 Nm
Connecting rod cap bolts
    Initial setting . . . .   21 Nm
    Final angle setting. . . . .   + 90°
Crankcase bolts
    Crankshaft journal 9 mm bolts
        Initial setting . . . .   18 Nm
        Final setting . . . .   32 Nm
    8 mm bolts . . . .   26 Nm
    6 mm bolts . . . .   11 Nm
Crankcase breather cover bolts. . . . .   10 Nm
Cylinder block nut . . . .   10 Nm
Cylinder head 6 mm bolts . . . .   10 Nm
Cylinder head 10 mm nuts and bolts
    Initial setting . . . .   25 Nm
    Final setting . . . .   37 Nm

Torque settings (continued)

Engine mounting bolts
- Upper rear mounting bolt nut .... 85 Nm
- Lower rear mounting bolt nut .... 88 Nm
- Cradle-to-frame bolts/nuts .... 50 Nm
- Cradle/frame-to-engine bolts (middle) .... 55 Nm
- Left-hand front mounting bracket-to-engine .... 55 Nm
- Left-hand front mounting bracket-to-frame .... 50 Nm
- Front mounting bolts/nuts .... 55 Nm
- Middle bracket-to-cradle/frame bolts .... 23 Nm

Gearchange selector drum cam centre bolt
- K2 models .... 10 Nm
- All other models .... 13 Nm

Gearchange stopper arm bolt .... 10 Nm
Main oil gallery plugs (below timing rotor cover and alternator cover) . 35 Nm
Main oil gallery plug (inside crankcase) .... 21 Nm
Sub oil gallery plug (in upper crankcase forward of timing rotor cover). 10 Nm
Sub oil gallery plug (in upper crankcase inside clutch housing) ...... 35 Nm
Oil control valve plug .... 35 Nm
Oil hose (external) banjo bolts .... 20 Nm
Oil hose union bolts .... 10 Nm
Oil pipe (internal) bolts .... 10 Nm
Oil strainer bolts .... 10 Nm
Oil sump bolts .... 11 Nm
Piston oil jet bolts .... 10 Nm
Starter clutch bolts .... 25 Nm
Timing rotor cover bolts .... 11 Nm

Valve cover bolts
- Centre (small head) bolts (M8 thread) .... 20 Nm
- Outer (large head) bolts (M7 thread) .... 14 Nm

1 General information

The engine is an air/oil-cooled in-line four. The valves are operated by double overhead camshafts which are chain driven off the middle of the crankshaft. The engine is constructed from aluminium alloy.

The crankcase is divided horizontally and incorporates a wet sump, pressure-fed lubrication system which uses a gear-driven, dual-rotor oil pump, an oil filter, pressure regulator and an oil pressure switch. The oil is cooled by a radiator matrix mounted on the frame downtubes.

Power from the crankshaft is routed to the transmission via the clutch, which is of the wet, multi-plate type and is gear-driven off the crankshaft. The clutch is operated hydraulically. The transmission is a six-speed constant-mesh unit. Final drive to the rear wheel is by chain and sprockets.

2 Component access

Operations possible with the engine in the frame

The components and assemblies listed below can be removed without having to remove the engine from the frame. If however, a number of areas require attention at the same time, removal of the engine is recommended.

Valve cover
Cam chain tensioner
Camshafts
Cylinder head
Cylinder block
Pistons and rings
Starter motor (see Chapter 8)
Starter clutch and idle gear
Timing rotor and crankshaft position sensor (see Chapter 4)
Clutch
Gearchange mechanism
Alternator (see Chapter 8)
Oil sump, oil strainer and pressure regulator
Balancer weight and shaft
Selector drum and forks (but see text)
Oil cooler

Operations requiring engine removal

It is necessary to remove the engine from

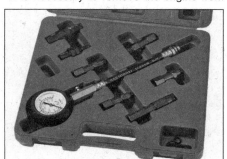

3.3 Compression gauge and adapter set

the frame to gain access to the following components.

Cam chain and tensioner blade
Crankshaft and connecting rods
Transmission shafts
Oil pump

3 Engine wear assessment

1 Poor engine performance may be caused by leaking valves, incorrect valve clearances, a leaking head gasket, or worn pistons, piston rings or cylinder walls. A cylinder compression check will highlight these conditions and can also indicate the presence of excessive carbon deposits in the cylinder head, and a leakdown test (for which special equipment is needed – consult a Suzuki dealer) will pinpoint the actual cause(s) of the problem.

2 If there is any doubt about the performance of the engine lubrication system an oil pressure check must be carried out. The check provides useful information about the state of wear of the engine.

Cylinder compression check

Special tool: A compression gauge is required to perform this test.

3 The only tools required are a compression gauge (with a threaded adapter to fit the spark plug hole in the cylinder head), and a spark plug socket **(see illustration)**. Suzuki provide a gauge and adapter (Pt Nos. 09915-64510 and 09913-10750) for this purpose, or one can

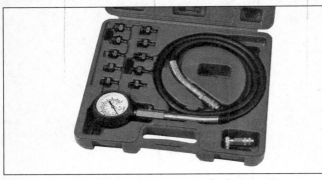

3.13 Oil pressure gauge and adapter set

3.14 Main oil gallery plug (arrowed)

be obtained commercially. Depending on the outcome of the initial test, a squirt-type oil can may also be needed.

4 Make sure the battery is fully charged (see Chapter 8), the valve clearances are correctly set (see Chapter 1), and that the cylinder head nuts and bolts are tightened to the correct torque setting (see Section 9).

5 Run the engine until it is at normal operating temperature. Remove the spark plugs (see Chapter 1). Fit the plugs back into the coils and earth them against the engine away from the plug hole – if the plug is not earthed the ignition system could be damaged.

6 Fit the adaptor and gauge into the No. 1 cylinder spark plug hole.

7 With the ignition switch ON, the kill switch set to RUN, the spark plugs earthed, the clutch lever pulled in and the throttle held fully open turn the engine over on the starter motor until the gauge reading has built up and stabilised.

8 Compare the reading on the gauge to the cylinder compression figure specified at the beginning of the Chapter. Repeat for the remaining cylinders.

9 If the reading is low, it could be due to a worn cylinder bore, piston or rings, failure of the head gasket, or worn valve seats. To determine which is the cause, pour a small quantity of engine oil into the spark plug hole to seal the rings, then repeat the compression test. If the figures are noticeably higher the cause is worn cylinder, piston or rings. If there is no change the cause is a leaking head gasket or worn valve seats.

10 Although unlikely, if the reading is high there could be a build-up of carbon deposits in the combustion chamber. Remove the cylinder head and scrape all deposits off the pistons and the combustion chambers.

Engine oil pressure check

11 The oil pressure warning light should illuminate when the ignition (main) switch is turned ON, and should extinguish when the engine is started – this serves as a check that the LED is working. If the oil pressure light comes on whilst the engine is running, low oil pressure is indicated – stop the engine immediately and carry out an oil level check (see *Pre-ride checks*).

12 An oil pressure check must be carried out

if the warning light comes on when the engine is running yet the oil level is good. It can also provide useful information about the condition of the engine's lubrication system.

13 To check the oil pressure, a suitable gauge, hose and adapter (which screws into the crankcase) will be needed **(see illustration)**. Suzuki produce service tools Pt. Nos. 09915-77330, 09915-74520 and 09915-74540 for this purpose. If not already assembled connect the hose to the gauge.

14 Put the bike on its sidestand. Position a suitable container below the main oil gallery plug on the left-hand side of the engine to catch any spilled oil **(see illustration)**. Unscrew the plug and screw the adapter into the oil gallery, then fit the hose onto the adapter. If any oil is lost, replenish it to the correct level before proceeding (see *Pre-ride checks*).

15 Warm the engine up to normal operating temperature (between 10 and 20 minutes running at 2000 rpm) then increase the engine speed to 3000 rpm whilst watching the gauge reading. The oil pressure should be similar to that given in the Specifications at the beginning of this Chapter.

16 If the pressure is significantly lower than the standard, either the pressure regulator is stuck open, the oil pump is faulty, the oil strainer or filter is blocked, or there is other engine damage. Begin diagnosis by checking the oil filter, strainer, regulator, then the oil pump. If these items are good, it is likely the bearing oil clearances are excessive and the engine needs to be overhauled.

17 If the pressure is too high, either an oil

4.7 Disconnect the fan switch wiring connector

passage is clogged, the regulator is stuck closed or the wrong grade of oil is being used.

18 Turn the engine OFF. Disconnect the hose and gauge from the adapter and unscrew the adapter from the crankcase.

> ⚠ *Warning: Be careful when removing the pressure gauge adapter as the exhaust pipes, the engine and the oil itself can cause severe burns.*

19 Fit a new sealing washer onto the main oil gallery plug and tighten it to the torque setting specified at the beginning of this Chapter **(see illustration)**. Check the engine oil level (see *Pre-ride checks*).

4 Engine removal and installation

> ⚠ *Warning: The engine is very heavy. Removal and installation should be carried out with the aid of at least one assistant; personal injury or damage could occur if the engine falls or is dropped. If available, an hydraulic or mechanical floor jack should be used to support and lower or raise the engine.*

Removal

1 Support the bike on its centrestand. Work can be made easier by raising the machine to a suitable working height on an hydraulic ramp or a suitable platform. Make sure the motorcycle is secure and will not topple over (see *Tools and Workshop Tips* in the Reference section).

2 If the engine is dirty, particularly around its mountings, wash it thoroughly before starting any major dismantling work. This will make work much easier and rule out the possibility of dirt falling into some vital component.

3 Remove the seat and the side panels (see Chapter 7).

4 Remove the fuel tank (see Chapter 4).

5 Remove the battery (see Chapter 8).

6 Drain the engine oil (see Chapter 1). If required, remove the oil filter (see Chapter 1).

7 Remove the oil cooler along with its hoses (see Chapter 3). Disconnect the wiring connector from the oil cooler fan switch **(see illustration)**.

4.12a Release the clamp (arrowed) and detach the hose from each side

4.12b Release the clamp (arrowed) and detach the hose from the breather

4.13 Disconnect the wiring connectors

8 Remove the exhaust system (see Chapter 4).

9 Remove the ignition HT coils (see Chapter 4).

10 Remove the throttle bodies (see Chapter 4). Plug the engine intake manifolds with clean rag to prevent debris falling into the engine.

11 Remove the camshaft position sensor (see Chapter 4).

12 Detach the PAIR system hoses from their unions on the valve cover **(see illustration)**. Detach the crankcase breather hose from the breather housing **(see illustration)**.

13 Disconnect the oil temperature sensor and crankshaft position (CKP) sensor/oil pressure switch wiring connectors – they are between the frame and the air filter housing on the right-hand side **(see illustration)**.

14 Disconnect the earth lead wiring connector **(see illustration)**. Feed the main lead through to the top of the crankcase, noting its routing.

15 Disconnect the gear position sensor (white) and sidestand switch (green) wiring connectors – they are between the frame and the air filter housing on the left-hand side **(see illustration)**.

16 Pull back the boot on the starter motor terminal, then undo the terminal nut **(see illustration)**.

17 Make an alignment mark between the slit in the gearchange linkage arm clamp and the end of the gearchange shaft, then unscrew the pinch bolt and slide the arm off the shaft **(see illustration)**.

18 Remove the front sprocket cover (see

Chapter 6). Displace the clutch release cylinder (see Section 17). Remove the clutch pushrod for safekeeping **(see illustration)**. Remove the front sprocket (see Chapter 6).

19 Disconnect the alternator wiring connector **(see illustration)**.

20 Make sure that all engine wiring is free of any clips and ties on the frame, and that all loom wiring is free from any clips and ties on the engine. Note the routing of all wiring, and where necessary feed it through to its source or secure it clear of the engine.

21 At this point, position an hydraulic or mechanical jack under the engine with a block of wood between the jack head and sump. Make sure the jack is centrally positioned so the engine will not topple in any direction when the last mounting bolt is removed. Take

4.14 Disconnect the earth lead wiring connector (arrowed)

4.15 Disconnect the wiring connectors (arrowed)

4.16 Pull back the boot then unscrew the nut and detach the lead

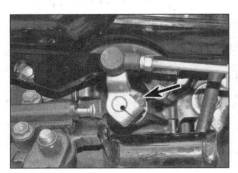

4.17 Make an alignment mark with the slit, then unscrew the bolt (arrowed) and slide the arm off

4.18 Remove the clutch pushrod

4.19 Disconnect the alternator wiring connector

4.21 Support the weight of the engine on a jack

4.22a Remove the blanking caps then unscrew the bolts at the rear of the cradle . . .

4.22b . . . and those at the top and front (arrowed)

4.22c Unscrew the bolt and remove the special nut

4.22d Support the cradle as you withdraw the bolt . . .

4.22e . . . then free the wiring clip from the cradle

the weight of the engine on the jack **(see illustration)**.

22 To remove the engine, the cradle section of the frame on the right-hand side must be separated from the main frame. First remove the blanking caps from the bolts securing the cradle to the frame at the rear, top and front, then unscrew the bolts **(see illustrations)**. Unscrew the bolt securing the cradle to the engine in the middle, noting the shaped nut that locates against the engine **(see**

illustration). Unscrew the nut on the bolt securing the cradle to the engine at the front, then support the cradle, withdraw the bolt, displace the cradle, and free the wiring clip **(see illustrations)**.

23 Unscrew the nut on the left-hand front engine mounting bolt then withdraw the bolt **(see illustration)**. Unscrew the bolts securing the bracket and remove it.

24 Unscrew the bolt securing the frame to the engine in the middle on the left-hand side,

noting the shaped nut that locates against the engine **(see illustration)**.

25 Unscrew the nuts on the upper and lower rear mounting bolts **(see illustration)**.

26 Check that the engine is properly supported by the jack. Withdraw the upper rear mounting bolt. Withdraw the lower rear mounting bolt, noting the washer. Check that all wiring, cables and hoses are well clear, then carefully lower the jack and manoeuvre the engine so the drive chain can be slipped

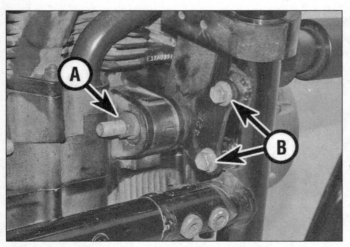

4.23 Unscrew the nut (A) and withdraw the bolt, then unscrew the bolts (B) and remove the bracket

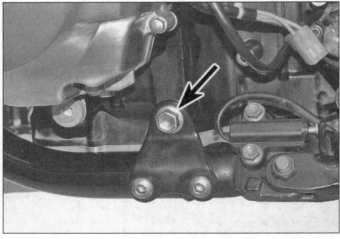

4.24 Unscrew the bolt (arrowed) and remove the special nut

4.25 Unscrew the nuts (arrowed)

4.27 Check the front mounting dampers (arrowed)

off the end of the output shaft. Fully lower the jack, then lift the engine, remove the jack, and manoeuvre the engine out to the right-hand side.

27 Check the condition of the front mount bushes and replace them with new ones if they are damaged, deformed or deteriorated **(see illustration)**.

Installation

28 Manoeuvre the engine into position under the frame and lift it onto the jack **(see illustration 4.21)**. Raise the engine, taking care not to catch any part on the frame, and loop the drive chain around the output shaft as early as possible. Raise and move the engine as required to align the rear mounting bolt holes. Note that it may be necessary to adjust the jack as the bolts are installed.

29 Slide the rear bolts through from the left-hand side, not forgetting to fit the washer with the lower bolt.

30 If removed fit the bushes into the engine front mounts **(see illustration 4.27)**. Fit the left-hand front mounting bracket with its bolts and nut and tighten them finger-tight **(see illustration 4.23)**. Fit the left-hand middle bolt with its shaped nut and tighten it finger-tight **(see illustration 4.24)**. Fit the wiring clip into the engine cradle then locate it on the frame, install all its bolts and nuts and tighten them finger-tight **(see illustrations 4.22e, d, c, and b)**.

31 Apply a thread locking compound to the rear mounting bolt threads then fit the nuts and tighten them to the torque setting specified at the beginning of the Chapter **(see illustration 4.25)**.

32 Tighten all the cradle-to frame bolts/nuts to the specified torque setting. Tighten the left-hand front mounting bracket-to-frame bolts to the specified torque.

33 Tighten the cradle-to-engine and frame-to-engine bolts/nuts at the front and in the middle to the specified torque settings. Go

round and check that all engine mounting bolts and nuts are now tightened to the specified torque. Fit the blanking caps into the cradle-to-frame bolts **(see illustration 4.22a)**.

34 The remainder of the installation procedure is the reverse of removal, noting the following points:

● Use new gaskets on the exhaust pipe connections.
● When fitting the gearchange linkage arm onto the gearchange shaft, align the mark made on removal with the slit in the clamp **(see illustration 4.17)**.
● Make sure all wires, cables and hoses are correctly routed and connected, and secured by any clips or ties.
● Refill the engine with oil (see Chapter 1) and check the level (see *Pre-ride checks*).
● Adjust the throttle cable freeplay.
● Adjust the drive chain (see Chapter 1).
● Start the engine and check that there are no oil leaks. Adjust the idle speed (see Chapter 1).

5 Engine overhaul information

1 Before beginning the engine overhaul, read through the related procedures to familiarise yourself with the scope and requirements of the job. Overhauling an engine is not all that difficult, but it is time consuming. Check on the availability of parts and make sure that any necessary special tools are obtained in advance.

2 Most work can be done with typical workshop hand tools, although a number of precision measuring tools are required for inspecting parts to determine if they are worn.

3 To ensure maximum life and minimum trouble from a rebuilt engine, everything must be assembled with care in a spotlessly clean environment.

Disassembly

4 Before disassembling the engine clean and degrease its external surfaces. This will prevent contamination of the engine internals, and will also make working a lot easier and cleaner. Use a proprietary engine cleaner such as Gunk or alternatively a high flash-point solvent, such as paraffin (kerosene). Use a brush to work the cleaner into the recesses of the engine casings. Take care not to get solvent or water into the electrical components and intake and exhaust ports.

 Warning: The use of petrol (gasoline) as a cleaning agent should be avoided because of the risk of fire.

5 When clean and dry, position the engine on the workbench, leaving suitable clear area for working. Make sure the engine is stable – some strategically placed blocks of wood under the crankcase or engine covers will help support it and keep it stable while you work. Gather a selection of small containers, plastic bags and some labels so that parts can be grouped together in an easily identifiable manner. Also get some paper and a pen so that notes can be taken. You will also need a supply of clean rag, which should be as absorbent as possible.

6 Before commencing work, read through the appropriate section so that some idea of the necessary procedure can be gained. When removing components it should be noted that great force is seldom required. In many cases, a component's reluctance to be removed is indicative of an incorrect approach or removal method – if in any doubt, re-check with the text. In cases where fasteners have corroded, apply penetrating oil or WD40 before disassembly.

7 When disassembling the engine, keep 'mated' parts together (e.g. valve assemblies, pistons, rings and connecting rods, clutch plates, bearing shells and journals etc. that have been in contact with each other during engine operation). These 'mated' parts must be reused or renewed as assemblies.

8 Disassembly should be done in the following general order with reference to the appropriate Sections.

    Remove the valve cover
    Remove the cam chain tensioner
    Remove the camshafts
    Remove the cylinder head
    Remove the cylinder block
    Remove the pistons
    Remove the timing rotor and crankshaft
        position sensor (see Chapter 4)

6.3 Disconnect the CMP sensor wiring connector

    Remove the clutch
    Remove the gearchange mechanism
    Remove the alternator (see Chapter 8)
        and starter clutch
    Remove the starter motor (see Chapter 8)
    Remove the oil sump, oil pipes and
        strainer
    Remove the balancer shaft/weight
    Remove the selector drum and forks
    Separate the crankcase halves
    Remove the crankshaft and connecting
        rod assemblies
    Remove the transmission shafts/gears
    Remove the oil pump

Reassembly

9 Reassembly is accomplished by reversing the general disassembly sequence.

6   Valve cover

Note: *This procedure can be carried out with the engine in the frame. If the engine has been removed, ignore the steps which do not apply.*

Removal

1 Remove the fuel tank (see Chapter 4).

2 Remove the ignition HT coils (see Chapter 4).

3 Disconnect the camshaft position sensor wiring connector **(see illustration)**.

4 Remove the PAIR control valve along with its hoses (see Chapter 4).

5 Refer to Chapter 3 and displace the oil cooler – there is no need to detach the hoses, but unscrew the bolt securing the hose guide bracket. Either tie it to the bottom yoke or rest it on the front mudguard, using rag to cushion it.

6 Unscrew the two bolts securing each oil hose union to the rear of the cover and displace the hoses **(see illustration)**. Discard the O-rings as new ones must be used. If the engine is being completely disassembled, also unscrew the two bolts securing the hose union to the crankcase behind the cylinder block and remove the hoses **(see illustration)**.

7 Unscrew the valve cover bolts and remove them along with their sealing washers **(see illustration)**. Discard the copper washers as new ones must be used. The large washers with the outer bolts can be re-used if they are in good condition, but replace them with new ones if necessary.

8 Lift the valve cover off the cylinder head **(see illustration)**. If it is stuck, do not try to lever it off with a screwdriver. Tap around

6.6a Unscrew the oil hose union bolts (arrowed) on the valve cover . . .

6.6b . . . and if required on the crankcase

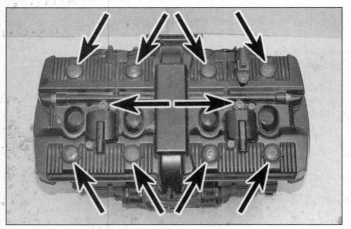

6.7 Unscrew the bolts (arrowed) . . .

6.8 . . . and remove the cover

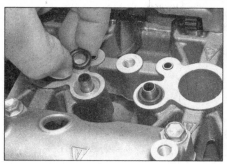

6.9 Remove the O-rings and dowels

6.12a Fit the new gasket onto the cover

6.12b Apply sealant to the cut-outs (arrowed) for the end caps

6.13a Fit new sealing washers with the centre bolts

6.13b Lubricate the outer bolt sealing washers

6.14a Fit a new O-ring onto the crankcase union if detached

the joint with a soft-faced mallet to dislodge it. Discard the cover gasket as a new one must be fitted on reassembly.

9 Remove the four air passage dowels and their O-rings from the cylinder head or cover if they are loose – discard the O-rings as new ones must be used **(see illustration)**.

Installation

10 Clean the mating surfaces of the cylinder head and cover with a suitable solvent to remove all traces of old sealant and gasket.

11 Fit the four air passage dowels and new O-rings into the cylinder head **(see illustration 6.9)**.

12 Lay the new gasket onto the valve cover, making sure it locates correctly and using dabs of grease to hold it in place **(see illustration)**. Apply a sealant (Suzuki 1216B or equivalent)

to the cut-outs in the cylinder head where the gasket half-circles fit **(see illustration)**.

13 Position the cover on the cylinder head, making sure the gasket stays in place and the cover locates correctly onto the dowels **(see illustration 6.8)**. Install the centre (small head) bolts with new copper sealing washers **(see illustration)**. Smear the outer (large head) bolt sealing washers with oil (using new ones if necessary) **(see illustration)**. Tighten the bolts evenly and in a criss-cross sequence, starting from the centre bolts and working outwards, to the torque settings specified at the beginning of this Chapter.

14 Fit the oil hose unions onto the valve cover, and onto the crankcase if detached, using new O-rings smeared with grease **(see illustrations)**. Tighten the union bolts to the specified torque setting.

15 Install the remaining components in the reverse order of removal.

7 Cam chain tensioner

Note: *This procedure can be carried out with the engine in the frame. If the engine has been removed, ignore the steps which do not apply.*

Removal

1 Unscrew the tensioner cap bolt and withdraw the spring from the tensioner **(see illustration)**. Note that there is a ball between the end of the spring and the tensioner plunger – make sure you don't lose it when

6.14b Make sure the hose is the correct way round

6.14c Fit a new O-ring onto each valve cover union

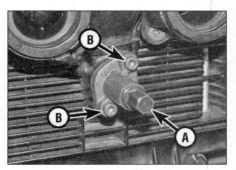

7.1 Tensioner cap bolt (A) and mounting bolts (B)

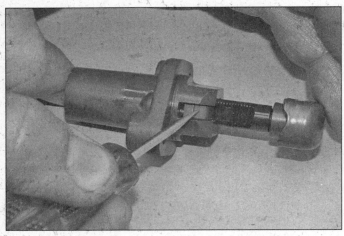

7.4 Lift the catch to retract the tensioner pushrod

7.5a Install the tensioner using a new gasket . . .

7.5b . . . and tighten the bolts to the specified torque

removing the tensioner (see illustration 7.6a). Discard the sealing washer as a new one must be used.

2 Undo the tensioner mounting bolts and withdraw the tensioner from the back of the cylinder head (see illustration 7.1). Discard the gasket as a new one must be fitted on reassembly. Tip the ball out of the tensioner body.

Caution: Do not rotate the engine with the cam chain tensioner removed.

Inspection

3 Examine the tensioner components for signs of wear or damage. Check the ratchet teeth on the plunger for wear, and make sure

the plunger cannot be pushed back into the tensioner with the catch engaged. If any components are worn or damaged replace them with new ones.

4 Release the catch and push the plunger into the tensioner body – the plunger should move smoothly and freely, and the catch should return onto the plunger and engage with the ratchet teeth when released (see illustration). Fit the ball and spring into the tensioner and check that the plunger extends easily under spring pressure with the catch clicking over the ratchet teeth.

Installation

5 Release the catch and push the plunger into the tensioner body (see illustration 7.4). Fit a new gasket onto the body and fit it onto the cylinder head with the UP mark facing up (see illustration). Tighten the mounting bolts to the torque setting specified at the beginning of this Chapter (see illustration).

6 Fit the ball into the tensioner (see illustration). Install the spring and the cap bolt with a new sealing washer and tighten the bolt to the specified torque (see illustration). Note that a clicking noise will be heard as the cap bolt is installed – this is the plunger extending.

7 Refer to Section 8, Steps 1 to 3 and 30, and make sure that all valve timing marks

are in correct alignment as described as it is possible for the chain to jump teeth on the sprockets with the tensioner removed. Then follow Steps 35, 38 and 39.

8 Camshafts and followers

Note: *This procedure can be carried out with the engine in the frame. If the engine has been removed, ignore the steps which do not apply.*

Removal

1 Remove the valve cover (see Section 6). Remove the spark plugs (see Chapter 1).

2 Unscrew the timing rotor cover bolts, noting the sealing washer fitted with the top bolt and remove the cover (see illustration). Discard the gasket as new one must be fitted on reassembly.

3 Turn the engine clockwise using a socket or spanner on the timing rotor (use the large hex cast into the rotor itself, do not use the timing rotor bolt) until the line on the timing rotor aligns with the sensing tip on the crankshaft position (CKP) sensor, and the lines on the right-hand end of each camshaft are flush with the cylinder head top

7.6a Fit the ball into the tensioner . . .

7.6b . . . then fit the cap bolt assembly using a new sealing washer

8.2 Unscrew the bolts (arrowed) and remove the cover

8.3a Turn the crankshaft in a clockwise direction using a spanner on the hex

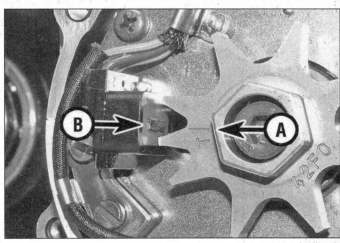

8.3b Align the scribe line (A) with the sensor (B) . . .

surface and pointing away from each other **(see illustrations)**. Observe the positions of the numbered arrows on the camshaft sprockets **(see illustration 8.30)**. This is how everything must be positioned on installation.

4 Remove the cam chain tensioner (see Section 7) and the top cam chain guide (Section 11).

5 Before disturbing the camshaft holders, check for identification markings, which should be the letters A, B, C and D, one for each holder, cast into their top surface, inside a triangle that points to the front, and corresponding to the mark on the cylinder head **(see illustration)**. These markings ensure that the holders can be matched to their original location on installation. If no markings are visible, mark your own using a felt pen.

6 Unscrew the bolts securing the holders, slackening them **evenly and a little at a time** in a criss-cross pattern, then remove them

8.3c . . . and make sure the lines and cam lobes are positioned as described

(see illustration). Retrieve the dowels from either the holders or the cylinder head if they are loose **(see illustration)**.

Caution: If the bolts are loosened carelessly and the holders do not come away from the head squarely, a holder is likely to break. If this happens the complete cylinder head

8.5 Camshaft holder identification – the letter is cast into the holder and on the head

assembly must be replaced with a new one; the holders are matched to the head and cannot be replaced separately. Also, a camshaft could be damaged if the holder bolts are not loosened evenly and the pressure from a depressed valve causes the shaft to bend.

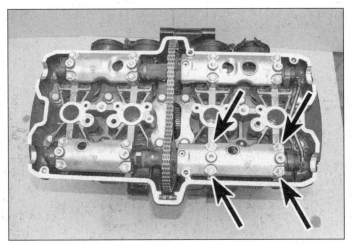

8.6a Each holder is secured by four bolts (arrowed)

8.6b Lift the holder off the camshaft, noting the dowels (arrowed)

8.7a Remove the intake camshaft first . . .

8.7b . . . then the exhaust camshaft

7 Remove the intake camshaft first. Pull up on the cam chain and carefully guide the intake camshaft out, disengaging the cam chain from the sprocket as you do **(see illustration)**. Now remove the exhaust camshaft **(see illustration)**.

8 The camshafts are marked for identification – IN (intake camshaft), and EX (exhaust camshaft) but if these marks are unclear

make your own so they do not get muddled **(see illustration 8.29a)**. **Note**: *Don't remove the sprockets from the camshafts unless absolutely necessary.*

9 Lay the cam chain across the centre plate.

10 Obtain a container which is divided into sixteen compartments, and label each compartment with the location of its corresponding valve in the cylinder head. If a

container is not available, use labelled plastic bags. **Note:** *It is essential that the followers and shims are stored according to and fitted back on their original valves otherwise all the clearances will be wrong.* Lift each cam follower out of the cylinder head using a magnet or suction tool (such as a valve lapping tool) **(see illustration)**. Retrieve the shim from either the inside of the follower or pick it out of the top of the valve, using a magnet or a small screwdriver with a dab of grease on it (the shim will stick to the grease) or a suitable pair of pliers **(see illustrations)**. Do not allow the shim to fall into the engine. Store each shim with its respective follower.

11 Cover the cylinder head to prevent anything falling into the engine.

Inspection

12 Inspect the bearing surfaces of the head and the holders and the corresponding journals on the camshaft. Look for score marks, deep scratches and evidence of spalling (a pitted appearance) **(see illustration)**.

13 Check the camshaft lobes for heat

8.10a Lift out each follower . . .

8.10b . . . and remove the shim (arrowed) from inside it . . .

8.10c . . . or from the top of the valve

8.12 Inspect the camshaft journals and corresponding surfaces for wear and damage

8.13a Inspect the camshaft lobes for wear . . .

8.13b . . . here's an example of spalling

8.13c Measuring a camshaft lobe with a micrometer

discoloration (blue appearance), score marks, chipped areas, flat spots and spalling **(see illustrations)**. Measure the height of each lobe with a micrometer and compare the results to the Specifications at the beginning of this Chapter **(see illustration)**. If damage is noted or wear is excessive, the camshaft must be replaced with a new one.

14 Check camshaft runout by supporting each end of the camshaft on V-blocks, and measuring any runout at the journals using a dial gauge (see *Tools and Workshop Tips* in the Reference section). If the runout exceeds the specified limit the camshaft must be replaced with a new one.

15 Inspect the outer surfaces of the cam followers for evidence of wear, scoring or other damage. If the surface of a follower is in poor condition, it is probable that its bore in the head is also worn or damaged. Remove the valve(s) (see Section 10) and check the follower bore(s) for wear. If the bore is worn or damaged the cylinder head will have to be replaced with a new one.

 HAYNES HiNT *Refer to Tools and Workshop Tips in the Reference section for details of how to read a micrometer and dial gauge.*

16 The camshaft journal oil clearance should now be checked. There are two possible ways of doing this, either by direct measurement

(see Steps 17 to 19) or by the use of a product known as Plastigauge (see Steps 20 to 23). If Plastigauge is used and the oil clearance is excessive, the direct measurement method then has to be used to determine whether it is the camshaft or the holder that is worn.

17 If direct measurement is to be used, make sure the camshaft holder dowels are fitted **(see illustration 8.6b)** then fit the holders, making sure they are in their correct location **(see illustration 8.5)**. Install the holder bolts and tighten them **evenly and a little at a time** in a criss-cross sequence, to the torque setting specified at the beginning of the Chapter.

18 Make a chart or sketch of the cylinder head so that a note of each measurement can be made against the appropriate bearing surface. Using telescoping gauges and a micrometer (see *Tools and Workshop Tips*), measure the internal diameter of each holder journal and record it on the chart. Now measure the diameter of the corresponding camshaft journals with a micrometer **(see illustration)**.

19 To determine the journal oil clearance, subtract the camshaft journal diameter from the internal holder journal diameter. Compare the result to the clearance specified. If the clearance is greater than specified, compare the individual measurements of the camshaft journal and the holder to those specified and replace whichever component is beyond its service limit with a new one.

20 If the Plastigauge method is to be used, clean the camshaft being checked and the

bearing surfaces in the cylinder head and camshaft holders with a clean, lint-free cloth. Lay the camshaft in place in the cylinder head, making sure the timing marks are correctly aligned (see Step 3).

21 Cut strips of Plastigauge and lay one piece on each camshaft journal, along the camshaft centreline **(see illustration)**. Make sure the camshaft holder dowels are in position then fit the holders, making sure each is in its correct location **(see illustration 8.6b and 8.5)**. Install the holder bolts and tighten them **evenly and a little at a time** in a criss-cross sequence, to the torque setting specified at the beginning of the Chapter. **Note:** *The camshaft must not rotate during this procedure.*

22 Now unscrew the bolts, slackening them **evenly and a little at a time** in a criss-cross pattern, then remove the holders, again making sure the camshaft does not turn.

23 To determine the oil clearance, compare the crushed Plastigauge (at its widest point) on each journal to the scale printed on the Plastigauge container **(see illustration)**. Compare the results to this Chapter's Specifications. If the oil clearance is greater than specified, follow Steps 18 and 19 to determine which component is worn beyond its service limit.

24 Check each sprocket for cracks and other damage, replacing them with new ones if necessary – the sprockets are available separately. If the sprocket teeth are worn, the cam chain is also worn, as will be the

8.18 Measuring a camshaft journal with a micrometer

8.21 Lay a strip of Plastigauge across each journal, along the camshaft centreline

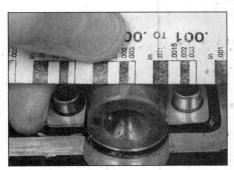

8.23 Compare the width of the crushed Plastigauge with the scale provided

8.24 Inspect the camshaft sprockets for wear and chipped teeth. Camshaft sprocket bolts (arrowed)

8.26 Fit the follower onto the valve

drive sprocket on the crankshaft. If wear this severe is apparent, the entire engine should be disassembled for inspection. To remove a sprocket unscrew its bolts **(see illustration)**.

Installation

25 If removed, fit each sprocket onto its camshaft, making sure they are installed with the numbered side facing the notched end of

8.29a Each camshaft is easily identified by its IN or EX mark

the camshaft and so that the numbers on the sprocket and the timing lines on the camshaft align as shown **(see illustration 8.30)**. Apply a smear of a suitable non-permanent thread locking compound to the sprocket bolts before installing them, and tighten them to the torque setting specified at the beginning of the Chapter **(see illustration 8.24)**.
26 If removed, lubricate each shim with

8.29b Make sure the No. 1 and No. 2 arrows are positioned as shown

molybdenum disulphide oil (a 50/50 mixture of molybdenum disulphide grease and engine oil) and fit it into its recess in the top of the valve, with the size marking on each shim facing up **(see illustration 8.10c)**. Check that the shim is correctly seated, then lubricate and install the follower **(see illustration)**. **Note:** *It is most important that the shims and followers are returned to their original valves otherwise the valve clearances will be inaccurate.*
27 Check that the cam chain is engaged around the lower sprocket teeth on the crankshaft and that the crankshaft is positioned as described in Step 3 – if you need to turn the engine pull up on the cam chain to prevent it binding between the bottom sprocket and the crankcase.
28 Make sure the bearing surfaces in the cylinder head, on the camshafts and in the holders are clean, then liberally apply molybdenum disulphide oil (a 50/50 mixture of molybdenum disulphide grease and engine oil) to each of them. Also apply oil to the camshaft lobes.
29 Install the exhaust camshaft (identified by EX) first **(see illustration)**. Pull up on the front run of the cam chain and keep it taut, then fit the camshaft through the cam chain with the sprocket bolts facing the right-hand side of the engine **(see illustration 8.7b)**, aligning it so that the timing line points forwards **(see illustration 8.3c)**, and so that the arrow marked 1 on the sprocket points forwards and is flush with the top of the cylinder head mating surface, and the arrow marked 2 points vertically upwards **(see illustration)**. Check that the chain is tight at the front so that there is no slack between the crankshaft sprocket and the exhaust camshaft sprocket – move the chain around the sprocket so that the slack is taken up if required, then check that all marks are still correctly aligned.
30 Fit the intake camshaft (identified by IN) through the cam chain with the sprocket bolts facing the right-hand side of the engine **(see illustration 8.7a)**, aligning it so that the timing line points backwards, and so that the arrow marked 3 on the sprocket points up. Starting with and including the cam chain pin that is directly above the arrow marked 2 on the exhaust camshaft sprocket, count twenty-four pins along the chain towards the intake side, then engage the sprocket with the chain so that the arrow marked 3 on the sprocket aligns with the twenty-fourth pin **(see illustration)**. Again check that the chain is tight at the front and between the sprockets – any slack in the chain must lie in the portion of the chain in the back of the engine so that it can be taken up by the tensioner.
31 Before proceeding further, check that everything aligns as described in Steps 3, 29 and 30. If it doesn't, the valve timing will be inaccurate and the valves will contact the pistons when the engine is turned over.
32 Ensure the camshaft holder dowels are installed then fit the holders **(see illustration 8.6b)**, making sure they are in their proper

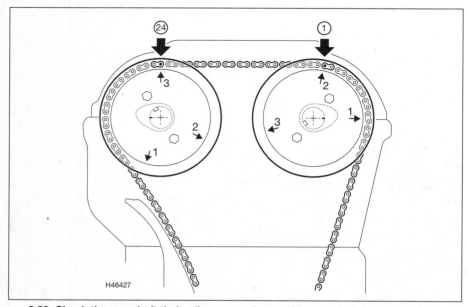

8.30 Check the camshaft timing lines, sprocket markings and chain pin count are correct – 1st pin above No. 2 arrow, 24th pin above No. 3 arrow

8.38a Apply some sealant to the grommet (arrowed) and crankcase joints . . .

8.38b . . . then fit the cover using a new gasket

positions as noted on removal (Step 5) **(see illustration 8.5)**. Tighten the cap bolts on one camshaft **evenly and a little at a time** in a criss-cross sequence, until the specified torque setting is reached. Repeat for the other camshaft.

33 With all holders tightened down, check that the valve timing marks still align (see Steps 3, 29 and 30). If they don't, unscrew the sprocket bolts, slip the sprocket off its mount on the shaft, then disengage it from the chain and move it round the required number of teeth in the correct direction, then realign the camshaft so that the bolt holes align and fit the sprocket back onto the shaft. Apply a smear of a suitable non-permanent thread locking compound to the sprocket bolts before installing them, and tighten them to the torque setting specified at the beginning of the Chapter. Assuming that the previous pin-count described in Step 33 was correct you will now have to perform the same procedure on the other camshaft to bring that into alignment and re-instate the correct pin count. If the pin count was initially incorrect you may only have to adjust one camshaft to re-instate it. On

completion check the alignment of all marks again, and make sure the chain pin-count is correct.

34 When you are sure that all marks are correctly aligned and that all slack in the chain is between the intake camshaft and the crankshaft, install the cam chain tensioner (see Section 7).

35 Turn the engine clockwise through two full turns (720°) using a spanner or socket on the timing rotor hex, then check the timing marks and the pin-count again.

Caution: If the marks are not aligned exactly as described, the valve timing will be incorrect and the valves may strike the pistons, causing extensive damage to the engine.

36 Install the top cam chain guide (see Section 11).

37 Check the valve clearances and adjust them if necessary (see Chapter 1).

38 Apply a suitable sealant (Suzuki Bond 1207B or equivalent) to the CKP sensor wiring grommet and to the crankcase joints **(see illustration)**. Install the timing rotor cover using a new gasket and tighten the bolts to

the torque setting specified at the beginning of the chapter, not forgetting the sealing washer with the top bolt **(see illustration)**.

39 Install the valve cover (see Section 6) and the spark plugs (see Chapter 1).

9 Cylinder head removal and installation

Note: *This procedure can be carried out with the engine in the frame. If the engine has been removed, ignore the steps which do not apply.*

Removal

1 Remove the exhaust system and the throttle bodies (see Chapter 4).

2 Remove the camshafts, cam followers and shims (see Section 8).

3 Remove the front cam chain guide (see Section 11).

4 Unscrew the external oil hose banjo bolts and remove the hose **(see illustration)**. Discard the sealing washers as new ones must be used. Unscrew the internal oil pipe bolts and remove the pipe **(see illustration)**.

9.4a Unscrew the bolts (arrowed) and remove the external pipe

9.4b Unscrew the bolts (arrowed) and remove the internal pipe

9.6a Undo and remove the 6 mm bolts in the back of the head . . .

9.6b . . . and those at the front

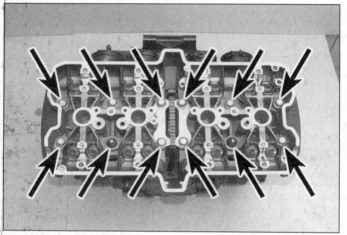

9.6c Cylinder head 10 mm bolts and nuts (arrowed)

9.6d Remove the plate from under the cam chain

5 If required, undo the screws securing the intake ducts and remove them, noting which fits where according to their markings **(see illustration 9.19)**. Discard the O-rings as new ones must be used. Check the condition of the ducts and replace them with new ones if they are damaged, deformed or deteriorated.

6 The cylinder head is secured by two 10 mm domed nuts with copper washers, four 10 mm bolts with a common plate, four

9.7 Carefully lift the head up off the block

10 mm bolts with copper washers, and four 6 mm bolts. Unscrew the four 6 mm bolts **(see illustrations)**. Slacken the 10 mm bolts and nuts evenly and a little at a time in a criss-cross pattern starting from the outside and working to the centre until they are all slack **(see illustration)**. Remove the bolts and nuts and their washers, taking great care not to drop any of them into the crankcase. Also remove the plate from the centre of the cylinder head **(see illustration)**. With the plate removed, don't allow the chain to drop into its tunnel.

7 Pull the cylinder head up off the block and the oil drain tubes **(see illustration)**. If the head is stuck, tap around the joint faces of the cylinder head with a soft-faced mallet to free the head, but take care not to strike any of the cooling fins as they break easily, especially on the corners. Do not attempt to free the head by inserting a screwdriver between the head and cylinder block – you'll damage the sealing surfaces.

8 As you remove the head pass the cam chain down through it and lay it over the front of the block. Do not let the chain fall into the

crankcase – tie it to the tensioner blade with a piece of wire or a cable-tie to prevent it from doing so **(see illustration 9.15b)**. Remove the old cylinder head gasket and the two dowels if they are loose **(see illustrations 9.15a and 9.14)**. Stuff a clean rag into the cam chain tunnel to prevent any debris falling into the engine. Discard the gasket as a new one must be used.

9 Remove the O-ring from the top of each oil drain tube and discard them as new ones must be used **(see illustration 9.12)**.

10 Check the cylinder head gasket and the mating surfaces on the cylinder head and block for signs of leakage, which could indicate warpage. Refer to Section 10 and check the cylinder head.

11 Clean all traces of old gasket material from the cylinder head and block. If a scraper is used, take care not to scratch or gouge the soft aluminium. Be careful not to let any of the gasket material drop into the crankcase, the cylinder bore or the oil passages. Unless you are removing the cylinder block, cover it with a clean rag to prevent any debris falling into the engine.

9.12 Fit a new O-ring into the groove in the top of each tube

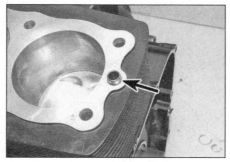

9.14 There is a dowel (arrowed) in each end

9.15a Free the cam chain from the blade

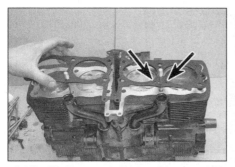

9.15b Fit the new gasket making sure all bolt holes align and it locates over the dowels – note the letters UP (arrowed)

9.16 Make sure the drain tubes locate correctly

9.17a Lubricate the copper washers, threads of the 10 mm head bolts . . .

Installation

12 Fit a new O-ring smeared with grease onto the top of each oil drain tube **(see illustration)**.
13 Lubricate the cylinder bores with engine oil.
14 If removed, fit the two dowels into the cylinder block **(see illustration)**.
15 Ensure both cylinder head and block mating surfaces are clean. Free the cam chain from the tensioner blade and hold it up **(see illustration)**. Lay the new head gasket in place on the cylinder block, making sure all the holes are correctly aligned and that the UP letters stamped out of the gasket read correctly, and that it locates over the dowels **(see illustration)**. Never re-use the old gasket.
16 Carefully lower the cylinder head over the

studs and onto the block, passing the cam chain up through the tunnel as you do – it is helpful to have an assistant do this and to slip a piece of wire through it to prevent it falling back into the engine **(see illustration 9.7)**. Keep the chain taut to prevent it becoming disengaged from the crankshaft sprocket. Make sure the oil drain tubes locate correctly into their holes in the underside of the cylinder head **(see illustration)**.
17 Fit the cylinder head plate, making sure the cam chain is looped over it, then allow the chain to rest on it **(see illustration 9.6d)**. Lubricate the bolt and stud threads and the copper washers with engine oil, then fit the bolts and nuts with their washers and tighten them finger-tight **(see illustrations)**. Now tighten the bolts and nuts in two stages, first to the initial torque setting specified at the

beginning of the chapter, then to the final torque setting, tightening them in a criss-cross pattern starting from the middle (i.e. the bolts with the plate) and working to the ends.
18 Now fit the 6 mm bolts and tighten them to the specified torque setting **(see illustrations 9.6b and a)**. If the cylinder block was removed tighten the nut to the specified torque **(see illustration 12.3)**.
19 If removed, install the intake ducts, fitting a new O-ring smeared with grease into the groove in each duct. Each duct is coded with its cylinder number – fit them in the correct position with the UP mark at the top and apply a suitable non-permanent thread locking compound to the screws **(see illustration)**.
20 Fit the external oil hose using new sealing washers and tighten the banjo bolts to the specified torque setting **(see illustration)**. Fit

9.17b . . . and the threads of the studs for the domed nuts

9.19 Make sure each duct is matched to its cylinder according to the number (arrowed)

9.20a Use new sealing washers on each side of the banjo unions

9.20b The white mark (arrowed) on the internal pipe goes at the front

the internal oil pipe with the white paint mark to the front (exhaust side), then fit the bolts with their washers and tighten them to the specified torque **(see illustration)**.
21 Install the front cam chain guide (see Section 11).
22 Install the shims, followers and camshafts (see Section 8).
23 Install the exhaust system and the throttle bodies (see Chapter 4).

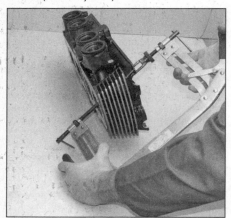

10.6a Fit the valve spring compressor . . .

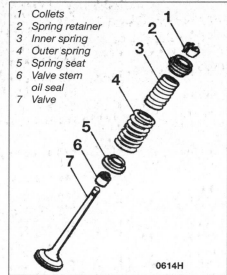

1 Collets
2 Spring retainer
3 Inner spring
4 Outer spring
5 Spring seat
6 Valve stem oil seal
7 Valve

0614H

10.5 Valve components

10 Cylinder head and valve overhaul

1 Because of the complex nature of this job and the special tools and equipment required, most owners leave servicing of the valves, valve seats and valve guides to a professional. However, you can make an initial assessment of whether the valves are seating correctly, and therefore sealing, by pouring a small amount of solvent into each of the valve ports. If the solvent leaks past any valve into the combustion chamber area the valve is not seating correctly and sealing.
2 With the correct tools (a valve spring compressor is essential – make sure it is suitable for motorcycle work), you can also remove the valves and associated components

from the cylinder head, clean them and check them for wear to assess the extent of the work needed, and, unless seat cutting or guide replacement is required, grind in the valves and reassemble them in the head.
3 A dealer service department or specialist can replace the guides and re-cut the valve seats.
4 After the valve service has been performed, be sure to clean it very thoroughly before installation on the engine to remove any metal particles or abrasive grit that may still be present from the valve service operations. Use compressed air, if available, to blow out all the holes and passages.

Disassembly

5 Before proceeding, arrange to label and store the valves along with their related components in such a way that they can be returned to their original locations without getting mixed up **(see illustration)**. Either use the same container as the cam followers and shims are stored in (see Section 8), or obtain a separate container and label each compartment accordingly. Alternatively, labelled plastic bags will do just as well.
6 Compress the valve springs on the first valve with a spring compressor, making sure it is correctly located onto each end of the valve assembly. On the top of the valve the adaptor needs to be about the same size as the spring retainer – if it is too big it will contact the follower bore and mark it, and if it is too small it will be difficult to remove and install the collets **(see illustration)**. On the underside of the head make sure the plate on the compressor only contacts the valve and not the soft aluminium of the head **(see illustrations)** – if the plate is too big for the valve, use a spacer between them. Do not compress the springs any more than is absolutely necessary.
Caution: Take great care not to mark the cam follower bore with the spring compressor.

10.6b . . . making sure it locates correctly on the spring retainer . . .

10.6c . . . and on the valve

10.7a Remove the collets . . .

10.7b . . . and the spring retainer and springs (arrowed) . . .

7 Remove the collets, using either needle-nose pliers, tweezers, a magnet or a screwdriver with a dab of grease on it **(see illustration)**. Carefully release the valve spring compressor and remove the spring retainer, noting which way up it fits, the inner and outer springs, and the valve **(see illustrations)**. If the valve binds in the guide and won't pull through, push it back into the head and deburr the area around the collet groove with a very fine file or whetstone **(see illustration)**.

8 Pull the valve stem seal off the top of the valve guide and discard it (the old seals should never be reused) **(see illustration)**. Remove the spring seat, noting which way up it fits – using a magnet is the easiest way to remove the seat from the head **(see illustration)**.

9 Repeat the procedure for the remaining valves. Remember to keep the parts for each valve together so they can be reinstalled in the same location.

10 Clean the cylinder head with solvent and dry it thoroughly. Compressed air will speed

10.7c . . . then draw the valve out from the underside of the head

the drying process and ensure that all holes and recessed areas are clean. **Note:** *Do not use a wire brush mounted in a drill motor to clean the combustion chambers as the head material is soft and may be scratched or eroded away by the wire brush.*

11 Clean all of the valve springs, collets, retainers and spring seats with solvent and dry

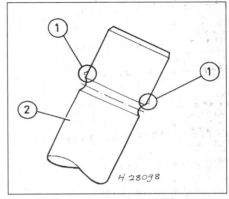

10.7d Remove any burrs (1) if the valve stem (2) won't pull through the guide

them thoroughly. Do the parts from one valve at a time so that no mixing of parts between valves occurs.

12 Scrape off any deposits that may have formed on the valve, then use a motorised

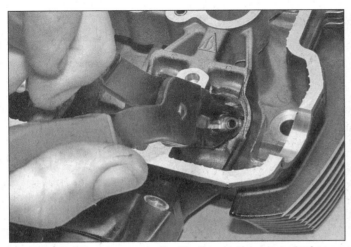

10.8a Pull the stem seal off with pliers or the proper tool as shown . . .

10.8b . . . then remove the spring seat

10.15 Examine the valve seat (arrowed) and measure its width

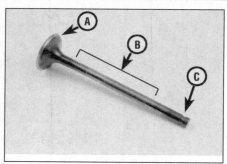

10.16a Examine the valve face (A), stem (B) and collet groove (C)

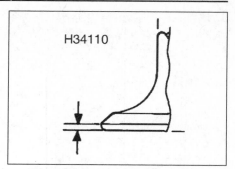

10.16b Measure the valve margin thickness

wire brush to remove deposits from the valve heads and stems. Again, make sure the valves do not get mixed up.

Inspection

13 Inspect the cylinder head very carefully for cracks and other damage. If cracks are found, a new head will be required. Check the cam bearing surfaces for wear and evidence of seizure **(see illustration 8.12)**. Check the camshafts for wear as well (see Section 8).
14 Using a precision straight-edge and a feeler gauge, check the head gasket mating surface for warpage. Refer to *Tools and Workshop Tips* in the Reference section for details of how to use the straight-edge. If the head is warped beyond the limit specified at the beginning of this Chapter, consult your Suzuki dealer or take it to a specialist repair shop for rectification.
15 Examine the valve seats in the combustion chamber **(see illustration)**. If they are pitted, cracked or burned, the head will require work

beyond the scope of the home mechanic. Measure the valve seat width and compare it to this Chapter's Specifications. If it exceeds the service limit, or if it varies around its circumference, consult your Suzuki dealer or take the head to a specialist repair shop for rectification.
16 Examine each valve face for cracks, pits and burned spots. Measure the valve margin thickness and compare it to this Chapter's Specifications **(see illustrations)**. If it exceeds the service limit, or if it varies around its circumference, replace the valve with a new one.
17 Check the valve stem and the collet groove area for wear and damage **(see illustration 10.16a)**. Rotate the valve and check for any obvious indication that it is bent. Check the end of the stem for pitting and excessive wear.
18 Using V-blocks and a dial gauge, measure the valve stem runout and the valve head runout and compare the results to the

Specifications **(see illustration)**. If either measurement exceeds the service limit, a new valve must be fitted.
19 Clean the valve guides to remove any carbon build-up, then install each valve in its guide in turn so that its face is 10 mm above the seat. Mount a dial gauge against the side of the valve face and measure the amount of side clearance (wobble) between the valve stem and its guide in two directions **(see illustration)**.
20 If the side clearance exceeds the limit specified, remove the valve and measure the valve stem diameter in three places along the stem **(see illustration)**. If the stem has worn beyond its limits replace it with a new one. If the valve stem has not worn, have the guide replaced with a new one. If required measure the inside diameter of the guide with a small hole gauge and micrometer **(see illustration)**. Measure the guides at each end and at the centre to determine if they are worn unevenly. Subtract the stem diameter from the valve guide inside diameter to obtain the valve stem-to-guide clearance. If the stem-to-guide clearance is greater than specified, replace whichever of the components is worn beyond its specifications. If the valve guide is within specifications, but is worn unevenly, it should be replaced with a new one.
21 Check the end of each valve spring for wear. Measure the spring free length and compare it to that listed in the specifications **(see illustration)**. If any spring is shorter than specified it has sagged and must be replaced with a new one.

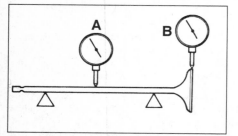

10.18 Measure the valve stem runout (A) and valve head runout (B)

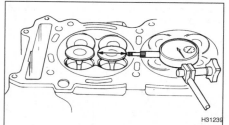

10.19 Measure the amount of 'wobble' as shown

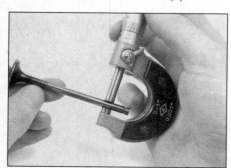

10.20a Measuring the valve stem diameter with a micrometer

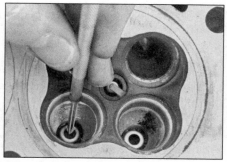

10.20b Measuring the valve guide inside diameter with a small hole gauge

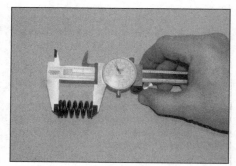

10.21 Measuring valve spring free length

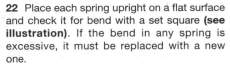

10.22 Check that the springs are not bent

10.26 Apply the grinding compound in small dabs to the valve face only

10.27a Rotate the grinding tool back-and-forth between the palms of your hands

22 Place each spring upright on a flat surface and check it for bend with a set square **(see illustration)**. If the bend in any spring is excessive, it must be replaced with a new one.

23 Check the spring retainers and collets for wear and damage. Any questionable parts should not be reused, as extensive damage will occur in the event of failure during engine operation.

24 If the inspection indicates that no overhaul work is required, the valve components can be reinstalled in the head.

Reassembly

25 Unless a valve service has been performed, before installing the valves in the head they should be ground in (lapped) to ensure a positive seal between the valves and seats. **Note:** *Suzuki advise against grinding in the valves after the seats have been recut. The valve seat must be soft and unpolished for final seating to occur when the engine is first run.* Valve grinding requires coarse and fine grinding compound and a valve grinding tool (either hand-held or drill driven – note that some drill-driven tools specify using only a fine grinding compound). If a grinding tool is not available, a piece of rubber or plastic hose can be slipped over the valve stem (after the valve has been installed in the guide) and used to turn the valve.

26 Apply a small amount of coarse grinding compound to the valve face, then lubricate the valve stem seal with molybdenum disulphide oil and slip the valve into the guide **(see**

10.27b The grinding process should leave the valve face (arrowed) . . .

illustration)**. Note:** *Make sure each valve is installed in its correct guide and be careful not to get any grinding compound on the valve stem.*

27 If a hand tool is being used rotate the tool between the palms of your hands. Use a back-and-forth motion (as though rubbing your hands together) rather than a circular motion (i.e. so that the valve rotates alternately clockwise and anti-clockwise rather than in one direction only) **(see illustration)**. If a motorised tool is being used, follow its instructions for use and take note of the correct drive speed for it – if your drill runs too fast and is not variable, use a hand tool instead. Lift the valve off the seat and turn it at regular intervals to distribute the grinding compound properly. Continue the grinding procedure until the valve and seat contact area is of uniform width, and unbroken around the entire circumference **(see illustrations)**.

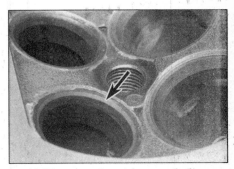

10.27c . . . and seat (arrowed) as an unbroken ring of uniform width

28 Carefully remove the valve from the guide and wipe off all traces of grinding compound. Use solvent to clean the valve and wipe the seat area thoroughly with a solvent-soaked cloth.

29 Repeat the procedure with fine valve grinding compound, then repeat the entire procedure for the remaining valves.

30 Working on one valve at a time, lay the spring seat in place in the cylinder head with its shouldered side facing up so that it will fit into the base of the spring **(see illustrations)**.

31 Coat the valve stem with molybdenum disulphide oil, then slip it into its guide **(see illustration 10.7c)**. Check that the valve moves up and down freely in the guide. Lubricate the new valve stem seal with molybdenum disulphide oil and fit it over the valve stem and onto the valve guide **(see illustration)**. Use an appropriate size deep socket to push the seal

10.30a Fit the valve seat shouldered side up . . .

10.30b . . . and use a rod to help locate it over the guide

10.31a Fit the new oil seal onto the valve stem . . .

10.31b . . . and press it onto the guide with a suitably sized socket

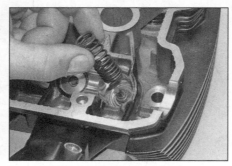

10.32a Fit the inner spring . . .

10.32b . . . then the outer spring

10.35 Tap each valve stem lightly to seat the collets

squarely over the end of the guide until it is felt to clip into place **(see illustration)**.

32 Next, fit the inner and outer valve springs with their closer-wound coils facing down into the cylinder head **(see illustrations)**. Fit the spring retainer with its shouldered side facing down into the top of the springs **(see illustration 10.7b)**.

33 Apply a small amount of grease to the collets to help hold them in place. Compress the spring with the valve spring compressor and install the collets **(see illustration 10.7a)**. When compressing the spring, depress it only as far as is absolutely necessary to slip the collets into place. Make certain that the collets

are securely located in the collet groove and release the spring compressor.

34 Repeat the procedure for the remaining valves. Remember to keep the parts for each valve together and separate from the other

> **HAYNES HiNT** *Check for proper sealing of the valves by pouring a small amount of solvent into each of the valve ports. If the solvent leaks past any valve into the combustion chamber the valve grinding operation on that valve should be repeated.*

valves so they can be reinstalled in the same location.

35 Support the cylinder head on blocks so the valves can't contact the work surface, then tap the end of each valve stem lightly to seat the collets in their grooves **(see illustration)**.

36 After the cylinder head and camshafts have been installed, check the valve clearances and adjust as required (see Chapter 1).

11 Cam chain, tensioner blade and guides

Note: *To remove the cam chain and the cam chain tensioner blade the engine must be removed from the frame and the crankcases separated. The top and front guides can be removed with the engine in the frame.*

1 Except in cases of oil starvation, the cam chain wears very little. If the chain has stretched excessively and can no longer be correctly tensioned by the cam chain tensioner, it is likely that the chain guides and tensioner blade will be worn and in need of renewal as well. Also check the condition of the camshaft sprockets (see Section 8) and crankshaft sprocket. **Note:** *Check the operation of the cam chain tensioner if the chain is slack but appears to be in good condition.*

Cam chain guides

Removal

2 To access the top guide remove the valve cover (see Section 6). Unscrew the bolts and remove the guide **(see illustration)**.

3 To access the front guide remove the exhaust camshaft (see Section 8). Lift the blade out of the front of the cam chain tunnel, noting which way round it fits and how it locates in the cut-outs in the cylinder head **(see illustration)**.

Inspection

4 Examine the sliding surface of the guides

11.2 Unscrew the bolts (arrowed) and remove the top guide

11.3 Lift the front guide out of its cut-out

for signs of wear or damage, and replace them with new ones if necessary.

Installation

5 Fit the front guide blade into the front of the cam chain tunnel **(see illustration 11.3)** – make sure it locates correctly in its seat and its lugs locate in their cut-outs in the cylinder head **(see illustration)**. Install the exhaust camshaft (see Section 8).

6 Fit the top guide onto the camshaft holders and tighten the bolts to the torque setting specified at the beginning of the Chapter **(see illustration)**.

7 Install the valve cover (see Section 6).

Cam chain and tensioner blade

Removal

8 Separate the crankcase halves (see Section 22) and remove the crankshaft (see Section 24).

9 Slip the cam chain off the crankshaft **(see illustration 11.9)**.

10 Remove the two rubber cushions from the upper crankcase half, noting which way up and round they fit, then push the cam chain tensioner blade up from the underside and out of its cut-outs in the crankcase, noting which way round it fits **(see illustration)**. Note the pivot pin which fits into the bottom of the blade.

Inspection

11 Examine the sliding surface of the tensioner blade for signs of wear or damage, and replace it with a new one if necessary. Check the condition of the rubber cushions and replace them with new ones if they are damaged or deteriorated.

Installation

12 If removed, fit the pivot pin into the bottom of the blade. Fit the tensioner blade into the upper crankcase half, making sure it is the correct way round and its pin locates correctly in the cut-outs **(see illustration 11.10)**. Fit the rubber cushions into the cut-outs with their rounded ends facing away from the tensioner blade pin and with the arrows facing front and back, not side to side.

13 Slip the cam chain onto its sprocket on the

11.5 Make sure the lugs locate correctly

11.9 Disengage the chain from the sprocket

crankshaft, making sure it is properly engaged **(see illustration 11.9)**.

14 Install the crankshaft (see Section 24) and reassemble the crankcase halves (see Section 22).

12 Cylinder block

Note: *The block can be removed with the engine in the frame. If the engine has been removed, ignore the steps that don't apply.*

Removal

1 Remove the cylinder head (see Section 9).

2 Clean any dirt and grit from around the base of each oil drain tube to prevent it falling in the crankcase, then pull them out of their holes

11.6 Fit the top guide onto the holders

11.10 Remove the rubber cushions then draw the blade (arrowed) out

(see illustration). Discard the O-rings as new ones must be used.

3 Unscrew the single nut which secures the front of the block to the crankcase **(see illustration)**.

4 Lift the cylinder block off the studs, supporting the pistons so the connecting rods do not knock against the block **(see illustration)**. If the block is stuck, tap around the joint faces of the block with a soft-faced mallet to free it from the crankcase, but take care not to strike any of the cooling fins as they break easily, especially on the corners. Don't attempt to free the block by inserting a screwdriver between it and the crankcase – you'll damage the sealing surfaces. When the block is removed, stuff clean rags around the connecting rods to support them and protect the crankcase and to prevent anything falling into the engine.

12.2 Remove the two oil tubes

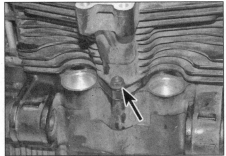

12.3 Unscrew the single nut (arrowed)

12.4 Lift the block up off the crankcase and the studs

12.5 Remove the gasket, then remove the dowels (arrowed) if loose

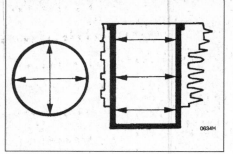

12.10a Measure the cylinder bore in the directions shown . . .

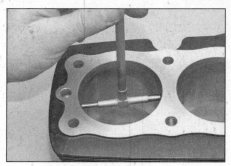

12.10b . . . with a telescoping gauge, then measure the gauge with a micrometer

5 Remove the gasket. Remove the two dowels from around the studs or from the bottom of the block if they are loose **(see illustration)**.

6 Check the base gasket and the mating surfaces on the cylinder head and block for signs of leakage, which could indicate warpage. Refer below and check the block.

7 Clean all traces of old gasket material from the cylinder block and crankcase. If a scraper is used, take care not to scratch or gouge the soft aluminium. Be careful not to let any of the gasket material drop into the crankcase or the oil passages.

Inspection

8 Using a precision straight-edge and a feeler gauge, check the head gasket mating surface for warpage. Refer to *Tools and Workshop Tips* in the Reference section for details of how to use the straight-edge. If the block is warped beyond the limit specified at the beginning of this Chapter, consult your Suzuki dealer or take it to a specialist repair shop for rectification.

9 Check the cylinder walls carefully for scratches and score marks. The bores are electro-plated with Suzuki's SCEM (Suzuki Composite Electro-chemical Material), a highly wear resistant nickel-phosphorus silicon-carbide coating which should last the life of the engine. If any cylinder is badly scratched, scuffed or scored, the cylinder block must be renewed. The bore surface should not be honed.

10 The standard bore diameter range is given in the specifications. Suzuki do not specify

a service limit for bore wear, but you can use telescoping gauges and a micrometer (see *Tools and Workshop Tips*) to check the dimensions of each cylinder to assess the amount of wear, taper and ovality. Measure near the top (but below the level of the top piston ring at TDC), centre and bottom (but above the level of the oil ring at BDC) of the bore, both parallel to and across the crankshaft axis **(see illustrations)**. Compare the results to the standard bore diameter range in the specifications at the beginning of this Chapter. Also use these measurements in conjunction with the piston diameter to assess the piston-to-bore clearance (see Section 13, Step 10).

11 If the precision measuring tools are not available, take the block to a Suzuki dealer or specialist motorcycle repair shop for assessment.

Installation

12 Check that the mating surfaces of the cylinder block and crankcase are free from oil or pieces of old gasket.

13 If removed, fit the dowels over the studs and into the crankcase, and push them firmly home **(see illustration 12.5)**.

14 Remove the rags from around the connecting rods, taking care not to let them fall against the rim of the crankcase. Lay the new base gasket in place over the studs, making sure it locates over the dowels (if they are in the crankcase) and all the holes are correctly aligned, and the UP mark stamped out of the gasket reads the correct way round **(see illustrations)**. Never re-use the old gasket.

15 Ensure the piston ring end gaps are positioned correctly before fitting the cylinder block **(see illustration 14.11)**. If required, fit piston ring compressors onto the pistons to ease their entry into the bores as the block is lowered. This is not essential as there is a good lead-in, enabling the piston rings to be hand-fed into the bores. If possible, have an assistant support the block while this is done.

 Rotate the crankshaft until the inner pistons (2 and 3) are uppermost and feed them into the block first. Access to the lower pistons (1 and 4) is easier since they are on the outside.

16 Release the cam chain then rotate the crankshaft so that the inner pistons are higher than the outer pistons, then tie the chain back onto the tensioner blade. It is useful to place a support under the pistons so that they remain steady while the block is fitted, otherwise the downward pressure could turn the crankshaft and the pistons will drop. Lubricate the cylinder bores, pistons and piston rings with clean engine oil.

17 Carefully lower the block onto the inner pistons until the crowns fit into their bores **(see illustration)**.

18 Gently push the cylinder down, holding the underside of the pistons if you are not using a support to prevent them dropping, and making sure they enter the bore squarely and do not get cocked sideways. If you are

12.14a Fit the new gasket . . .

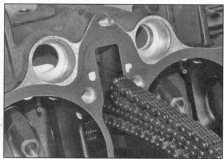

12.14b . . . making sure the UP letters stamped out of the gasket read correctly

12.17 Carefully lower the block and guide the inner pistons in . . .

12.18 . . . and compress the rings so they enter the bore

12.19 Repeat the process for the outer pistons

12.21a Fit a new ring onto the bottom of each tube . . .

12.21b . . . then fit them into the crankcase

doing this without a piston ring compressor, carefully compress and feed each ring into the bore as the cylinder is lowered **(see illustration)**. Do not use force if it appears to be stuck as the piston and/or rings will be damaged. If necessary, use a soft mallet to gently tap the block down. If a compressor was used, remove it once the rings are in the bore.

19 When the inner pistons are correctly located in the cylinders, carefully press the block down until the outer piston crowns then enter the bore **(see illustration)**. Feed the rings on the outer pistons into their bores in the same way as before. When all pistons are correctly located press the block onto the base gasket, making sure it locates on the dowels.

20 Install the single nut which secures the front of the block to the crankcase and tighten it finger-tight only at this stage **(see**

illustration 12.3)** – tighten it to the specified torque setting after the cylinder head has been tightened down.

21 Fit a new O-ring smeared with grease onto the bottom of each oil drain tube, then press the tubes into their holes in the crankcase **(see illustrations)**.

22 Install the cylinder head (see Section 9).

13 Pistons

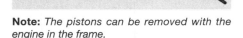

Note: *The pistons can be removed with the engine in the frame.*

Removal

1 Remove the cylinder block (see Section 12).

2 Before removing a piston from its connecting rod, ensure it is marked with its

cylinder identity. Cylinders are numbered 1 to 4, from the left to right side of the engine. If the piston is going to be cleaned, scratch the identity lightly on the inside of the piston skirt. Each piston must be installed in its original cylinder on reassembly. Note the indent on the top of each piston which faces the front (exhaust side) of the engine **(see illustration 13.16)**; if this is not visible due to carbon build-up, mark the piston accordingly so that it can be installed the correct way round.

3 Carefully prise out the circlip on one side of the piston using needle-nose pliers or a small flat-bladed screwdriver inserted into the notch **(see illustration)**. Push the piston pin out from the other side with a suitably sized socket to free the piston from the connecting rod **(see illustration)**. Remove the other circlip and discard them as new ones must be used. When the piston has been removed, fit its pin back into its bore so that related parts do not get mixed up.

> **HAYNES HINT** *If a piston pin is a tight fit in the piston bosses, heat the piston gently with a hot air gun – this will expand the alloy piston sufficiently to release its grip on the pin. If the piston pin is particularly stubborn, extract it using a drawbolt tool, but be careful to protect the piston's working surfaces – see Tools and Workshop Tips in the Reference section.*

4 Using your thumbs or a piston ring removal and installation tool, carefully remove the rings from the pistons, working on one piston at a time (see Section 14). Do not nick or gouge the pistons in the process. Carefully note which way up each ring fits and in which groove as they must be installed in their original positions if being re-used. The upper surface of the top two rings should have a manufacturer's mark at one end, with the top ring marked N and the 2nd ring marked 2N on original equipment rings **(see illustration 14.2a)** – if the mark on each ring is different, note which mark is for the top ring and which is for the second. The rings can also be identified by their different cross-section **(see illustration 14.2b)**. **Note:** *It is good practice to replace the piston rings with new ones when an engine is being overhauled.*

5 Clean all traces of carbon from the tops of the pistons. A hand-held wire brush or a piece of fine emery cloth can be used once most of the deposits have been scraped away. Do not, under any circumstances, use a wire brush mounted in a drill motor; the piston material is soft and will be eroded away by the wire brush.

6 Use a piston ring groove cleaning tool to remove any carbon deposits from the ring grooves. If a tool is not available, a piece broken off an old ring will do the job. Be very careful to remove only the carbon deposits.

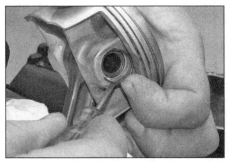

13.3a Remove the circlip using a screwdriver inserted in the notch . . .

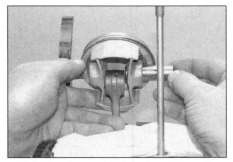

13.3b . . . then push the pin out from the other side and remove the piston

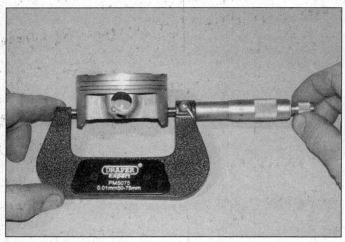

13.10 Measure the piston diameter at the specified distance from the bottom of the skirt

13.11 Measuring the piston ring-to-groove clearance with a feeler gauge

Do not remove any metal and do not nick or gouge the sides of the ring grooves.

7 Once the carbon has been removed, clean the pistons with a suitable solvent and dry them thoroughly. If the identification previously marked on the piston is cleaned off, be sure to re-mark it with the correct identity. Make sure the oil return holes at the back of the oil ring groove are clear.

Inspection

8 Carefully inspect each piston for cracks around the skirt, at the pin bosses and at the ring lands. Normal piston wear appears as even, vertical wear on the thrust surfaces of the piston and slight looseness of the top ring in its groove. If the skirt is scored or scuffed, the engine may have been suffering from overheating and/or abnormal combustion, which caused excessively high operating temperatures. The oil pump should be checked thoroughly.

9 A hole in the top of the piston, in one extreme, or burned areas around the edge of the piston crown, indicate that pre-ignition or knocking under load have occurred. If you find evidence of any problems the cause must be corrected or the damage will occur again (see *Fault Finding* in the Reference section).

10 Check the piston-to-bore clearance by measuring the bore (see Section 12) and

the piston diameter. Make sure each piston is matched to its correct cylinder. Measure the piston 15 mm up from the bottom of the skirt and at 90° to the piston pin axis **(see illustration)**. Subtract the piston diameter from the bore diameter to obtain the clearance. If it is greater than the service limit specified at the beginning of this Chapter, check whether it is the bore or piston that is worn. If the piston diameter is less that the service limit, new pistons and rings should be fitted.

11 Measure the piston ring-to-groove clearance by fitting each ring in its groove and slipping a feeler gauge in beside it **(see illustration)**. Make sure you have the correct ring for the groove (see Step 4). Check the clearance at three or four locations around the groove. If the clearance is greater than specified, renew both the piston and rings as a set. If new rings are being used, measure the clearance using the new rings. If the clearance is greater than that specified, the piston is worn and must be renewed.

12 Apply clean engine oil to the piston pin, fit it into the piston and check for any freeplay between the two **(see illustration)**. Measure the pin external diameter and the pin bore in the piston and compare the results to the Specifications at the beginning of this Chapter **(see illustration)**. Repeat the measurements

between the pin and the connecting rod small-end (see Section 25, Step 7). Replace components that are worn beyond the specified limits with new ones.

Installation

13 Work on one piston at a time. Inspect and install the piston rings (see Section 14).

14 Fit a new circlip into the groove in one side of the piston – when installing the circlips, compress them only just enough to fit them in the piston, make sure they are properly seated in their grooves with the open end away from the removal notch, and never re-use old circlips.

15 Lubricate the piston pin, the piston pin bore and the connecting rod small-end bore with clean engine oil.

16 Locate the piston on its correct connecting rod, making sure the indent on the top of the piston is to the front (exhaust side) of the engine and on the opposite side to the ID code marked across the big-end (which should be to the rear – if not the connecting rod has been fitted the wrong way round on the crankshaft) **(see illustration)**. Insert the piston pin from the side without the circlip **(see illustration 13.3b)**. Secure the pin with the other new circlip **(see illustration 13.3a)**.

17 Fit the remaining pistons onto their rods. Install the cylinder block (see Section 12).

13.12a Slip the pin into the piston and check for freeplay between them

13.12b Measure the external diameter of the pin and the internal diameter of the bore in the piston

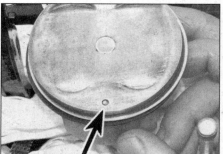

13.16 Fit the piston with the indent (arrowed) at the front

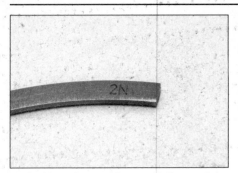

14.2a Note the marking on the top surface of the second ring . . .

14.2b . . . and the different profile of the top ring

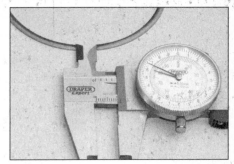

14.3 Measure the piston ring free end gap

14 Piston rings

Inspection

1 It is good practice to replace the piston rings with new ones when an engine is being overhauled. Before installing the new piston rings, the compression ring (top and 2nd ring) end gaps must be checked, both free and installed.

2 Lay out each piston with its ring set so the rings will be matched with the same piston and cylinder during the measurement procedure. The upper surface of the top two rings should have a manufacturer's mark at one end, with the top ring marked N and the 2nd ring marked 2N on original equipment. On the model photographed only the second ring was marked **(see illustration)**. However the top ring can be identified by its different cross-section, having a chamfered top inner rim **(see illustration)**. If the marks on each ring are different, note which is the top ring and which is the second.

3 To measure the free end gap, lay the ring on a flat surface and measure the gap between the ends using a Vernier caliper **(see illustration)**. Compare the results to specifications at the beginning of this Chapter and replace any ring that is outside its service limit with a new one.

4 To measure the installed end gap, insert the ring into the bottom of the cylinder and square it up with the cylinder walls by pushing it in with the top of the piston **(see illustrations)**. The ring should be a minimum of 15 mm below the bottom edge of the cylinder. Slip a feeler gauge between the ends of the ring to measure the gap and compare the result to the Specifications at the beginning of this Chapter **(see illustration)**.

5 If the gap is larger or smaller than specified, check that you have the correct rings before proceeding. Excess end gap is not critical unless it exceeds the service limit. Again, check that you have the correct rings for your engine.

6 Repeat the procedure for the other compression ring and then the compression rings in the other cylinders. Remember to keep the rings together with their matched pistons.

Installation

7 The oil control ring (lowest on the piston) is installed first. It is composed of three separate components; the expander and the upper and lower side rails. Slip the expander into the groove, positioning its ends so that they touch yet do not overlap **(see illustration)**. Install

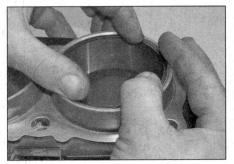

14.4a Carefully fit the ring into the bottom of the bore . . .

14.4b . . . then square it up using the piston . . .

14.4c . . . and measure the installed end gap

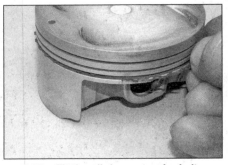

14.7a Fit the oil ring expander in its groove . . .

14.7b . . . then fit one side rail . . .

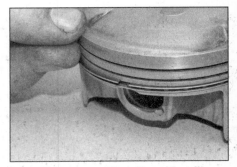

14.7c . . . and the other side rail

14.9 Fit the middle ring into its groove . . .

14.10 . . . then fit the top ring

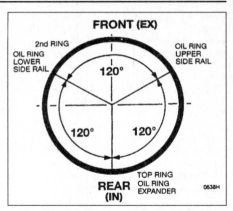

14.11 Arrange the ring end gaps as shown

the lower side rail **(see illustration)**. Do not use a piston ring installation tool on the oil ring side rails as they may be damaged. Instead, place one end of the side rail into the groove between the expander and the ring land. Hold it firmly in place and slide a finger or thin blade around the piston while pushing the rail into the groove. Next, install the upper side rail in the same manner **(see illustration)**.

8 After the oil control ring has been installed, check that both its upper and lower side rails can be turned smoothly in the ring groove.

9 Fit the second compression ring into the middle groove in the piston with its mark (2N) facing up (see Step 2). Do not expand the ring any more than is necessary to slide it into place **(see illustration)**. To avoid breaking the ring, use a piston ring installation tool or a feeler gauge blade as shown.

10 Install the top compression ring in the

same manner into the top groove in the piston **(see illustration)**. If the top ring has no mark its chamfered edge must be uppermost **(see illustration 14.2b)**.

11 Once the rings are correctly installed, check they move freely without snagging and stagger their end gaps as shown **(see illustration)**.

15 Starter clutch and gears

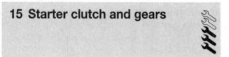

Note: *The starter clutch can be removed with the engine in the frame.*

Check

1 The operation of the starter clutch can be checked while it is in situ. Remove the

starter motor (see Chapter 8). Check that the starter idle/reduction gear is able to rotate freely clockwise as you look at it via the starter motor aperture, but locks when rotated anti-clockwise. If not, the starter clutch is faulty and should be removed for inspection.

Removal

2 Remove the alternator rotor (see Chapter 8) – the starter driven gear should come with it. If not slide it off the end of the crankshaft **(see illustration)**.

Inspection

3 If separated fit the starter driven gear into the back of the alternator rotor, turning the gear anti-clockwise as you do to spread the clutch sprags and allow it to enter. With the alternator rotor face down on a workbench, check that the starter driven gear rotates freely in an anti-clockwise direction and locks against the rotor in a clockwise direction **(see illustration)**. If it doesn't, the starter clutch should be dismantled for further investigation.

4 Withdraw the starter driven gear from the starter clutch. If the gear appears stuck, rotate it anti-clockwise as you withdraw it to free it from the sprags.

5 Check the condition of the sprags inside the clutch housing and the corresponding surface on the driven gear hub **(see illustration)**. If they are damaged, marked or flattened at any point, new ones should be fitted – the starter clutch components (sprag assembly, housing and starter driven gear) come as an assembly and are not available individually. To separate the clutch housing and sprag assembly from the rotor, hold the rotor using a suitable spanner on its boss or using a holding strap and unscrew the bolts inside the rotor **(see illustration)**. Remove the sprag assembly from the housing, noting which way round it fits and how it locates. Install the new assembly in a reverse sequence, making sure the sprag assembly flange locates in the rim in the housing and faces the rotor when

15.2 Slide the starter driven gear off if necessary

15.3 Check that the gear turns freely anti-clockwise

15.5a Check the sprags (A) and the driven gear hub (B) for wear and damage

15.5b The starter clutch bolts are on the inside of the rotor

fitted onto it. Apply a suitable non-permanent thread locking compound to the bolts and tighten them to the torque setting specified at the beginning of the Chapter. Apply clean engine oil to the sprags.

6 Check the bush in the starter driven gear hub and its corresponding surface on the crankshaft **(see illustration)**. If the bush surfaces show signs of excessive wear (i.e. the oil retaining holes are barely visible) replace the starter clutch with a new one.

7 Check the teeth of the starter motor drive shaft, idle/reduction gear and starter driven gear **(see illustration)**. If worn or chipped teeth are discovered on related gears replace the relevant components with new ones. Check the idle gear shaft for damage, and check that the gear is not a loose fit on it.

Installation

8 Install the alternator rotor (see Chapter 8).

16 Clutch

Note: *The clutch can be removed with the engine in the frame.*

15.6 Check the bush for wear – the oil holes should be easily visible

15.7 Check all gear teeth for wear and damage

Removal

1 Drain the engine oil (see Chapter 1).

2 Working in a criss-cross pattern, evenly slacken the clutch cover bolts **(see illustration)**. Lift the cover away from the engine, being prepared to catch any residual oil. Note that there is a leverage point on the front edge of the cover at the bottom if it is difficult to displace. Never lever between the cover and crankcase mating surfaces as you could gouge them and cause a leak.

3 Remove the gasket and discard it **(see illustration 16.33b)**. Note the positions of

the two locating dowels and remove them for safe-keeping if they are loose – they could be in either the crankcase or the cover.

4 Working in a criss-cross pattern, and holding the clutch housing to prevent it turning, gradually slacken the clutch pressure plate bolts until spring pressure is released, then remove the bolts and springs, and the pressure plate **(see illustrations)**. Remove the thrust washer, bearing and pressure plate lifter **(see illustration)**.

5 Remove the clutch friction and plain plates, keeping them in order, and using a bent piece of wire to hook them out where necessary **(see**

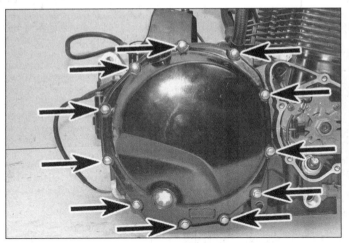

16.2 Clutch cover bolts (arrowed)

16.4a Unscrew the bolts . . .

16.4b . . . and remove the springs . . .

16.4c . . . and the pressure plate

16.4d Remove the thrust washer, bearing and pressure plate lifter

16.5 Remove the clutch plates as described

16.6 Withdraw the pushrod from the shaft

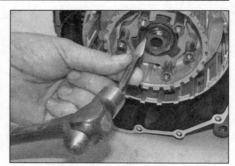

16.7a Unstake the clutch nut . . .

illustration). Keep the plates assembled in their original order, even if you are replacing them with new ones, as there are different types – the old ones can be used as a guide to installing the new ones. Remove the anti-judder spring and spring seat **(see illustrations 16.29a)**.

6 If the release cylinder has been displaced from the left-hand side of the engine, push the exposed short pushrod into the input shaft **(see illustration 16.18b)** and withdraw the long pushrod from the right-hand end **(see illustration)**. Do not attempt to withdraw the long pushrod from the left-hand side as it has a knurled section on each end which will damage the oil seal (and you have to separate the crankcase halves to replace the oil seal). If the release mechanism is in place use a magnet or a hooked piece of wire to draw the pushrod out.

7 Using a suitable drift and hammer unstake the rim of the clutch nut from the indent in the shaft **(see illustration)**. To remove the

clutch nut the transmission input shaft must be locked. This can be done in several ways. If the engine is in the frame, engage 6th gear and have an assistant hold the rear brake on hard with the rear tyre in firm contact with the ground. Alternatively, the Suzuki service tool (Pt. No. 09920-53740) or a commercially available (and inexpensive) equivalent can be used to stop the clutch centre from turning whilst the nut is slackened **(see illustration)**. Locate the shaped ends of the tool arms into opposed grooves in the clutch centre. With the clutch centre held, unscrew the clutch nut, then remove the spring washer. If the rim of the nut is badly distorted replace it with a new one, otherwise it can reused.

8 Slide the clutch centre off the shaft **(see illustration 16.27)**. Remove the back-torque limiter drive and driven cams from the clutch centre, noting how they fit **(see illustrations 16.26b and a)**.

9 Slide the thrust washer off the shaft **(see illustration 16.25)**.

10 Support the clutch housing and ease the needle bearing and spacer out of its centre using a magnet, then draw them off the shaft **(see illustration)**. Remove the housing, noting how it engages with the primary drive gear on the crankshaft and the oil pump driven gear **(see illustration 16.24a)**. Note the oil pump drive gear on the back of the clutch housing and remove it if required, noting which way up it fits **(see illustration 16.23)**.

11 Slide the thrust washer off the shaft **(see illustration)**.

Inspection

12 After an extended period of service the clutch friction plates will wear and promote clutch slip. Measure the thickness of each friction plate using a Vernier caliper **(see illustration)**. If any plate has worn to or beyond the service limit given in the Specifications at the beginning of the Chapter, the friction plates must be replaced with new ones as a set. Also, if any of the plates smell burnt or are glazed, they must be replaced as a set. Note that there are three different types of friction plate– ensure the correct quantity of each are supplied according to the Suzuki parts list.

13 Also measure the width of the friction plate tabs and replace any plates that are worn beyond the service limit specified with new ones.

14 The plain plates should not show any signs of excess heating (bluing). Check for warpage using a flat surface and feeler gauges **(see illustration)**. If any plate exceeds the

16.7b . . . then unscrew it as described – here a commercially available holding tool is being used

16.10 Draw the spacer and bearing out from the centre of the housing

16.11 Slide the thrust washer off

16.12 Measure the thickness of the friction plates and the width of the tabs

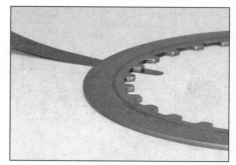

16.14 Check the plain plates for warpage

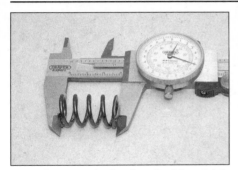

16.15 Measure the free length of the clutch springs and check that they are square

16.16a Check the friction plate tabs and clutch housing slots as described

16.16b Check the plain plate tongues and the clutch centre slots as described

maximum amount of warpage, or shows signs of bluing, all plain plates must be replaced as a set.

15 Measure the free length of each clutch spring using a Vernier caliper **(see illustration)**. If any spring is below the service limit specified, replace all the springs with new ones as a set. Also place the spring upright on a flat surface and check it for bend by placing a ruler against it, or alternatively lay it against a set square **(see illustration 10.22)**. If the bend in any spring is excessive, all springs must be replaced with new ones.

16 Inspect the edges of the tabs on the friction plates and the corresponding slots in the clutch housing for burrs and indentations **(see illustration)**. Similarly check for wear between the inner teeth of the plain plates and the slots in the clutch centre **(see illustration)**. Wear of this nature will cause clutch drag and slow disengagement during gear changes as

the plates will snag when the pressure plate is lifted. With care a small amount of wear can be corrected by dressing with a fine file, but if wear is excessive new components should be installed.

17 Check the needle bearing, its bearing surface in the clutch housing and the spacer it runs on, and the section of shaft the spacer runs on for signs of damage or scoring and excessive play, and replace them with new ones if necessary **(see illustration)**.

18 Check the clutch pressure plate, the lifter, the bearing and the thrust washer for signs of roughness, wear or damage, and replace any parts with new ones as necessary **(see illustration)**. Check the pushrods for bend and damaged ends – to access the short pushrod displace the release cylinder (see Section 17). Withdraw the pushrod **(see illustration)**.

19 Check the pushrod oil seal on the left-hand side of the engine for signs of leakage and

replace it with a new one it if necessary. To do this you have to separate the crankcase halves as the seal sits in a lipped rim in the crankcases – refer to Section 22.

20 Check the back-torque limiter drive and driven cams for wear of the engagement dogs and their slots, and replace them with a new set if necessary **(see illustration)**. Also check that the clutch spring bolt holders are tight in the driven cam – if any are loose, unscrew them all, then clean their threads, apply a suitable non-permanent thread-locking compound to them and tighten them to the torque setting specified at the beginning of the Chapter **(see illustration)**.

21 Check the teeth of the primary driven gear on the back of the clutch housing and the corresponding teeth of the primary drive gear on the crankshaft **(see illustration)**. Replace the clutch housing and/or crankshaft with new ones if worn or chipped teeth are discovered

16.17 Check the spacer, bearing and clutch housing as described

16.18a Check the lifter, its bearing and the other components as described

16.18b Withdraw the short pushrod and check it as described

16.20a Check the dogs and slots for wear and damage . . .

16.20b . . . and make sure the bolt holders are tight

16.21 Check the teeth on the various related gears for wear and damage

16.23 Fit the gear onto the housing, making sure it is the correct way round

16.24a Locate the clutch housing, engaging the gear teeth . . .

16.24b . . . then slide the bearing and spacer onto the shaft and into the housing

16.24c Check that the gear teeth have engaged correctly

16.25 Slide the thrust washer onto the shaft

16.26a Fit the driven cam into the clutch centre . . .

(refer to Section 24 for the crankshaft). Similarly check the oil pump drive gear on the back of the housing and its driven gear on the pump shaft – the drive gear is not listed as being available as a separate component from the clutch housing, but check with a Suzuki dealer before buying a whole new housing.

Installation

22 Remove all traces of old gasket from the crankcase and clutch cover surfaces.
23 Slide the thrust washer onto the shaft with its chamfered side facing in **(see illustration 16.11)**. If removed, fit the oil pump drive gear onto the back of the clutch housing with

the recessed side facing the housing **(see illustration)**.
24 Smear the spacer (inside and out) and the needle bearing with molybdenum disulphide oil (50% molybdenum grease and 50% engine oil). Locate the clutch housing on the input shaft, engaging the teeth on the oil pump drive gear with those on the driven gear, and the teeth on the primary driven gear with those on the primary drive gear **(see illustration)**. Slide the spacer and bearing together into the centre of the housing **(see illustration)**. Try to turn the oil pump driven gear by hand to check that it has engaged correctly with the drive gear **(see illustration)**.

25 Slide the thrust washer onto the shaft **(see illustration)**.
26 Fit the back-torque limiter driven cam into the clutch centre, locating the cut-outs on its inner side over the raised sections in the centre **(see illustration)**. Now fit the drive cam into the driven cam, locating the dogs in the slots and aligning the punch mark on the drive cam with that on the driven cam **(see illustration)**.
27 Slide the clutch centre onto the shaft, engaging the splines in the centre of the drive cam with those on the shaft **(see illustration)**.
28 Slide the spring washer onto the shaft so that its inner rim is raised away from the

16.26b . . . then fit the drive cam into the driven cam, aligning the punch marks

16.27 Slide the clutch centre onto the shaft

16.28a Fit the spring washer . . .

16.28b . . . then fit the clutch nut . . .

16.28c . . . and tighten it to the specified torque

engine **(see illustration)**. Fit the clutch nut with its thin rim facing out, and using the method employed on removal to lock the input shaft (see Step 7), tighten the nut to the torque setting specified at the beginning of the Chapter **(see illustrations)**. **Note:** *Check that the clutch centre rotates freely after tightening the clutch nut.* Stake the rim of the nut into one of the indents on the shaft **(see illustration)**.

29 Fit the anti-judder spring seat over the clutch centre, then fit the spring so that its outer rim is raised off the spring seat **(see illustrations)**.

30 There are three different types of friction plate which must be identified before installation so they are correctly fitted: one plate has a larger internal diameter – this is the innermost friction plate and it locates over the anti-judder spring and seat; of the remaining nine, one has friction pads that are smaller than those on the other eight and there are more of them, and this is the outermost plate **(see illustration)**. The remaining eight plates are identical. Coat each clutch friction and plain plate with engine oil before installing it and build them up in the housing as follows. First fit the innermost friction plate with the larger internal diameter, locating it around the anti-judder spring and seat **(see illustration)**. Next fit a plain plate, then alternate standard friction plates (of which there are eight) and plain plates until all are installed **(see illustration)**. Now fit the outermost friction plate, locating its tabs in the shallow slots in the housing so they are offset from the others **(see illustration)**.

16.28d Stake the rim of the clutch nut against the shaft indent

31 If removed, smear molybdenum grease onto each end of the pushrod and slide it into the input shaft **(see illustration 16.6)**. Lubricate the pressure plate lifter, the bearing and thrust washer with clean oil, then fit the

16.29a Fit the spring seat and the spring . . .

bearing and the washer onto the lifter and slide the assembly into the shaft **(see illustration 16.4d)**.

32 Fit the pressure plate into the clutch centre, aligning the circular indent on its

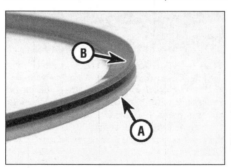

16.29b . . . as shown – spring seat (A), spring (B)

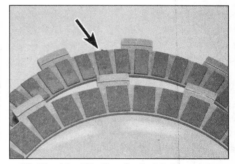

16.30a Identify the single friction plate with smaller and more friction pads (arrowed) – this is the outermost plate

16.30b Fit the innermost friction plate around the anti-judder spring and seat . . .

16.30c . . . then alternate between plain plates and friction plates . . .

16.30d . . . fitting the tabs on the outermost plate in the shallow slots (arrowed)

16.32 Fit the pressure plate aligning the indents

16.33b ... then fit the gasket onto the dowels (arrowed) ...

16.33a Apply the sealant around the joints ...

16.34 ... and install the cover

rim with one of the two triangular indents on the clutch centre rim, making sure the plate seats correctly with its inner rim castellations locating in the slots in the centre **(see illustration)** – if there is any clearance between the clutch plates as you push on the pressure plate then it has not located properly. Fit the clutch springs and bolts and tighten the bolts evenly in a criss-cross sequence to the specified torque setting **(see illustrations 16.4b and a).**

33 Apply a smear of sealant (Suzuki Bond 1207B or equivalent) to the area around the crankcase joints as shown **(see illustration)**. If removed, insert the clutch cover dowels into the crankcase, then place a new gasket onto the crankcase, making sure it locates correctly over the dowels **(see illustration)**.

34 Install the clutch cover and tighten its bolts evenly in a criss-cross sequence **(see illustration)**.

35 Refill the engine with oil to the correct level (see Chapter 1 and *Pre-ride checks*).

36 Check the action of the release mechanism.

17 Clutch release mechanism

⚠ **Warning: Do not, under any circumstances, use petroleum-based solvents to clean the clutch release mechanism parts. Use clean brake/clutch fluid or denatured alcohol only. Use care when working with brake/clutch fluid as it can injure your eyes and it will damage painted surfaces and plastic parts – cover surrounding components with rag, wipe up any spills immediately and wash the area with soap and water. Overhaul must be done in a spotlessly clean work**

area to avoid contamination and possible failure of the hydraulic release mechanism components.*

Master cylinder

Note: *If the entire clutch release mechanism is being overhauled (i.e. release cylinder as well as master cylinder), or if you intend to change the clutch fluid as part of the master cylinder overhaul (which is advisable), drain the fluid completely from the system (after displacing the piston from the release cylinder if applicable), as opposed to retaining the old fluid within it by blocking the hose as described (Step 6).*

1 If the master cylinder is leaking fluid, or if the clutch does not work properly when the lever is applied, and bleeding the system does not help, and the hydraulic hose is in good condition, then master cylinder overhaul is recommended.

2 Before disassembling the master cylinder, read through the entire procedure and make sure that you have the correct rebuild kit. Also, you will need some new DOT 4 hydraulic brake and clutch fluid, some clean rags and internal circlip pliers.

Removal

Note: *If the master cylinder is being displaced from the handlebar and not being removed completely or overhauled, follow Steps 4 and 7 only.*

3 Place the bike on its centrestand and turn the handlebars as required so that the top of the reservoir is level. Remove the mirror (see Chapter 7). Slacken the reservoir cover screws, then lightly tighten them again **(see illustration)**.

4 Disconnect the clutch switch wiring connectors **(see illustration)**. If required, remove the clutch switch (see Chapter 8).

5 If the master cylinder is being overhauled, remove the clutch lever (see Chapter 5). If it is just being displaced it can remain in situ.

6 If the master cylinder is being completely removed or overhauled, unscrew the clutch hose banjo bolt and separate the hose from the cylinder, noting its alignment **(see illustration)**. Wrap Clingfilm around the banjo union and secure the hose in an upright position to minimise fluid loss. Discard the sealing washers as they must be replaced

17.3 Slacken the screws

17.4 Disconnect the wiring connectors (arrowed)

17.6 Clutch hose banjo bolt (arrowed)

17.7 Master cylinder clamp bolts (arrowed)

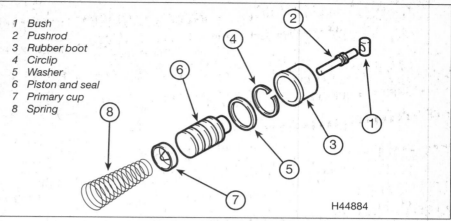

1 Bush
2 Pushrod
3 Rubber boot
4 Circlip
5 Washer
6 Piston and seal
7 Primary cup
8 Spring

H44884

17.9 Clutch master cylinder components

with new ones. If the master cylinder is just being displaced and not completely removed, do not disconnect the hose.

7 Unscrew the master cylinder clamp bolts, then lift the master cylinder and reservoir away from the handlebar **(see illustration)**.

Caution: Do not tip the master cylinder or brake fluid will run out.

8 Remove the reservoir cover, diaphragm plate and rubber diaphragm **(see illustration 17.24)**. If the system hasn't been drained, tip the brake fluid from the reservoir into a suitable container. Wipe any remaining fluid out of the reservoir with a clean rag.

Overhaul

Note: *If required, refer to the illustrations for front brake master cylinder overhaul in Chapter 6.*

9 Draw the pushrod out of the master cylinder, noting how it locates in the rubber boot – the boot may come away with the pushrod **(see illustration)**.

10 If it didn't come with the pushrod, remove the rubber boot from the end of the cylinder.

11 Push the piston in and, using circlip pliers, remove the circlip, then slide out the washer, piston and seal, cup and spring, noting how they fit. Lay the parts out in the proper order and way round to prevent confusion during reassembly.

12 Clean all parts with clean brake/clutch fluid. Do not dry or wipe the components with a rag.

13 Check the master cylinder bore for corrosion, scratches, nicks and score marks. If damage or wear is evident, the master cylinder must be replaced with a new one. If the master cylinder is in poor condition, then the release cylinder should be checked as well. Check that the fluid inlet and outlet ports in the master cylinder are clear.

14 The dust boot, circlip, washer, seal, piston, cup and spring are all included in the rebuild kit. Use all of the new parts, regardless of the apparent condition of the old ones. Fit all components according to the layout of the old ones. Lubricate the bore, seal, piston, primary cup and spring with clean brake/clutch fluid.

15 Fit the dished side of the primary cup into the narrow end of the spring. Fit the spring into the master cylinder, wide end first, making sure the cup lips do not turn inside.

16 If not already done, fit the seal onto the piston. Fit the piston into the master cylinder, making sure it is the correct way round and the seal lips do not turn inside out. Slide the washer into the cylinder. Depress the piston and install the new circlip, making sure that it locates in the groove.

17 Apply some silicone grease to the inside of the rubber boot and to the pushrod ends. Fit the boot, making sure the wide rim locates correctly in the end of the master cylinder. Fit the pushrod into the boot, locating its end against the piston, and locating the narrow rim of the boot into the groove.

18 Inspect the reservoir rubber diaphragm and replace it with a new one if it is damaged or deteriorated.

Installation

19 Locate the master cylinder on the handlebar and fit the clamp with its UP mark facing up **(see illustration 17.7)**, aligning the clamp mating surfaces with the punch mark on the underside of the handlebar. Tighten the upper bolt first, then the lower bolt, to the torque setting specified at the beginning of the Chapter.

20 If detached, connect the clutch hose to the master cylinder, using new sealing washers on each side of the union, and aligning the hose so the elbow butts against the lug **(see illustration 17.6)**. Tighten the banjo bolt to the specified torque setting.

21 If removed, install the clutch switch (see Chapter 8). Connect the clutch switch wiring connectors **(see illustration 17.4)**.

22 If removed, install the clutch lever (see Chapter 5).

23 Fill the fluid reservoir with new DOT 4 brake/clutch fluid (see Pre-ride checks). Bleed the air from the system (see below).

24 Fit the rubber diaphragm onto the master cylinder reservoir, making sure it is correctly seated, and the diaphragm plate **(see illustration)**. Fit the cover and tighten its screws (do not overtighten) **(see illustration 17.3)**.

25 Check the operation of the clutch before riding the motorcycle.

Clutch release cylinder

Note: *If the entire clutch release mechanism is being overhauled (i.e. master cylinder as well as release cylinder), or if you intend to change the clutch fluid as part of the release cylinder overhaul (which is advisable), drain the fluid completely from the system after displacing the piston, as opposed to retaining the old fluid within it by blocking the hose as described (Step 29).*

26 If the release cylinder is leaking fluid, or if the clutch does not work properly when the lever is applied, and bleeding the system does not help (see below), and the hydraulic hose and master cylinder are in good condition, then release cylinder overhaul is recommended.

27 Before disassembling the release cylinder, read through the entire procedure and make sure that you have a new seal. Also, you will need some new DOT 4 hydraulic brake and clutch fluid, and some clean rags.

Removal

28 Remove the front sprocket cover (see Chapter 6).

29 If the release cylinder is being completely removed or overhauled, unscrew the clutch hose guide/wiring clamp bolt, then unscrew the banjo bolt and detach the hose, noting its alignment **(see illustration)**. Wrap Clingfilm around the banjo union and secure the hose

17.24 Make sure the diaphragm is properly seated in the reservoir

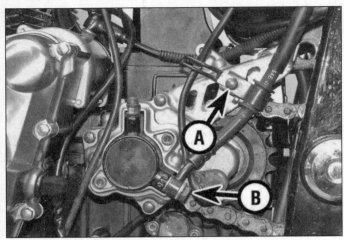

17.29 Clutch hose guide/wiring clamp bolt (A), clutch hose banjo bolt (B)

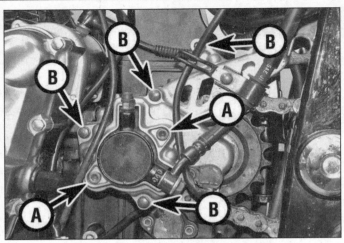

17.30 Release cylinder bolts (A), housing bolts (B)

in an upright position to minimise fluid loss. Discard the sealing washers as they must be replaced with new ones. If the release cylinder is just being displaced and not completely removed, do not disconnect the hose.

30 Slacken the two release cylinder bolts **(see illustration)**. Unscrew the release cylinder housing bolts and detach the assembly from the engine. Note the dowels and remove them if they are loose – they could be in either the housing or the engine **(see illustration 17.42a)**.

31 Undo the two screws securing the cover on the inside of the housing and remove the cover **(see illustration)**. Unscrew the release cylinder bolts and withdraw the cylinder, noting the dowels. Do not operate the clutch lever with the release cylinder removed.

32 Withdraw the short pushrod from the engine **(see illustration 16.18b)**.

Overhaul

33 Have a supply of clean rags on hand, then displace the piston by directing compressed air into the fluid inlet – take care to apply the compressed air gradually and progressively, starting with a fairly low pressure, until the piston is displaced, and have the piston against the work surface so that the compressed air lifts the cylinder off it.

17.31 Undo the screws (arrowed) and remove the cover

⚠️ *Warning: Use only low air pressure, otherwise the piston may be forcibly expelled and cause damage or injury. Never place your fingers in front of the piston in an attempt to catch or protect it when applying compressed air, as serious injury could result. Do not try to remove the piston by levering it out.*

34 Tip any residual fluid from the cylinder into a suitable container or onto a wad of rag.

35 Separate the spring from the piston, noting how it fits, or withdraw it from the cylinder if it is still in there **(see illustration)**. Remove the seal from its groove in the piston, noting which way round it fits, and taking care not to mark the piston if using a metal tool. Discard it as a new one should be used.

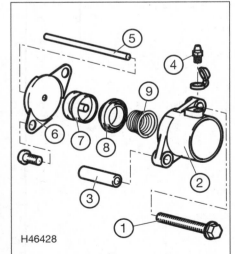

17.35 Clutch release cylinder components

1	Bolts	6 Cover
2	Release cylinder	7 Piston
3	Dowel	8 Piston seal
4	Bleed valve	9 Spring
5	Pushrod	

36 Clean the piston and release cylinder bore with DOT 4 hydraulic fluid.

37 Inspect the piston and bore for signs of corrosion, nicks and burrs and loss of plating. If surface defects are found, or if wear is evident, the piston and cylinder should be replaced with new ones (they are not available individually). If the release cylinder is in poor condition the master cylinder should also be overhauled (see above).

38 Check that the pushrod is straight by rolling it on a flat surface – if it is bent, replace it with a new one. Clean off any corrosion from the outer end of the rod. Check the pushrod oil seal for signs of leakage and replace it with a new one it if necessary. To do this you have to separate the crankcase halves as the seal sits in a lipped rim in the crankcases – refer to Section 22.

39 Lubricate the new piston seal with clean hydraulic fluid and fit it into the groove in the piston with the wider side facing its inner end. Fit the narrow end of the spring over the lug on the inner end of the piston. Lubricate the cylinder bore, piston and seal with DOT 4 hydraulic fluid and insert the assembly into the cylinder, making sure the spring stays in place on the piston and the rim of the seal does not turn inside out. Use your thumbs to press it fully in.

Installation

40 Lubricate the pushrod with molybdenum disulphide oil (a 50/50 mixture of molybdenum disulphide grease and engine oil) then slide it through the seal and into the engine **(see illustration 16.18b)**. Wipe the outer end of the pushrod clean and smear some silicon grease onto it.

41 Fit the release cylinder into the housing, making sure the dowels are in place and they locate correctly, and finger-tighten its bolts to hold it there. Fit the inner cover and tighten its screws **(see illustration 17.31)**.

42 Clean the speed sensor tip on the inside of the clutch release cylinder housing. Make

17.42a **Make sure the dowels (arrowed) are in place**

17.42b **Make sure the pushrod locates in the hole (arrowed)**

17.50 **Clutch release cylinder bleed valve (arrowed)**

sure the housing dowels are fitted in either the housing or the engine **(see illustration)**. Fit the housing onto the engine, locating the pushrod in its hole, and tighten the bolts **(see illustration)**. Now fully tighten the release cylinder bolts.

43 If detached, connect the clutch hose to the release cylinder, using new sealing washers on each side of the union, and aligning the hose as noted on removal **(see illustration 17.29)**. Tighten the banjo bolt to the specified torque setting.

44 Fill the fluid reservoir to the correct level with new DOT 4 brake/clutch fluid (see *Pre-ride checks*). Bleed the air from the system (see below).

45 Install the sprocket cover (see Chapter 6).

Clutch release mechanism bleeding

 Warning: Use care when working with hydraulic fluid as it can injure your eyes and it will damage painted surfaces and plastic parts.

Bleeding

46 Bleeding the clutch is simply the process of removing all the air bubbles from the fluid reservoir, the hose and the release cylinder. Bleeding is necessary whenever a hydraulic connection is loosened, when a component or hose is replaced, or when the master cylinder or release cylinder is overhauled. Leaks in the system may also allow air to enter, but leaking fluid will reveal their presence and warn you of the need for repair.

47 To bleed the clutch, you will need some new DOT 4 brake/clutch fluid, a length of clear vinyl or plastic tubing, a small container partially filled with clean brake/clutch fluid, some rags and a ring spanner to fit the release cylinder bleed valve. Note that a 'one-man type bleeding kit' will simplify the operation.

48 Remove the front sprocket cover (see Chapter 6). Cover the areas surrounding the master and release cylinder with rag to prevent damage in the event that brake fluid is spilled.

49 Place the bike on its centrestand and turn the handlebars so that the top of the reservoir is level. Undo the reservoir cover screws and remove the cover, diaphragm plate and diaphragm **(see illustration 17.3)**. Slowly pump the clutch lever a few times until no

air bubbles can be seen floating up from the holes in the bottom of the reservoir. Doing this bleeds the air from the master cylinder end of the line. Loosely refit the reservoir cover.

50 Remove the rubber cap from the top of the bleed valve **(see illustration)**. If using a ring spanner (which is preferable as you can leave it fitted over the bleed valve throughout the procedure), fit it over the bleed valve now. Attach one end of the clear vinyl or plastic tubing to the bleed valve and submerge the other end in the brake fluid in the container.

51 Check the fluid level in the reservoir – do not allow it to drop below the lower mark during the bleeding process.

52 Carefully pump the clutch lever three or four times and hold it in while opening the release cylinder bleed valve. When the valve is opened, clutch fluid will flow into the clear tubing and the lever will move toward the handlebar.

53 Retighten the bleed valve, then release the clutch lever gradually. Repeat the process until no air bubbles are visible in the fluid leaving the release cylinder. On completion, disconnect the bleeding equipment, then tighten the bleed valve to the torque setting specified at the beginning of the chapter. Fit the rubber cap onto the top of the bleed valve.

54 Fit the rubber diaphragm onto the master cylinder reservoir, making sure it is correctly seated, and the diaphragm plate. Fit the cover and tighten its screws (do not overtighten) **(see illustration 17.24)**. Wipe up any spilled brake fluid and check the entire system for leaks. Install the sprocket cover (see Chapter 6).

 If it's not possible to shift air from the hose, let the fluid in the system stabilise for a few hours and then repeat the procedure when the tiny bubbles in the system have settled out. Also check to make sure that there are no 'high-spots' in the clutch hose in which an air bubble can become trapped – this will occur most often in an incorrectly mounted hose union or badly routed hose. Displacing and moving the offending component around will normally dislodge any trapped air.

Changing the fluid

55 Changing the clutch fluid is a similar process to bleeding the clutch and requires the same materials, plus a suitable tool for siphoning the fluid out of the master cylinder reservoir (such as a syringe, though if one isn't available it is no problem to displace the reservoir and tip the fluid out). Ensure that your container is large enough to take all the old fluid when it is flushed out of the system.

56 Follow Steps 47, 48, 49 and 50, but after removing the reservoir cover, diaphragm plate and diaphragm, siphon or tip the old fluid out of the reservoir. Clean the reservoir and fill it with new brake fluid, then follow Step 52.

57 Retighten the bleed valve, then release the lever gradually. Keep the reservoir topped-up with new fluid to above the LOWER level at all times or air may enter the system and greatly increase the length of the task. Repeat the process until new fluid can be seen emerging from the bleed valve.

 Old fluid is invariably darker in colour than new fluid, making it easy to see when all old fluid has been expelled from the system.

58 Disconnect the hose, then tighten the bleed valve to the specified torque setting and fit the rubber cap.

59 Top-up the reservoir then install the diaphragm, plate and cover. Wipe up any spilled fluid and check the entire system for leaks.

60 Check the operation of the clutch before riding the motorcycle.

18 Gearchange mechanism

Note: *This procedure can be carried out with the engine in the frame. If the engine has been removed, ignore the steps which do not apply.*

Removal

1 Remove the clutch (see Section 16). Make sure the transmission is in neutral.

18.2 Remove the circlip (arrowed) and slide the washer off

18.3 Withdraw the gearchange shaft, noting the thrust washer

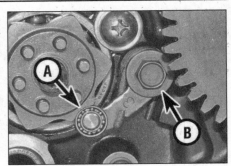

18.4 Note how the stopper arm (A) locates in the neutral detent and how the return spring ends locate, then unscrew the bolt (B)

2 Make an alignment mark between the slit in the gearchange linkage arm clamp and the end of the gearchange shaft, then unscrew the pinch bolt and slide the arm off the shaft **(see illustration 4.17)**. Remove the circlip from the end of the shaft and slide off the washer **(see illustration)**.

3 Working on the right-hand side of the engine, note how the gearchange shaft return spring ends fit on each side of the locating pin in the crankcase, and how the selector arm pawls engage with the pins on the gearchange cam **(see illustration 18.16)**. Withdraw the gearchange shaft from the crankcase, noting the thrust washer on the shaft **(see illustration)**.

4 Note how the stopper arm roller locates in the neutral detent on the gearchange cam **(see illustration)**. Undo the stopper arm pivot bolt and remove the bolt, stopper arm, washer and return spring.

5 If required remove the gearchange cam from the end of the selector drum – counter-hold the cam using a screwdriver between two pins and unscrew the centre bolt **(see illustration)**. Remove the locating pin from the end of the selector drum and store it with the cam for safekeeping.

Inspection

6 Inspect the stopper arm return spring and the gearchange shaft return spring **(see illustration)**. If they are fatigued, worn or damaged they must be replaced with new ones. The shaft return spring is retained by a circlip. To remove the circlip, slide it down the length of the shaft after releasing it from the groove, do not stretch it over the shaft. Note which way round the spring is fitted and how it locates on the tab on the selector arm. Ensure the circlip is correctly located in its groove.

7 Check that the gearchange shaft return

spring locating bolt is tight **(see illustration 18.5)**; if loose, remove it, then clean the threads and apply a suitable non-permanent thread-locking compound before tightening it.

8 Check the gearchange shaft for straightness and damage to the splines. If the shaft is bent you can attempt to straighten it but it is better to replace it with a new one, and if the splines are damaged the shaft must be replaced with a new one.

9 Check the condition of the shaft oil seal in the left-hand side of the crankcase. If it is damaged or deteriorated or shows signs of leakage it must be replaced with a new one. Lever out the old seal **(see illustration)**. With the seal removed check the bearing behind it and the one in the opposite side of the crankcase, replacing them with new ones if necessary (see Step 10). Press or drive the new seal in squarely, with its marked side facing out, using a seal driver or suitable socket, until it seats against the bearing **(see illustration)**.

10 Check that the gearchange shaft needle bearings (one in each side of the crankcase) rotate smoothly and freely and have no sign of freeplay between them and the crankcase **(see illustration)**. To remove the bearings, draw them out of the crankcase with a bearing puller, noting that once removed they cannot be re-used. Drive the new bearings into place, making sure they enter squarely. Refer to *Tools and Workshop Tips* in the Reference Section for more information on bearings and how to remove and install them.

18.5 Gearchange cam bolt (A). Gearchange shaft return spring locating pin (B)

18.6 Gearchange shaft return spring is retained by a circlip (arrowed)

18.9a Lever out the old seal . . .

18.9b . . . and press the new one into place

18.10 Check the bearing (arrowed) on each side of the crankcase

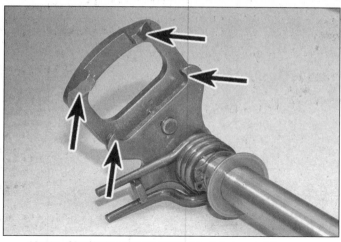

18.11a Check the selector arm pawls (arrowed) for wear

18.11b The outer arm is retained by a circlip (arrowed)

11 Check the selector arm pawls for wear **(see illustration)**. The outer arm can be replaced with a new one separately by removing the circlip, washer and spring and drawing the arm off the shaft **(see illustration)**. Note that the arm is fitted with the pawls facing inwards. The inner arm is integral with the gearchange shaft.

12 Inspect the lobes and the pins on the gearchange cam **(see illustration 18.5)**. Check that the stopper arm roller turns freely **(see illustration)**. Check that the stopper arm is a light fit on the pivot bolt with no appreciable freeplay between them. Replace any worn or damaged parts with new ones as necessary.

Installation

13 If removed, fit the pin in the end of the selector drum, then install the gearchange cam, locating the pin in the recess in the back of the cam. Clean the threads of the centre bolt, then apply a suitable non-permanent thread-locking compound. Install the bolt and tighten it to the torque setting specified at the beginning of this Chapter **(see illustration 18.5)**.

14 Ensure the selector drum is in the neutral position with the neutral detent on the cam as shown **(see illustration 18.4)**. Slide the

18.12 Make sure the roller (arrowed) turns freely and smoothly

stopper arm and its washer onto the pivot bolt, and apply a suitable non-permanent thread locking compound to the bolt threads. Fit the return spring over the lug in the crankcase, then install the stopper arm and tighten the pivot bolt to the specified torque setting **(see illustrations)**. Ensure the spring locates against the cut-out in the arm and the roller is in the neutral detent on the cam **(see illustration 18.4)**.

15 Slide the thrust washer onto the shaft and check that the gearchange shaft return spring is properly positioned and that the circlip is in its groove **(see illustration 18.6)**. Lightly

18.14a Fit the return spring onto the lug . . .

grease the inside of the gearchange shaft oil seal and slide the shaft into place from the right-hand side **(see illustration 18.3)**.

16 Locate the selector arm pawls onto the pins on the selector cam and the ends of the return spring onto each side of the locating pin **(see illustration)**.

17 Fit the washer and circlip onto the left-hand end of the gearchange shaft **(see illustration 18.2)**.

18 Slide the gearchange linkage arm onto the shaft, aligning the mark made on removal with the slit in the clamp **(see illustration 4.17)**. Install the clutch (see Section 16).

18.14b . . . then fit the stopper arm, locating the hooked end of the spring in its cut-out in the bottom edge . . .

18.14c . . . and locating the roller in the neutral detent as you tighten the bolt

18.16 Make sure the return spring ends and arm locate correctly

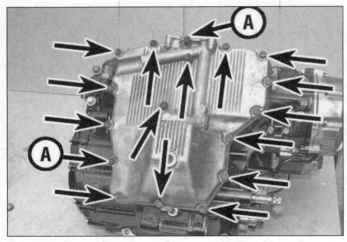

19.3 Sump bolts (arrowed) – note the bolts with sealing washers (A)

19.4 Unscrew the bolts (arrowed) and remove the strainer and its O-ring

19 Oil sump, strainer, pressure regulator and pipes

Note: *This procedure can be carried out with the engine in the frame. If the engine has been removed, ignore the steps which do not apply.*

Removal

1 Remove the exhaust system (see Chapter 4).

2 Drain the engine oil (see Chapter 1).

3 Unscrew the sump bolts, loosening them evenly in a criss-cross pattern to prevent distortion, and remove the sump, noting the position of the bolts with the sealing washers **(see illustration)**. Discard the sealing washers and the gasket as new ones must be fitted on reassembly.

4 Undo the bolts securing the oil strainer and remove the strainer **(see illustration)**. Discard the O-ring as a new one must be fitted.

5 Remove the oil outlet shim and its O-ring from the underside of the crankcase just ahead of the oil strainer **(see illustration 19.17)**. Discard the O-ring as a new one must be fitted whenever the sump is removed.

6 Pull the pressure regulator out of its socket **(see illustration)**. **Note:** *Suzuki do not list a replacement O-ring for the valve so take care not to distort or loose it. If necessary check with your Suzuki dealer as to the availability of a suitable replacement O-ring.*

7 If required unscrew the oil control valve plug and withdraw the spring and plunger **(see illustrations)**. Discard the plug sealing washer.

8 If required remove the main oil gallery pipe by pulling it out **(see illustration)**. Discard its O-rings. Also remove the oil return pipe, noting how it locates **(see illustration)**.

9 Remove all traces of old gasket from the sump and crankcase mating surfaces with a suitable solvent. If a scraper is used, take care not to scratch or gouge the soft aluminium.

Inspection

10 Clean the sump thoroughly, squirting solvent through all oil passages then blowing through them with compressed air.

11 Unscrew the oil strainer housing bolts and

19.6 Pressure regulator is a press fit in sump

19.7a Unscrew the plug . . .

19.7b . . . and withdraw the spring and plunger

19.8a Remove the oil gallery pipe, using a screwdriver to ease it out if necessary . . .

19.8b . . . and remove the oil return pipe

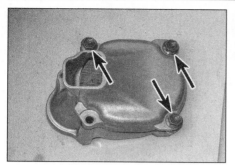

19.11 Oil strainer housing bolts (arrowed)

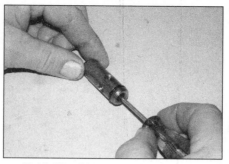

19.12 Checking the operation of the pressure regulator

19.14a Make sure the tab (arrowed) locates correctly over the support

separate the halves **(see illustration)**. Remove the strainer mesh. Discard the gasket. Wash the oil strainer and with a suitable solvent and remove any debris caught in the mesh, using compressed air if available. Inspect the strainer for any signs of wear or damage and replace it with a new one if necessary. Fit the mesh and a new gasket, then join the housing halves and tighten the bolts.

12 Clean the pressure regulator. Push the plunger into the regulator body and check that it moves freely against the spring pressure **(see illustration)**. If not replace it with a new one.

Installation

13 Coat the oil control valve plunger with oil and fit it into the sump closed end first, then fit the spring into the open end of the plunger **(see illustration 19.7b)**. Fit a new sealing washer onto the plug and tighten it to the torque setting specified at the beginning of the Chapter **(see illustration 19.7a)**.

14 Fit the oil return pipe, making sure it locates correctly **(see illustration)**. Fit new O-rings smeared with grease into the grooves in the main oil gallery pipe, then locate the pipe into its sockets and push it in **(see illustration)**.

15 Smear the pressure regulator O-ring with general purpose grease and press the regulator firmly into its recess in the sump **(see illustration 19.6)**.

16 Smear the new oil strainer O-ring with grease and fit it into the groove in the strainer **(see illustration)**. Install the strainer, making sure it is fitted the correct way round, and

tighten the bolts to the specified torque setting **(see illustration)**.

17 Fit a new O-ring smeared with grease into the oil outlet in the underside of the crankcase, then install the shim **(see illustration)**.

18 Lay a new gasket onto the crankcase or sump, making sure the holes align **(see illustration)**.

19 Position the sump on the crankcase **(see illustration)**. Install the bolts, using new sealing washers where fitted **(see illustration 19.3)**. Tighten the bolts evenly in a criss-cross pattern to the specified torque setting.

20 Install the exhaust system (see Chapter 4).

21 Replenish the engine with oil and check the level (see Chapter 1 and *Pre-ride checks*). Start the engine and check that there are no leaks around the sump).

19.14b Fit the pipe using new O-rings

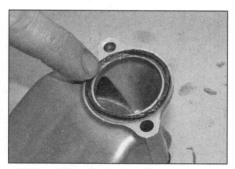

19.16a Fit the O-ring into the groove and smear it with grease . . .

19.16b . . . then fit the strainer

19.17 Grease the O-ring then fit the shim into it

19.18 Align the new gasket with the bolt holes . . .

19.19 . . . and install the sump

20.1 Unscrew the bolts and remove the cover

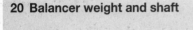

20 Balancer weight and shaft

Note: *The balancer weight and shaft can be removed with the engine in the frame. If the engine has been removed or partially disassembled, ignore the steps which don't apply.*

Removal

1 Remove the sump and main oil gallery pipe (see Section 19). Unscrew the balancer cover bolts and remove the cover **(see illustration)**.
2 Remove the spark plugs to allow the engine to be turned over easier (see Chapter 1).
3 Unscrew the timing rotor cover bolts, noting the sealing washer fitted with the top bolt and remove the cover **(see illustration 8.2)**. Discard the gasket as new one must be fitted on reassembly.

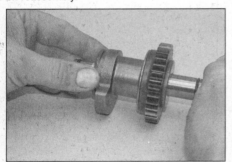

20.7a Check the run of the shaft in the bearings

20.7c . . . then slide the bearings and spacer out

20.5a Unscrew the holder bolt . . .

4 Turn the engine clockwise using a socket or spanner on the timing rotor (use the large hex cast into the rotor itself, do not use the timing rotor bolt) until the line on the timing rotor aligns with the sensing tip on the crankshaft position (CKP) sensor **(see illustrations 8.3a and b)**, and the punch mark and scribe line on the balancer shaft align with the mark on the crankcase **(see illustration 20.12)** – this is how the crankshaft and balancer shaft must be positioned for installation later.
5 Unscrew the shaft holder mounting bolt **(see illustration)**. Hold the balancer gear/weight assembly in the crankcase and slide the holder and shaft out, then remove the balancer gear/weight assembly, noting the washer on each end **(see illustration)**. Leave the holder on the shaft if possible then there is no chance of upsetting the existing backlash setting. Discard the shaft O-rings as a new one must be used.
6 If you need to separate the shaft from its

20.7b Remove the washer on each end . . .

20.8 Separate the weight and the gear, noting the alignment marks (arrowed)

20.5b . . . then grasp the holder, draw the shaft out and remove the balancer

holder, make an alignment mark between the holder and the slot in the end of the shaft – this will give a good indication as to the starting point for the backlash setting when the shaft is installed (the shaft provides an eccentric adjustment to allow the backlash between the balancer gear and its drive gear on the crankshaft to be optimised to reduce noise) **(see illustration)**. Slacken the pinch bolt and slide the holder off the shaft.

Inspection

7 Slide the shaft back into the weight and check that it runs freely and smoothly in the bearings, and that the shaft is a good fit **(see illustration)**. Remove the washer from each end of the gear/weight assembly **(see illustration)**. Replace the bearings with new ones if necessary – they are a sliding fit with a spacer between them **(see illustration)**. If there is any evidence of wear on the shaft, or if it is still a sloppy fit in the new bearings, replace the shaft with a new one – slacken the holder pinch bolt and slide the holder off it (if not already done), but do not fit the holder onto the new shaft until later. Check for wear on the faces of each washer and replace them with new ones if necessary.
8 Separate the weight from the gear, noting their alignment **(see illustration)**. Inspect the teeth on the gear for signs of wear or damage, and replace it with a new one if necessary. If damage is found, check the teeth on the drive gear on the crankshaft.
9 Check the condition of the rubber damper assembly in the gear for damage, deformation and deterioration, and replace them with new ones if necessary **(see illustration)**.

20.9 Check the rubber dampers

20.10 Balancer weight and gear assembly components

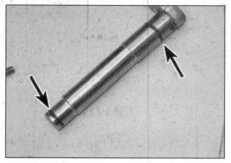

20.11 Fit new O-rings (arrowed) onto the shaft

20.12 Make sure the scribed line (A), punch mark (b) and crankcase mark (C) are all aligned

10 On reassembly of the shaft/weight assembly, lubricate each part with molybdenum disulphide oil (a 50/50 mixture of molybdenum disulphide grease and clean engine oil) **(see illustration)**. Fit the rubber dampers into the gear, butting each one against a lug **(see illustration 20.9)**. Fit the balancer weight into the gear, slotting the tabs into the gaps between the dampers, and making sure the scribe line on the weight aligns with the punch mark on the gear **(see illustration 20.8)**. Do not forget to fit the spacer between the needle bearings **(see illustration 20.7c)**.

Installation

11 Fit new O-rings onto the balancer shaft and smear the shaft with molybdenum disulphide oil (a 50/50 mixture of molybdenum disulphide grease and clean engine oil) **(see illustration)**. Check that the crankshaft is still positioned correctly, and realign it if necessary (see Step 4) – if the engine has been disassembled you will need to temporarily install the CKP sensor and timing rotor (see Chapter 4) in order to align the crankshaft correctly.

12 Make sure the washers are correctly fitted on each end of the balancer gear/weight **(see illustration 20.7b)**. Position the gear/weight assembly in the crankcase so that the punch mark and scribe line align with the mark on the crankcase **(see illustration)**, then slide in the shaft, if fitted aligning the holder with its mounting bolt hole in the crankcase **(see illustration 20.5b)**. If not already fitted, slide the holder onto the end of the shaft. In all cases apply a suitable non-permanent thread

locking compound to the holder mounting bolt and tighten it to the torque setting specified at the beginning of the Chapter **(see illustration 20.5a)**. If the shaft is difficult to install (because the gears are meshed too tight) turn it until it becomes easier.

13 If the holder was removed from the original shaft and no new components have been installed, turn the shaft using a screwdriver in the slot in its end until the alignment mark between the shaft holder and the slot in the end of the shaft made earlier align. Temporarily tighten the shaft pinch bolt **(see illustration 20.19)**.

14 In all cases carry out the backlash adjustment procedure (see below).

15 Turn the engine clockwise through 360° (one full turn) and check that the crankshaft and balancer marks still align (see Step 4).

16 Apply a suitable non-permanent thread locking compound to the balancer cover bolts, then fit the cover and tighten the bolts to the specified torque setting **(see illustration 20.1)**. Install the oil gallery pipe and the sump (see Section 19).

17 Apply a suitable sealant (Suzuki Bond 1207B or equivalent) to the CKP sensor wiring grommet and to the crankcase joints **(see illustration 8.38a)**. Install the timing rotor cover using a new gasket and tighten the bolts to the torque setting specified at the beginning of the chapter, not forgetting the sealing washer with the top bolt **(see illustration 8.38b)**.

18 Install the spark plugs (see Chapter 1).

Backlash adjustment

Note: *A backlash adjustment is provided so that the balancer shaft drive and driven gears mesh at their optimum point for quiet running with minimal wear. If the amount of backlash is too great, the shafts will clatter. If the gears are running tight, they will whine, and wear very quickly. At the optimum point the gears will run very quietly – it is easy to tell the difference with the engine running. Adjustment is possible due to the offset on the shaft which allows eccentric movement of the balancer gear in relation to its drive gear when the shaft is turned.*

Note: *This procedure must be carried out when the engine is cold.*

19 Slacken the balancer shaft holder pinch bolt **(see illustration)**.

20 Turn the shaft slightly anti-clockwise, then turn it clockwise until it stops – at this point backlash between the gears has been eliminated. Now turn the shaft anti-clockwise 1½ to 2 graduations as marked on the holder, then tighten the pinch bolt.

21 Selector drum and forks

Note: *Removal and installation of the selector drum and forks is easier with the engine removed and upside down a bench, though you can do so with the engine in the frame. Bear in mind that the engine itself is very heavy and manoeuvring it out of and into the frame requires the help of at least one extra person.*

Removal

1 Remove the gearchange mechanism and stopper arm (see Section 18), the sump and oil strainer (see Section 19), and the gear position sensor (see Chapter 4).

2 Before removing the selector forks, it is best to mark them according to their location and orientation as an aid to installation.

3 Undo the fork shaft and selector drum retaining screws **(see illustration)**.

20.19 Slacken the pinch bolt (arrowed)

21.3 Undo the shaft and bearing retaining screws (arrowed)

21.4a Withdraw the front shaft . . .

21.4b . . . and the rear shaft . . .

21.5a . . . then pivot the forks away from the selector drum . . .

4 Withdraw the fork shafts from the right-hand side of the crankcase **(see illustrations)**.

5 Pivot the forks out of their tracks in the selector drum then withdraw the selector drum from the right-hand side **(see illustrations)**.

6 Withdraw the forks, noting how they locate **(see illustration)**. Once removed from the crankcase, slide the forks back onto the shafts in their correct order and way round. Note that the two forks for the output shaft pinions are identical, and different to the fork for the input shaft pinion.

Inspection

7 Inspect the selector forks for any signs of wear or damage, especially around the fork ends where they engage with the groove in

the pinion. Check that each fork fits correctly in its pinion groove. Check closely to see if the forks are bent. If the forks are in any way damaged they must be replaced with new ones.

8 With the fork engaged in its pinion groove, measure the fork-to-groove clearance using a feeler gauge, and compare the result to the specifications at the beginning of the Chapter **(see illustration)**. If the clearance exceeds the service limit specified, measure the thickness of the fork ends and the width of the groove and compare the readings to the specifications **(see illustration)**. Replace whichever components are worn beyond their specifications with new ones.

9 Check each fork fits correctly on its shaft **(see illustration)**. They should move freely

with a light fit but no appreciable freeplay. Check that the fork shaft holes in the crankcases are not worn or damaged.

10 Check that the selector fork shafts are straight by rolling them along a flat surface. A bent rod will cause difficulty in selecting gears and make the gearchange action heavy. Replace the shafts with new ones if bent.

11 Inspect the selector drum grooves and selector fork guide pins for signs of wear or damage **(see illustration)**. If any components shows signs of wear or damage they must be replaced with new ones.

12 Check that the selector drum bearings (there is a ball bearing on the drum and a needle bearing in the crankcase) rotate freely and smoothly with no sign of freeplay between them and the drum or crankcase

21.5b . . . and withdraw the drum

21.6 Lift the forks out of their pinions

21.8a Measure fork-to-groove clearance

21.8b Measure the thickness of the fork ends and the width of the gear pinion groove

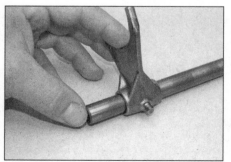

21.9 Forks should slide freely on the shafts

21.11 Check the drum grooves and fork guide pins for wear and damage

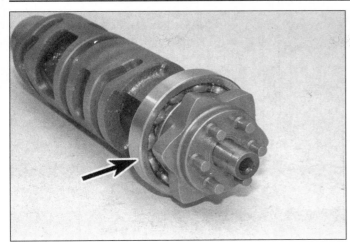

21.12a Check the bearing (arrowed) on the drum . . .

21.12b . . . and the bearing (arrowed) in the crankcase

(see illustrations). Replace the bearings with new ones if necessary – refer to *Tools and Workshop Tips* in the Reference Section for information on bearing checks and removal and installation methods. To remove the ball bearing first remove the cam (Section 18, Step 5 for removal, noting that you should counter-hold the drum by inserting a rod through one of the holes in the drum, and Step 13 to install) **(see illustration)**. Note that once the needle bearing has been removed it cannot be re-used.

Installation

13 Make certain of the correct order and way round for the forks before you install them to make sure you get it right – the two forks for the output shaft pinions are identical, and different to the fork for the input shaft pinion. Fit each selector fork in turn into the groove in its pinion, making sure they are in the correct position and the right way round **(see illustration 21.6)**. Pivot the forks forward and back so they will not get in the way of the drum when it is installed **(see illustration 21.5a)**.
14 Slide the drum into position in the crankcase **(see illustration 21.5b)**. Rotate the drum into the neutral position, so that the neutral detent in the cam, identifiable by its

shallower depth, points to the bottom of the engine.
15 Pivot each selector fork onto the drum, locating the guide pins into the drum tracks. Lubricate the selector fork shafts with clean engine oil and slide them into their bores in the crankcase and through the fork(s) **(see illustration)**.
16 Apply a suitable thread locking compound to the fork shaft and selector drum retaining screws and tighten them **(see illustration 21.3)**.
17 Install the gear position sensor (see Chapter 4), the oil strainer and sump (see Section 19), and the stopper arm and gearchange mechanism (Section 18).

22 Crankcase separation and reassembly

Note: *When the engine is upside down, referrals to the right and left-hand ends or sides of the transmission shafts or components are made as though the engine is the correct way up. Therefore the right-hand end of a shaft or side of a crankcase will actually be on your left as you look down onto the underside of the crankcase assembly.*

Separation

1 To access the oil pump, crankshaft, cam chain and tensioner blade, connecting rods and transmission shafts, the crankcase must be split into two parts.
2 To enable the crankcases to be separated, the engine must be removed from the frame (see Section 4). Before the crankcases can be separated the following components must be removed:
   a) Cam chain tensioner (Section 7).
   b) Camshafts (Section 8).
   c) Cylinder head (Section 9).
   d) Cylinder block (Section 12).
   e) Timing rotor and crankshaft position (CKP) sensor (Chapter 4)
   f) Clutch (Section 16).
   g) Gearchange mechanism (Section 18).
   h) Alternator (Chapter 8).
   i) Starter motor (Chapter 8).
   j) Oil filter (Chapter 1).
   k) Oil sump and oil strainer (Section 19).
   l) Balancer weight/shaft (Section 20).
   m) Selector drum and forks (Section 21).
Note: *If the crankcases are being separated to inspect or access the transmission components, or to inspect the crankshaft without removing it, the engine top-end components (cam chain tensioner, camshafts, cylinder head, cylinder block) can remain in situ. However, if removal of the crankshaft and connecting rod assemblies is intended, full disassembly of the top-end is necessary.*
3 Make a cardboard template punched with holes to match all the bolts in each crankcase half – as each crankcase bolt is removed, store it in its relative position in the template **(see illustration)**. This will ensure all bolts and washers and any wiring clamps are installed in the correct location on reassembly. Note that new copper sealing washers should be used on assembly where fitted, though keep the old ones with the bolts for the time being as a pattern for the new ones.
4 Unscrew the single 6 mm and the five

21.15 Locate the fork guide pins in their grooves then slide the shafts in and guide them through the forks

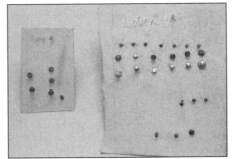

22.3 Cardboard templates of the crankcase halves for storing the bolts

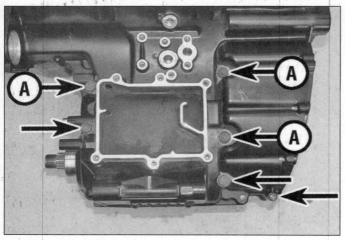

22.4 Upper crankcase bolts (arrowed) – note the bolts with copper washers (A)

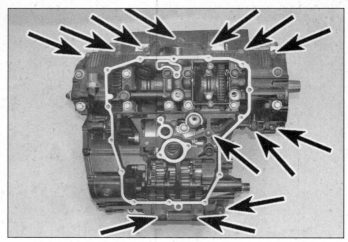

22.6 Lower crankcase 6 mm and 8 mm bolts (arrowed)

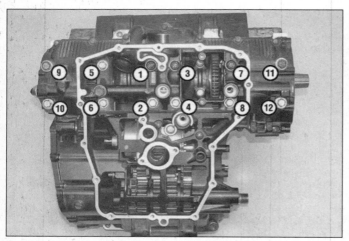

22.7 Crankshaft journal 9 mm bolt TIGHTENING sequence – nos 9, 10, 11 and 12 have copper washers

22.8 Lift the lower crankcase off the upper crankcase

8 mm upper crankcase bolts and fit them in the cardboard template **(see illustration)**.

5 Turn the engine upside down and support it on wood blocks so that no strain is placed on the cylinder studs.

6 Unscrew the twelve 6 mm and the single 8 mm lower crankcase bolts and fit them in the cardboard template **(see illustration)**.

7 Working in a **reverse** of the tightening sequence shown or as marked on the crankcase, slacken the twelve 9 mm crankshaft journal bolts a little a time until they are all finger-tight, then remove the bolts and fit them into the template **(see illustration)**.

8 Carefully lift the lower crankcase half off the upper half, using a soft-faced hammer to tap around the joint to initially separate them if necessary **(see illustration)**. **Note:** *If the halves do not separate easily, make sure all fasteners have been removed. Do not try and separate the halves by levering against the crankcase mating surfaces as they are easily scored and will leak oil.* The lower crankcase half will come away with the oil pump, leaving

the crankshaft, cam chain tensioner blade and transmission shafts in the upper crankcase half.

9 Remove the four locating dowels from the crankcase if they are loose (they could be in either crankcase half), noting their locations **(see illustration)**. Also remove the three oil passage O-rings from the upper crankcase

half **(see illustration)**. Discard these as new ones must be used.

10 Remove the clutch pushrod oil seal from the crankcase and discard it as a new one should be used **(see illustration 22.26)**.

11 Remove the crankshaft and connecting rods (Section 23) and the transmission shafts (Section 26) from the upper crankcase half

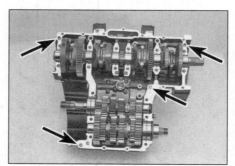

22.9a Remove the dowels . . .

22.9b . . . and the O-rings

22.13 Crankcase breather bolts (arrowed) – note the earth lead and wiring clamp (A)

22.14a Unscrew the bolt securing each oil jet (arrowed) – there are four

22.14b Unscrew the transmission oil jets (arrowed)

22.15 Main oil gallery plug (arrowed)

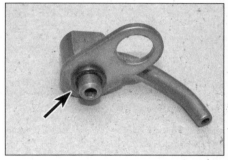

22.23 Fit a new O-ring onto each oil jet

and the oil pump from the lower (Section 28).

12 Remove the oil pressure switch (see Chapter 8), the oil temperature sensor and the cooling fan switch (Chapter 4).

13 Undo the bolts securing the crankcase breather cover, noting the positions of the engine earth lead and wiring clamp, and remove the cover **(see illustration)**. Discard the gasket as a new one must be fitted.

14 Undo the bolts securing the piston oil jets in the upper crankcase and remove the jets, noting how they fit **(see illustration)**. Remove the O-rings and discard them as new ones must be fitted. Unscrew the transmission oil jets **(see illustration)**.

15 Unscrew the oil galley plugs **(see illustration)**. Discard the sealing washers as new ones must be fitted.

16 Remove all traces of old sealant from the mating surfaces with a suitable solvent. Minor damage to the surfaces can be cleaned up with a fine file or sharpening stone.

Caution: Be very careful not to nick or gouge the crankcase mating surfaces or oil leaks will result. Check the crankcases very carefully for cracks and other damage.

17 Clean the crankcases thoroughly with clean solvent and dry them with compressed air. Blow through all oil passages and oil jets with compressed air.

Inspection

18 Small cracks or holes in aluminium castings may be repaired with an epoxy resin adhesive as a temporary measure. Permanent repairs can only be effected by argon-arc

22.24 Fit the breather cover using a new gasket

welding, and only a specialist in this process is in a position to advise on the economy or practical aspect of such a repair. If any damage is found that can't be repaired, a new set of crankcases is needed.

19 Damaged threads can be economically reclaimed by using a thread insert, which are easily fitted after drilling and tapping the affected thread.

20 Sheared studs and screws can usually be removed with the correct tools, or by employing the skills of a local engineering shop.

> **HAYNES HINT** *Refer to Tools and Workshop Tips for details of installing a thread insert and using screw extractors.*

21 Always clean the crankcases thoroughly after any repair work to ensure no dirt or metal

22.26 Fit a new clutch pushrod oil seal

swarf is trapped inside when the engine is rebuilt.

Reassembly

22 Fit new sealing washers to the oil gallery plugs then install the plugs and tighten them to the specified torque settings.

23 Fit a new O-ring onto the base of each piston oil jet and smear it with clean engine oil **(see illustration)**. Push each jet into its bore in the upper crankcase, making sure the oil nozzle points up into the cylinder **(see illustration 22.14a)**. Apply a suitable non-permanent thread locking compound to the jet bolts and tighten them to the specified torque setting. Install the transmission oil jets **(see illustration 22.14b)**.

24 Fit a new crankcase breather cover gasket and install the cover **(see illustration)**. Tighten the bolts to the specified torque setting, not forgetting the earth lead and wiring clamp **(see illustration 22.13)**.

25 Install the oil pressure switch (see Chapter 8), the oil temperature sensor and the cooling fan switch (Chapter 4).

26 Install the transmission shafts using a new oil seal on the output shaft (Section 26). Fit a new clutch pushrod oil seal **(see illustration)**.

27 Install the crankshaft and connecting rods (Section 23), and the oil pump (Section 28).

28 Ensure that all components and their bearings are in place in the upper and lower crankcase halves. Check that the crankshaft thrust bearings and the transmission bearing locating pins and half-ring retainers are all correctly located, and that the cam chain tensioner blade, its cushions, and all oil jets have been installed, if removed.

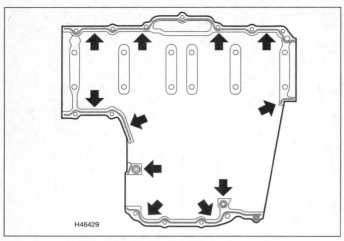

22.32 Apply sealant to the shaded areas

22.35 Fit new copper washers with the outer bolts

29 Generously lubricate the transmission shafts, selector drum and forks, and the crankshaft, particularly around the bearings, with clean engine oil, then use a rag soaked in high flash-point solvent to wipe over the mating surfaces of both halves.

30 Fit the four locating dowels into one crankcase half **(see illustration 22.9a)**.

31 Fit new O-rings into the oil passage holes in the upper crankcase half **(see illustration 22.9b)**.

32 Apply a small amount of suitable sealant to the mating surfaces of the lower crankcase half **(see illustration)**.

Caution: Do not apply an excessive amount of sealant as it will ooze out when the case halves are assembled and may obstruct oil passages. Do not apply the sealant on or too close to any of the bearing shells or surfaces.

33 Check again that all components are in position, particularly that the bearing shells are still correctly located in the lower crankcase half. Carefully fit the lower crankcase half down onto the upper crankcase half, making sure the dowels all locate correctly and the O-rings stay in place **(see illustration 22.8)**.

34 Check that the lower crankcase half is correctly seated. **Note:** *The crankcase halves should fit together without being forced. If the casings are not correctly seated, remove the lower crankcase half and investigate the problem. Do not attempt to pull them together using the crankcase bolts as the casing will crack and be ruined.*

35 Clean the threads of the 9 mm crankshaft journal bolts and insert them in their original locations **(see illustration 22.7)** – use new copper washers with bolt Nos. 9, 10, 11 and 12 **(see illustration)**. Secure all bolts finger-tight at first, then tighten them evenly and a little at a time in the numerical sequence shown first to the initial torque setting specified at the beginning of the Chapter, then to the final setting **(see illustration 22.7)**.

36 Clean the threads of the lower crankcase

bolts and insert them in their original locations **(see illustration 22.6)**. Tighten the bolts evenly and a little at a time to their specified torque settings, being sure to distinguish between the 6 mm bolts and the 8 mm bolt.

37 Turn the engine over. Install the upper crankcase bolts, using new sealing washers where fitted **(see illustration 22.4)**. Tighten the bolts evenly and a little at a time to their specified torque settings, again being sure to distinguish between the 6 mm bolt and the 8 mm bolts.

38 With all crankcase bolts tightened, check that the crankshaft and transmission shafts rotate smoothly and easily. Check the operation of the transmission in each gear by turning the selector drum by hand as you turn the input shaft. If there are any signs of undue stiffness, tight or rough spots, or of any other problem, the fault must be rectified before proceeding further.

23 Connecting rod and main bearing information

1 Even though new main and connecting rod bearings are generally fitted during engine overhaul, the old bearings should be retained for close examination as they may reveal valuable information about the condition of the engine.

2 Bearing failure occurs mainly because of lack of lubrication, the presence of dirt or other foreign particles, overloading the engine and/or corrosion. Regardless of the cause of bearing failure, it must be corrected before the engine is reassembled to prevent it from happening again.

3 When examining the bearing shells, lay them out on a clean surface in the same general position as their location on the crankshaft journals. This will enable you to match any noted bearing problems with the corresponding crankshaft journal.

4 Dirt and other foreign particles get into the engine in a variety of ways. They may be left in the engine during assembly or they may pass through filters or breathers, then get into the oil and from there into the bearings. Metal chips from machining operations and normal engine wear are often present. Abrasives are sometimes left in engine components after reconditioning operations, especially when parts are not thoroughly cleaned using the proper cleaning methods. Whatever the source, foreign objects often end up imbedded in the soft bearing material and are easily recognised. Large particles will not imbed in the bearing and will score or gouge the bearing and journal. The best prevention for this cause of bearing failure is to clean all parts thoroughly and keep everything spotlessly clean during engine reassembly. Regular oil and filter changes are also recommended.

5 Lack of lubrication or lubrication breakdown has a number of interrelated causes. Excessive heat (which thins the oil), overloading (which squeezes the oil from the bearing face) and oil leakage or throw off (from excessive bearing clearances, worn oil pump or high engine speeds) all contribute to lubrication breakdown. Blocked oil passages will starve a bearing of lubrication and destroy it. When lack of lubrication is the cause of bearing failure, the bearing material is wiped or extruded from the steel backing of the shell. Temperatures may increase to the point where the steel backing and the journal turn blue from overheating.

Refer to Tools and Workshop Tips for bearing fault finding.

6 Riding habits can have a definite effect on bearing life. Full throttle low, speed operation, or labouring the engine, puts very high loads on bearings, which tend to squeeze out the oil film. These loads cause the bearings to flex,

24.2 Measuring the clearance between the crank and the outer thrust bearing

24.3a Remove the thrust bearings as described

24.3b Carefully lift the crankshaft out

which produces fine cracks in the bearing face (fatigue failure). Eventually the bearing material will loosen in pieces and tear away from the steel backing. Short trip riding leads to corrosion of bearings, as insufficient engine heat is produced to drive off the condensed water and corrosive gases produced. These products collect in the engine oil, forming acid and sludge. As the oil is carried to the engine bearings, the acid attacks and corrodes the bearing material.

7 Incorrect bearing installation during engine assembly will lead to bearing failure as well. Tight fitting bearings which leave insufficient bearing oil clearances result in oil starvation. Dirt or foreign particles trapped behind a bearing shell result in high spots on the bearing which lead to failure.

8 To avoid bearing problems, clean all parts thoroughly before reassembly, double check all bearing clearance measurements and lubricate the new bearings with clean engine oil during installation.

24 Crankshaft and bearings

Note: *To remove the crankshaft the engine*

must be removed from the frame and the crankcases separated.

Removal

1 Separate the crankcase halves (see Section 22).
2 Before removing the crankshaft check the thrust bearing clearance. The thrust bearings are located on each side of the No. 2 main bearing housing between cylinders 1 and 2. Pull the crankshaft as far as it will go toward the alternator (left-hand) end (this eliminates play in the inner bearing). Insert a feeler gauge between the crankshaft and the outer (left-hand) thrust bearing and record the clearance **(see illustration)**. Compare the measurement with this Chapter's Specifications. If the clearance is excessive, refer to Steps 10 and 11 for selection of replacement bearings.
3 Remove the thrust bearings by pushing one end round with a small screwdriver then drawing the other end out, noting how and where they fit – do not get the inner and outer bearing mixed up **(see illustration)**. Lift the crankshaft together with the connecting rods and cam chain out of the upper crankcase half **(see illustration)**. If the crankshaft appears stuck, tap it gently using a soft faced mallet.
4 If required remove the main bearing shells

from their housings **(see illustration)**. Keep the bearing shells in order.
5 If required, separate the connecting rods from the crankshaft (see Section 25), and disengage the cam chain from its sprocket.

Inspection

6 Clean the crankshaft with solvent, squirting it through the oil passages. If available, blow the crank dry with compressed air, and also blow through the oil passages. Check the balancer drive gear, cam chain sprocket and primary drive gear for wear or damage **(see illustration)**. If any of the sprocket or gear teeth are excessively worn, chipped or broken, the crankshaft must be replaced with a new one. Similarly check the driven sprockets on the camshafts, the primary driven gear on the clutch housing and the balancer driven gear. If a new crankshaft is installed, make sure you select the correct new bearing shells to go with it (see Steps 23 and 24).
7 Refer to Section 23 and examine the main bearing shells. If they are scored, badly scuffed or appear to have been seized, new bearings must be installed. Always replace the main bearings as a set. If they are badly damaged, check the corresponding crankshaft journals. Evidence of extreme heat, such as discoloration, indicates that lubrication failure

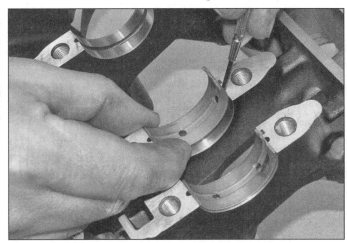

24.4 Remove the bearing shells if required

24.6 Balancer drive gear (A), cam chain sprocket (B), primary drive gear (C)

has occurred. Be sure to thoroughly check the oil pump and pressure regulator as well as all oil holes and passages before reassembling the engine.

8 Inspect the crankshaft journals, paying particular attention where damaged bearings have been discovered. If the journals are scored or pitted in any way a new crankshaft will be required.

9 Place the crankshaft on V-blocks and check for runout at the main bearing journals using a dial gauge. Compare the reading to the maximum specified at the beginning of the Chapter. If the runout exceeds the limit, the crankshaft must be replaced with a new one.

Thrust bearing selection

10 If the thrust bearing clearance was excessive (see Step 2), measure the thickness of the inner thrust bearing, and compare the result to the specifications at the beginning of the Chapter **(see illustration)**. If the thickness measured is below the service limit specified, the inner thrust bearing must be replaced with a new one. There is only one size of replacement inner bearing, and it is colour-coded green. Install the replacement and check the clearance again (see Step 2). If the clearance is still excessive, or if the inner bearing was within specifications, select a replacement outer bearing as follows:

11 With the crankshaft in place fit the inner thrust bearing but do not fit the outer bearing. Push the crankshaft as far as it will go toward the alternator (left-hand) end to eliminate any clearance. Insert a feeler gauge between the crankshaft and the main bearing housing where the outer bearing fits, and record the clearance. Using the table below, select a replacement outer thrust bearing according

24.10 Measuring the thickness of the inner (right-hand) thrust bearing

to the clearance measured. For example, if the clearance recorded was 2.475 mm, the bearing colour-code required is black. Re-check the clearance with the new bearings (see Step 2).

Main bearing oil clearance check

12 Whether new bearing shells are being fitted or the original ones are being re-used, the main bearing oil clearance should be checked before the engine is reassembled. Main bearing oil clearance is measured with a product known as Plastigauge.

13 Clean the backs of the bearing shells and the bearing housings in both crankcase halves.

14 Press the bearing shells into their cut-outs, ensuring that the tab on each shell engages in the notch in the crankcase **(see illustration)**. Make sure the bearings are fitted in the correct locations and take care not to touch any shell's bearing surface with your fingers.

15 Ensure the shells and crankshaft are clean

and dry. Lay the crankshaft in position in the upper crankcase **(see illustration 24.3b)**. If removed fit the dowels into one crankcase half **(see illustration 22.9a)**.

16 Cut several lengths of the appropriate size Plastigauge (they should be slightly shorter than the width of the crankshaft journals). Place a strand of Plastigauge on each (cleaned) journal **(see illustration)**. Make sure the crankshaft is not rotated.

17 Carefully fit the lower crankcase half onto the upper half **(see illustration 22.8)**. Check that the lower crankcase half is correctly seated. **Note:** *Do not tighten the crankcase bolts if the casing is not correctly seated.* Install the crankshaft journal 9 mm bolts numbers 1 to 12 **(see illustration 22.7)** in their original locations, with the copper washers on bolts 9 to 12. Secure all bolts finger-tight at first, then tighten them evenly and a little at a time in the numerical sequence shown first to the initial torque setting specified at the beginning of the Chapter, then to the final setting. Make sure that the crankshaft does not rotate as the bolts are tightened.

18 Slacken each bolt in reverse sequence starting at number 12 and working backwards to number 1. Slacken each bolt a little at a time until they are all finger-tight, then remove the bolts. Carefully lift off the lower crankcase half, making sure the Plastigauge is not disturbed.

19 Compare the width of the crushed Plastigauge on each crankshaft journal to the scale printed on the Plastigauge envelope to obtain the main bearing oil clearance **(see illustration)**. Compare the reading to the specifications at the beginning of the Chapter.

20 On completion carefully scrape away all traces of the Plastigauge material from the crankshaft journal and bearing shells; use a fingernail or other object which is unlikely to score them.

21 If the oil clearance falls into the specified range, no bearing shell replacement is required (provided they are in good condition). If the clearance exceeds the service limit, refer to the marks on the case and the marks on the crankshaft and select new bearing shells (see Steps 23 and 24). Install the new shells and check the oil clearance once again (the new

Outer bearing clearance (bearing removed)	Bearing colour-code required	Bearing thickness
2.430 to 2.460 mm	Red	2.350 to 2.375 mm
2.460 to 2.485 mm	Black	2.375 to 2.400 mm
2.485 to 2.510 mm	Blue	2.400 to 2.425 mm
2.510 to 2.535 mm	Green	2.425 to 2.450 mm
2.535 to 2.560 mm	Yellow	2.450 to 2.475 mm
2.560 to 2.585 mm	White	2.475 to 2.500 mm

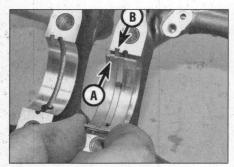

24.14 Ensure tab (A) locates in notch (B)

24.16 Lay a strip of Plastigauge along the centreline of each journal

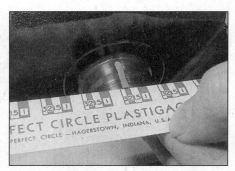

24.19 Compare the width of the crushed Plastigauge with the scale provided

24.22 Measuring a crankshaft journal

24.23a Crankshaft journal size letters are on the outside of the web . . .

24.23b . . . and are repeated on the top

shells may bring bearing clearance within the specified range).

22 If the clearance is greater than the service limit listed in this Chapter's Specifications with new shells, measure the diameter of the crankshaft journals with a micrometer and compare your findings with this Chapter's Specifications **(see illustration)**. By measuring the diameter at a number of points around each journal's circumference, you'll be able to determine whether or not the journal is out-of-round. Also take a measurement at each end of the journal, near the crank throws, as well as in the middle, to determine if the journal is tapered. If the journals are worn replace the crankshaft with a new one, then select the appropriate shells for it.

Main bearing shell selection

23 Replacement bearing shells for the main bearings are supplied on a selected fit basis. Numbers stamped on the crankshaft and crankcase are used to identify the correct replacement bearings. The crankshaft main bearing journal size letters, one letter for each journal (A, B or C), are stamped on the outside of the crankshaft left-hand web and are repeated on the top of the web **(see illustrations)**. The corresponding main bearing housing size letters (A or a B), are

stamped into the rear of the upper crankcase half **(see illustration)**. The first letter of each set of six is for the outer left-hand journal, the second for the middle left-hand, the third for the inner left-hand, the fourth for the inner right-hand, the fifth for the middle right-hand and the sixth for the outer right-hand. **Note:** *Reference to left- and right-hand are made as though the engine is the correct way up. Do not confuse the two if the engine is upside down.*

24 A range of bearing shells is available. To select the correct bearing for a particular journal, using the table below cross-refer the main bearing journal size letter (stamped on the crank web) with the main bearing housing size letter (stamped on the crankcase) to determine the colour code of the bearing required. For example, if the journal code is C, and the housing code is B, then the bearing required is Yellow. The colour is marked on the side of the shell **(see illustration 25.22)**.

Installation

25 If removed, fit the connecting rods onto the crankshaft (see Section 25), and loop the cam chain around its sprocket **(see illustration 11.9)**.
26 Clean the backs of the bearing shells and the bearing cut-outs in both crankcase halves.

If new shells are being fitted, ensure that all traces of the protective grease are cleaned off using paraffin (kerosene). Wipe the shells and crankcase halves dry with a lint-free cloth. Make sure all the oil passages and holes are clear, and blow them through with compressed air if it is available.
27 Lubricate each shell with molybdenum disulphide oil (a 50/50 mixture of molybdenum disulphide grease and engine oil). Press the bearing shells into their locations. Make sure the tab on each shell engages in the notch in the casing **(see illustration 24.14)**. Make sure the bearings are fitted in the correct locations and take care not to touch any shell's bearing surface with your fingers.
28 Lower the crankshaft into position in the upper crankcase, feeding the cam chain down through its tunnel **(see illustration 24.3b)**.
29 Lubricate each thrust bearing with molybdenum disulphide oil (a 50/50 mixture of molybdenum disulphide grease and engine oil). Slide the thrust bearings into place (do not mix up the inner with the outer – the inner is always colour-coded green), making sure that the oil grooves face out (i.e. towards the crankshaft web, away from the main journal housing) **(see illustrations)**.
30 Reassemble the crankcase halves (see Section 22).

	Crankshaft journal		
Main bearing housing	**A (39.992 to 40.000 mm)**	**B (39.984 to 39.992 mm)**	**C (39.976 to 39.984 mm)**
A (43.000 to 43.008 mm)	Green (1.480 to 1.484 mm)	Black (1.484 to 1.488 mm)	Brown (1.488 to 1.492 mm)
B (43.008 to 43.016 mm)	Black (1.484 to 1.488 mm)	Brown (1.488 to 1.492 mm)	Yellow (1.492 to 1.496 mm)

24.23c Main bearing housing size letters (arrowed)

24.29a Fit the inner thrust bearing with the green colour mark (arrowed) . . .

24.29b . . . then the outer, with the grooves facing out

25.2 Measuring big-end side clearance with a feeler gauge

25.4a Unscrew the bolts (arrowed) . . .

25.4b . . . and separate the cap and rod from the crankpin

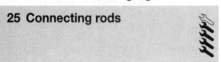

25 Connecting rods

Note: *To remove the connecting rods the engine must be removed from the frame and the crankcases separated.*

Removal

1 Remove the crankshaft (see Section 24).
2 Before separating the rods from the crankshaft, measure the side clearance on each rod with a feeler gauge **(see illustration)**. If the clearance on any rod is greater than the service limit listed in this Chapter's Specifications, measure the big-end and crankpin widths as described in Step 8.
3 Using paint or a felt marker pen, mark the relevant cylinder identity on each connecting rod. Mark across the join between rod and

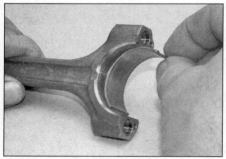

25.5 Remove the bearing shells if required

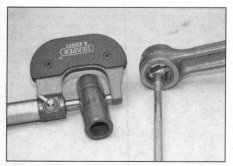

25.7b Measuring the external diameter of the pin and the internal diameter of small-end bore

cap and note which side of the rod faces the front of the engine to ensure they are fitted the correct way around on reassembly. Note that the number already across the rod and cap indicates bearing size code, not cylinder number, and that this number faces the rear of the engine **(see illustration 25.21c)**.
4 Unscrew the big-end cap bolts and separate the rod and cap from the crankpin **(see illustrations)**. Keep the rod, cap, bolts, and (if they are to be reused) the bearing shells together in their correct positions to ensure correct installation. Note that although the bolts are of the stretch type, they can be re-used. However if the engine is used in racing, has been tuned for extra power, or is regularly stripped and rebuilt, the bolts should be replaced with new ones after every third use. Note that new connecting rods should come fitted with new bolts.
5 If required remove the big-end bearing shells

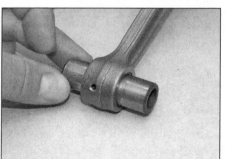

25.7a Check for freeplay between the piston pin and connecting rod

25.8 Measure the width of the connecting rod and the corresponding crankpin

from the caps and rods **(see illustration)**. Keep the bearing shells in order.

Inspection

6 Check the connecting rods for cracks and other obvious damage.
7 If not already done (see Section 13), apply clean engine oil to the piston pin, insert it into the connecting rod small-end and check for any freeplay between the two **(see illustration)**. Measure the pin external diameter and the small-end bore internal diameter and compare the measurements to the specifications at the beginning of the Chapter **(see illustration)**. Replace components that are worn beyond the specified limits.
8 If the side clearance measured in Step 2 exceeds the service limit specified, measure the width of the connecting rod big-end and the width of the crankpin **(see illustration)**. Compare the results to the specifications at the beginning of the Chapter, and replace whichever component exceeds those specifications with a new one.
9 Refer to Section 23 and examine the connecting rod bearing shells. If they are scored, badly scuffed or appear to have seized, new shells must be installed. Always replace the shells in the connecting rods as a set. If they are badly damaged, check the corresponding crankpin. Evidence of extreme heat, such as discoloration, indicates that lubrication failure has occurred. Be sure to thoroughly check the oil pump and pressure regulator as well as all oil holes and passages before reassembling the engine.
10 Have the rods checked for twist and bend by a Suzuki dealer if you are in doubt about their straightness.

Oil clearance check

11 Whether new bearing shells are being fitted or the original ones are being re-used, the connecting rod bearing oil clearance should be checked prior to reassembly. Check one rod at a time.
12 Clean the backs of the bearing shells and the bearing locations in both the connecting rod and cap. Also clean the crankpin journal on the crankshaft.
13 Press the bearing shells into their locations, ensuring that the tab on each shell engages the notch in the connecting rod/cap

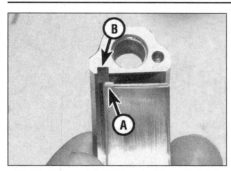

25.13 Ensure tab (A) locates in notch (B)

25.18 Measuring a crankpin journal

25.21a Crankpin journal size letters are on the outside of the web . . .

(see illustration). Make sure the bearings are fitted in the correct locations and take care not to touch any shell's bearing surface with your fingers.

14 Cut a length of the appropriate size Plastigauge (it should be slightly shorter than the width of the crankpin) and place it on the crankpin journal **(see illustration 24.16)**. Fit the connecting rod and cap **(see illustration 25.4b)**. Make sure they are fitted the correct way around so the previously made markings align. Fit the bolts and tighten them in two stages, first to the initial torque setting specified at the beginning of the Chapter, and then in one movement through the angle specified, whilst ensuring that the connecting rod does not rotate – use a degree disc to tighten through the specified angle, or alternatively after tightening to the initial torque setting make two marks, one on one of the ridges on the bolt head and one on the rod three ridges (which corresponds to 90°) clockwise from the mark on the bolt, then tighten the bolt until the marks align **(see illustrations 25.23 and 25.24a and b)**. Slacken the bolts and remove the connecting rod, again taking great care not to rotate the crankshaft.

15 Compare the width of the crushed Plastigauge on the crankpin to the scale printed on the Plastigauge envelope to obtain the connecting rod bearing oil clearance **(see illustration 24.19)**. Compare the reading to

the specifications at the beginning of the Chapter.

16 On completion carefully scrape away all traces of the Plastigauge material from the crankpin and bearing shells using a fingernail or other object which is unlikely to score the shells.

17 If the clearance is within the range listed in this Chapter's Specifications and the bearings are in perfect condition, they can be reused. If the clearance is beyond the service limit, replace the bearing shells with new ones (see Steps 21 and 22). Check the oil clearance once again (the new shells may be thick enough to bring bearing clearance within the specified range). Always replace all of the inserts at the same time.

18 If the clearance is still greater than the service limit listed in this Chapter's Specifications, measure the diameter of the crankpin journal with a micrometer and compare your findings with this Chapter's Specifications **(see illustration)**. Also, by measuring the diameter at a number of points around the journal's circumference, you'll be able to determine whether or not the journal is out-of-round. Also take a measurement at each end of the journal, near the crank throws, as well as in the middle, to determine if the journal is tapered.

19 If any journal has worn down past the service limit, replace the crankshaft with a new one.

20 Repeat the bearing selection procedure for the remaining connecting rods.

Bearing shell selection

21 Replacement bearing shells for the big-end bearings are supplied on a selected fit basis. Numbers stamped on the crankshaft and connecting rod are used to identify the correct replacement bearings. The crankpin journal size numbers (1, 2 or 3) are stamped on the outside of the crankshaft left-hand web and are repeated on the top of the inner left-hand web **(see illustrations)**. The number coming immediately after the L is for the outer left-hand big-end (cyl no. 1), the next number is for the inner left-hand big-end (cyl no. 2), the next for the inner right-hand (cyl no. 3) and the number coming before the R is for the outer right-hand big-end cyl no. 4). The connecting rod size number (1 or 2) is marked on the flat face of the connecting rod and cap **(see illustration)**.

22 A range of bearing shells is available. To select the correct bearing for a particular big-end, using the table below cross-refer the crankpin journal size number (stamped on the web) with the connecting rod size number (stamped on the rod) to determine the colour code of the bearing required. For example, if the connecting rod size is 2, and the crankpin size is 3, then the bearing required is Yellow. The colour is marked on the side of the shell **(see illustration)**.

Connecting rod number	Crankpin journal number		
	1 (37.992 to 38.000 mm)	**2** (37.984 to 37.992 mm)	**3** (37.976 to 37.984 mm)
1 (41.000 to 41.008 mm)	Green (1.480 to 1.484 mm)	Black (1.484 to 1.488 mm)	Brown (1.488 to 1.492 mm)
2 (41.008 to 41.016 mm)	Black (1.484 to 1.488 mm)	Brown (1.488 to 1.492 mm)	Yellow (1.492 to 1.496 mm)

25.21b . . . and are repeated on the top

25.21c Connecting rod size number

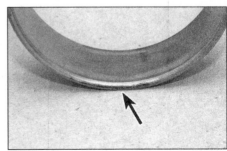

25.22 The colour code is marked on the side of the shell

25.23 Fit the bolts

25.24a Tighten the cap bolts as described, using an angle gauge . . .

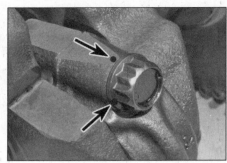

25.24b . . . or by marking the bolt and the rod as described

Installation

23 Fit the bearing shells in the connecting rods and caps, aligning the notch in the bearing with the groove in the rod or cap (see illustration 25.13). Lubricate the shells with molybdenum disulphide oil (a 50/50 mixture of molybdenum disulphide grease and engine oil). Assemble each connecting rod and cap on its correct crankpin so that the previously made matchmarks align and the connecting rod size letter is facing the rear of the engine when the crankshaft is installed (see illustration 25.4b and 25.21c). Install the bolts, using new ones if required (see Step 4) and tighten them finger-tight at this stage (see illustration). Check to make sure that all components have been returned to their original locations using the marks made on disassembly.

24 Tighten the bearing cap nuts or bolts in two stages, first to the initial torque setting specified at the beginning of the Chapter, and then in one movement through the angle specified – use a degree disc to tighten through the specified angle, or alternatively after tightening to the initial torque setting make two marks, one on one of the ridges on the bolt head and one on the rod three ridges (which corresponds to 90º) clockwise from the mark on the bolt, then tighten the bolt until the marks align (see illustrations).

25 Check that the rods rotate smoothly and freely on the crankpin. If there are any signs of roughness or tightness, remove the rods and re-check the bearing clearance. Sometimes tapping the bottom of the connecting rod cap will relieve tightness, but if in doubt, recheck the clearances.

26 Install the crankshaft (see Section 24).

26 Transmission shaft removal and installation

Note: *To remove the transmission shafts the engine must be removed from the frame and the crankcases separated.*

Note: *Referrals to the right and left-hand ends of the transmission shafts are made as though the engine is the correct way up, even though throughout this procedure it is upside down. Therefore the right-hand end of a shaft will actually be on your left as you look down onto the underside of the upper crankcase assembly.*

Removal

1 Separate the crankcase halves (see Section 22). If not already done, remove the clutch pushrod oil seal from the crankcase and discard it as new a one should be used (see illustration 22.26).

2 Lift the output shaft out of the crankcase, then the input shaft, noting their relative positions in the crankcase and how they fit together (see illustrations). If they are stuck, use a soft-faced hammer and gently tap on the ends of the shafts to free them.

3 Remove the retainer for the input shaft ball bearing from its slot in the upper crankcase half, and remove the needle bearing dowels from their holes (see illustrations). The retainer for the output shaft ball bearing is part of the bearing (see illustration 26.4). If they are not in their slot or holes in the crankcase, remove them from the bearings themselves on the shafts.

4 Remove the output shaft oil seal from the left-hand end of the output shaft and discard it as a new one should be used (see illustration). If necessary, the input shaft and output shaft can be overhauled (see Section 27).

26.2a Remove the output shaft . . .

26.2b . . . then the input shaft

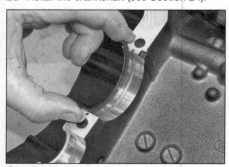

26.3a Remove the bearing retainer . . .

26.3b . . . and the dowel pins

26.4 Remove the output shaft oil seal. The retainer (arrowed) is part of the bearing

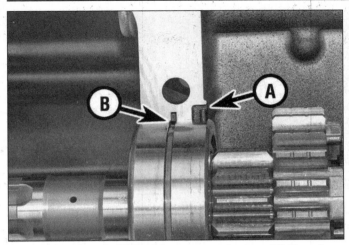

26.6 Locating pin (A) fits into recess and groove (B) fits onto half-ring retainer

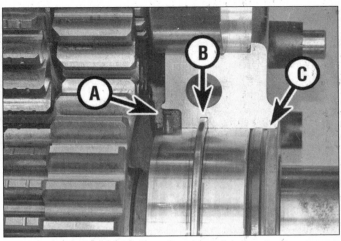

26.7 Locating pin (A) fits into recess, retainer locates in groove (B), and oil seal (C) seats squarely

Installation

5 Fit the needle bearing dowels into their holes in the upper crankcase half (see illustration 26.3b). Fit the retainer for the input shaft ball bearing into its slot (see illustration 26.3a). Make sure the retainer for the output shaft ball bearing is in place (see illustration 26.4). Fit a new oil seal, its lips lubricated with grease, onto the left-hand end of the output shaft (see illustration 26.4).

6 Lower the input shaft into position in the upper crankcase, making sure the hole in the needle bearing engages correctly with the dowel (see illustration 26.2b), the ball bearing locating pin faces forward and locates in its recess, and the groove in the bearing engages correctly with the bearing half-ring retainer (see illustration).

7 Lower the output shaft into position in the crankcase half, making sure the hole in the needle bearing engages correctly with the dowel (see illustration 26.2a), the ball bearing locating pin faces forwards and locates in its recess, the bearing retainer engages correctly with the groove in the crankcase, and the oil seal seats correctly (see illustration).

8 Make sure both transmission shafts are correctly seated and their related pinions are correctly engaged.

Caution: If the ball bearing locating pins and half-ring retainers or needle bearing dowel pins are not correctly engaged, the crankcase halves will not seat correctly.

9 Position the gears in the neutral position and check the shafts are free to rotate easily and independently (i.e. the input shaft can turn whilst the output shaft is held stationary) before proceeding further.

10 Fit a new clutch pushrod oil seal into its cut-out in the crankcase (see illustration 22.26). Smear some grease into the hole for the pushrod.

11 Reassembly the crankcase halves (see Section 22).

27 Transmission shaft overhaul

Note: *References to the right- and left-hand ends of the transmission shafts are made as though they are installed in the engine and the engine is the correct way up.*

HAYNES HiNT *When disassembling the transmission shafts, place the parts on a long rod or thread a wire through them to keep them in order and facing the proper direction.*

1 Remove the transmission shafts from the crankcase (see Section 26). Always disassemble the transmission shafts separately to avoid mixing up the components (see illustration).

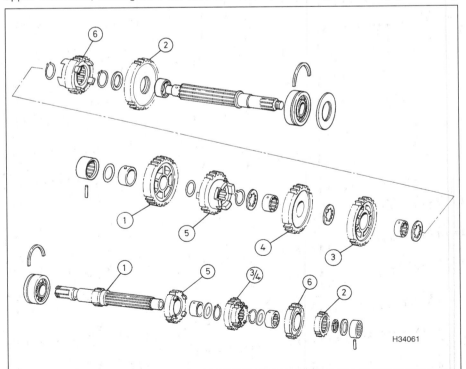

27.1 Transmission shaft components
Numbers indicate gears

27.3a Slide the circlip towards the 3rd/4th gear pinion

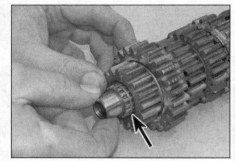

27.3b Slide the gears back to expose the snap-ring (arrowed) . . .

27.3c . . . and remove the snap-ring

Input shaft disassembly

2 Remove the needle bearing and oil seal from the left-hand end of the shaft, noting which way round the seal fits **(see illustrations 27.20b and a)**.

3 Reach behind the 6th gear pinion with circlip pliers, spread the circlip and slide it toward the 3rd/4th gear pinion **(see illustrations)**. Slide the 6th and 2nd gear pinions back to expose the snap-ring on the end of the shaft, then remove it **(see illustration)**. Slide the 2nd gear pinion off the shaft, noting which way round it fits or having marked its outer face as a guide, then slide the 6th gear pinion off the shaft, followed by the splined washer and the splined bush **(see illustrations 27.19a and 27.18c, b and a)**.

4 Remove the circlip, then slide the combined 3rd/4th gear pinion off the shaft **(see illustrations 27.17b and a)**.

5 Remove the circlip securing the 5th gear pinion, then slide the thrust washer, the pinion and its bush off the shaft **(see illustrations 27.16d, c, b and a)**.

6 The 1st gear pinion is integral with the shaft **(see illustration)**.

Input shaft inspection

7 Wash all of the components in clean solvent and dry them off.

8 Check the gear teeth for cracking chipping, pitting and other obvious wear or damage **(see illustration)**. Any pinion that is damaged as such must be renewed.

9 Inspect the dogs and the dog holes in the gears for cracks, chips, and excessive wear especially in the form of rounded edges. Make sure mating gears engage properly. Renew the paired gears as a set if necessary.

10 Check for signs of scoring or bluing on the pinions, bushes and shaft. This could be caused by overheating due to inadequate lubrication. Check that all the oil holes and passages are clear. Replace any damaged pinions or bushes with new ones.

11 Check that each pinion moves freely on the shaft or bush but without undue freeplay. Check that each bush moves freely on the shaft but without undue freeplay.

12 The shaft is unlikely to sustain damage unless the engine has seized, placing an unusually high loading on the transmission, or the machine has covered a very high mileage. Check the surface of the shaft, especially where a pinion turns on it, and renew the shaft if it has scored or picked up, or if there are any cracks. Damage of any kind can only be cured by renewal.

13 Check that the transmission shaft bearings rotate freely and smoothly and are tight on the shaft **(see illustrations)**. Remove the old bearings and fit new ones if necessary (see *Tools and Workshop Tips* in the Reference Section).

14 Discard all the circlips and the snap-ring as new ones must be used.

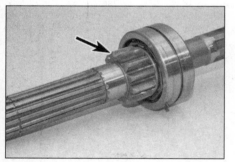

27.6 The 1st gear pinion is integral with the shaft

27.8 Check all gear teeth and engagement dogs and slots

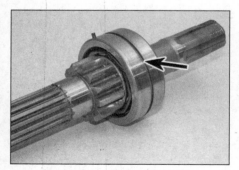

27.13a Check the ball bearings (arrowed) . . .

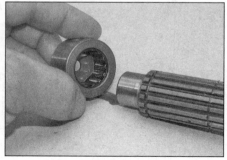

27.13b . . . and the needle bearings

Input shaft reassembly

15 During reassembly, apply molybdenum disulphide oil (a 50/50 mixture of molybdenum disulphide paste or grease and clean engine oil) to the mating surfaces of the shaft, pinions and bushes. When installing the circlips, use new ones and do not expand the ends any further than is necessary. Install the stamped circlips so that their chamfered side faces the pinion it secures, i.e. so that its sharp edge faces the direction of thrust load (see *correct fitting of a stamped circlip* illustration in Tools and Workshop Tips of the Reference section).

16 Slide the 5th gear pinion bush onto the left-hand end shaft, then slide the pinion onto the bush with its dogs facing away from the integral 1st gear **(see illustrations)**. Slide the thrust washer against the pinion, then fit the

27.16a Slide on the 5th gear bush . . .

27.16b . . . the 5th gear pinion . . .

27.16c . . . and the washer . . .

circlip, making sure that it locates correctly in its groove **(see illustrations)**.

17 Slide the combined 3rd/4th gear pinion onto the shaft, so that the larger (4th gear) pinion faces the 5th gear pinion dogs **(see illustration)**. Fit the circlip onto the shaft but do not locate it in its groove – slide it past the groove and as far towards the 3rd/4th gear pinion as possible **(see illustrations)**.

18 Slide the splined washer onto the shaft, followed by the splined bush, aligning the oil holes **(see illustrations)**. Slide the 6th gear pinion onto the bush, with its dog holes facing the dogs on the 3rd gear pinion **(see illustration)**.

27.16d . . . and secure them with the circlip . . .

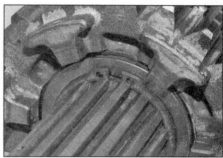

27.16e . . . making sure it locates in its groove

27.17a Slide on the 3rd /4th gear pinion

27.17b Slide the circlip onto the shaft . . .

27.17c . . . and beyond its groove (arrowed)

27.18a Slide on the splined washer . . .

27.18b . . . followed by the bush, aligning the oil holes . . .

27.18c . . . then fit the 6th gear pinion onto the bush

27.19a Slide the 2nd gear pinion onto the shaft . . .

27.19b . . . and secure it with the snap-ring

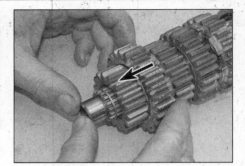

27.19c Slide the pinions along over the snap-ring . . .

27.19d . . . then slide the circlip into its groove . . .

27.19e . . . making sure it locates correctly

27.20a Fit the oil seal . . .

19 Slide the 2nd gear pinion onto the shaft with the slightly shouldered side facing in then fit the snap-ring, making sure it is properly seated in its groove **(see illustrations)**. Now slide the 6th and 2nd gear pinions along so the recess in the outer face of the 2nd gear pinion fits over the snap ring and the groove for the 3rd/4th gear pinion circlip is exposed, then move the circlip along the shaft and fit it into the groove **(see illustrations)**.

20 Slide the oil seal onto the shaft making sure it is the correct way round – the outer rim should be slightly raised away from the pinion **(see illustration)**. Lubricate the needle bearing and slide it onto the end of the shaft **(see illustration)**.

21 Check that all components have been correctly installed **(see illustration)**.

Output shaft disassembly

22 Remove the needle bearing and the thrust washer from the right-hand end of the shaft **(see illustrations 27.37 and 27.36c)**.

23 Slide the 1st gear pinion and its bush off the shaft, followed by the thrust washer and the 5th gear pinion **(see illustrations 27.36b and a, 27.35b and a)**.

24 Remove the circlip securing the 4th gear pinion, then slide the splined washer, 4th gear pinion and its bush off the shaft **(see illustrations 27.34b and a, 27.33c and b)**.

25 Slide off the splined washer, followed by

the 3rd gear pinion and its bush, and another splined washer **(see illustrations 27.33a, 27.32c, b and a)**.

26 Remove the circlip securing the 6th gear pinion, and slide the pinion off the shaft **(see illustration 27.31b and a)**.

27 Remove the circlip securing the 2nd gear pinion, then slide the thrust washer, the 2nd gear pinion and its bush off the shaft **(see illustrations 27.30d, c, b and a)**.

Output shaft inspection

28 Refer to Steps 7 to 14 above.

Output shaft reassembly

29 During reassembly, apply clean engine oil to the mating surfaces of the shaft, pinions

27.20b . . . then the needle bearing

27.21 The completed input shaft should look like this

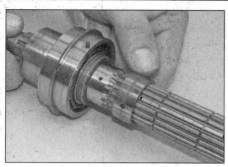

27.30a Slide on the 2nd gear bush . . .

27.30b . . . the 2nd gear pinion . . .

27.30c . . . and the washer . . .

and bushes. When installing the circlips, do not expand their ends any further than is necessary. Install the stamped circlips so that their chamfered side faces the pinion it secures (see Correct fitting of a stamped circlip illustration in *Tools and Workshop Tips* in the Reference Section).

30 Slide the 2nd gear bush all the way onto the shaft, then slide the 2nd gear pinion (flat side faces towards the bearing) onto the bush, followed by the thrust washer **(see illustrations)**. Secure them in place with the circlip, making sure it is properly seated in its groove **(see illustrations)**.

31 Slide the 6th gear pinion onto the shaft with its selector fork groove facing away from the 2nd gear pinion, and secure it in place with the circlip, making sure it is properly seated in its groove **(see illustrations)**.

27.30d . . . and secure them with the circlip . . .

32 Slide on the splined washer and the 3rd gear pinion bush, aligning the oil hole in the bush with the hole in the shaft **(see**

27.30e . . . making sure it locates correctly in the groove

illustrations). Fit the 3rd gear pinion on the bush so that its open side faces the 6th gear pinion **(see illustrations)**.

27.31a Slide on the 6th gear pinion . . .

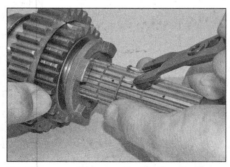

27.31b . . . and secure it with the circlip . . .

27.31c . . . making sure it locates correctly in the groove

27.32a Slide on the splined washer . . .

27.32b . . . followed by the bush, aligning the oil holes . . .

27.32c . . . then fit the 3rd gear pinion onto the bush

27.33a **Slide on the splined washer . . .**

27.33b **. . . followed by the bush, aligning the oil holes . . .**

27.33c **. . . then fit the 4th gear pinion onto the bush**

27.34a **Slide on the splined washer . . .**

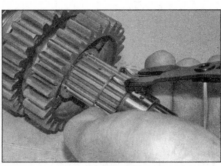

27.34b **. . . and secure it with the circlip . . .**

33 Slide on the splined washer and the 4th gear pinion bush, aligning the oil hole in the bush with the hole in the shaft **(see illustration)**. Fit the 4th gear pinion on the bush so that its open side faces away from the 3rd gear pinion **(see illustrations)**.

34 Slide on the splined washer, then install the circlip making sure it is properly seated in its groove **(see illustrations)**.

35 Slide the 5th gear pinion onto the shaft with its selector fork groove facing the 4th gear pinion, followed by the thrust washer **(see illustrations)**.

36 Slide on the 1st gear pinion bush and pinion with its open side facing the 5th gear pinion, followed by the thrust washer **(see illustrations)**.

27.34c **. . . making sure it locates correctly in the groove**

27.35a **Slide on the 5th gear pinion . . .**

27.35b **. . . and the thrust washer**

27.36a **Slide on the bush . . .**

27.36b **. . . the 1st gear pinion . . .**

27.36c **. . . and the thrust washer**

27.37 Install the bearing

27.38 The completed output shaft should look like this

37 Fit the needle bearing onto the end of the shaft **(see illustration)**.
38 Check that all components have been correctly installed **(see illustration)**.

28 Oil pump

Note: *To remove the oil pump the engine must be removed from the frame and the crankcases separated.*

Pressure check

1 Perform an oil pressure check (see Section 3). If the pressure is as specified at the beginning of the Chapter then the pump is good. If the pressure is lower than it should be, and all other possible causes (as listed in Section 3) have been eliminated, then the pump is worn or faulty and a new one must be installed. No individual components are available.

Removal

2 Separate the crankcase halves (see Sec-

tion 22). The oil pump is located inside the lower half.
3 Remove the circlip from the end of the oil pump drive shaft, then remove the outer washer **(see illustrations)**. Turn the oil pump driven gear so the drive pin is horizontal then remove the gear, noting how it locates over the drive pin **(see illustration)**. Withdraw the drive pin from the shaft and remove the inner washer **(see illustrations)**.
4 Unscrew the three bolts securing the pump to the crankcase, then remove the pump **(see illustration)**. Remove the O-rings from

28.3a Remove the circlip . . .

28.3b . . . the outer washer . . .

28.3c . . . and the gear . . .

28.3d . . . then remove the pin . . .

28.3e . . . and the inner washer

28.4 Unscrew the bolts (arrowed) and remove the pump

28.7a Fit the round O-ring into the crankcase . . .

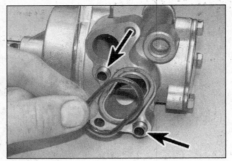

28.7b . . . and the oval O-ring onto the pump. Make sure the dowels (arrowed) are fitted

28.8 Fit the pump into the crankcase

the pump and the crankcase and discard them as new ones must be used **(see illustrations 28.7b and a)**. Also remove the two dowels from either the crankcase or the pump if they are loose.

Inspection

5 Inspect the pump body for any obvious damage such as cracks or distortion, and check that the shaft rotates smoothly and freely and without any side-to-side play or excessive end-float.
6 The oil pump fitted to this machine is not serviceable and Suzuki provide no specifications for it, and even go to the extent of advising that it should not be disassembled for cleaning. If the pump is suspected of being faulty a new one must be installed.

Installation

7 Fit a new O-ring smeared with grease into the groove in the crankcase **(see illustration)**. Fit a new O-ring smeared with grease into the groove on the pump, and if removed fit the dowels into their holes in the crankcase, making sure they are secure **(see illustration)**.
8 Prime the pump with some clean oil and turn the shaft to distribute it. Install the pump, making sure the dowels locate correctly **(see illustration)**. Apply a suitable non-permanent thread locking compound to the threads of the pump bolts and tighten them – fit the longer bolt into the rear left hole **(see illustration 28.4)**.

9 Slide the inner washer onto the shaft then fit the drive pin through it **(see illustrations 28.3e and d)**. Locate the gear over the drive pin, then fit the outer washer and secure them with the circlip, making sure it locates in the groove **(see illustrations 28.3c, b and a)**.
10 Reassemble the crankcase halves (see Section 22).

29 Running-in procedure

1 Make sure the engine oil level is correct (see *Pre-ride checks*). Make sure there is fuel in the tank.
2 Start the engine and let it run at fast idle until it reaches normal operating temperature. Check carefully that there are no oil leaks.

> ⚠ **Warning: If the oil pressure warning light doesn't go off, or it comes on while the engine is running, stop the engine immediately.**

3 If a lubrication failure is suspected, stop the engine immediately and try to find the cause. If an engine is run without oil, even for a short period of time, severe damage will occur.
4 Make sure the transmission and controls, especially the throttle and brakes, function

properly before road testing the machine.
5 Treat the machine gently for the first few miles to make sure oil has circulated throughout the engine and any new parts installed have started to seat.
6 Even greater care is necessary if a major engine overhaul has been undertaken. In the case of a new crankshaft or piston and connecting rod assemblies, the bike will have to be run in as when new. This means greater use of the transmission and a restraining hand on the throttle until at least 1000 miles (1600 km) have been covered. There's no point in keeping to any set speed limit – the main idea is to keep from labouring the engine and to gradually increase performance up to the 1000 mile (1600 km) mark. These recommendations can be lessened to an extent when only a top-end overhaul has been undertaken. Experience is the best guide, since it's easy to tell when an engine is running freely. The following maximum engine speed limitations (above), which Suzuki provide for new motorcycles, can be used as a guide.
7 Upon completion of the road test, and after the engine has cooled down completely, recheck the valve clearances (Chapter 1) and check the engine oil level (see *Pre-ride checks*).

Up to 500 miles (800 km)	4500 rpm max	Vary throttle position/speed
500 to 1000 miles (800 to 1600 km)	6700 rpm max	Vary throttle position/speed. Use full throttle for short bursts
Over 1000 miles (1600 km)	9000 rpm max	Do not exceed tachometer red line

Chapter 3
Oil cooling system

Contents

Degrees of difficulty

Easy, suitable for novice with little experience		**Fairly easy,** suitable for beginner with some experience		**Fairly difficult,** suitable for competent DIY mechanic		**Difficult,** suitable for experienced DIY mechanic		**Very difficult,** suitable for expert DIY or professional	

Specifications

Engine oil

Type and quantity.. see Chapter 1

Fan switch

Cooling fan cut-in temperature .... 120°C approx.
Cooling fan cut-out temperature .... 108°C approx.

Oil temperature sensor

Resistance
  @ 20°C .... 61.3 K-ohms approx.
  @ 50°C .... 17.8 K-ohms approx.
  @ 80°C .... 6.2 K-ohms approx.
  @ 100°C .... 3.4 K-ohms approx.
  @ 110°C .... 2.5 K-ohms approx.

Torque settings

Oil cooler hose union bolts................................ 10 Nm
Cooling fan switch .... 17 Nm
Engine oil temperature (EOT) sensor retaining plate bolts........... 10 Nm

1 General information

The oil used to lubricate the engine also acts as a coolant. It absorbs heat from the engine before passing through the cooler radiator where it is cooled by the airflow. The cooled oil then returns to the engine. A temperature-controlled fan mounted behind the cooler radiator assists cooling at extreme temperature.

Oil temperature information is supplied to the engine control module (ECM) by the engine oil temperature (EOT) sensor mounted on the top of the crankcase behind the cylinder block. When the oil is cold fuel injector opening time is increased to richen the fuel/air mixture. The sensor is part of the engine management system, the fault diagnosis for which is covered in Chapter 4. The function of the sensor itself is covered in Section 4 of this Chapter.

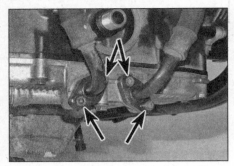

2.2a Unscrew the sump union bolts (arrowed) . . .

2.2b . . . the hose guide bracket bolt . . .

2.2c . . . and if required the cooler union bolts (arrowed) on each end

2 Oil cooler and hoses

Removal

1 Drain the engine oil (see Chapter 1).
2 Unscrew the bolts securing each hose union to the sump **(see illustration)**. Discard the O-rings as new ones must be used. Unscrew the bolt securing the hose guide bracket **(see illustration)**. If required, unscrew the bolts securing each hose union to the cooler and remove the hoses **(see illustration)** – note that the cooler can be removed with the hoses still attached.
3 Unscrew the two bolts securing the cooler to the frame, then lift the cooler out of its bottom mounting lugs, displacing the rubber dampers as you do to give more freedom of movement **(see illustrations)**. Manoeuvre the cooler down so the top of the fan shroud clears the frame, then disconnect the fan wiring connector and remove the cooler **(see illustrations)**.
4 Take care not to lose the U-shaped rubber mounts from the lugs, and replace them with new ones if they are damaged, deformed or deteriorated **(see illustration)**. Note the collars inside the bolt mounting grommets, and how the cooling fan and fan guard locate. Replace the grommets with new ones if necessary.

Installation

5 Installation is the reverse of removal. Make sure the fan guard on the top of the cooler is correctly located. Make sure the rubber mounts are correctly located **(see illustration 2.4)**. Always use new O-rings smeared with grease when installing the hoses **(see illustration)**. Tighten the hose union bolts to the torque settings specified at the beginning of the Chapter.

3 Cooling fan and fan switch

1 If the engine is overheating and the cooling fan isn't coming on, first check the cooling fan circuit fuse (see Chapter 8). If the fuse is blown, check the fan circuit for a short to earth (see *Wiring diagrams* at the end of Chapter 8). If the fuse is good check the fan switch, then the fan motor.

2.3a Unscrew the bolts (arrowed) . . .

2.3b . . . then displace the cooler from the bottom lugs (arrowed) . . .

2.3c . . . manoeuvre it down . . .

2.3d . . . and disconnect the wiring connector

2.4 Check the rubber mounts (arrowed), and make sure they are correctly located on installation

2.5 Fit a new O-ring onto each union

3.2 Disconnect the fan switch wiring connector

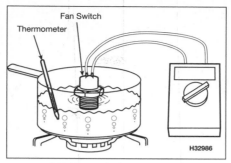

3.5 Fan switch test set-up

3.8 Cooling fan switch (arrowed)

Cooling fan switch

Check

2 The switch is on the bottom front right-hand corner of the engine. Disconnect the wiring connector from the switch **(see illustration)**.

3 Using a jumper wire, connect across the terminals in the wiring connector and turn the ignition ON. If the fan comes on, the switch is defective and must be replaced with a new one (see Steps 7 to 10). If it does not come on, make sure all the wiring, terminals and connectors are good, then test the fan motor (see Steps 11 and 12).

4 If the fan stays on all the time the ignition is ON, disconnect the fan switch wiring connector. The fan should stop. If it does, the switch is defective and must be replaced with a new one. If it doesn't, check the wiring between the switch and the fan motor for a short to earth.

5 If the fan works but is suspected of cutting in at the wrong temperature, a more comprehensive test of the switch can be made as follows. Remove the switch (see Steps 7 to 10). Fill a small heatproof container with oil and place it on a stove. Connect the probes of an ohmmeter or continuity tester to the switch terminals, and using some wire or other support, suspend the switch in the oil so that just the sensing portion and the threads are submerged **(see illustration)**. Also place a thermometer capable of reading temperatures up to 130°C in the oil so that its bulb is close to the switch. **Note:** *None of the components should be allowed to touch the container directly.*

6 Initially there should be no continuity (infinite resistance) indicating that the switch is open (OFF). Heat the oil slowly, stirring it gently.

⚠ *Warning: This must be done very carefully to avoid the risk of personal injury.*

When the temperature reaches around 120°C there should be continuity (zero resistance), indicating that the switch has closed (ON). Now turn the heat off. As the temperature falls to around 108°C there should again be no continuity (infinite resistance), indicating that the switch has opened (OFF). If the test results are different, or they are obtained at different temperatures, then the switch is faulty and must be replaced with a new one.

Removal and installation

⚠ *Warning: The engine must be completely cool before carrying out this procedure.*

7 The switch is on the bottom front right-hand corner of the engine. Drain the engine oil (see Chapter 1).

8 Disconnect the wiring connector from the switch **(see illustration 3.2)**. Unscrew the switch and withdraw it from the engine **(see illustration)**. Discard the sealing washer as a new one must be used.

9 Fit the switch with a new sealing washer and tighten it to the torque setting specified at the beginning of the Chapter. Take care not to overtighten the switch.

10 Reconnect the switch wiring and replenish the oil (see Chapter 1 and *Pre-ride checks*).

Cooling fan

Check

11 If the engine is overheating and the fan does not come on (and the fan switch is good), the fault lies in either the cooling fan motor or the relevant wiring. Test all the wiring and connections as described in Chapter 8.

12 To test the fan motor, displace the cooler (see above, but do not detach the hose unions), then disconnect the wiring connector **(see illustration 2.3d)**. Using a 12 volt battery and two jumper wires, connect the battery positive (+) terminal to the blue wire terminal on the fan side of the wiring connector and the battery negative (-) terminal to the black wire terminal. Once connected the fan should operate. If it does not, and the wiring is all good, then the fan motor is faulty.

Removal and installation

13 Remove the cooler (see Section 2).

14 Displace the fan assembly from the cooler, noting how the lugs locate in the grommets **(see illustration)**.

15 Installation is the reverse of removal. Replace the grommets with new ones if they are damaged, deformed or deteriorated.

---

4 Engine oil temperature (EOT) sensor

Check

1 The engine oil temperature (EOT) sensor is located in the top of the crankcase behind the cylinder block **(see illustration)**. If a sensor fault is indicated by the fuel injection system diagnostic process (see Chapter 4), carry out the preliminary checks as described in Chapter 4, Section 10.

2 To check the sensor resistance remove it from the engine (see Steps 6 and 7).

3 Fill a small heatproof container with oil and place it on a stove. Using an ohmmeter set to the K-ohms scale, connect the meter probes to the sensor terminals in the wiring connector, and using some wire or other support, suspend the sensor in the oil so that just the sensing portion and the threads are submerged **(see illustration 3.5)**. Also place a

3.14 Detach the cooling fan, noting how it locates

4.1 Oil temperature sensor (arrowed)

thermometer capable of reading temperatures up to 130°C in the oil so that its bulb is close to the switch. **Note:** *None of the components should be allowed to touch the container directly.*

4 Check the meter reading and compare the result with the specifications at the beginning of this Chapter, then heat the oil slowly, stirring it gently.

 Warning: This must be done very carefully to avoid the risk of personal injury.

5 As the temperature of the oil rises, the sensor resistance should fall. Check that the specified resistance is obtained at the correct temperature (see Specifications at the beginning of this Chapter). If the readings obtained are different, or are obtained at different temperatures, the sensor is faulty and must be replaced with a new one. If the readings are as specified, the fault could lie in the ECM (see Chapter 4).

Removal and installation

 Warning: The engine must be completely cool before carrying out this procedure.

4.6 Disconnect the wiring connector

4.7 Unscrew the retaining plate bolts and remove the sensor. Fit a new O-ring (arrowed) on installation

6 The engine oil temperature (EOT) sensor is located in the top of the crankcase behind the cylinder block **(see illustration 4.1)**. Remove the right-hand side panel (see Chapter 7) and disconnect the sensor wiring connector (black 2-pin) **(see illustration)**. Feed the wiring to the sensor, noting its routing.

7 Unscrew the sensor retaining plate bolts, then displace the plate and withdraw the sensor **(see illustration)**. Discard the O-ring as a new one must be fitted on reassembly. Take care not to drop or knock the sensor as an impact could damage it.

8 Installation is the reverse of removal, noting the following:
● Fit a new O-ring to the sensor.
● Tighten the sensor retaining plate bolts to the torque setting specified at the beginning of this Chapter.

Chapter 4
Engine management system

Contents

Degrees of difficulty

| **Easy,** suitable for novice with little experience | | **Fairly easy,** suitable for beginner with some experience | | **Fairly difficult,** suitable for competent DIY mechanic | | **Difficult,** suitable for experienced DIY mechanic | | **Very difficult,** suitable for expert DIY or professional | |

Specifications

General information

Cylinder identification (from left to right-hand side of the bike)	1–2–3–4
Firing order	1–2–4–3
Spark plugs	see Chapter 1
Rev limiter cut-in	9200 rpm

Fuel

Grade
European models	Unleaded, minimum octane rating 91 RON (Research Octane Number)
Canada model	Unleaded, minimum octane rating 87 ((R+M) /2 method)
Fuel tank capacity (including reserve)	22 litres

Fuel supply system

Operating pressure	43 psi (3.0 Bar)

Fuel level sensor

Resistance
   In full position . . . . 4 to 10 ohms
   In empty position . . . . 90 to 100 ohms

Throttle body

Identification marking 42F0
Bore diameter . . . . 34 mm
Engine idle speed
   Normal idle (engine hot) . . . . 1100 ± 100 rpm
   Fast idle (engine cold) . . . . 1600 ± 100 rpm

Component test data

Air pressure (AP) sensor
   Input voltage . . . . 4.5 to 5.5 V
   Output voltage . . . . approx. 4.0 V @ 760 mmHg
Camshaft position (CMP) sensor
   Peak voltage . . . . min. 3.7 V
Crankshaft position (CKP) sensor
   Resistance . . . . 134 to 202 ohms
   Peak voltage . . . . min. 2.7 V
Engine oil temperature (EOT) sensor
   Input voltage . . . . 4.5 to 5.5 V
   Resistance . . . . 61.3 K-ohms @ 20°C
Gear position (GP) sensor voltage . . . . min. 0.6 V
Injector voltage . . . . Battery voltage (12 V approx)
Injector resistance . . . . 12 to 18 ohms @ 20°C
Intake air pressure (IAP) sensor
   Input voltage . . . . 4.5 to 5.5 V
   Output voltage . . . . approx 2.5 V @ idle speed
Intake air temperature (IAT) sensor
   Input voltage . . . . 4.5 to 5.5 V
   Resistance
      @ 20°C . . . . 2.6 K-ohms approx.
      @ 50°C . . . . 0.8 K-ohms approx.
      @ 80°C . . . . 0.3 K-ohms approx.
      @ 110°C . . . . 0.2 K-ohms approx.
Secondary throttle position (STP) sensor
   Input voltage . . . . 4.5 to 5.5 V
   Output voltage
      Closed . . . . 0.8 V approx
      Open . . . . 4.0 V approx
   Resistance
      Closed . . . . 0.8 K-ohms approx
      Open . . . . 3.9 K-ohms approx
Secondary throttle valve (STV) servo resistance . . . . 4.8 to 7.2 ohms approx
Throttle position (TP) sensor
   Input voltage . . . . 4.5 to 5.5 V
   Output voltage
      Closed . . . . 1.1 V approx
      Open . . . . 4.3 V approx
   Resistance
      Closed . . . . 1.1 K-ohms approx
      Open . . . . 4.3 K-ohms approx
Tip over (TO) sensor
   Resistance . . . . 60 to 64 K-ohms
   Voltage
      Upright . . . . 3.8 V approx
      At 43° angle or greater . . . . zero V

Ignition HT coils

Primary winding resistance . . . . 2 to 4 ohms
Secondary winding resistance (with plug caps) . . . . 25 to 40 K-ohms
Spark plug cap resistance . . . . 11 K-ohms approx
Primary peak voltage . . . . min 150 V
Spark performance . . . . min 8 mm

Torque settings

Camshaft position (CMP) sensor bolt	8 Nm
Exhaust system	
Downpipe clamp bolts	20 Nm
Downpipe flange bolts	23 Nm
Downpipe assembly mounting bolt	23 Nm
Silencer mounting bolt nut	23 Nm
Silencer clamp bolt	24 Nm
Fuel rail screws.	5 Nm
Fuel level sensor bolts	10 Nm
Fuel pump bolts	10 Nm
Intake air temperature (IAT) sensor.	18 Nm
PAIR system reed valve cover bolts	10 Nm
Secondary throttle position (STP) sensor screws	3.5 Nm
Throttle position (TP) sensor screws	3.5 Nm
Timing rotor bolt.	25 Nm
Timing rotor cover bolts	11 Nm

1 General information and precautions

General information

Fuel system

The fuel system consists of the fuel tank, incorporating the fuel pump and filter, the fuel hose to the fuel rail on the throttle bodies, and the injector that is located in each throttle body – one for each cylinder. The fuel pump is activated by the ignition switch via the fuel pump relay and safety interlock circuit and delivers fuel whilst the engine is running. Fuel pressure is controlled within the pump by a pressure regulator. In the event of the machine falling over, a tip-over sensor cuts power to the fuel pump, injectors and ignition HT coils.

The entire fuel injection system is controlled by the engine control module (ECM) which monitors data sent from the various system sensors and adjusts fuel delivery to the engine accordingly. If a fault develops in the injection system, the FI warning LED on the instrument cluster comes on or flashes (according to the severity of the problem) and FI is displayed on the LCD (either alternately with the odometer reading or by itself, again according to the severity of the problem). In the case of a minor fault the engine will continue to run in a fail-safe mode enabling the machine to be ridden, although performance will be significantly reduced. In the case of a major fault the engine will stop and cannot be restarted. For comprehensive fault diagnosis and certain service procedures, a Suzuki mode select switch (Pt. No. 09930-82710) is required – this switch converts the system from user mode to dealer mode, allowing access to the fault codes which are then displayed on the LCD in the instrument cluster.

The SDTV (Suzuki Dual Throttle Valve) fuel injection system uses two throttle valves in each throttle body. The main valve is actuated by the throttle cables from the handlebar twistgrip, the secondary valve is actuated by a servo controlled by the ECM for the purpose of smoothing airflow into the throttle body.

The air filter housing is under the seat, and the air is drawn through the filter before going into the throttle bodies. An automatic fast idle system that receives signals from the intake air and oil temperature sensors controls the start-up and running of the engine when cold.

The exhaust system is a four-into-two design on K2 to K4 models and a four-into-one on K5 models onward. A PAIR system introduces filtered air into the exhaust ports to promote the burning of excess fuel in the exhaust gases.

Ignition system

The transistorised electronic ignition system is combined with the fuel injection system, both being controlled by the ECM (engine control module). The ignition system comprises a timing rotor, crankshaft position sensor (CKP sensor), engine control module (ECM) and ignition HT coils.

The triggers on the rotor, which is fitted to the right-hand end of the crankshaft, generate a signal in the CKP sensor as the crankshaft rotates. The CKP sensor sends that signal to the ECM which, in conjunction with information received from the camshaft position, throttle position, gear position and engine oil temperature sensors, calculates the ignition timing and supplies the ignition HT coils with the power necessary to produce a spark at the plugs. There is no provision for checking or adjusting the ignition timing.

There are two ignition HT coils, one providing for cylinders 1 and 4, the other for cylinders 2 and 3, using the wasted spark principle.

The system incorporates a safety interlock circuit which will cut the ignition if the sidestand is put down whilst the engine is running and in gear, or if a gear is selected whilst the engine is running and the sidestand is down (see Chapter 8).

Maximum engine speed is restricted by the ECM to prevent engine damage.

Note: Individual engine management system components can be checked but not repaired. If system troubles occur, and the faulty component can be isolated, the only cure for the problem in most cases is to replace the part with a new one. Keep in mind that most electronic parts, once purchased, cannot be returned. To avoid unnecessary expense, make very sure the faulty component has been positively identified before buying a new part.

Precautions

 Warning: Petrol (gasoline) is extremely flammable, so take extra precautions when you work on any part of the fuel system. Don't smoke or allow open flames or bare light bulbs near the work area, and don't work in a garage where a natural gas-type appliance is present. If you spill any fuel on your skin, rinse it off immediately with soap and water. When you perform any kind of work on the fuel system, wear safety glasses and have a fire extinguisher suitable for a class B type fire (flammable liquids) on hand.

Always perform service procedures in a well-ventilated area to prevent a build-up of fumes.

Never work in a building containing a gas appliance with a pilot light, or any other form of naked flame. Ensure that there are no naked light bulbs or any sources of flame or sparks nearby.

Do not smoke (or allow anyone else to smoke) while in the vicinity of petrol (gasoline) or of components containing it. Remember the possible presence of vapour from these sources and move well clear before smoking.

Check all electrical equipment belonging to the house, garage or workshop where work is being undertaken (see the Safety first! section of this manual). Remember that certain electrical appliances such as drills, cutters etc. create sparks in the normal course of operation and must not be used near petrol (gasoline) or any component containing it. Again, remember the possible presence of fumes before using electrical equipment.

Always mop up any spilt fuel and safely dispose of the rag used.

Any stored fuel that is drained off during servicing work must be kept in sealed containers that are suitable for holding petrol (gasoline), and clearly marked as such; the containers themselves should be kept in a safe place. Note that this last point applies equally to the fuel tank if it is removed from the machine; also remember to keep its filler cap closed at all times.

Read the Safety first! section of this manual carefully before starting work.

2 Fuel tank

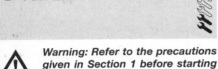

Warning: Refer to the precautions given in Section 1 before starting work.

Raise

1 Make sure the fuel cap is secure. Remove the seat and the side panels (see Chapter 7).
2 Undo the bolts securing the rear of the fuel tank **(see illustration)**. Remove the rubber bushes from each side of the lug, noting the collar in each bottom bush **(see illustrations 2.9b and a)**. Raise the rear of the tank and draw it back a bit, then place a suitable prop such as a block of wood under it **(see illustration)**.

Removal

3 Make sure the ignition switch is OFF. Disconnect the fuel tank wiring connector **(see illustration)**.

4 Place a rag underneath the fuel rail hose union on the throttle bodies to catch any residual fuel. Press the fuel hose connector clips in and pull the hose off the union **(see illustration)**.
5 Note the routing of the breather/overflow hose down the right-hand side of the air filter housing. Lift the tank away, bringing the hose with it **(see illustration)**. Inspect the tank rubber bushes for signs of damage or deterioration and replace them with new ones if necessary.

Installation

6 Make sure the ignition switch is OFF. Check that the tank mounting rubbers are fitted. Carefully lower the fuel tank into position on the frame, making sure it locates around the rubber bushes at the front **(see illustration 2.5)**. Feed the breather/overflow hose down between the frame and the air filter housing on

2.2a Fuel tank mounting bolts (arrowed)

the right-hand side then behind the centre of the swingarm pivot so it finishes in the holder on the frame.
7 Push the fuel hose connector onto its union on the throttle bodies so that the clip locates in the cut-outs in the connector **(see illustration)**. Make sure the hose is secure by trying to pull it back off.
8 Connect the fuel tank wiring connector **(see illustration 2.3)**.
9 Make sure the collars are in place in the rubber bushes, then fit the lower and upper bushes and the bolts and tighten them **(see illustrations)**.
10 Start the engine and check that there is no sign of fuel leakage, then turn it OFF.
11 Install the side panels and seat (see Chapter 7).

Cleaning and repair

12 All repairs to the fuel tank should be carried

2.2b Support the tank as shown using a block of wood

2.3 Disconnect the fuel tank wiring connector

2.4 Press the clips in and pull the hose off

2.5 Lift the tank away – note that if it is full of fuel it will be heavy

2.7 Push the hose onto the union until the connector engages with the clips

2.9a Fit the bushes with the collars into the lugs from the underside . . .

2.9b . . . then fit the upper bushes and the bolts with their washers

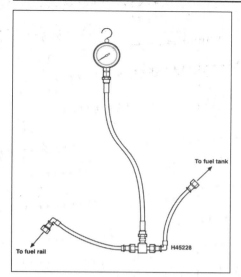

3.2 Fuel pressure gauge and hose set-up

out by a professional who has experience in this critical and potentially dangerous work. Even after cleaning and flushing the fuel system, explosive fumes can remain and ignite during repair of the tank.

13 If the fuel tank is removed from the bike, it should not be placed in an area where sparks or open flames could ignite the fumes coming out of the tank. Be especially careful inside garages where a natural gas-type appliance is located, because the pilot light could cause an explosion.

3 Fuel pressure check

![warning] **Warning: Refer to the precautions given in Section 1 before starting work.**
Special Tool: A fuel pressure gauge is required for this procedure.

1 To check the fuel pressure, a suitable gauge, gauge hose and adapters will be needed to connect. Suzuki provides service tools (Pt. Nos. 09915-77330, 09915-74520, 09940-40211 and 09940-40220) for this purpose.
2 Raise the fuel tank, then disconnect the fuel hose from the fuel rail on the throttle bodies (see Section 2). Use the adapters to connect the gauge between the fuel tank and the throttle bodies as shown **(see illustration)**.
3 Turn the ignition switch ON and check the pressure reading on the gauge. The pressure should be as specified at the beginning of this Chapter.
4 Turn the ignition OFF and disconnect the gauge and adapters. Use a rag to catch any residual fuel as before. Reconnect the fuel hose to the fuel rail (see Section 2).
5 If the pressure is too low, there could be a leak in the fuel supply system, a blocked fuel filter, a faulty pressure regulator or a faulty fuel pump.
6 If the pressure is too high, either the pressure regulator or the fuel pump check valve is faulty.

7 Suzuki provides no test procedure for the pressure regulator. Remove the pump to inspect it (see Section 5). The fuel filter cartridge and pressure regulator come as an assembly so it is worth fitting a new one then checking the pressure again before doing anything else. The fuel check valve is an integral part of the pump and is not available separately.

4 Fuel pump relay

1 Remove the left-hand side panel (see Chapter 7) – the relay is behind it below the fusebox **(see illustration)**.
2 Pull the relay off its mounting lugs and disconnect the wiring connector **(see illustrations)**.
3 Using a multimeter or test light, check for continuity between terminals 1 and 2 on the relay **(see illustration)**. There should be no continuity. Now use jumper wires to connect the positive (+) terminal of a fully charged 12 volt battery to terminal 3 on the relay and the negative (-) battery terminal to relay terminal 4. There should now be continuity shown across terminals 1 and 2. If the relay fails either of the checks, replace it with a new one.

5 Fuel pump

![warning] **Warning: Refer to the precautions given in Section 1 before starting work.**

Check

1 The fuel pump is located inside the fuel tank. When the ignition is switched ON, it should be possible to hear the pump run for a few seconds until the system is up to pressure. If you can't hear anything, first check the fuses (see Chapter 8), then check the relay (see Section 4). If they are good, raise the fuel tank (see Section 2) and check the fuel tank main wiring connector and the fuel pump wiring connector and their terminals for physical damage or loose or corroded connections and rectify as necessary (see the Wiring Diagrams at the end of Chapter 8). If the pump still will not run, check the tip-over (TO) sensor (see Section 10). If that is good, and assuming the ECM is OK, fit a new pump.

Removal

2 The fuel pump is located inside the fuel tank. Remove the tank (see Section 2). Turn it upside down and rest it on plenty of clean rag to soak up any fuel that may leak or spill and to protect the paintwork. Mark an arrow on the pump base pointing to the front to show which way round it fits.

4.1 Fuel pump relay (arrowed)

4.2a Pull the relay off its mount . . .

4.2b . . . and disconnect the wiring connector

4.3 Fuel pump relay terminal identification

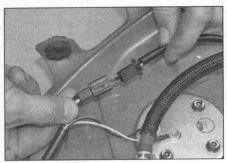

5.3a Disconnect the wiring connector . . .

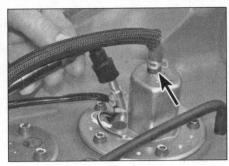

5.3b . . . then detach the fuel hose and the return hose (arrowed)

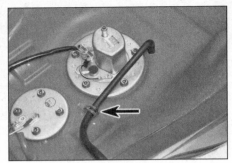

5.3c Release the hose guide (arrowed)

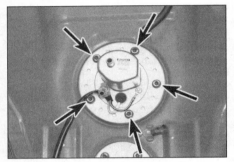

5.4a Undo the bolts (arrowed) . . .

5.4b . . . and lift out the pump

5.7a Undo the nut (arrowed) . . .

5.7b . . . and the screws (arrowed) . . .

3 Disconnect the pump wiring connector **(see illustration)**. Press the fuel hose connector clips in and pull the hose off the union **(see illustration)**. Release the fuel return hose clamp and detach the hose from its union on the pump. Release the breather/overflow hose from its guide **(see illustration)**.

4 Undo the bolts securing the base to the underside of the tank and carefully lift out the pump **(see illustrations)**. Discard the O-ring as a new one must be fitted on reassembly.

5 If required, disassemble the pump assembly to clean the strainer or replace the filter/regulator assembly (see Steps 7 to 12).

6 Check that all the wiring terminals are tight.

Disassembly

7 Undo the nut on the pump base and the screws on the holding arms and detach the wires, noting the washers fitted with the nut **(see illustrations)**. Remove the clip-nuts from the arms **(see illustration)**.

8 Pull the pump assembly out of the base **(see illustration)**. Discard the O-ring on the base fuel union as a new one must be fitted on reassembly. Clean any sediment out of the pump base.

9 Clean any sediment off the strainer gauze with a soft brush or low pressure compressed air. If the strainer is damaged, or if there is

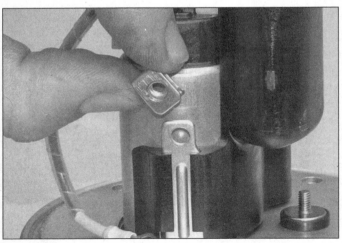

5.7c . . . and remove the clip nuts

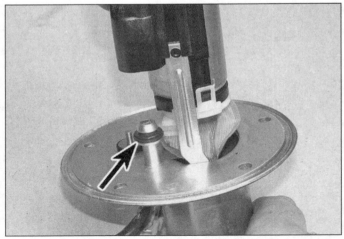

5.8 Pull the pump assembly out of the base. Discard the O-ring (arrowed)

5.9a Release the clips and remove the seat . . .

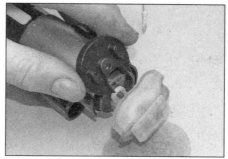

5.9b . . . and the cushion . . .

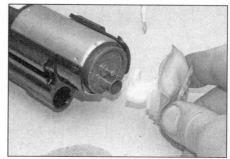

5.9c . . . then detach the strainer

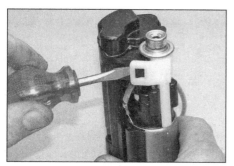

5.10a Release the clip . . .

5.10b . . . and remove the holder . . .

5.10c . . . then detach the regulator

sediment inside it, a new one should be fitted – release the clips and remove the fuel pump seat and rubber cushion, then remove the strainer from the bottom of the pump **(see illustrations)**.

10 If required (but note that the filter cartridge and regulator come as an assembly) release the pressure regulator holder clip, then remove the holder, noting how it locates, and pull the regulator off **(see illustrations)**. Discard the O-ring as a new one must be fitted on reassembly.

11 Carefully separate the pump from the fuel filter cartridge **(see illustration)**. Discard the rubber bush as a new one must be used **(see illustration)**.

12 Install the components in the reverse order of disassembly, noting the following:

● Fit a new rubber bush between the filter cartridge and the pump **(see illustration 5.11b)**.

● If disassembled fit the new O-ring onto the regulator and smear it with engine oil, then press the regulator into place and secure it with the holder, making sure the clips locate **(see illustrations 5.10c, b and a)**.

● Fit a new O-ring to the pump base fuel union and smear it with engine oil **(see illustration 5.8)**.

● Ensure the clip nuts are in place on both holding arms for the wire terminal and retaining screws **(see illustration 5.7c)**.

● Make sure the star washer and spring washer are correctly fitted with the wire terminal on the pump base **(see illustration)**.

Installation

13 Smear the new O-ring lightly with grease and fit it into the recess around the aperture on the underside of the fuel tank **(see illustration)**.

14 Install the pump with the arrow mark made

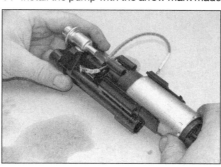

5.11a Pull the pump and filter assembly apart . . .

5.12 Make sure the star washer and spring washer are fitted on each side of the terminal

on the base pointing to the front of the tank and align the holes in the base with those in the tank – if no mark was made, make sure the pump is installed as shown **(see illustrations 5.4b and a)**. Apply a suitable thread locking

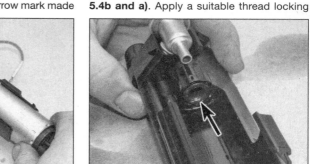

5.11b . . . and remove the bush (arrowed)

5.13 Fit the new O-ring into the groove

compound to the bolts and install them finger-tight, then tighten them evenly and a little at a time in a criss-cross pattern to the torque setting specified at the beginning of this Chapter.

15 Secure the breather/overflow hose in its clamp **(see illustration 5.3c)**. Fit the return hose onto its union and secure it with the clamp **(see illustration 5.3b)**. Push the fuel hose connector onto its union until the clips engage. Connect the pump wiring connector **(see illustration 5.3a)**.

16 Install the fuel tank (see Section 2). Ensure there are no signs of fuel leakage around the pump base.

6 Fuel level sensor

⚠️ **Warning: Refer to the precautions given in Section 1 before starting work.**

Note: *When the ignition is switched ON the low fuel warning LED will come on, then either extinguish or flash according to the level of fuel in the tank. The low fuel warning LED will flash when the volume of fuel in the tank drops below 6.0 litres. The fuel level is also indicated by the number of segments displaced between E and F on the display. When only one segment is displayed the level has dropped to 6.0 litres. When this segment flashes the level has dropped to 1.75 litres. Refer to Chapter 8 for the instrument function of the low fuel warning circuit.*

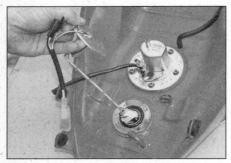

6.4b . . . then twist the base as required to get the sensor . . .

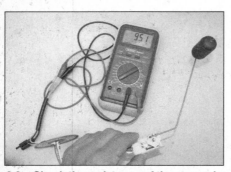

6.6a Check the resistance of the sensor in its empty position . . .

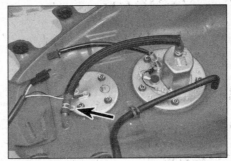

6.3 Release the clamp (arrowed) and detach the hose

Removal

1 The level sensor is located inside the fuel tank. Remove the tank (see Section 2). Make sure the fuel cap is secure.

2 Turn it upside down and rest it on plenty of clean rag to soak up any fuel that may leak or spill and to protect the paintwork. Mark an arrow on the sensor base pointing to the front to show which way round it fits.

3 Disconnect the fuel pump wiring connector **(see illustration 5.3a)**. Release the fuel return hose clamp and detach the hose from its union on the tank **(see illustration)**.

4 Unscrew the bolts securing the sensor base to the underside of the tank and manoeuvre the sensor out **(see illustrations)**. Discard the O-ring as a new one must be used on reassembly.

Inspection

5 Connect an ohmmeter between the yellow/

6.4c . . . and the float out of the hole

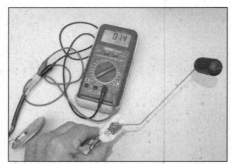

6.6b . . . and then in the full position

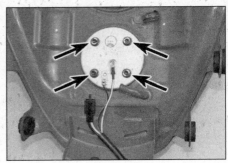

6.4a Unscrew the bolts (arrowed) . . .

black and black/white wire terminals in the sensor side of the fuel tank wiring connector.

6 With the sensor float in its lowest (empty) position the meter should show a resistance of between 90 and 100 ohms **(see illustration)**. Carefully raise the float to its highest (full) position – the meter should now show a resistance of between 4 and 10 ohms **(see illustration)**.

7 If no readings are obtained, or if they differ greatly from those specified, replace the sensor with a new one.

8 If the tests show the sensor to be good, check for voltage at the yellow/black wire terminal on the loom side of the fuel tank wiring connector with the ignition on. If there is voltage, check for continuity to earth in the black/white wire. If there is no voltage, check the wiring between the sensor and the instrument cluster, then check the cluster itself (see Chapter 8).

Installation

9 Smear the new O-ring lightly with grease and fit it into the recess around the aperture on the underside of the fuel tank **(see illustration)**.

10 Manoeuvre the sensor into the tank so that the arrow mark made on the base will point to the front of the tank – if no mark was made, make sure the sensor is installed as shown **(see illustrations 6.4c, b and a)**. Apply a suitable thread locking compound to the bolts and install them finger-tight, then tighten them evenly and a little at a time in a criss-cross pattern to the torque setting specified at the beginning of this Chapter.

11 Fit the return hose onto its union and

6.9 Fit the new O-ring into the groove

secure it with the clamp **(see illustration 6.3)**. Connect the fuel pump wiring connector **(see illustration 5.3a)**.

12 Install the fuel tank (see Section 2). Ensure there are no signs of fuel leakage around the pump base.

7 Air filter housing

Note: *Removal of the air filter is covered in Chapter 1, Section 2.*

1 Remove the engine from the frame (see Chapter 2).

2 Disconnect the intake air temperature (IAT) sensor wiring connector **(see illustration)**. If required remove the sensor from the housing (see Section 10).

3 Make a note of the routing of the drain hose on the left-hand side of the housing. Draw the housing forwards and remove it, bringing the drain hose with it **(see illustration)**.

4 If required detach the drain hose from the left-hand side of the housing and the crankcase breather hose from the front.

5 Installation is the reverse of removal.

8 Fuel injection system description

1 The fuel injection system consists of two main component groups, the fuel supply circuit and the electronic control circuit.

2 The fuel supply circuit consists of the tank, the pump, filter and pressure regulator, the injectors and the throttle bodies. Fuel is pumped under pressure from the tank to the fuel rail, from which the individual injectors are fed. Operating pressure is maintained initially by the pump check valve and, once the engine is running, by the pressure regulator. The injectors spray pressurised fuel into the throttle bodies where it mixes with air and vaporises, before entering the cylinders where it is compressed and ignited.

3 The electronic control circuit consists of the engine control module (ECM), which operates and co-ordinates both the fuel injection and ignition systems, and the various sensors

7.2 Disconnect the intake air temperature (IAT) sensor wiring connector

which provide the ECM with information on engine operating conditions.

4 The ECM monitors signals from the following sensors:

Intake air temperature (IAT) sensor
Intake air pressure (IAP) sensor
Throttle position (TP) sensor
Secondary throttle position (STP) sensor
Camshaft position (CMP) sensor
Crankshaft position (CKP) sensor
Engine oil temperature (EOT) sensor
Atmospheric pressure (AP) sensor
Gear position (GP) sensor
Tip-over (TO) sensor

5 Based on the information it receives, the ECM calculates the appropriate ignition and fuel requirements of the engine. By varying the length of the electronic pulse it sends to each injector, the ECM controls the length of time the injectors are held open and thereby the amount of fuel that is supplied to the engine. Fuel supply varies according to the engine's needs for starting, warming-up, idling, cruising and acceleration.

6 In the event of an abnormality in any of the sensor signals, the ECM will determine whether the engine can still be run safely. If it can, a back-up mode replaces the sensor signal with a fixed signal, restricting performance but allowing the bike to be ridden home or to a dealer. When this occurs, the LCD display in the instrument cluster will indicate the letters FI every two seconds (alternating with the odometer reading), and the FI LED will come on. If the unit decides that the fault is too serious, the appropriate system will be shut down and the engine will not run. When this occurs, the LCD display in

7.3 Remove the housing from the frame

the instrument cluster will indicate the letters FI continuously, and the FI LED will flash. See Section 9 for fault finding.

7 The system incorporates two safety circuits. When the ignition is switched ON, the fuel pump runs for three seconds and pressurises the system. Thereafter the pump automatically switches off until the engine is started. The second circuit incorporates a tip-over sensor, which automatically switches off the fuel pump and cuts the ignition and injection circuits if the motorcycle falls over.

9 Fuel injection system fault diagnosis

1 The system incorporates a self-diagnostic function whereby any faults are stored in the ECM memory. To access the appropriate fault code, a Suzuki mode select switch (Pt. No. 09930-82720) is required – this switch converts the system from user mode to dealer mode, allowing access to the fault codes which are then displayed on the LCD in the instrument cluster. The mode select switch is inexpensive and is required for a number of testing procedures.

2 Remove the seat (see Chapter 7), then unclip and remove the storage tray **(see illustration)**. Locate the mode select switch wiring connector which is next to the ECM wiring connectors **(see illustration)**. Remove the connector cover, ensure the ignition and the select switch are OFF, then connect the select switch **(see illustration)**.

9.2a Remove the storage tray, noting how it locates

9.2b Mode select switch wiring connector (arrowed)

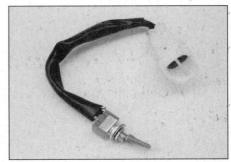

9.2c The Suzuki mode select switch

3 Start the engine, or if it will not start, crank the engine on the electric starter for at least 4 seconds. Turn the mode select switch ON. The fault code(s) will be displayed on the LCD panel on the instrument cluster, in ascending order if there are more than one. Note the codes and identify the faults from the table.

Note: *Do not disconnect the battery, main fuse or ECM wiring connectors before recording the fault codes – the ECM memory is erased when they are disconnected.*

4 To check the fuel injection system components see Section 10.

5 Once the fault has been corrected, turn the ignition switch OFF (if not already done), then turn it ON. If the fault has been cleared, the instrument display with indicate the code C00. Turn the mode select switch OFF and ignition switch OFF and disconnect the mode select switch. Refit the wiring connector cover and install the storage tray and seat (see Chapter 7).

Fault code	Faulty component – symptoms	Possible causes
CHEC	No ECM signal – engine will not run	Kill switch OFF Faulty wiring or wiring connector Faulty ignition safety interlock system (clutch switch, sidestand switch, diode or gear position switch) Damaged ignition fuse
C00	No fault.	System clear
C11	Camshaft position sensor – engine will continue to run and can be restarted	Faulty wiring or wiring connector Damaged sensor or intake cam pin
C12	Crankshaft position sensor – engine will not run	Faulty wiring or wiring connector Damaged sensor or timing rotor
C13	Intake air pressure sensor – engine will run, air pressure signal fixed at 760 mmHg	Faulty wiring or wiring connector Damaged sensor
C14	Throttle position sensor – engine will run, throttle position signal and ignition timing fixed	Faulty wiring or wiring connector Damaged sensor
C15	Engine oil temperature sensor – engine will run, oil temperature signal fixed at 80°C	Faulty wiring or wiring connector Damaged sensor
C21	Intake air temperature sensor – engine will run, air temperature signal fixed at 40°C	Faulty wiring or wiring connector Damaged sensor
C22	Atmospheric pressure sensor – engine will run, atmospheric pressure signal fixed at 760 mmHg	Faulty wiring or wiring connector Damaged sensor
C23	Tip-over sensor – engine will not run	Faulty wiring or wiring connector Damaged sensor
C24	Nos. 1 and 4 cylinder ignition HT coil – engine will run on cylinders 2 and 3, ignition signal to Nos. 1 and 4 cylinders cut	Faulty wiring or wiring connector Damaged ignition coil Faulty power supply for the ignition system (see Sections18 and 19 for details)
C25	Nos. 2 and 3 cylinder ignition HT coil – engine will run on cylinders 1 and 4, ignition signal to Nos. 2 and 3 cylinders cut	Faulty wiring or wiring connector Damaged ignition coil Faulty power supply for the ignition system (see Sections18 and 19 for details)
C28	Secondary throttle valve servo – engine will run, valve fixed in half-open position	Faulty wiring or wiring connector Damaged servo motor
C29	Secondary throttle position sensor – engine will run, valve fixed in half-open position	Faulty wiring or wiring connector Damaged sensor
C31	Gear position sensor – engine will run, signal fixed to 6th gear	Faulty wiring or wiring connector Damaged sensor Faulty gearchange mechanism
C32	No. 1 cylinder fuel injector – engine will run on other cylinders	Faulty wiring or wiring connector Damaged fuel injector
C33	No. 2 cylinder fuel injector – engine will run on other cylinders	Faulty wiring or wiring connector Damaged fuel injector
C34	No. 3 cylinder fuel injector – engine will run on other cylinders	Faulty wiring or wiring connector Damaged fuel injector
C35	No. 4 cylinder fuel injector – engine will run on other cylinders	Faulty wiring or wiring connector Damaged fuel injector
C41	Fuel pump control system – engine will not run	Faulty wiring or wiring connector to pump and/or pump relay Faulty pump relay (see Section 4) Damaged fuel pump (see Section 5)
C42	Ignition switch – engine will not run	Faulty wiring or wiring connector Damaged switch (see Chapter 8 for details)

10.5a Disconnect the wiring connector, then unscrew the bolt (arrowed) . . .

10.5b . . . and remove the sensor. Discard the O-ring and fit a new one (arrowed)

10.7 Crankshaft position (CKP) sensor wiring connector

10 Fuel injection system components

1 If a fault is indicated on any of the system components, first check the wiring and connectors between the appropriate component and the engine control module (ECM); refer to Electrical system fault finding and the Wiring Diagrams in Chapter 8. A continuity test of all wires will locate a break or short in any circuit. Inspect the terminals inside the wiring connectors and ensure they are not loose or corroded. Spray the inside of the connectors with a proprietary electrical terminal cleaner before reconnection. Also remove the sensor and check the sensor head, and clean it if it is dirty – an accumulation of dirt could affect the signal it transmits.

2 It is possible to undertake some checks on system components using a multimeter and comparing the results with the specifications at the beginning of this Chapter. Note: Different meters may give slightly different results to those specified even though the component being tested is not faulty – do not consign a component to the bin before having it double-checked. However, some faults will only become evident when a component is tested with a peak voltage tester, in which case the checks should be undertaken by a Suzuki dealer.

3 If after a thorough check the source of a fault has not been identified, it is possible that the ECM itself is faulty. Suzuki provides no test specifications for the ECM. In order to determine conclusively that the unit is defective, it should be substituted with a known good one (Section 20). If the problem is then rectified, the original unit is faulty.

Camshaft position (CMP) sensor

4 Have the sensor peak voltage tested by a Suzuki dealer.
5 To remove the sensor raise, or for best access remove, the fuel tank (see Section 2). The sensor is on the left-hand side of the valve cover. Disconnect the wiring connector, then unscrew the bolt and remove the sensor (see illustrations). Discard the O-ring and use a new one smeared with grease. On installation tighten the bolt to the torque setting specified at the beginning of the Chapter.
6 To inspect the sensor trigger on the intake camshaft, remove the valve cover (see Chapter 2).

Crankshaft position (CKP) sensor and timing rotor

Check

7 Make sure the ignition is OFF. Raise the fuel tank (see Section 2). The CKP sensor is

on the right-hand end of the crankshaft. Trace the wiring from behind the top of the timing rotor cover and disconnect it at the connector (see illustration). Using an ohmmeter or multimeter set to the ohms scale, measure the resistance between the blue and yellow wire terminals on the sensor side of the connector. If the result is as specified, check that there is no continuity between each terminal and earth (ground).
8 If the results are good, have the sensor peak voltage tested by a Suzuki dealer.

Removal

9 Make sure the ignition is OFF. Raise the fuel tank (see Section 2).
10 Unscrew the timing rotor cover bolts, noting the sealing washer fitted with the top bolt and remove the cover (see illustration). Discard the gasket as a new one must be fitted on reassembly.
11 Counter-hold the timing rotor using a ring spanner on the hex and unscrew the bolt in its centre (see illustration). Remove the rotor, noting how it locates on the pin (see illustration 10.18a).
12 Undo the oil pressure switch wire screw and detach the wire (see illustration).
13 Trace the wiring from behind the top of the timing rotor housing and disconnect it at the 3-pin connector above the air filter housing (see illustration 10.7). Free the wiring from any clips or ties and feed it through to the housing, noting its routing.

10.10 Unscrew the bolts (arrowed) and remove the cover

10.11 Counter-hold the rotor hex and unscrew the bolt

10.12 Undo the screw and detach the wire

10.14a Undo the plate mounting screws . . .

10.14b . . . then displace the plate and draw the wiring through

10.16 Fit the grommet (arrowed) into its recess then locate the plate

14 Undo the screws securing the CKP sensor mounting plate **(see illustration)**. Detach the plate, then free the rubber wiring grommet from its recess and draw the wiring through **(see illustration)**.

15 Examine the rotor triggers for signs of damage and replace it with a new one if necessary.

Installation

16 Feed the wiring through the hole in the timing rotor housing, then smear some sealant (Suzuki Bond 1207B or equivalent) into the grooved side of the grommet and fit it into its recess **(see illustration)**. Mount the sensor plate onto the crankcase and tighten its screws.

17 Route the wiring back to the connector and reconnect it **(see illustration 10.7).**

Connect the wire to the oil pressure switch **(see illustration 10.12)**.

18 Fit the timing rotor onto the end of the crankshaft, locating the cut-out over the pin **(see illustration)**. Apply some thread locking compound to the rotor bolt **(see illustration)**. Counter-hold the rotor and tighten the bolt to the torque setting specified at the beginning of the Chapter **(see illustration 10.11)**.

19 Apply a suitable sealant (Suzuki Bond 1207B or equivalent) to the wiring grommet and to the crankcase joints **(see illustration)**. Install the timing rotor cover using a new gasket and tighten the bolts to the torque setting specified at the beginning of the chapter, not forgetting the sealing washer with the top bolt **(see illustration)**.

20 Lower the fuel tank (see Section 2).

Intake air pressure (IAP) sensor

21 Make sure the ignition is OFF. Remove the fuel tank (see Section 2). The IAP sensor is on the top of the frame. Displace the sensor from its mount and check the condition of the vacuum hose between the sensor and the throttle bodies **(see illustrations)**. If the hose is cracked or perished replace it with a new one. Make sure the hose is a tight fit on the sensor union and the throttle bodies.

22 Disconnect the sensor wiring connector and turn the ignition ON. Connect the positive (+) probe of a voltmeter to the red wire terminal on the loom side of the wiring connector and the negative (-) probe first to earth (ground), then to the black/brown wire terminal to check the input voltage. Turn the ignition OFF. If the input voltage is not as specified in both cases,

10.18a Locate the cut-out in the back of the rotor over the pin (arrowed) in the crankshaft

10.18b Apply threadlock to the bolt

10.19a Apply some sealant to the grommet (arrowed) and crankcase joints . . .

10.19b . . . then fit the cover using a new gasket

10.21a Displace the sensor . . .

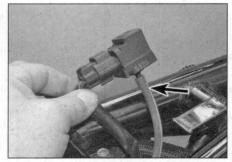

10.21b . . . and check the vacuum hose (arrowed)

10.25 Throttle position (TP) sensor (arrowed)

10.33a Engine oil temperature (EOT) sensor (arrowed)

10.33b EOT sensor wiring connector

check the wiring to the ECM connectors for continuity, and check the ECM terminals.

23 If the input voltage is good, reconnect the wiring to the sensor, then start the engine and allow it idle. Insert the positive (+) probe of a voltmeter (using needle probes or bits of solid copper wire as extensions to crocodile clip probes) into the green/black wire terminal in the back of the connector and the negative (-) probe into the black/brown wire terminal to check the output voltage. If the result is as specified, take the sensor to a Suzuki dealer for vacuum testing. If the output voltage is not as specified, check the wiring to the ECM connectors for continuity, and check the ECM terminals.

24 To remove the IAP sensor, displace it from its mount and disconnect the vacuum hose and the wiring connector **(see illustrations 10.21a and b)**. On installation, ensure the wiring connector terminals are clean and that the vacuum hose is a tight fit on the union.

Throttle position (TP) sensor

Check

25 Make sure the ignition is OFF. Remove the fuel tank (see Section 2). The TP sensor is located on the left-hand end of the throttle bodies **(see illustration)**. Trace the wiring from the sensor and disconnect it at the black wiring connector. Turn the ignition ON. Connect the positive (+) probe of a voltmeter to the red wire terminal on the loom side of the wiring connector and the negative (-) probe first to earth (ground), then to the black/brown wire terminal to check the input voltage. Turn the ignition OFF. If the input voltage is not as specified in both cases, check the wiring to the ECM connectors for continuity, the sensor wiring connector, the multi-pin wiring connector for the throttle body loom and the ECM terminals.

26 If the input voltage is good, check for continuity between the yellow wire terminal on the sensor side of the wiring connector and earth (ground). There should be no continuity.

27 Using an ohmmeter set to the K-ohms scale, measure the resistance between the yellow and black wire terminals on the sensor side of the wiring connector, first with the throttle closed, then turn the twistgrip so that the throttle is fully open. If the results are as specified, reconnect the wiring connector.

If the results are close to but not exactly as specified refer to Step 32 and adjust the position of the sensor.

28 Turn the ignition ON and connect the probes of a voltmeter (using needle probes or bits of solid copper wire as extensions to crocodile clip probes) between the yellow and black wire terminals in the connector (with the connector connected and probes inserted from the back) to check the output voltage, first with the throttle closed, then turn the twistgrip so that the throttle is fully open. Turn the ignition OFF.

29 If the results are not as specified, the sensor is faulty.

Removal, installation and adjustment

30 Make sure the ignition is OFF. Remove the fuel tank (see Section 2). The TP sensor is located on the left-hand end of the throttle bodies **(see illustration 10.25)**. Trace the wiring from the sensor and disconnect it at the black wiring connector. Free the wiring from any ties. Mark the position of the sensor to aid installation, then undo the screws and remove the sensor. Note how the end of the throttle shaft engages the sensor. If the secondary throttle position (STP) sensor is also being removed note which is which – the TP sensor has a black connector, the STP sensor a white connector.

31 Installation is the reverse of removal. Ensure that the throttle shaft engages correctly in the slot in the sensor and align any register marks before tightening the screws to the torque setting specified at the beginning of this Chapter. Ensure the wiring connector terminals are clean.

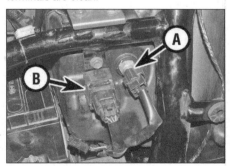

10.36 IAT sensor (A) and AP sensor (B)

32 To check and adjust the position of the TP sensor, first check the engine idle speed and adjust it if necessary (see Chapter 1). Following the procedure in Step 27, make sure the resistance with the throttle closed is as specified at the beginning of the Chapter. If not, loosen the sensor screws and adjust its position until the resistance is correct, then tighten the screws.

Engine oil temperature (EOT) sensor

33 Make sure the ignition is OFF. The EOT sensor is located in the top of the crankcase behind the cylinder block **(see illustration)**. Remove the right-hand side panel (see Chapter 7) and disconnect the sensor wiring connector (black 2-pin) **(see illustration)**. Turn the ignition ON. Connect the positive (+) probe of a voltmeter to the black/blue wire terminal on the loom side of the connector and the negative (-) probe first to earth (ground), then to the black/brown wire terminal to check the input voltage. Turn the ignition OFF. If the input voltage is not as specified in both cases, check the wiring to the ECM connectors for continuity, and check the ECM terminals.

34 Using an ohmmeter or multimeter set to the K-ohms scale, measure the resistance between the terminals on the sensor side of the connector with the engine cold. If the result is not as specified, the sensor is faulty.

35 If the sensor is working correctly, the resistance should drop as the engine warms up. A check for sensor performance is described in Chapter 3, along with removal and installation details.

Intake air temperature (IAT) sensor

36 Make sure the ignition is OFF. Remove the right-hand side panel (see Chapter 7). The IAT sensor is on the right-hand side of the air filter housing **(see illustration)**. Disconnect the sensor wiring connector and turn the ignition ON **(see illustration 7.2)**. Connect the positive (+) probe of a voltmeter to the dark green wire terminal on the loom side of the wiring connector and the negative (-) probe first to earth (ground), then to the black/brown wire terminal to check the input voltage. Turn the ignition OFF. If the input voltage is not as specified in both cases, check the wiring to the ECM connectors for continuity, and check the ECM terminals.

37 Using an ohmmeter or multimeter set to the K-ohms scale, measure the resistance between the terminals on the sensor itself. If the result is not as specified, the sensor is faulty. The IAT sensor resistance should drop as temperature increases. If required test the sensor in the same way as described in Chapter 3 for the oil temperature sensor – the resistance/temperature values should be as specified at the beginning of this Chapter.

38 The sensor screws into the air filter housing. To remove the sensor, first disconnect the wiring connector, then unscrew the sensor **(see illustration 7.2)**. Note the seal on the sensor body and replace it with a new one on installation if it is damaged. Tighten the sensor to the torque setting specified at the beginning of the Chapter.

Atmospheric pressure (AP) sensor

39 Make sure the ignition is OFF. Remove the right-hand side panel (see Chapter 7). The AP sensor is on the right-hand side of the air filter housing **(see illustration 10.36)**.

40 Disconnect the sensor wiring connector and turn the ignition ON **(see illustration)**. Connect the positive (+) probe of a voltmeter to the red wire terminal on the loom side of the wiring connector and the negative (-) probe first to earth (ground), then to the black/brown wire terminal to check the input voltage. Turn the ignition OFF. If the input voltage is not as specified in both cases, check the wiring to the ECM connectors for continuity, and check the ECM terminals.

41 If the input voltage is good, reconnect the wiring to the sensor, then turn the ignition ON. Insert the positive (+) probe of a voltmeter (using needle probes or bits of solid copper wire as extensions to crocodile clip probes)

10.40 Disconnect the wiring connector

into the green/yellow wire terminal in the back of the connector and the negative (-) probe into the black/brown wire terminal to check the output voltage. Turn the ignition OFF.

42 If the output voltage is not as specified, the AP sensor air passage may be clogged with dirt. Disconnect the wiring connector and remove the sensor **(see illustration)**. Clean the outside of the sensor with a damp cloth and check the air passage for any obstruction, then retest the output voltage (see Step 41).

43 If the output voltage is as specified, take the sensor to a Suzuki dealer for vacuum testing.

Tip-over (TO) sensor

44 Make sure the ignition is OFF. Remove the right-hand side panel (see Chapter 7). The TO sensor is behind the rear brake fluid reservoir **(see illustration)** – unscrew the bolt and displace the reservoir for access **(see illustration)**. Note the arrow that points up marked on the sensor sleeve.

45 Disconnect the sensor wiring connector **(see illustration 10.44a)**. Using an ohmmeter or multimeter set to the K-ohms scale, measure the resistance between the black and black/white wire terminals on the sensor side of the connector. Compare the result to that given in the Specifications at the beginning of

10.42 Remove the sensor and check the air passage (arrowed)

this Chapter; if the result is good, reconnect the wiring connector.

46 Turn the ignition ON and insert the positive (+) probe of a voltmeter (using needle probes or bits of solid copper wire as extensions to crocodile clip probes) into the brown wire terminal in the back of the connector and the negative (-) probe into the black/brown wire terminal to check the voltage. If the result is as specified for the upright position, carefully displace the sensor and check the voltage reading when the sensor is tilted beyond 43° to one side and then to the other, this simulates the cut-off point reached if the motorcycle falls over – at each point the voltage should drop to zero. If not the sensor is faulty.

47 To remove the sensor, displace the reservoir **(see illustration 10.44b)**, then disconnect the wiring connector **(see illustration 10.44a)**. Release the sensor from its bracket, noting which way up and round it fits. Installation is the reverse of removal – make sure the arrow on the sensor sleeve faces the front and points up **(see illustration 10.44a)**.

Secondary throttle valve (STV) servo

48 Make sure the ignition is OFF. The STV servo is in the middle of the throttle bodies

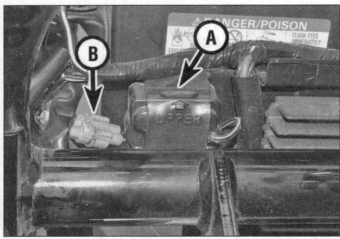

10.44a TO sensor (A) and its wiring connector (B), viewed from the front . . .

10.44b . . . unscrew the bolt (arrowed) and displace the reservoir for access

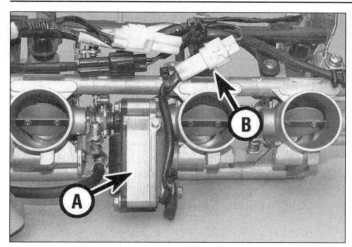

10.48 Secondary throttle valve (STV) servo (A) and its wiring connector (B)

10.52 Secondary throttle position (STP) sensor (arrowed)

(see illustration). Remove the fuel tank (see Section 2).

49 Disconnect the STV servo wiring connector and check that there is no continuity between the red wire terminal on the servo side of the connector and earth (ground).

50 Using an ohmmeter or multimeter set to the ohms scale, measure the resistance between the red and yellow wire terminals on the servo side of the connector. If the result is not as specified, the STV servo is faulty. If the result is as specified, have the ECM checked by a Suzuki dealer.

51 The servo is an integral part of the throttle body assembly and must not be removed from it. The servo is not available separately, and so if it is faulty a new throttle body assembly must be obtained (though it is worth checking with a Suzuki dealer first).

Secondary throttle position (STP) sensor

Check

52 Make sure the ignition is OFF. Remove the fuel tank (see Section 2). The STP sensor is mounted on the right-hand end of the throttle bodies **(see illustration)**.

53 Trace the wiring from the sensor and disconnect it at the white wiring connector. Turn the ignition ON. Connect the positive (+) probe of a voltmeter to the red wire terminal on the loom side of the wiring connector and the negative (-) probe first to earth (ground), then to the black/brown wire terminal to check the input voltage. Turn the ignition OFF. If the input voltage is not as specified in both cases, check the wiring to the ECM connectors for continuity, and check the ECM terminals.

54 If the input voltage is good, check for continuity between the yellow wire terminal on the sensor side of the wiring connector and earth (ground). There should be no continuity.

55 Remove the air filter (see Chapter 1). Using an ohmmeter or multimeter set to the K-ohms scale, connect the positive (+) probe to the yellow wire terminal on the sensor side of the connector and the negative (-) probe to the black wire terminal, and measure the sensor resistance with the secondary throttle valves in both the closed and open positions, accessing the valves from inside the air filter housing and moving them using finger pressure. If the results are as specified, reconnect the sensor wiring connector. If the results are close to but not exactly as specified refer to Step 60 and adjust the position of the sensor.

56 Turn the ignition ON and connect the probes of a voltmeter (using needle probes or bits of solid copper wire as extensions to crocodile clip probes) between the yellow and black wire terminals in the connector (with the connector connected and probes inserted from the back) to check the output voltage, while carefully closing and opening the throttle valves by finger pressure.

57 If the results are not as specified, the sensor is faulty.

Removal, installation and adjustment

58 Make sure the ignition is OFF. Remove the fuel tank (see Section 2). The STP sensor is mounted on the right-hand end of the throttle bodies **(see illustration 10.52)**. Trace the wiring from the sensor and disconnect it at the white wiring connector. Free the wiring from any ties. Mark the position of the sensor to aid installation, then undo the screws and remove the sensor. Note how the end of the throttle shaft engages the sensor. If the throttle position (TP) sensor is also being removed note which is which – the STP sensor has a white connector, the TP sensor a black connector.

59 Installation is the reverse of removal. Ensure that the throttle shaft engages correctly in the slot in the sensor and align any register marks before tightening the screws to the torque setting specified at the beginning of this Chapter. Ensure the wiring connector terminals are clean.

60 To check and adjust the position of the STP sensor, following the procedure in Step 55, make sure the resistance with the secondary throttle valve closed is as specified at the beginning of the Chapter. If not, loosen the sensor screws and adjust its position until the resistance is correct, then tighten the screws. If the sensor cannot be adjusted so the resistance is correct, turn the adjuster screw on the STV servo as required until the resistance on the STP sensor is correct. If it still cannot be adjusted correctly it is faulty.

Gear position (GP) sensor

61 Support the bike on the centre stand and raise the sidestand. The GP sensor is located on the left-hand side of the engine between the front sprocket and the gearchange shaft.

62 Make sure the engine kill switch is in the RUN position. Remove the left-hand side panel (see Chapter 7). Trace the wiring from the sensor to the connector **(see illustration)**. Turn the ignition switch ON and insert the positive (+) probe of a voltmeter (using needle probes or bits of solid copper wire as extensions to crocodile clip probes) into the pink wire terminal in the connector (with the connector connected and probe inserted from the back) and connect the negative (-) probe to earth (ground) to check the output voltage. Select each gear in turn and check that the voltage is above the specified minimum in each gear. Turn the ignition OFF.

10.62 Gear position sensor wiring connector (arrowed)

10.64a Unscrew the bolts (arrowed) and remove the sensor

10.64b Remove the plungers and springs for safekeeping

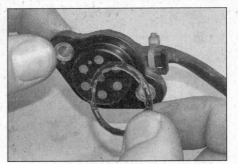

10.64c Clean the contacts and fit a new O-ring . . .

10.64d . . . before installing the sensor

10.65a To access the outer wiring connector remove the end cover, secured by a screw (arrowed) . . .

10.65b . . . and securing the wiring clamp for the STP sensor on the right-hand end

63 If the output voltage is not as specified, check the pink and blue wires to the ECM connector for continuity, and check the ECM terminal. Also check the black/white wire for continuity to earth. If the wiring is good the sensor is faulty.

64 To remove the GP sensor remove the front sprocket cover (see Chapter 6) and the left-hand side panel (see Chapter 7). Trace the wiring from the sensor to the connector and disconnect it **(see illustration 10.62)**. Feed the wiring down to the sensor, noting its routing. Unscrew the bolts and remove the sensor – note that there are two sprung plungers in the

end of the selector drum which could fall out **(see illustrations)**. On installation make sure the plungers are correctly installed. Clean the contacts on the inner face of the sensor, then fit a new O-ring smeared with grease **(see illustration)**. Fit the sensor and tighten the bolts.

Fuel injectors

65 Make sure the ignition is OFF. Remove the fuel tank (see Section 2). The injectors are numbered 1 to 4 from left to right – identify the faulty injector by the fault code and disconnect the injector wiring connector – you may need

to remove the end covers to disconnect the outer wiring connectors, noting how the right-hand one secures the STP sensor wiring clamp **(see illustrations)**. Using an ohmmeter or multimeter set to the ohms scale, measure the resistance between the terminals on the injector **(see illustration)**. If the result is as specified, check that there is no continuity between each terminal and earth (ground).

66 Connect the positive (+) probe of a voltmeter to the yellow/red wire terminal on the loom side of the wiring connector and the negative (-) probe to earth (ground), then turn the ignition ON to check the input voltage.

10.65c Disconnect the wiring connector from the injector

10.65d Measure the resistance of the sensor

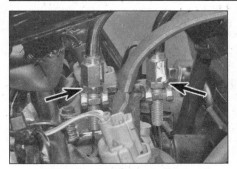

11.2 Slacken the locknuts (arrowed)

11.3a Detach the IAP sensor vacuum hose . . .

11.3b . . . and the PAIR control valve air hose . . .

Note: *Injector input voltage can only be detected for 3 seconds after the ignition has been turned ON.* Turn the ignition OFF. If the input voltage is not as specified, refer to the Wiring Diagrams at the end of Chapter 8 and check for a fault in the yellow/red wire.

67 If the input voltage is as specified check, refer to the Wiring Diagrams at the end of Chapter 8 and check for a fault in the individual injector wires.

68 Refer to Section 13 for removal and installation of the injectors.

---

11 Throttle body removal and installation

⚠️ **Warning: Refer to the precautions given in Section 1 before starting work.**

Removal

1 Remove the fuel tank (see Section 2).
2 Slacken the locknuts securing the throttle cable elbows in the bracket **(see illustration)**.
3 Disconnect the IAP sensor vacuum hose from the 3-way hose union **(see illustration)**. Disconnect the PAIR control valve air hose

from the air filter housing and the vacuum hose from its union on the No. 3 throttle body **(see illustrations)**.

4 Release the cable-tie which secures the throttle body wiring loom to the left-hand frame tube **(see illustration)**. Disconnect the throttle body loom connector **(see illustration)**.

5 Unscrew the bolts securing the fuse box/relay bracket on the left-hand side of the air filter housing and displace the bracket **(see illustration)**. Unscrew the bolt securing the air filter housing on each side **(see illustration)**.

6 Loosen the clamp screws securing the air filter housing to the throttle bodies **(see**

11.3c . . . and vacuum hose

11.4a Release the cable-tie . . .

11.4b . . . and disconnect the wiring connector

11.5a Unscrew the bolts (arrowed) and displace the bracket

11.5b Unscrew the air filter housing bolt (arrowed) on each side

11.6 Air filter housing-to-throttle body clamp screws (A), throttle body-to-intake adapter clamp screws (B)

11.7 Manoeuvre the throttle bodies out to the left-hand side

11.9 Moving the clamps out of the way makes throttle body removal easier

illustration). Move the clamps back out of their grooves so they are against the housing (see illustration 11.9). Move the air filter housing back off the throttle bodies as far as it will go, moving the wiring, connectors and hoses between the housing and frame on each side aside if they get in the way (see illustration 10.62).

7 Loosen the clamp screws securing the throttle bodies to the intake adapters (see illustration 11.6). Move the clamps forwards out of their grooves (see illustration 11.9).

Ease the throttle bodies out of the adapters and draw them out to the left-hand side (see illustration).

8 Disconnect the throttle cables (see Section 14).

Installation

9 Installation is the reverse of removal, noting the following:

● Refer to Section 14 and connect the throttle cables before installing the throttle bodies, but do not tighten the elbow locknuts so the cables align themselves freely, and for freeplay adjustment.

● Move all the clamps forwards or backwards out of their grooves so they do not get in the way of the throttle bodies (see illustration).

● Ensure the throttle bodies are fully engaged with the intake adapters on the cylinder head before tightening the clamps.

● Ensure the terminals in the connector are clean.

● Make sure the vacuum hoses and air hose are securely connected.

● Check the operation of the throttle cables and adjust them as necessary (see Chapter 1).

● Check the engine idle speed and adjust as necessary (see Chapter 1).

12 Throttle body overhaul

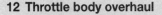

> **Warning: Refer to the precautions given in Section 1 before starting work.**

Disassembly

1 Undo the screw securing each end cover and remove the covers, noting how the right-hand one secures the STP sensor wiring clamp (see illustrations 10.65a and b).

2 Disconnect the vacuum hoses for the intake air pressure (IAP) sensor from the union on each throttle body and remove the IAP hose assembly (see illustration).

3 Cut the cable-tie securing the wiring to the fuel rail (see illustration). Disconnect the wiring connectors from the fuel injectors, the throttle position (TP) sensor, secondary throttle position (STP) sensor and secondary throttle valve (STV) servo, then remove the throttle body assembly wiring loom, noting the routing of the individual wires.

4 Remove the fuel rail and injectors (see Section 13).

12.2 Detach the IAP sensor hose assembly from each union (arrowed)

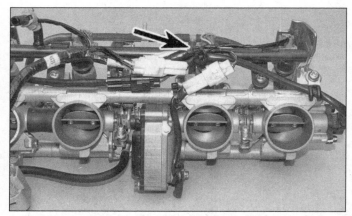

12.3 Cut the cable-tie (arrowed) and disconnect all the wiring connectors

5 If required, remove the TP sensor and STP sensor (see Section 10).

Caution: The throttle valves and secondary throttle valves must not be removed from the valve shafts.

Cleaning

Caution: Use only a petroleum based solvent or dedicated injector cleaner for throttle body cleaning. Don't use caustic cleaners.

6 Ensure that only metal components are submerged in cleaning solvent and always follow manufacturer's recommendations as to cleaning time. If a spray cleaner is used, direct the spray into all passages.

7 After the cleaner has loosened and dissolved most of the varnish and other deposits, use a nylon-bristled brush to remove the stubborn deposits. Rinse the throttle bodies again, then dry them with compressed air.

8 Use compressed air to blow out all of the fuel and air passages.

Caution: Never clean the jets or passages with a piece of wire or a drill bit, as they will be enlarged, causing the fuel and air metering rates to be upset.

Inspection

9 Check the throttle bodies for cracks or any other damage which may result in air getting in.

10 Check that the throttle valves move smoothly and freely in the bodies. Inspect the valve shafts and throttle bodies for wear. Check the condition of the valve shaft springs.

11 Check all the springs, levers and screws in the throttle and secondary throttle linkage.

Reassembly

12 If removed, install the TP and STP sensors (see Section 10).

13 Install the fuel injectors and fuel rail (see Section 13).

14 Connect the throttle body assembly wiring loom to the TP sensor, STP sensor and STV servo, and the fuel injectors. Secure the wiring to the fuel rail using a new cable-tie **(see illustration 12.3)**.

15 Check the vacuum hose assembly for the intake air pressure (IAP) sensor and replace any damaged, deformed or deteriorated hoses with new ones. Connect the hose assembly to

the union on each throttle body – note that the outer union on No. 3 is for the PAIR control valve vacuum hose **(see illustration 12.2)**.

16 Fit the end covers, securing the STP sensor wiring clamp with the screw for the right-hand cover.

13 Fuel rail and injectors

> **Warning: Refer to the precautions given in Section 1 before starting work.**

Removal

Note: The fuel injectors can be removed with the throttle bodies in place. If the bodies have been removed, ignore the Steps which do not apply.

1 Disconnect the battery negative terminal (see Chapter 8). Remove the fuel tank (see Section 2).

2 Undo the screw securing each end cover and remove the covers, noting how the right-hand one secures the STP sensor wiring clamp **(see illustration 10.65a and b)**.

3 Cut the cable-tie securing the wiring to the fuel rail **(see illustration 12.3)**. Disconnect the individual fuel injector wiring connectors **(see illustration 10.65c)**.

4 Undo the fuel rail screws and carefully lift the rail off the throttle bodies – the injectors will come away with it **(see illustrations)**.

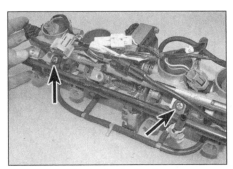

13.4a Undo the fuel rail screws (arrowed) . . .

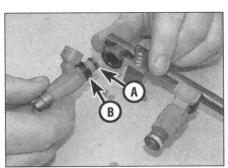

13.4c Remove the seals from the throttle bodies or injectors

Remove and discard the injector seals as new ones must be fitted on reassembly – if they are not in the injector sockets in the throttle bodies they will be on the injectors themselves **(see illustration or 13.8)**.

5 Pull each injector out of the fuel rail, noting how it fits. Remove and discard the injector O-rings and cushions as new ones must be fitted on reassembly **(see illustration)**.

6 Modern fuels contain detergents which should keep the injectors clean and free of gum or varnish from fuel residue. If an injector is suspected of being blocked, clean it through with injector cleaner. If the injector is clean but its performance is suspect, take it to a Suzuki dealer for assessment.

Installation

Note: Apply a smear of clean engine oil to all new seals and O-rings before reassembly.

7 Fit a new cushion and O-ring onto each injector, then carefully fit each injector into its fuel rail, seating the connector socket between the tabs on the rail **(see illustration 13.5)**. Do not twist the injectors when pushing them in as this may damage the O-rings.

8 Fit a new seal onto the bottom of each injector **(see illustration)**. Fit the fuel rail and injectors onto the throttle bodies, making sure each injector is correctly aligned before pressing the assembly into place **(see illustration 13.4b)**. Install the fuel rail screws and tighten them to the specified torque setting **(see illustration 13.4a)**.

9 Connect the individual injector wiring

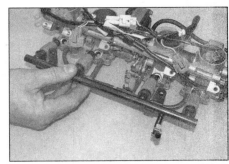

13.4b . . . and carefully remove the fuel rail assembly

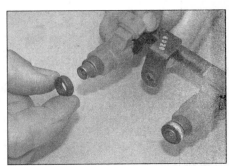

13.8 Fit a new seal onto each injector

13.5 Pull each injector out of the fuel rail and discard the O-ring (A) and cushion (B)

connectors and secure the wiring to the fuel rail with a new cable-tie **(see illustration)**.

10 Fit the end covers, securing the STP sensor wiring clamp with the screw for the right-hand cover **(see illustrations 10.65a and b)**.

11 Install the fuel tank and connect the battery lead. On completion, start the engine and check carefully that there are no fuel leaks.

14 Throttle cables

Removal

1 Refer to Section 11, Steps 1 to 7 and displace the throttle bodies.

2 Before removing the cables note which fits where – the throttle opening cable has gold coloured elbows, and the throttle closing cable has silver coloured elbows.

3 If not already done slacken the locknuts securing the throttle cable elbows in the bracket on the throttle bodies **(see illustration 11.2)**. Turn the adjusters out to thread the bottom nuts down and free the elbows from the bracket, noting how they fit **(see illustrations 14.8d and b)**. Disconnect the cable ends from the throttle pulley – detach the opening cable end first, and hold the pulley or the throttle butterflies in the open position when detaching the closing cable **(see illustrations 14.8c and a)**.

4 Pull the rubber boot off the cable housing

14.7a Fit the closing cable end into its socket . . .

14.7c . . . then locate the housing on the underside of the pulley

13.9 Reconnect the wiring connectors and secure the wiring

14.4b . . . then undo the housing screws (arrowed)

on the handlebar **(see illustration)**. Undo the housing screws and separate the halves **(see illustration)**. Free the cable elbows from the housing and detach the ends from the twistgrip pulley, noting how they fit **(see illustrations 14.7d, c, b and a)**.

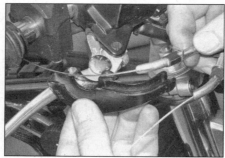

14.7b . . . and the elbow into the housing . . .

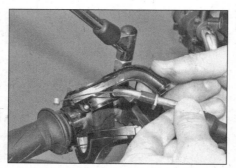

14.7d Fit the opening cable into the housing . . .

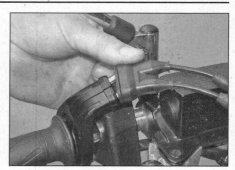

14.4a Pull the boot off the housing . . .

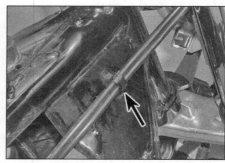

14.5 Free the cables from the guide (arrowed)

5 Remove the cables, freeing them from the guide on the right-hand side of the frame and noting their routing **(see illustration)**.

Installation

6 Route the cables from the handlebars to the throttle bodies, fitting them into the guide on the frame and making sure they are correctly routed **(see illustration 14.5)** – they must not interfere with any other component and should not be kinked or bent sharply. Apply some grease to the cable ends.

7 Fit the throttle closing cable (with the silver elbow) end into its socket in the twistgrip pulley, then fit the elbow into the lower half of the housing **(see illustrations)**. Turn the twistgrip forwards so that the cable routes around the underside of the pulley, seating in its channel, and locate the housing half under the pulley **(see illustration)**. Now fit the opening cable end into its socket

14.7e . . . and the pulley

14.7f Locate the housing . . .

14.7g . . . aligning the mating surfaces with the punch mark (arrowed) . . .

14.7h . . . and fit the screws

and the elbow into the housing. Locate the housing halves around the pulley and onto the handlebar, aligning the mating surfaces with the punch mark **(see illustrations)**. Fit and tighten the screws **(see illustration)**.
8 At the throttle body end fit the throttle closing cable (with the silver elbow) end into the rear socket in the throttle pulley, holding the pulley or the throttle butterflies in the open position, then fit the elbow into the rear of the bracket, leaving it loose at this stage **(see illustrations)**. Now fit the opening cable end into its socket and the elbow into the bracket **(see illustrations)**.
9 Install the throttle bodies (see Section 11).
10 Adjust the cables as described in Chapter 1.
11 Install the fuel tank (see Section 2).
12 Start the engine and check that the idle

speed does not rise as the handlebars are turned. If it does, correct the problem before riding the motorcycle.

15 Fast idle system

1 The fast idle system is automatic in operation and pre-set at the factory. Fast idle speed is controlled by the ECM in conjunction with the secondary throttle valve servo according to data received from the engine oil temperature sensor. The servo opens the secondary throttle valves as required, and this causes a train of cams to open the main throttle valves. The fast idle speed should be

as specified at the beginning of the Chapter and should cancel automatically after a period determined by ambient and engine temperatures and lapsed time (30 seconds @ 20ºC and 5 mins @ -10ºC).
2 If the fast idle speed is incorrect (see Specifications) check the engine oil temperature (EOT) sensor and the throttle position (TP) sensor (see Section 10).

16 Exhaust system

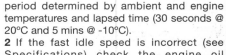 **Warning: If the engine has been running the exhaust system will be very hot. Allow the system to cool before carrying out any work.**
Note: *It is possible to remove the complete exhaust system as one – to do this, simply leave the silencers attached to the downpipe assembly. However it should be noted that the system is heavy and it is best to only do so if you have help from an assistant.*

Silencer(s)

Removal

1 Slacken the clamp bolt securing the silencer to the downpipe assembly **(see illustration)**.
2 Unscrew the nut from the bolt securing the silencer to the passenger footrest bracket, then support the silencer and withdraw the

14.8a Fit the closing cable end into its socket . . .

14.8b . . . and the elbow into the bracket . . .

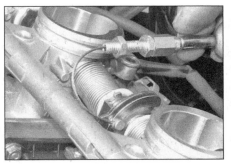

14.8c . . . then fit the opening cable end into its socket . . .

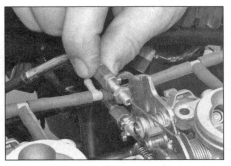

14.8d . . . and the elbow into the bracket

16.1 Slacken the silencer clamp bolt (arrowed)

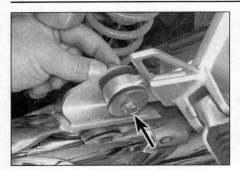

16.2 Unscrew the nut, withdraw the bolt (arrowed) and remove the silencer

16.10 Unscrew the downpipe flange bolts . . .

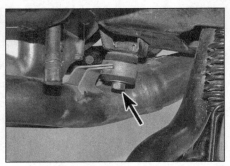

16.11 . . . and the mounting bolt (arrowed) on the underside

bolt with its washer (see illustration). Pull the silence back off the downpipe assembly.

3 Check the condition of the sealing ring and replace it with a new one if necessary – you will have to dig the old one out which will ruin it, and bear in mind that it is easy to damage a new one when fitting it.

4 Note the collar fitted in the rubber mounting bush in the footrest bracket. Replace the bush with a new one if it is damaged, deformed or deteriorated.

Installation

5 If removed fit the collar into the bush in the footrest bracket from the inner side.

6 Fit the silencer onto the downpipe assembly, taking care not to damage the sealing ring, then align the silencer mounting bracket with the footrest bracket and slide the bolt through from the outside. Fit the nut and tighten it and the clamp bolt to the torque settings specified at the beginning of the Chapter.

7 Run the engine and check that there are no exhaust gas leaks.

Downpipe assembly

Removal

8 Refer to Chapter 3 and displace the oil cooler forwards, resting it on the front brake hoses and mudguard, using plenty of rag to prevent scratches – there is no need to detach the oil hoses from either the engine or the cooler, but you do need to remove the guide bracket and disconnect the fan wiring connector.

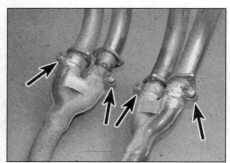

16.13 Separate the downpipes from the collector by slackening the clamp bolts (arrowed)

9 Remove the silencer(s) (Steps 1 to 4).

10 Unscrew the downpipe flange bolts, noting the washers (see illustration). Draw the flanges off the studs.

11 Unscrew the downpipe assembly mounting bolt, then detach the downpipes from the cylinder head and manoeuvre the assembly out from under the bike (see illustration).

12 Remove the gaskets from the cylinder head exhaust ports and discard them as new ones must be fitted on reassembly.

13 If required slacken the downpipe clamp bolts and remove the pipes from the collector piece, marking each one according to its location (see illustration). Check the condition of the sealing rings and replace them with new ones if necessary – you will have to dig the old ones out which will ruin them, and bear in mind that it is easy to damage the new ones when fitting them.

Installation

14 If detached fit the downpipes into the collector piece, using new sealing rings if necessary and making sure each pipe is returned to its original location (see illustration 16.13). Do not tighten the clamp bolts yet as the pipes will have to be aligned once the assembly is fitted.

15 Apply a smear of grease to the new exhaust port gaskets to keep them in place, then place the gaskets in the ports (see illustration).

16 Manoeuvre the downpipe assembly into position so that each pipe is located in its

16.15 Fit a new gasket into each exhaust port

port, then support the assembly and fit the mounting bolt, tightening it finger-tight (see illustration 16.11). Fit the flanges onto the studs, then fit the bolts with their washers and tighten them to the torque setting specified at the beginning of the Chapter (see illustration 16.10). Now tighten the mounting bolt to the specified torque, and if required the downpipe clamp bolts.

17 Install the silencer(s) (see Steps 5 and 6). Remount the oil cooler (see Chapter 3). Run the engine and check that there are no exhaust gas leaks.

---

17 PAIR (pulse air injection) system

General information

1 To reduce the amount of unburned hydrocarbons released in the exhaust gases, a pulse air injection (PAIR) system is fitted. The system consists of the control valve (mounted under the fuel tank), the reed valves (incorporated in the valve cover) and the hoses. The control valve is actuated by a vacuum sourced from the No. 3 throttle body.

2 Under normal operating conditions, the PAIR control valve allows filtered air to be drawn through it, the reed valves and cylinder head passages and into the exhaust ports. The air mixes with the exhaust gases, causing any unburned particles of fuel in the mixture to be burnt in the exhaust port/pipes. This process changes a considerable amount of hydrocarbons and carbon monoxide into relatively harmless carbon dioxide and water. When manifold depression increases, for example when the throttle is closed and the engine is on overrun, the vacuum produced closes the control valve and the air supply to the exhaust ports is cut off – this prevents exhaust popping. The reed valves are fitted to prevent the flow of exhaust gases back into the control valve and air filter housing.

3 The system is not adjustable and requires no maintenance, except to ensure that the hoses are in good condition and are securely connected at each end, and that there is no build-up of carbon fouling the reed valves.

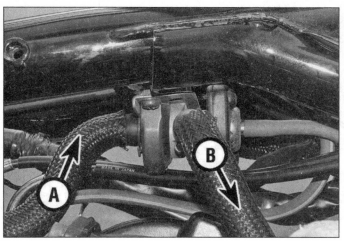

17.5 Air blown up hose (A) should flow out each side hose (B)

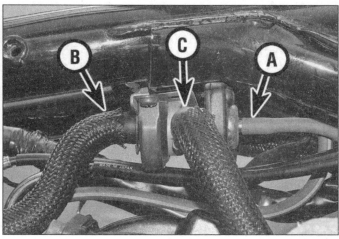

17.10a Vacuum hose (A), air filter housing hose (B), reed valve hose (C)

Replace any hoses that are cracked, split or generally deteriorated with new ones. The reed valves can be checked for any build-up of carbon by removing the reed valve housing covers on the valve cover (see Steps 12 and 13) – if any is found, clean up the valves and their housings.

Testing

Control valve

4 Disconnect the PAIR control valve air hose from the air filter housing and the vacuum hose from its union on the No. 3 throttle body **(see illustrations 11.3b and c)**.

5 Check the operation of the control valve by blowing through the air filter housing hose; air should flow freely through the valve and out of the reed valve hoses **(see illustration)**.

6 Now apply a vacuum of 280 to 390 mmHg to the vacuum hose and repeat the check; no air should now flow through the valve if it is functioning correctly.

Reed valves

7 Remove the fuel tank (see Section 2).

8 Disconnect each reed valve hose from the control valve (see illustration 17.10). Check the valve by blowing and sucking on the hose end. Air should flow through the hose only

when blown down it and not when sucked back up. If this is not the case the reed valve is faulty. Check the other valve in the same way.

Component renewal

Control valve

9 Remove the fuel tank (see Section 2).

10 Detach the vacuum hose and the air filter housing hose from the front and back of the valve **(see illustration)**. Detach the reed valve hoses from each side. Unscrew the two bolts on the top of the bracket to release the holder on the underside of the valve and remove the valve **(see illustration)**.

11 Installation is the reverse of removal. Make sure the hoses are securely connected at each end.

Reed valves

12 Remove the fuel tank (see Section 2).

13 Release the clamp and detach the hose from the reed valve housing cover **(see illustration)**. Unscrew the bolts and remove the cover **(see illustration)**. Remove the reed valve, noting which way around it is fitted **(see illustration)**.

14 Installation is the reverse of removal. Make sure the reed valves are clean and correctly fitted. Tighten the cover bolts to the torque setting specified at the beginning of the Chapter.

17.10b Unscrew the bolts (arrowed) and remove the valve

17.13a Release the clamp (arrowed) and detach the hose

17.13b Remove the cover . . .

17.13c . . . and remove the reed valve

18 Ignition system check

⚠ *Warning: The energy levels in electronic systems can be very high. On no account should the ignition be switched on whilst the plugs or plug caps are being held. Shocks from the HT circuit can be most unpleasant. Secondly, it is vital that the engine is not turned over or run with any of the plug*

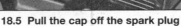

18.5 Pull the cap off the spark plug

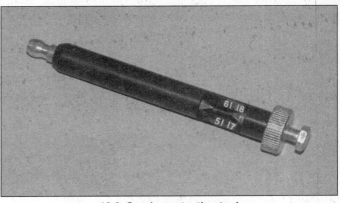

18.8 Spark gap testing tool

caps removed, and that the plugs are soundly earthed (grounded) when the system is checked for sparking. The system components can be seriously damaged if the HT circuit becomes isolated.

1 As no means of adjustment is available, any failure of the system can be traced to failure of a system component or a simple wiring fault. Of the two possibilities, the latter is by far the most likely. In the event of failure, check the system in a logical fashion, as described below.

2 Remove the fuel tank (see Section 2). Referring to Section 10, trace the wiring from the cam position (CMP), crankshaft position (CKP), throttle position (TP), engine oil temperature (EOT) and gear position (GP) sensors to their respective wiring connectors and then to the ECM. Ensure that the connector terminals are clean and that the connectors are secure. Also refer to Chapter 8 and check the sidestand switch and relay circuit.

3 Check the battery condition and the ignition circuit fuse (see Chapter 8).

4 Refer to Section 20 and disconnect the ECM multi-pin wiring connector(s), then turn the ignition ON. Connect the probes of a voltmeter between the orange/white (orange/green on K4 models onward) and the black/white wire terminals on the loom side of the wiring connector and check for battery input voltage (12V approx). Turn the ignition OFF. If the input voltage is not as specified, check the ignition switch, side stand relay and engine stop switch, and the wiring and connectors between them (see Chapter 8).

5 Starting with the No. 1 cylinder, pull the spark plug cap off the spark plug (see illustration).

6 Connect the cap to a known good spark plug and hold the plug threads against the ignition coil bracket so the plug is earthed. If necessary, hold the spark plug with an insulated tool.

⚠ **Warning: Do not remove any of the spark plugs from the engine to perform this check – atomised fuel being pumped out of the open spark plug hole could ignite, causing severe injury!**

7 Having observed the above precautions, check that the engine stop switch is in the RUN position and the transmission is in neutral, then turn the ignition switch ON, pull the clutch lever in and turn the engine over on the starter motor. If the system is in good condition a regular, fat blue spark should be evident at the plug electrodes. If the spark appears thin or yellowish, or is non-existent, further investigation will be necessary. Repeat the check for the other cylinders.

8 The ignition system must be able to produce a spark at each plug which is capable of jumping a particular size gap. Suzuki specify that a healthy system should produce a spark capable of jumping 8 mm. Use a commercially available adjustable ignition spark gap test tool to check the strength of the spark (see illustration).

9 Set the gap on the tool at the 8 mm mark. Connect one of the caps to the protruding electrode on the test tool, and hold the tool against the ignition coil bracket so it is earthed. Check that the engine stop switch is in the RUN position, turn the ignition switch ON, pull the clutch lever in and turn the engine over on the starter motor. If the system is in good condition a regular, fat blue spark should be seen to jump the gap between the test tool electrodes. Repeat the test on the other caps. Before proceeding further, turn the ignition OFF and disconnect the test equipment.

10 Ignition faults can be divided into two categories, namely those where the ignition system has failed completely, and those which are due to a partial failure. The likely faults are listed below, starting with the most probable source of failure. Work through the list systematically, referring to the relevant sections for details of the necessary checks and tests. Note that if cylinders 1 and 4 have no spark the fault can be isolated to the left-hand HT coil or its wiring circuit, and if 2 and 3 have no spark concentrate on the right-hand HT coil. If cylinder 1 has no spark but 4 does, then the fault is in the HT lead or plug cap for that plug, or the plug itself, and vice versa, and likewise for plugs 2 and 3.

● Loose, corroded or damaged wiring connections, broken or shorted wiring

between any of the component parts of the ignition system (see Chapter 8).
● Faulty spark plug, dirty or damaged plug electrodes, incorrect gap between electrodes, incorrect spark plug (see Chapter 1).
● Faulty ignition HT coil, HT lead or plug cap (see Section 19).
● Faulty ignition switch or engine stop switch (see Chapter 8).
● Faulty clutch, neutral or sidestand switch (see Chapter 8).
● Faulty crankshaft position sensor or damaged rotor (see Section 10).
● Faulty engine control module (see Section 20).

11 If the above checks don't reveal the cause of the problem, have the ignition system tested by a Suzuki dealer.

19 Ignition HT coils

Removal

1 Disconnect the battery negative (-) lead (see Chapter 8). Remove the fuel tank (see Section 2). The left-hand coil is for cylinders 1 and 4, and the right-hand is for cylinders 2 and 3. Each coil bracket is marked L or R accordingly (see illustration) – if you separate the coil from its bracket mark it as well as they are different.

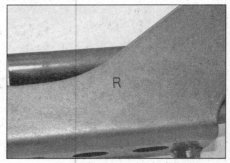

19.1 Each bracket is marked according to its side

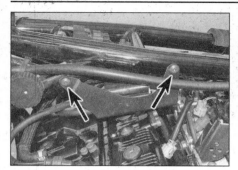

19.3a Undo the screws (arrowed) . . .

19.3b . . . then disconnect the wiring connector and remove the coil

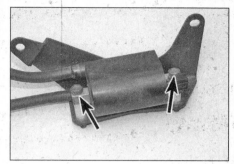

19.3c HT coil mounting bolts (arrowed)

2 Pull the spark plug caps off the spark plugs **(see illustration 18.5)**.

3 Undo the coil bracket screws and displace the coil assembly, then disconnect the primary wiring connector and remove the coil **(see illustrations)**. If required separate the coil from its bracket by unscrewing the bolts, noting the collars **(see illustration)**.

Check

4 Ensure the primary circuit terminals on the coil and the spark plug terminal inside the cap are undamaged and free from corrosion.

5 Using an ohmmeter or multimeter set to the ohms scale, measure the coil primary resistance between the primary circuit terminals **(see illustration)**. Compare the result with the specifications at the beginning of this Chapter.

6 Now set the meter to the K-ohms scale and measure the coil secondary resistance by inserting one meter probe into each spark plug cap – make sure they are long enough to reach the plug terminal, and use extensions if necessary **(see illustration)**. Compare the result with the specifications at the beginning of this Chapter.

7 If the secondary resistance reading is not

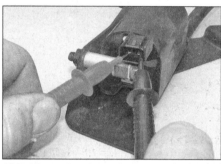

19.5 Measuring the coil primary resistance

as specified, unscrew the plug caps from the HT leads and measure the resistance of each cap by inserting a probe into each end **(see illustrations)**. If the result is not as specified fit a new cap or caps as required. With the caps removed, check the secondary resistance of the coil again by inserting a probe into each HT lead end, then subtract the resistance of the two plug caps from the secondary resistance specified and see if your result matches this.

8 If the results are not as specified the coil is probably faulty. Have the coil peak voltage tested by a Suzuki dealer to confirm this.

19.6 Measuring the coil secondary resistance

Installation

9 If separated fit each coil onto its bracket, not forgetting the collars, and tighten the bolts – the coil for cylinders 1 and 4 fits onto the bracket marked L. Make sure the HT leads and primary wiring socket and correctly positioned in relation to the bracket as shown **(see illustration 19.3c)**.

10 Connect the primary wiring connector, then fit the coil bracket and tighten the screws **(see illustrations 19.3b and a)**. Fit the caps onto the spark plugs **(see illustration 18.5)**.

11 Install the fuel tank (Section 2) and connect the battery negative (-) lead (Chapter 8).

19.7a Unscrew the cap from the lead . . .

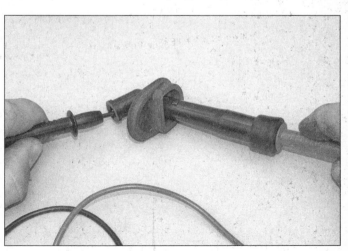

19.7b . . . and check the cap

20.2 Remove the seat and the storage tray

20.3a Lift the ECM out . . .

20.3b . . . then disconnect the wiring connectors

20 Engine control module (ECM)

1 If the testing procedures described in this Chapter indicate that all ignition and fuel injection system components are functioning correctly, yet a fault exists, take the machine to a Suzuki dealer for testing. No details are available for checking the ECM on home workshop equipment.
2 To access the ECM, remove the seat (see Chapter 7), then unclip and remove the storage tray **(see illustration)**. Disconnect the battery negative (-) lead (see Chapter 8).
3 The ECM is located behind the battery. Lift the ECM out then disconnect the wiring connector(s) **(see illustrations)**.
4 Installation is the reverse of removal. Make sure the wiring connector(s) is/are clean and secure.

21 Immobiliser

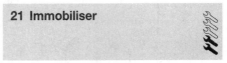

Note: *The immobiliser is fitted to K5 models onward.*
1 The immobiliser verifies the authenticity of the key being used by matching its code with that of the ECM, and will not allow the bike to start if the match is not made.
2 When the ignition switch is turned ON using the key and the engine stop switch is set to the RUN position, a transponder in the key communicates with the immobiliser antennae around the ignition switch, and that in turn communicates with the ECM. The immobiliser light on the receiver around the ignition switch will flash a few times, the number of flashes corresponding to the number of keys registered to the system. If the match is made the immobiliser light comes on for two seconds. If there is a non-match or a problem the light flashes rapidly. If this happens, turn the ignition OFF them ON again as it is possible for radio interference to affect the communication process. Note that on occasion in winter when battery performance is low the system may delay its immobiliser light flashing sequence until after the bike has been started.
3 No further information is provided for the system. If there is a problem with a key, all keys are lost or the bike will not start and all other possible causes have been eliminated, take the bike to a Suzuki dealer. Refer to Chapter 8 for details on the ignition switch should you need to fit a new receiver.

Chapter 5
Frame and suspension

Contents

Degrees of difficulty

Easy, suitable for novice with little experience	**Fairly easy,** suitable for beginner with some experience	**Fairly difficult,** suitable for competent DIY mechanic	**Difficult,** suitable for experienced DIY mechanic	**Very difficult,** suitable for expert DIY or professional

Specifications

Frame and cycle parts

Gearchange lever height	30 to 40 mm
Rear brake pedal height	35 to 45 mm

Front forks

Fork oil type	Suzuki L01 fork oil or equivalent
Fork oil capacity	644 cc
Fork oil level*	108 mm
Fork spring minimum free length	322.6 mm

Oil level is measured from the top of the tube with the fork spring removed and the leg fully compressed.

Rear suspension

Swingarm pivot bolt runout (max)	0.3 mm

Torque settings

Brake hose banjo bolt	23 Nm
Brake torque arm-to-swingarm bolt nut	28 Nm
Clutch master cylinder clamp bolts	10 Nm
Fork clamp bolts (top and bottom yoke)	23 Nm
Fork damper cartridge bolt	40 Nm
Fork top bolt	23 Nm
Front axle clamp bolts	23 Nm
Front brake master cylinder clamp bolts	10 Nm
Handlebar clamp bolts	23 Nm
Handlebar holder nuts	45 Nm
Rear shock absorbers	
Upper bolt	23 Nm
Lower bolt nut	34 Nm
Sidestand pivot bolt	50 Nm
Sidestand pivot bolt nut	40 Nm
Steering head bearing adjuster nut initial setting (see text)	45 Nm
Steering stem nut	65 Nm
Swingarm pivot bolt nut	120 Nm

1 General information

All models have a tubular steel cradle frame with a removable right-hand cradle section for engine removal.

All models are fitted with coil-sprung and hydraulically-damped telescopic forks that are adjustable for spring pre-load, rebound and compression damping.

At the rear, an alloy swingarm acts on twin shock absorbers. The shock absorbers are adjustable for spring pre-load, rebound and compression damping.

2 Frame

1 The frame should not require attention unless accident damage has occurred. In most cases, fitting a new frame is the only satisfactory remedy for such damage. A few frame specialists have the jigs and other equipment necessary for straightening frames to the required standard of accuracy, but even then

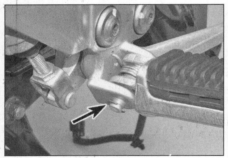

3.1 Remove the E-clip (arrowed) and withdraw the pivot pin. Note the position of the return spring ends

there is no simple way of assessing to what extent the frame may have been over stressed.
2 After a high mileage, the frame should be examined closely for signs of cracking or splitting at the welded joints. Loose engine mounting bolts can cause ovaling or fracturing of the mounting points. Minor damage can often be repaired by specialised welding, depending on the extent and nature of the damage.
3 Remember that a frame that is out of alignment will cause handling problems. If, as the result of an accident, misalignment is suspected, it will be necessary to strip the machine completely so the frame can be thoroughly checked.

3 Footrests, brake pedal and gearchange lever

Rider's footrests

Removal

1 Remove the E-clip from the bottom of the footrest pivot pin, then withdraw the pivot pin and remove the footrest, noting the fitting of the return spring and spacer **(see illustration)**.

3.2 Undo the screws (arrowed) to remove the rubber

Discard the E-clip if it is damaged and fit a new one on reassembly.
2 If required the rubber can be removed by undoing the two screws on the underside of the bar **(see illustration)** – the rubber is available separately.

Installation

3 Installation is the reverse of removal, noting the following:
● Make sure the spring ends are correctly positioned.
● Apply a small amount of grease to the pivot pin.
● Ensure the E-clip is properly located in the groove in the pivot pin.

Passenger footrests

Removal

4 Remove the E-clip from the bottom of the footrest pivot pin, then withdraw the pivot pin and remove the footrest, the detent plate, ball and spring – note how they fit and make sure the ball and spring do not ping away **(see illustration)**. Discard the E-clip if it is damaged and fit a new one on reassembly.
5 If required the rubber can be removed by undoing the two screws on the underside of the bar, noting the plate that fits between them **(see illustration)** – the rubber is available separately.

Installation

6 Installation is the reverse of removal, noting the following:
● Make sure the detent plate, ball and spring are correctly positioned.
● Apply a small amount of grease to the pivot pin.
● Ensure the E-clip is properly located in the groove in the pivot pin.

Brake pedal

Removal

7 Unhook the brake pedal return spring and brake light switch spring from the lug on the

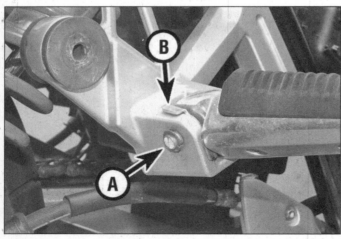

3.4 Remove the E-clip (A) and withdraw the pivot pin. Note the position of the detent plate, ball and spring (B)

3.5 Undo the screws (arrowed) to remove the rubber

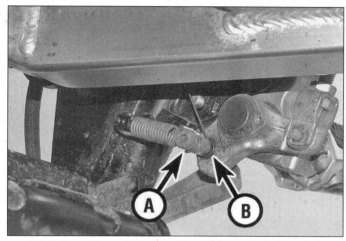

3.7 Unhook the pedal spring (A) and the brake light switch spring (B)

3.8 Remove the split pin and washer (A) then withdraw the clevis pin (B)

inside of the brake pedal, noting which fits where (see illustration).

8 Remove the split pin and washer from the clevis pin securing the brake pedal to the master cylinder pushrod (see illustration). Remove the clevis pin and separate the pedal from the pushrod.

9 Release the circlip and remove the washer, then slide the pedal off its pivot (see illustration).

Installation

10 Installation is the reverse of removal, noting the following:

3.9 Remove the circlip (arrowed) and washer

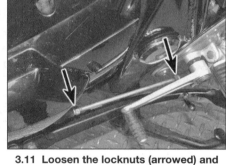

3.11 Loosen the locknuts (arrowed) and unscrew the rod

3.12 Remove the circlip (arrowed) and washer

● Apply grease to the brake pedal pivot and to the spring lugs.
● Use a new circlip to secure the pedal if the old one deformed on removal, and make sure it locates correctly in its groove (see illustration 3.9).
● Use a new split pin on the clevis pin securing the brake pedal to the master cylinder pushrod and bend the split pin ends round.
● Fit the brake light switch spring into the groove next to the pedal and the return spring into the groove near the end of the lug (see illustration 3.7).

● Check the operation of the rear brake light switch (see Chapter 1).
● Check the brake pedal height and adjust it if necessary (see Chapter 1, Section 10).

Gearchange lever

Removal

11 Loosen the gearchange linkage rod locknuts, then unscrew the rod and separate it from the lever and the gearchange arm (the rod is reverse-threaded on one end and so will simultaneously unscrew from both lever and arm) (see illustration). Note the how far the rod is threaded into the lever and arm as this determines the height of the lever relative to the footrest.

12 Release the circlip and remove the washer, then slide the pedal off its pivot (see illustration).

13 If required make an alignment mark between the slit in the gearchange linkage arm clamp and the end of the gearchange shaft, then unscrew the pinch bolt and slide the arm off the shaft (see illustration).

Installation

14 Installation is the reverse of removal, noting the following:
● If removed align the gearchange linkage arm with the shaft as noted on removal (see illustration 3.13).
● Apply grease to the gearchange lever pivot.
● Use a new circlip to secure the lever if the old one deformed on removal, and make sure it locates correctly in its groove (see illustration 3.12).
● Adjust the gearchange lever height (the distance of the gearchange lever tip below the top surface of the rider's footrest) as specified at the beginning of the chapter, or as preferred, by screwing the rod in or out of the lever and arm, then tighten the locknuts securely.

3.13 Unscrew the bolt (arrowed) and slide the arm off the shaft

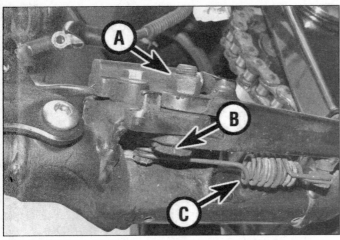

4.2 Undo the nut (A) then unscrew the pivot bolt (B) and release the springs (C)

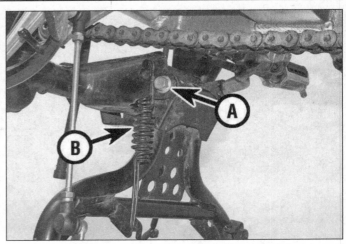

4.7 Centrestand pivot bolt (A) and springs (B)

4 Sidestand and centrestand

Sidestand

Removal

1 The sidestand pivots on a lug on the frame. Springs between the frame and the stand ensure the stand is held in the retracted or extended position.

2 Support the bike on its centrestand. Undo the pivot bolt nut, then undo the pivot bolt and remove the stand, releasing the springs as you do **(see illustration)**.

Installation

3 Apply grease to the pivot bolt shank, the contact surfaces of the stand and its lug, and the spring lugs. Locate the stand on its bracket, hooking up the springs as you do **(see illustration 4.2)**. Install the bolt and tighten it to the specified torque setting, then fit the nut and tighten it to the specified torque.

4 Check that the stand springs are correctly located and hold the stand securely up when not in use – an accident is almost certain to occur if the stand extends while the machine is in motion.

5 Check the operation of the sidestand switch (see Chapter 1).

Centrestand

Removal

6 The centrestand pivots on a bolt and spacer between two lugs on a bracket on the underside of the frame. Springs between the bracket and the stand ensure that it is held in the retracted or extended position.

7 Support the bike on its sidestand. Remove the spring clip from the end of the pivot bolt. Undo the pivot bolt nut, then withdraw the pivot bolt and remove the stand, releasing the

springs as you do **(see illustration)**. Note the spacer for the pivot bolt.

Installation

8 Apply grease to the pivot bolt and spacer and to the inner side of each mounting lug. Fit the spacer then locate the stand between the lugs, hooking up the springs as you do **(see illustration 4.7)**. Install the bolt then fit the nut and tighten it. Fit the spring clip through the hole in the end of the pivot bolt.

9 Check that the stand springs are correctly located and hold the stand securely up when not in use – an accident could occur if the stand extends while the machine is in motion.

5 Handlebar and levers

Handlebar removal

Note: *The handlebar can be displaced from the top yoke for access to the steering stem nut without displacing or removing the master cylinders or switch housings, though it is best to remove the mirrors – follow Steps 1 and 2 and 8 and 9 as required.*

1 To avoid the possibility of damaging the fuel tank should anything not go quite according

5.4 Handlebar end-weight screw (arrowed)

to plan, remove the fuel tank (see Chapter 4), or at least cover it in plenty of rag.

2 Remove the mirrors (see Chapter 7).

3 Release the throttle cables from the twistgrip pulley (see Chapter 4).

4 On K2 models slightly loosen each handlebar end-weight screw until the weight assembly can be withdrawn from the handlebar. On all other models undo each handlebar end-weight screw and remove the weight **(see illustration)**. On all models pull the throttle twistgrip off the right-hand end and remove the grip from the left-hand end. **Note:** *The grip will probably be stuck in place – it may be necessary to slit it with a sharp knife in order to remove it.*

5 Displace the handlebar switch housings (see Chapter 8) – there is no need to disconnect the wiring connectors.

6 Displace the front brake and clutch master cylinders and position them clear of the handlebar (see Chapter 6 and Chapter 2 respectively). Ensure no strain is placed on the hydraulic hoses and try to keep the reservoirs upright to prevent air entering the system.

7 If you are removing the handlebar holders from the yoke slacken the nuts on the underside slightly now.

8 Remove the blanking caps from the handlebar clamp bolts **(see illustration)**.

5.8a Remove the blanking caps . . .

5.8b . . . then unscrew the bolts (arrowed) . . .

5.8c . . . and lift the handlebars off the holders

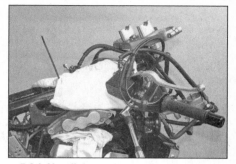

5.8d Handlebars shown displaced and resting behind the steering head

5.9a Unscrew the nut (arrowed) securing each holder

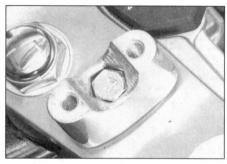

5.9b Note how the bolt head locates

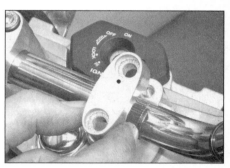

5.10a Make sure the punch mark on each holder is at the front . . .

Unscrew the bolts and remove the washers and clamps, then displace or remove the handlebars **(see illustration)** – if they are only being displaced rest them either in front of or behind the top yoke, on plenty of rag **(see illustration)**.

9 If required unscrew the handlebar holder nuts on the underside of the top yoke and remove the holders, noting the washer and rubber seat between each one and the yoke. Remove the bolts from the holders if required, noting how they locate **(see illustrations)**.

Handlebar installation

10 Installation is the reverse of removal, noting the following:

● If removed make sure the holder bolt heads are correctly located in the holders **(see illustration 5.9b)**. Fit the rubber seat and washers between each holder and the yoke. Only finger-tighten the holder bolt nuts at this stage to allow the handlebars to properly align the holders.

● Fit the handlebar clamps with the punch mark at the front **(see illustration)**. Align the bars so they are central in the clamps and with the punch mark on the front aligned with the left-hand holder/clamp mating surfaces **(see illustration)**. Fit the bolts with their washers, then tighten the front bolt first, then the rear, to the torque setting specified at the beginning of the Chapter

(see illustration). If necessary now tighten the handlebar holder nuts to the specified torque setting **(see illustration 5.9a)**.

● Refer to Chapters 6 and 2 for installation of the front brake and clutch master cylinders.

● Refer to Chapter 8 for installation of the switch housings.

● Refer to Chapter 4 for installation of the throttle cables.

● If new grips are being fitted, secure them using a suitable adhesive.

● Check the operation of the front brake light switch and clutch switch before riding the motorcycle.

5.10b . . . and align the clamp mating surfaces with the punch mark on the handlebar

5.10c Fit the bolts with their washers and tighten the front ones first

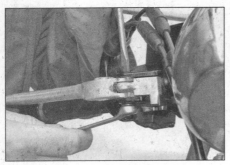

5.11a Unscrew the locknut . . .

5.11b . . . then unscrew the pivot bolt . . .

5.11c . . . and remove the lever

Brake and clutch levers

11 Unscrew the lever pivot bolt locknut on the underside of the lever, then unscrew the pivot bolt and remove the lever (see illustrations).
12 Installation is the reverse of removal. Apply grease to the pivot bolt shaft and the contact areas between the lever and its bracket, and apply silicone grease to the contact tip with the master cylinder pushrod. Counter-hold the pivot bolt when tightening the locknut (see illustration 5.11a). Check the setting of the lever span adjusters (see Chapter 1).

6 Fork removal and installation

Removal

1 Remove the front wheel (see Chapter 6) and the mudguard (see Chapter 7).
2 Work on each fork leg individually. Note the routing of the cables, hoses and wiring around the forks. If both fork legs are being removed, note which side they fit and mark them accordingly.
3 Loosen but do not remove the fork clamp bolt in the top yoke (see illustration).
4 If the fork oil is being changed, or if the forks are to be overhauled, loosen the fork top bolt while the leg is still clamped in the bottom yoke (see illustration 6.3).
5 Support the fork leg, then loosen but do not remove the clamp bolts in the bottom yoke (see illustration). Remove the fork by twisting it and pulling it downwards (see illustration).

Note how it passes through the headlight assembly holder.

> **HAYNES HiNT**
> *If the fork legs are seized in the yokes, spray the area with penetrating oil and allow time for it to soak in before trying again.*

Installation

6 Remove all traces of corrosion from the fork tubes and the yokes. Slide the fork leg up through the bottom yoke and headlight holder and into the top yoke, making sure the cables hoses and wiring are correctly routed round the fork (see illustration). Set the fork so the top of the inner tube (where the top bolt seats) is flush with the upper surface of the top yoke (see illustration).
7 Tighten the clamp bolts in the bottom yoke

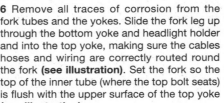

6.3 Loosen the fork clamp bolt (A) in the top yoke. Fork top bolt (B)

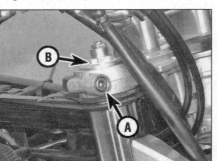

6.5b . . . and remove the fork

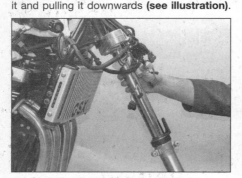

to the torque setting specified at the beginning of the Chapter (see illustration 6.5a). If the fork has been overhauled or if the fork oil has been changed, tighten the fork top bolt to the specified torque setting. Tighten the fork clamp bolt in the top yoke to the specified torque setting (see illustration 6.3).
8 Install the front mudguard (Chapter 7) and wheel (Chapter 6).
9 Make sure the forks are adjusted as required and both set the same (see Section 12), and check the operation of the forks and brakes, before taking the machine on the road.

7 Fork oil change

1 After a high mileage the fork oil will deteriorate and its damping and lubrication

6.5a Loosen the fork clamp bolts (arrowed) in the bottom yoke . . .

6.6a Do not forget to pass the fork through the headlight holder, and make sure everything is correctly routed

6.6b Set the fork in the top yoke with the top bolt rim protruding as shown

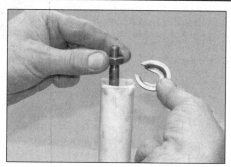

7.5a Remove the slotted washer . . .

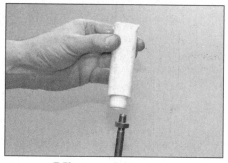

7.5b . . . and the spacer

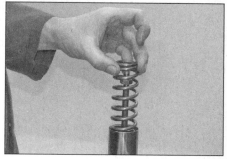

7.5c Withdraw the spring from the fork

qualities will be impaired. Always change the oil in both forks. Work on one fork at a time.

2 Remove the fork – make sure the top bolt is loosened while the leg is still clamped in the bottom yoke (see Section 6).

3 Support the fork upright and unscrew the top bolt from the top of the inner tube **(see illustrations 7.14b and a)**. Slide the inner tube down into the outer tube.

4 Using two spanners, one counter-holding the locknut at the base of the top bolt and one on the pre-load adjuster hex, unscrew the top bolt assembly and thread it off the damper rod **(see illustrations 7.13b and a)**. Draw the damping adjuster rod out of the damper rod **(see illustration 7.12)**.

5 On K2, K3 and K4 models remove the upper washer, the spacer and the lower washer **(see illustration 8.2)**. On K5 models onward remove the slotted washer and the spacer. On

all models withdraw the spring, noting which way up it fits **(see illustrations)**.

6 Invert the fork leg over a suitable container and pump the fork and damper rod to expel as much oil as possible **(see illustration)**.

7 Support the leg and allow it to drain for several minutes. Wipe any excess oil off the spring and spacer. If the fork oil contains metal particles inspect the fork components for signs of wear (see Section 8).

8 Slowly pour in the correct quantity and type of fork oil as specified at the beginning of this Chapter **(see illustration)**. Draw the damper rod out of the fork using long-nosed pliers and pump the rod several times to expel air from the damper cartridge. Secure the fork leg upright and allow it to stand for several minutes to allow all the air to escape. Now pump the rod several times again –once all the air is expelled you should feel stiff resistance

when pumping the rod. Take great care to ensure that all air is expelled from the damper cartridge at this stage.

9 Fully compress the inner tube and damper rod into the outer tube and measure the oil level from the top of the inner tube **(see illustration)**. Add or subtract oil until it is at the level specified at the beginning of this Chapter.

10 Draw the damper rod out of the fork using long-nosed pliers and hold it up. Install the spring with its narrower end downwards **(see illustration)** – on the K5 model photographed both ends of the spring were tapered. On K2, K3 and K4 models fit the lower washer, the spacer and the upper washer **(see illustration 8.2)**. On K5 models onward fit the spacer, then slide the slotted washer, dished side down, under the locknut and into the top of the spacer **(see illustrations)**.

7.6 Drain all the old oil from the fork

7.8 Pour the oil into the top of the tube

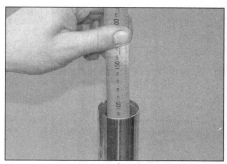

7.9 Measure the oil level with the fork held vertical

7.10a Fit the spring into the fork

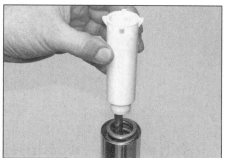

7.10b Make sure the narrow end of the spacer locates in the top of the spring . . .

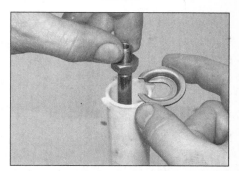

7.10c . . . and fit the washer with the dished side down into the top of the spacer

7.11 Make sure the locknut is correctly positioned

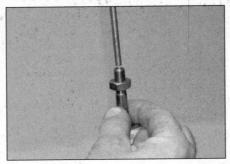

7.12 Slide the adjuster rod into the damper rod

14 Pull the inner tube up and carefully thread the top bolt into it, making sure it does not cross-thread, and tighten as far as possible holding the inner tube by hand **(see illustrations)** – it can be tightened to the specified torque setting after the fork leg has been installed and is securely clamped in the bottom yoke (see Section 6).
15 Install the fork (see Section 6).

8 Fork overhaul

Disassembly

1 Remove the fork – make sure the top bolt is loosened while the leg is still clamped in the bottom yoke (see Section 6).
2 Always dismantle the fork legs separately to avoid interchanging parts. Store all

11 Check the position of the locknut on the damper rod – its upper surface should be 11 mm below the top of the rod **(see illustration)**.
12 Slide the damping adjuster rod into the damper rod **(see illustration)**.
13 Make sure the top bolt O-ring is in good condition. Thread the top bolt assembly onto the damper rod and screw it all the way down onto the locknut **(see illustration)**. Counter-hold the locknut using one spanner and tighten the top bolt securely against it using another spanner on the pre-load adjuster hex **(see illustration)**.

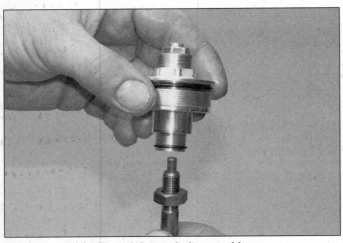

7.13a Thread the top bolt assembly on . . .

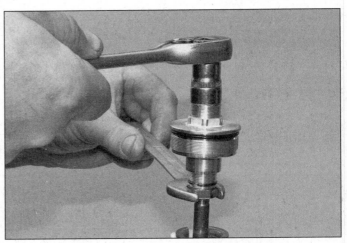

7.13b . . . and tighten it against the locknut

7.14a Thread the top bolt into the inner tube . . .

7.14b . . . and tighten as much as possible

components in separate, clearly marked containers (see illustration).

3 Remove the axle clamp bolts from the bottom of the right-hand fork (see illustration). Unscrew and remove the axle clamp bolts from the bottom of the left-hand fork and remove the axle nut (see illustration).

Remove the inner tube protector from the top of the outer tube, noting how it aligns and locates (see illustration).

4 Lay the fork flat with the caliper lugs to the left and loosen the damper cartridge bolt (see illustration). Do not loosen it too much as oil will come out, and lightly tighten it after

loosening it to prevent leakage. If the bolt does not loosen (i.e. the damper cartridge turns with it inside the fork), use an air wrench if available, or if not carry on and use a holding tool as described in Step 6.

5 Refer to Section 7, Steps 3 to 6, and drain the fork oil.

8.3a When working on the right-hand fork remove the axle clamp bolts

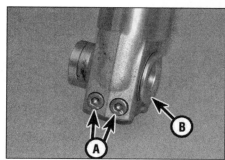

8.3b When working on the left-hand fork remove the axle clamp bolts (A) and the axle nut (B)

8.3c Remove the fork protector

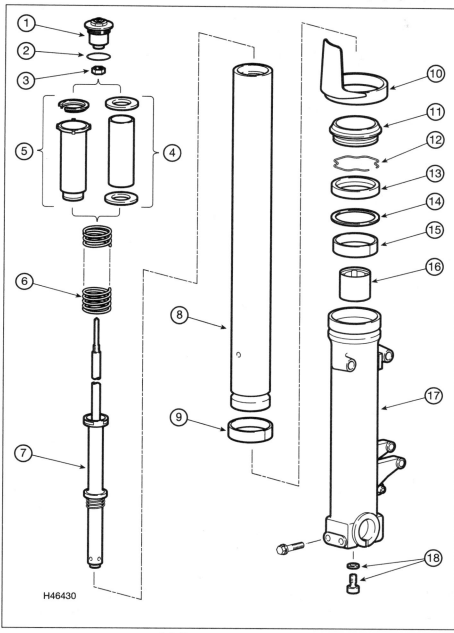

H46430

8.2 Front fork components

1 Top bolt
2 O-ring
3 Locknut
4 Upper washer, spacer and lower washer – K2, K3 and K4
5 Slotted washer and spacer – K5 onwards
6 Spring
7 Damper cartridge
8 Inner tube
9 Bottom bush
10 Inner tube protector
11 Dust seal
12 Retaining clip
13 Oil seal
14 Washer
15 Top bush
16 Damper cartridge seat
17 Outer tube
18 Damper cartridge bolt and washer

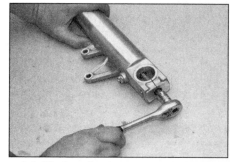

8.4 Slacken the damper cartridge bolt

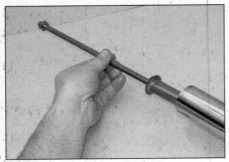

8.7 Withdraw the damper cartridge

8.8 Ease the dust seal out . . .

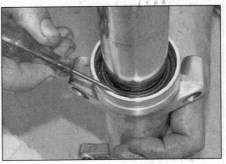

8.9 . . . then remove the retaining ring

6 Remove the previously loosened damper cartridge bolt and its sealing washer from the bottom of the outer tube **(see illustration 8.22a)**. Discard the washer as a new one must be fitted on reassembly. If the damper cartridge bolt was impossible to slacken in Step 4, note that a Suzuki service tool (Pt. No. 09940-30250) is available to hold the damper cartridge in place while the bolt is unscrewed – the tool passes down the inner tube, over the damper rod and engages the top of the cartridge body.

7 Withdraw the damper cartridge from inside the fork **(see illustration)**.

8 Carefully prise the dust seal from the top of the outer tube to gain access to the oil seal retaining clip **(see illustration)**. Discard the dust seal as a new one must be fitted on reassembly.

9 Carefully remove the retaining ring, taking care not to scratch the surface of the inner tube **(see illustration)**.

10 Grasp the inner tube in one hand and the outer tube in the other, then quickly and repeatedly draw the inner tube out until the oil seal and top bush are displaced from the top of the outer tube by the bottom bush on the bottom of the inner tube **(see illustrations)**. Draw the oil seal, washer and top bush off the inner tube. Discard the oil seal as a new one must be fitted on reassembly.

11 Do not remove the bottom bush unless it is to be replaced with a new one. To remove it spread its ends using a screwdriver to dislodge it from its seat and slide it off **(see illustration)**.

12 Tip the damper cartridge seat out of the outer tube, noting the spring fitted inside it **(see illustration)**.

Inspection

13 Clean all parts in a suitable solvent and blow them dry with compressed air, if available. Check the outer surface of the inner tube for score marks, scratches, flaking of the finish and excessive or abnormal wear, and for dents. Similarly check the inner surface of the outer tube. Replace the tubes with new ones if necessary.

14 Check the inner tube runout using V-blocks and a dial gauge. If the condition of the tube is suspect have it checked by a Suzuki dealer or suspension specialist. Suzuki provides no specifications for runout, but 0.2 mm is considered the limit.

⚠️ *Warning: If the inner tube is bent or exceeds the runout limit, it should not be straightened; renew it.*

15 Inspect the inner surface of the top bush and the outer surface of the bottom bush for score marks, scratches, and signs of excessive wear, in which case the grey Teflon outer coating will have worn away to expose the copper inner surface **(see illustration and 8.11)**. Replace the bushes with new ones if necessary, or if in doubt as to their condition.

16 Check the fork oil seal seat for nicks, gouges and scratches. If damage is evident, leaks will occur. Also check the oil seal washer for damage or distortion and replace it with a new one if necessary.

17 Check the spring for cracks and other damage. Measure the spring free length and compare the measurement to the specifications at the beginning of this Chapter

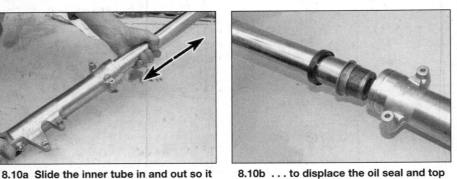

8.10a Slide the inner tube in and out so it acts as a slide-hammer . . .

8.10b . . . to displace the oil seal and top bush

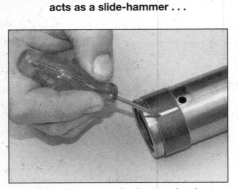

8.11 Removing the bottom bush

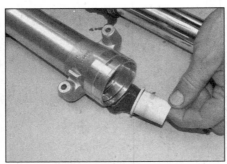

8.12 Tip the damper cartridge seat out

8.15 Check the working surface (arrowed) of each bush – top bush shown

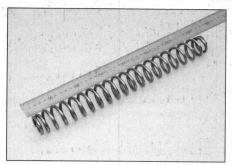

8.17 Measure the free length of the spring

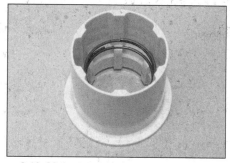

8.19 Make sure the bottom coil of the spring is clipped in place

8.20a Slide the cartridge into the inner tube . . .

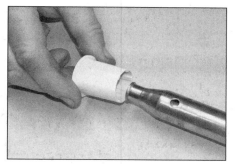

8.20b . . . then fit the seat onto the bottom . . .

8.20c . . . and push both up into the bottom of the tube

8.21 Fit the inner tube into the outer tube

(see illustration). If the spring is defective or has sagged below the service limit, fit new springs in both forks. Never replace only one spring.

18 Check the damper cartridge assembly for damage and wear. Hold the cartridge and gently pump the rod in and out. If the rod does not move smoothly the assembly must be replaced with a new one.

Reassembly

19 Make sure the spring is correctly located in the damper cartridge seat – the bottom coil locates in clips (see illustration). Make sure

the bottom bush is correctly located in its recess in the bottom of the inner tube (see illustration 8.11).

20 Insert the damper cartridge into the inner tube so its bottom end protrudes from the bottom of the tube (see illustration). Fit the damper cartridge seat onto the bottom of the cartridge, then push them up into the bottom of the tube (see illustrations).

21 Lubricate the bottom bush and the inner surface of the outer tube with the specified fork oil. Slide the inner tube into the outer tube and seat it at the bottom (see illustration).

22 Fit a new sealing washer onto the damper

cartridge bolt and apply a few drops of a suitable non-permanent thread locking compound (see illustration). Fit the bolt into the bottom of the outer tube and thread it into the bottom of the damper cartridge and tighten it to the torque setting specified at the beginning of this Chapter (see illustration). **Note:** *If the damper cartridge rotates inside the tube, the Suzuki service tool described in Step 6 can be used to hold the head of the cartridge body, or a suitable tool that will achieve the same result can be fabricated from a piece of tubing.*

23 Lubricate the inner and outer surfaces of

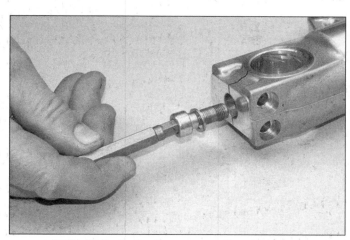

8.22a Fit the bolt using a new sealing washer . . .

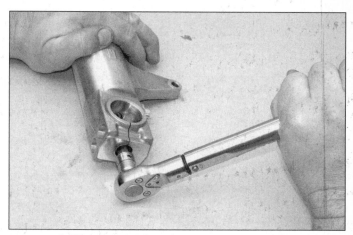

8.22b . . . and tighten it to the specified torque

8.23a Fit the top bush into the top of the outer tube . . .

8.23b . . . then slide the washer on top of it . . .

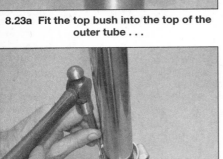

8.23c . . . and drive the bush into place . . .

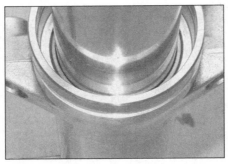

8.23d . . . until it has seated

the top bush with the specified fork oil. Slide the bush down the inner tube and press it as far as possible into the top of the outer tube by hand, making sure it fits squarely **(see illustration)**. Slide the washer onto the top of the bush, then carefully drive the bush

into place until it seats using a suitable drift or piece of tubing on the washer, using it as an interface to prevent damage to the upper rim of the bush **(see illustrations)**. Take care not to mark the inner tube when driving the bush in. Remove the washer and make sure

the bush has fully entered, in which case its upper rim will be flush with the oil seal seat **(see illustration)**. Refit the washer.

24 Lubricate the inner and outer surfaces of the new oil seal with the specified fork oil. Slide the seal, with its marked side facing up, down the inner tube and press it as far as possible into the top of the outer tube by hand, making sure it fits squarely **(see illustration)**. Carefully drive the seal into place until it seats using a suitable drift or piece of tubing, or the special service tool (Pt. No. 09940-52861) **(see illustration)**. Take care not to mark the inner tube when driving the bush in. Make sure the seal has fully entered, in which case the groove for the retaining ring will be fully exposed **(see illustration)**.

25 Fit the retaining ring, making sure it is correctly located in its groove **(see illustrations)**. Press the new dust seal into place **(see illustration)**.

26 Refer to Section 7, Steps 8 to 14, and put new oil into the fork.

27 Thread the front axle clamp bolts into the bottom of the right-hand fork, leaving them loose **(see illustration 8.3a)**. Fit the axle nut (making sure it is clean) into the bottom of the left-hand fork so that the flange contacts the outer surface **(see illustration 8.3b)**. Thread the front axle clamp bolts into the fork, then hold the axle nut against the fork and tighten the bolts to the specified torque setting.

28 Fit the inner tube protector onto the top of the outer tube, making sure the shield faces the front of the fork and the tab locates in the cut-out **(see illustration 8.3c)**.

29 Install the fork (see Section 6).

8.24a Fit the new oil seal . . .

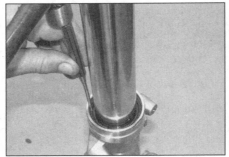

8.24b . . . and drive it in . . .

8.24c . . . until the retaining clip groove (arrowed) is fully exposed

8.25a Fit the retaining clip . . .

8.25b . . . making sure it locates in the groove . . .

8.25c . . . then fit the new dust seal

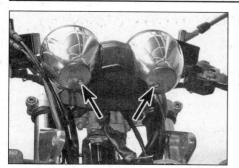

9.3a Undo the screws (arrowed) and remove the cowl

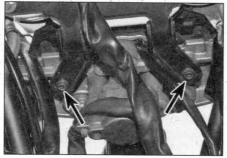

9.3b Unscrew the bolts (arrowed) and remove the instruments

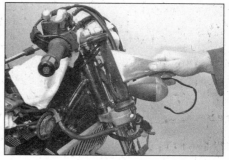

9.5 Pull the headlight holders from between the yokes

9 Steering stem

Removal

1 Remove the fuel tank to avoid the possibility of damage (see Chapter 4).
2 Remove the headlight and headlight shell (see Chapter 8).
3 Undo the instrument cowl screws and remove the cowl **(see illustration)**. Unscrew the instrument cluster bracket bolts and remove the instrument assembly **(see illustration)**.
4 Displace and support the handlebars so they are out of the way (see Section 5). Ensure no strain is placed on the brake or clutch hoses or the wiring. Keep the fluid reservoirs upright if possible to prevent air entering the system, and wrap them in rag.
5 Remove the front forks (see Section 6). Remove each headlight holder/turn signal assembly from between the yokes **(see illustration)**.
6 Unscrew and remove the steering stem nut and remove the washer **(see illustration)**. Lift the top yoke up off the steering stem **(see illustration)**.
7 Support the bottom yoke and unscrew the steering head bearing adjuster nut using either a C-spanner, a peg spanner or a suitable drift located in one of the notches **(see illustration)**.
8 Remove the bearing cover, then lower the steering stem out of the steering head **(see illustrations)**.

9 Remove the upper bearing inner race and the upper bearing from the top of the steering head – on K2 models caged ball bearings are fitted, and the inner race will come away separately from the ball bearing cage, while on all other models taper roller bearings are fitted, and on these the inner race is integral with the roller cage **(see illustration)**. On K2 models remove the lower bearing from the steering stem. **Note:** *Do not attempt to remove the outer races from the frame unless new ones are being installed. The same applies to the lower bearing inner race on K2 models, and the complete lower bearing on all other models.*
10 Remove all traces of old grease from the bearings and races and check them for wear or damage (see Section 10).

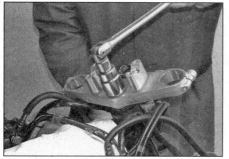

9.6a Unscrew the steering stem nut . . .

9.6b . . . and lift the top yoke off

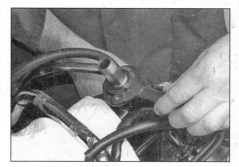

9.7 Unscrew the adjuster nut . . .

9.8a . . . then remove the bearing cover . . .

9.8b . . . and lower the steering stem out of the head

9.9 Remove the upper bearing – taper roller type shown

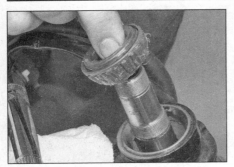

9.12 Fit the upper bearing

9.13 Thread the adjuster nut onto the steering stem and tighten as described

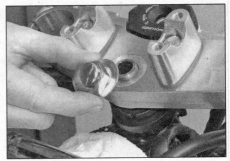

9.14 Fit the steering stem nut and washer

Installation

11 Apply general purpose grease to the bearing outer races in the steering head, and work grease well into both the upper and lower bearings. On K2 models fit the lower bearing onto its inner race on the steering stem.

12 Carefully lift the steering stem up through the steering head **(see illustration 9.8b)**. Fit the upper bearing in the top of the steering head, then on models with caged ball bearings fit the inner race **(see illustration)**. Fit the bearing cover **(see illustration 9.8a)**.

13 Thread the adjuster nut onto the steering stem **(see illustration)**. If the correct tools are available (Suzuki special tool part No. 09940-14911 or equivalent peg spanner and a torque wrench), tighten the nut to the initial torque setting specified at the beginning of this Chapter. If the tools are not available, tighten the adjuster nut carefully until all front to back freeplay is removed, then tighten it 1/2 a turn further **(see illustration 9.7)**. Whichever method is used, now turn the steering stem from lock to lock five or six times to settle the bearings, then loosen the adjuster nut by 1/4 to 1/2 a turn, so that the steering is able to move freely from lock to lock but without any front to back freeplay. Do not be too concerned about accurately setting the bearings at this stage, as the rest of the front end components need to be installed before making a final adjustment so their mass and inertia can be taken into account.

Caution: Take great care not to apply excessive pressure to the bearings as this will cause their premature failure. If new bearings have been fitted you may need to carry out the adjustment procedure several times to allow them to settle properly. The object is to set the adjuster nut so that the bearings are under a very light loading, just enough to remove any front to back freeplay.

14 Fit the top yoke onto the steering stem **(see illustration 9.6b)**. Fit the steering stem nut with its washer and tighten it finger-tight **(see illustration)**. Temporarily install one of the fork legs to align the top and bottom yokes, and secure it by tightening the bottom yoke clamp bolts only. Tighten the steering stem nut to the specified torque setting, then remove the fork leg.

15 Install the remaining components in the reverse order of removal.

16 Carry out a check of the steering head bearing adjustment as described in Chapter 1, and if necessary re-adjust.

10 Steering head bearings

Inspection

1 Remove the steering stem (see Section 9).
2 Remove all traces of old grease from the bearings and races and check them for wear or damage.

3 The races should be polished and free from indentations **(see illustration)**. Inspect the bearing balls (K2 model) or rollers (all other models) for signs of wear, pitting or discoloration, and examine the cages for signs of cracks or splits. Spin the bearings by hand. They should spin freely and smoothly. If there are any signs of wear on any of the above components, both upper and lower bearing assemblies must be renewed as a set. **Note:** *Do not attempt to remove the outer races from the frame unless new ones are being installed. The same applies to the lower bearing inner race on K2 models, and the complete lower bearing on all other models.*

Renewal

4 The outer races are an interference fit in the frame steering head – the top race can be tapped out with a suitable drift located on the exposed rim **(see illustrations)**. Tap firmly and evenly around the race to ensure that it is driven out squarely. To remove the bottom race may you may need to curve the end of the drift to get better purchase on the rim which is not as exposed as the top race.

5 Alternatively, the outer races can be removed using a slide-hammer type bearing extractor – these can often be hired from tool shops.

6 The new outer races can be installed in the steering head using a drawbolt arrangement

10.3 Check the races for wear

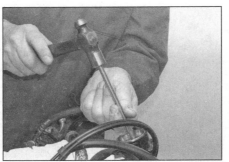

10.4a Drive the bearing outer races out with a brass drift . . .

10.4b . . . located as shown

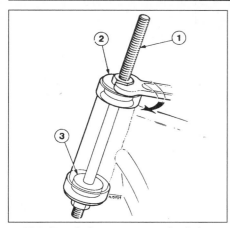

10.6 Drawbolt arrangement for fitting steering head bearing outer races

1 *Long bolt or threaded bar*
2 *Thick washer*
3 *Guide for lower outer race*

(see illustration), or by using a large diameter bearing driver. Ensure that the drawbolt washer or driver (as applicable) bears only on the outer edge of the race and does not contact the bearing seat. Alternatively, have the races installed by a Suzuki dealer equipped with the bearing race installing tools.

 Installation of new bearing outer races is made much easier if the races are left overnight in the freezer. This causes them to contract slightly making them a looser fit.

7 To remove the inner race/lower bearing from the steering stem, thread the steering stem nut onto the top to protect the threads, then place the yoke/steering stem on its side. Carefully tap the race free with a chisel, and/or use two screwdrivers placed on opposite sides to work it free **(see illustrations)**. If the race is firmly in place it will be necessary to use a bearing puller **(see illustration)**. Take the steering stem to a Suzuki dealer if required. Remove the dust seal and replace it with a new one.
8 Fit the new dust seal, then fit the new inner race/lower bearing onto the steering stem.

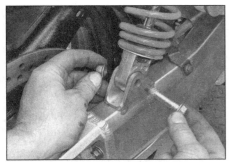

11.3 Unscrew the nut and withdraw the bottom bolt

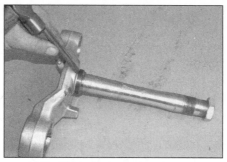

10.7a Work the lower bearing free carefully . . .

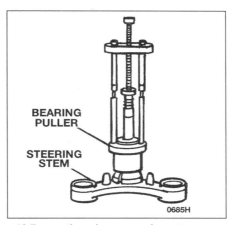

10.7c . . . though you may have to use a puller

A length of tubing with an internal diameter slightly larger than the steering stem will be needed to tap the race into position **(see illustration)**. Ensure that the drift bears only on the top rim of the race.
9 Install the steering stem (see Section 9).

11 Rear shock absorbers

Removal

1 Support the bike using on its centrestand. If both shock absorbers are being removed at the same time position a support under the rear wheel so that it does not drop when

11.4 Unscrew the top bolt . . .

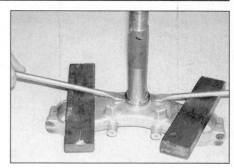

10.7b . . . using whatever method you find easiest . . .

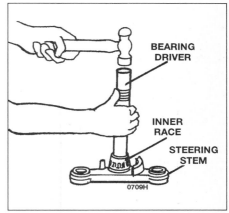

10.8 Install the lower bearing using a suitable driver or length of tubing

the second shock absorber is removed, but ensure that the weight of the machine is off the rear suspension so that the shocks are not compressed.
2 To improve access and avoid the possibility of damage, remove the silencer(s) (see Chapter 4).
3 Unscrew the nut and withdraw the bolt securing the bottom of the shock to the swingarm **(see illustration)**.
4 Unscrew the bolt securing the top of the shock to the frame, noting the bungee hook (or washers as shown) fitted with it **(see illustration)**.
5 Pivot the bottom of the shock back out of its bracket then slide the top off the mount and remove it **(see illustration)**. Remove

11.5a . . . then remove the shock absorber

11.5b Remove the washer from the lug . . .

11.5c . . . and the spacer from the bush

12 Suspension adjustment

Note: *The front and rear suspension on all models is adjustable for spring pre-load, rebound and compression damping. Refer to the suspension setting table in the owner's manual supplied with your motorcycle for recommended settings for solo and pillion riding.*

Front forks

1 **Spring pre-load** is adjusted using a suitable spanner on the adjuster hex **(see illustration)**. The adjuster is located in the fork top bolt; turn the adjuster clockwise to increase pre-load and anti-clockwise to decrease it. The amount of pre-load is indicated by lines on the adjuster which extend from the top bolt hex. The standard preload setting is with 5 lines visible. Maximum to minimum preload settings range from 0 to 8 lines. Always make sure the adjusters on both forks are set equally.

2 **Rebound damping** is adjusted using a flat-bladed screwdriver in the slot in the damping adjuster in the centre of the fork top bolt **(see illustration)**. Turn the adjuster clockwise to increase damping and anti-clockwise to decrease it. To establish the current setting, turn the adjuster in (clockwise) until it stops, counting the number of clicks. Reset it as required by turning it out (anti-clockwise). The standard position is eight clicks out. Always make sure the adjusters on both forks are set equally.

3 **Compression damping** is adjusted using a flat-bladed screwdriver in the slot in the damping adjuster in the bottom of the fork **(see illustration)**. Turn the adjuster clockwise to increase damping and anti-clockwise to decrease it. To establish the current setting, turn the adjuster in (clockwise) until it stops, counting the number of clicks. Reset it as required by turning it out (anti-clockwise). The standard position is seven clicks out. Always make sure the adjusters on both forks are set equally.

11.6 Check the shock for damage and look for leaks and pitting on the rod (arrowed)

11.8 Check the mounting bushes (arrowed)

the washer from the top mounting lug **(see illustration)**. Note the spacer in the bottom bush **(see illustration)**.

Inspection

6 Inspect the body of the shock absorber for physical damage and the coil spring for looseness, cracks or signs of fatigue **(see illustration)**.
7 Inspect the shock for signs of oil leakage.
8 Check the bush in each mount for wear and deterioration **(see illustration)**.
9 If a shock absorber is in any way damaged or worn a new pair of shocks must be installed. Individual components are not available from Suzuki although it is worth checking whether the shock can be rebuilt by a suspension specialist.
Caution: Take the old shocks to a Suzuki

dealer or suspension specialist for discharge of the nitrogen gas.

Installation

10 Installation is the reverse of removal, noting the following:
● Apply general purpose grease to the top mount and bush and the bottom spacer and bush.
● Fit the shock onto the upper mount first, then pivot it down onto the swingarm **(see illustration 11.5a)**.
● Tighten the upper mounting bolt and the lower mounting bolt nut to the torque settings specified at the beginning of this Chapter.
● Adjust the suspension as required (see Section 12).

12.1 Spring pre-load adjuster (arrowed)

12.2 Rebound damping adjuster (arrowed)

12.3 Compression damping adjuster (arrowed)

12.4 Spring pre-load adjuster (arrowed)

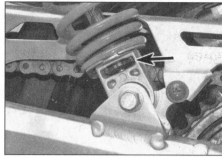

12.5 Rebound damping adjuster (arrowed)

12.6 Compression damping adjuster (arrowed)

Rear shock absorbers

4 Spring pre-load is adjusted by turning the adjuster knob on the shock absorber body **(see illustration)**. Turn the knob clockwise to increase pre-load and anti-clockwise to decrease it. The amount of pre-load is indicated by lines on the shock absorber. The standard preload setting is with 1.5 lines visible (i.e. between the first and second lines). Maximum to minimum preload settings range from 1 to 5 lines. Always make sure the adjusters on both shocks are set equally.

5 Rebound damping is adjusted by turning the dial on the bottom of the shock absorber **(see illustration)**. There are four settings, each indicated by a number and defined by a click.

13.1a Brake hose banjo bolt (arrowed)

The standard position is with the dial set to number 2. Minimum damping is at position 1, and maximum at position 4. Always make sure the adjusters on both shocks are set equally, and precisely, i.e. not between numbers.

6 Compression damping is adjusted by turning the dial on the gas reservoir **(see illustration)**. There are four settings, each indicated by a number and defined by a click. The standard position is with the dial set to number 2. Minimum damping is at position 1, and maximum at position 4. Always make sure the adjusters on both shocks are set equally, and precisely, i.e. not between numbers.

13 Swingarm

Removal

Note: *Due to the fact that the rear brake hose is routed through a closed riveted guide on the inside of the swingarm, it is necessary either to detach the hose from the rear brake caliper, and then draw the hose out of the guide (see Step 1), or to displace the rear brake master cylinder and its reservoir, and to remove the swingarm bringing the brake system with it (see Step 2). The method will depend upon your reason for removing the swingarm.*

1 If you are removing the swingarm without the brake system, unscrew the bolt securing the guide to the top of the swingarm. Unscrew the brake hose banjo bolt and detach the hose from the caliper, noting its alignment **(see illustration)**. Draw the hose out of the closed guide on the inside of the swingarm, taking care not to splash brake fluid around – have some rag on hand to quickly mop up any spills. Wrap some Clingfilm and rag tightly around the hose to minimise fluid loss and prevent dirt entering the system, and support it upright. Discard the sealing washers as new ones must be used on installation. Unscrew the nut on the brake torque arm front bolt, then withdraw the bolt and detach the arm – you can leave the caliper attached to the other end **(see illustration)**.

2 If you are removing the swingarm with the brake system, refer to Chapter 6 and displace the rear brake master cylinder and its reservoir – do not detach any of the hoses. Wrap them in some rag.

3 Remove the rear wheel (see Chapter 6).

4 Remove the rear shock absorbers if required, or alternatively just remove the bottom mounting bolts (see Section 11).

5 If required, undo the screws securing the chainguard and remove it – this can be done after removing the swingarm if preferred **(see illustration)**. Note the spacer and rubber grommet with the front screw.

13.1b Unscrew the nut (arrowed), withdraw the bolt and detach the arm

13.5 Undo the screws (arrowed) and remove the chainguard

13.6 Remove the blanking cap from each side . . .

13.7 . . . then unscrew the nut . . .

13.8 . . . withdraw the pivot bolt and remove the swingarm

6 Remove the blanking cap from each side of the frame **(see illustration)**.

7 Unscrew the nut on the right-hand end of the pivot bolt **(see illustration)**.

8 Support the swingarm, then withdraw the pivot bolt and ease the swingarm out of the back of the frame **(see illustration)**.

9 Remove the bearing cover from each side of the swingarm, noting the washer fitted on its inside, which should stay in place **(see illustration)**. Check to see if a thrust shim is fitted onto the inside of the right-hand pivot boss in the frame, and if so remove it for safe-keeping if it is loose. If required, undo the bolts securing the chain slider and remove it **(see illustration)**. Note the spacers with the bolts.

Inspection

10 Clean the swingarm with a suitable solvent, removing all traces of dirt, corrosion and grease.

11 Inspect the drive chain adjuster bolts and the bolt threads in the swingarm. Stripped threads in the swingarm can be repaired with a thread insert – see 'Tools and Workshop Tips' in the Reference section. Inspect the axle plate on the inside of the right-hand end of the swingarm on K2 models and the left-hand end on all other models and fit a new one if it is gouged or distorted **(see illustration)**.

12 Withdraw the spacers from the needle roller bearings in both ends of the swingarm pivot **(see illustration)**. Remove any corrosion from the spacers with steel wool. If necessary, wash old grease out of the bearings with a suitable solvent, then dry the bearings with compressed air, if available **(see illustration)**.

13 Inspect the pivot components closely, looking for obvious signs of wear such as scoring and pitting. Apply clean oil to the spacers, then slip each one back into its bearing and check that there is not an excessive amount of freeplay between the two. Ensure the bearings turn smoothly without binding or grating. If there is any doubt about the condition of the bearings have them checked by a Suzuki dealer or replace them with new ones (see below).

14 Clean the swingarm pivot bolt and check the bolt for wear where it passes through the frame and the bearing spacers. Slide the bearing spacers onto the pivot bolt and check that there is not an excessive amount of freeplay between the two.

15 Check the pivot bolt is straight by rolling it on a flat surface such as a piece of plate glass. If available, place the bolt in V-blocks and measure the runout using a dial gauge. If the runout exceeds the limit specified, fit a new one.

16 Lay the swingarm on the work surface and support it so that the pivot end is level (check this with a spirit level). Install the chain adjuster blocks and the axle and check the level of the axle. If the axle is not level, the swingarm is out of true and must be replaced with a new one.

Bearing renewal

Note: *The needle bearings should only be removed if new ones are going to be fitted – removal of the bearings will destroy them.*

17 Remove the spacers from the bearings **(see illustration 13.12a)**. Note the set position (depth) of the bearings before removing them.

13.9a Remove the bearing covers

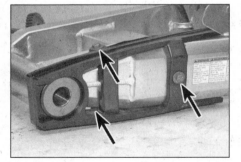

13.9b Chain slider bolts (arrowed)

13.11 Check the axle plate (arrowed)

13.12a Remove the spacers . . .

13.12b . . . and clean and check the bearings (arrowed)

18 Remove the bearings using an internal expanding knife-edged puller with slide-hammer attachment. Locate the bearing puller tool behind the inner edge of the first bearing to be removed, note that there is only a small clearance in which to locate the puller edges. Operate the puller to draw the bearing out of the swingarm. The centre spacer can now be removed from inside the swingarm. Now use the same procedure to remove the bearing from the other side of the swingarm.

19 The new bearings should be pressed or drawn into place so that they bottom against the seat inside the swingarm – do not drive them into position. In the absence of a press, a suitable drawbolt arrangement can be made up as described in *Tools and Workshop Tips (Section 5)* in the Reference section. Do not forget to install the centre spacer between the two bearings, and fit each bearing with its marked side facing outwards.

Installation

20 Clean the frame around the swingarm mountings. If removed, install the chain slider **(see illustration)**.

21 Lubricate the bearings, spacers and pivot with multi-purpose grease. Fit the bearing covers with their washers to each end of the swingarm pivot **(see illustration 13.9a)**. Where removed fit the thrust shim onto the inside of the right-hand pivot boss in the frame. If one was not present check the

thrust clearance after installing the swingarm, especially if a new swingarm is being fitted.

22 Offer up the swingarm, align the swingarm pivot with the frame mountings and slide the pivot bolt all the way in from the left-hand side **(see illustration 13.8)**. If no thrust shim is fitted, using a feeler gauge check the pivot thrust clearance between the outside of the right-hand bearing cover and the inside of the right-hand pivot boss in the frame using a feeler gauge – this is especially important if a new swingarm is fitted. If the clearance exceeds 0.9 mm, obtain the pivot thrust shim from a Suzuki dealer, then withdraw the pivot bolt, displace the swingarm and fit the shim onto the pivot boss. Refit the swingarm and slide the pivot bolt back in.

23 Fit the nut onto the right-hand end of the pivot bolt, then counter-hold the bolt head and tighten the nut to the torque setting specified at the beginning of the Chapter **(see illustration 13.7)**. Fit the blanking caps **(see illustration 13.6)**.

24 If removed, fit the chainguard **(see illustration 13.5)**.

25 Install the rear shock absorbers (see Section 11).

26 Install the rear wheel (see Chapter 6).

27 If you removed the swingarm with the brake system, install the rear brake master cylinder and reservoir (see Chapter 6).

28 If you removed the swingarm without the brake system, fit the brake torque arm onto

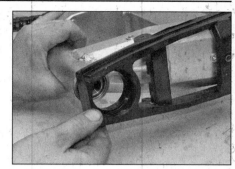

13.20 Fit the chain slider back onto the swingarm

the swingarm, then install the bolt and tighten the nut to the specified torque setting **(see illustration 13.1b)**. Route the brake hose down through its closed guide on the inside of the swingarm. Fit the guide onto the top of the swingarm and tighten its bolt. Connect the brake hose to the caliper, using new sealing washers on each side of the fitting. Align the hose as noted on removal **(see illustration 13.1a)**. Tighten the banjo bolt to the torque setting specified at the beginning of the Chapter. Refer to Chapter 7 and bleed the brakes.

29 Check and adjust the drive chain slack (see Chapter 1). Check the operation of the rear suspension and brake before taking the machine on the road.

Notes

Chapter 6
Brakes, wheels and final drive

Contents

Degrees of difficulty

| **Easy,** suitable for novice with little experience 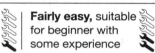 | **Fairly easy,** suitable for beginner with some experience | **Fairly difficult,** suitable for competent DIY mechanic | **Difficult,** suitable for experienced DIY mechanic | **Very difficult,** suitable for expert DIY or professional |

Specifications

Brakes

Brake fluid type . . . . DOT 4
Disc minimum thickness
  Front
    Standard. . . . . 4.8 to 5.2 mm
    Service limit . . . . 4.5 mm
  Rear
    Standard. . . . . 5.3 to 5.7 mm
    Service limit . . . . 5.0 mm
Disc maximum runout (front and rear, all models) . . . . 0.3 mm
Caliper bore ID
  Front
    Lower . . . . 24.000 to 24.076 mm
    Middle and upper . . . . 27.000 to 27.076 mm
  Rear . . . . 38.180 to 38.230 mm
Caliper piston OD
  Front
    Lower . . . . 23.925 to 23.975 mm
    Middle and upper . . . . 26.920 to 26.970 mm
  Rear . . . . 38.115 to 38.148 mm
Master cylinder bore ID
  Front . . . . 15.870 to 15.913 mm
  Rear . . . . 12.700 to 12.743 mm
Master cylinder piston OD
  Front . . . . 15.827 to 15.854 mm
  Rear . . . . 12.657 to 12.684 mm

Wheels

Maximum wheel runout (front and rear)
  Axial (side-to-side) . . . . 2.0 mm
  Radial (out-of-round) . . . . 2.0 mm
Maximum axle runout (front and rear) . . . . 0.25 mm

Tyres

Tyre pressures . . . .   see *Pre-ride checks*
Tyre sizes
   Front . . . .   120/70 ZR 17 58W
   Rear . . . .   190/50 ZR 17 73W
Refer to the owners handbook or the tyre information label on the swingarm for approved tyre brands.

Final drive

Drive chain slack and lubricant . . . .   see Chapter 1
Drive chain type . . . .   RK GB50GSVZ3 (116 links)
Sprocket sizes . . . .   18 tooth front, 41 tooth rear

Torque settings

Brake caliper bleed valves . . . .   8 Nm
Brake hose banjo bolts. . . . .   23 Nm
Brake torque arm-to-caliper bolt nut . . . .   34 Nm
Clutch release cylinder housing bolts . . . .   10 Nm
Front brake caliper body joining bolts . . . .   21 Nm
Front brake caliper mounting bolts . . . .   25 Nm
Front brake disc bolts . . . .   23 Nm
Front brake master cylinder clamp bolts . . . .   10 Nm
Front brake pad retaining pin . . . .   16 Nm
Front axle . . . .   100 Nm
Front axle clamp bolts and axle nut clamp bolts . . . .   23 Nm
Front sprocket nut . . . .   115 Nm
Rear axle nut . . . .   100 Nm
Rear brake caliper body joining bolts. . . . .   37 Nm
Rear brake caliper mounting bolts . . . .   26 Nm
Rear brake disc bolts . . . .   23 Nm
Rear brake master cylinder mounting bolts . . . .   10 Nm
Rear brake pad retaining pin . . . .   17 Nm
Rear sprocket nuts. . . . .   102 Nm
Speed sensor rotor bolt . . . .   20 Nm

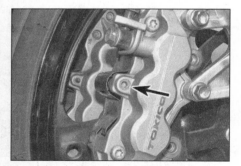

2.1 Slacken the pad pin (arrowed) . . .

2.2a . . . then unscrew the bolts (arrowed) . . .

2.2b . . . and slide the caliper off the disc

1 General information

All models have hydraulically operated disc brakes, with twin discs at the front and a single disc at the rear. All models have triple opposed-piston calipers at the front and a single opposed-piston caliper at the rear.

All models are fitted with cast alloy wheels designed for tubeless tyres only.

The drive to the rear wheel is by chain and sprockets.

Caution: Do not disassemble components unless absolutely necessary. If an hydraulic brake hose is loosened or disconnected, the union sealing washers must be renewed and the system bled upon reassembly. Do not use solvents on internal brake components. Solvents will cause the seals to swell and distort. Use only clean DOT 4 brake fluid for cleaning. Use care when working with brake fluid as it can injure your eyes and it will damage painted surfaces and plastic parts.

2 Front brake pads

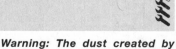

⚠ *Warning: The dust created by the brake system may contain asbestos, which is harmful to your health. Never blow it out with compressed air and don't inhale any of it. An approved filtering mask should be worn when working on the brakes.*

1 Slacken the pad retaining pin **(see illustration)**.

2 Unscrew the caliper mounting bolts and slide the caliper off the disc **(see illustrations)**.

3 Unscrew and remove the pad pin, then remove the pads from the bottom of the caliper

2.3a Unscrew the pin . . .

2.3b . . . and remove the pads

(see illustrations). The pad spring can stay in place – if you need to remove it undo the two bolts, but note they are prone to corrosion and may be seized **(see illustration)**. **Note:** *Do not operate the brake lever while the pads are out of the caliper.*

4 Inspect the surface of each pad for contamination and check that the friction material has not worn beyond its service limit (see Chapter 1, Section 10) **(see illustration)**. If any pad is worn down to, or beyond, the bottom of the grooves, is fouled with oil or grease, or is heavily scored or damaged, fit a complete set of new pads. **Note:** *It is not possible to degrease the friction material; if the pads are contaminated in any way they must be replaced with new ones.*

5 If the pads are in good condition clean them carefully, using a fine wire brush which is completely free of oil and grease to remove all traces of road dirt and corrosion. Using a pointed instrument, dig out any embedded particles of foreign matter. If required, spray with a dedicated brake cleaner to remove any dust.

6 Check the condition of the brake disc (see Section 4).

7 Remove all traces of corrosion from the pad pin and check it for wear and damage.

8 Clean around the exposed section of each piston to remove any dirt or debris that could cause the seals to be damaged **(see**

2.3c Pad spring bolts (arrowed)

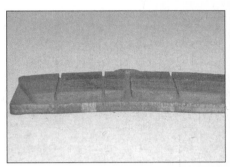

2.4 Check the pad material as described

illustration). If new pads are being fitted, now push the pistons all the way back into the caliper to create room for them; if the old pads are still serviceable push the pistons in a little way. To push the pads back use finger pressure or a piece of wood as leverage, or place the old pads back in the caliper and use a metal bar or a screwdriver inserted between them, or use grips and a piece of wood, rag or card to protect the caliper body **(see illustration)**. Alternatively obtain a proper piston-pushing tool from a good tool supplier **(see illustration)**. It may be necessary to remove the master cylinder reservoir cap, plate and diaphragm and siphon out some fluid (see *Pre-ride checks*). If the pistons are

difficult to push back, remove the bleed valve cap, then attach a length of clear hose to the bleed valve and place the open end in a suitable container, then open the valve and try again (see Section 11). Take great care not to draw any air into the system. If in doubt, bleed the brakes afterwards.

9 If any of the pistons appear seized, first block the other pistons using wood or other suitable item, then apply the brake lever and check whether the piston in question moves at all. If it moves out but can't be pushed back in the chances are there is some hidden corrosion stopping it. If it doesn't move at all, or to fully clean and inspect the pistons, overhaul the caliper (see Section 3).

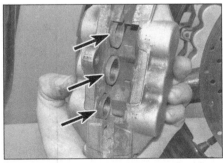

2.8a Clean the exposed part of each piston (arrowed)

2.8b Push the pistons in using one of the methods described

2.8c This is a commercially available piston pushing tool

2.11a Fit the pads into the caliper . . .

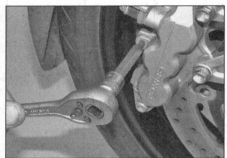

2.11b . . . then insert and tighten the pad pin

2.12 Fit the mounting bolts and tighten them to the specified torque . . .

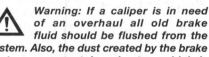

2.13 . . . then tighten the pad pin

10 If the pad spring was removed, fit it and tighten the bolts **(see illustration 2.3c)**. Lightly smear the back of the pad backing material and the edges of the backing material where it contacts the caliper body with copper-based grease, making sure that none gets on the friction material. Also smear the pad pin.

11 Fit the pads into the caliper so the friction material on each pad faces the other and press them up against the spring to align the holes, then insert the pad pin and tighten it finger-tight **(see illustrations)**.

12 Slide the caliper onto the disc making sure the pads locate correctly on each side **(see illustration 2.2b)**. Install the caliper mounting bolts and tighten them to the torque setting specified at the beginning of the Chapter **(see illustration)**.

13 Tighten the pad pin to the torque setting specified at the beginning of this Chapter **(see illustration)**.

14 Operate the brake lever until the pads contact with the disc. Check the level of fluid in the hydraulic reservoir and top-up if necessary (see *Pre-ride checks*).

15 Check the operation of the front brake before riding the motorcycle.

---

3 Front brake calipers

> ⚠ **Warning: If a caliper is in need of an overhaul all old brake fluid should be flushed from the system. Also, the dust created by the brake system may contain asbestos, which is harmful to your health. Never blow it out with compressed air and do not inhale any of it. An approved filtering mask should be worn when working on the brakes.**

Overhaul must be done in a spotlessly clean work area to avoid contamination and possible failure of the brake hydraulic system components. Do not, under any circumstances, use petroleum-based solvents to clean brake parts. Use clean DOT 4 brake fluid, dedicated brake cleaner or denatured alcohol only, as described. To prevent damage from spilled brake fluid, always cover paintwork when working on the braking system.

Removal

Note: *If the caliper is being overhauled (usually due to sticking pistons or fluid leaks) read through the entire procedure first and make sure that you have obtained all the new parts required, including some new DOT 4 brake fluid.*

1 If the caliper is being overhauled, slacken the brake pad retaining pin **(see illustration 2.1)**. If the caliper is just being displaced from the forks as part of the wheel removal procedure, the brake pads can be left in place.

2 If the caliper is just being displaced free the brake hose from its holder to give more freedom of movement if required – squirt some lubricant between the rubber and the holder then press the rubber out **(see illustration)**.

3 If the caliper is being completely removed or overhauled, unscrew the brake hose banjo bolt and detach the banjo union, noting its alignment with the caliper **(see illustration)**.

4 Wrap Clingfilm and rag around the banjo union and secure the hose in an upright position to minimise fluid loss. Discard the sealing washers, as new ones must be fitted on reassembly.

5 If the caliper body is to be split into its halves for overhaul, loosen the caliper body joining bolts and retighten them lightly **(see illustration)**.

6 Unscrew the caliper mounting bolts and slide the caliper off the disc **(see illustrations 2.2a and b)**. If the caliper is just being displaced, secure it to the motorcycle with a cable-tie to avoid straining the brake hose. **Note:** *Do not operate the brake lever while either caliper is off the disc. If the caliper is being overhauled, remove the brake pads (see Section 2).*

3.2 Free the hose to give freedom of movement

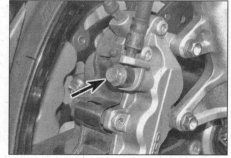

3.3 Brake hose banjo bolt (arrowed)

3.5 Caliper body joining bolts (arrowed)

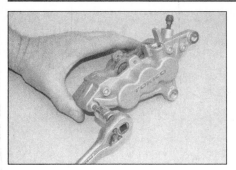

3.8a Unscrew the bolts . . .

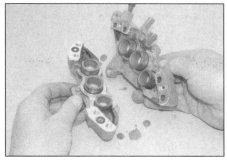

3.8b . . . and separate the halves

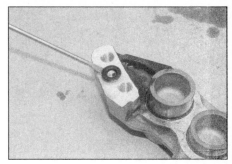

3.8c Remove the O-ring and discard it

Overhaul

7 Clean the exterior of the caliper with denatured alcohol or brake system cleaner. Have some clean rag ready to catch any spilled brake fluid.

8 Unscrew the caliper body joining bolts and separate the body halves, catching any residual fluid with the rag **(see illustrations)**. Remove the caliper body O-ring from whichever body half it is in and discard it – fit a new one on reassembly **(see illustration)**.

9 Place a caliper half piston-up on the bench. Find a suitable bolt and thread it into the banjo bolt bore in the outer half. Get a wad of rag and/or a block of wood hold it against the pistons as a cushion to protect your hand as the pistons are forced out. Apply compressed air gradually and progressively, starting with a fairly low pressure, to the fluid passage on the caliper joint and allow the pistons to ease out of their bores, controlling them with hand pressure **(see illustration)**. Make sure the

pistons are displaced evenly, using pressure to block one while another moves if necessary. Repeat the procedure for the other caliper half.

10 If a piston is stuck in its bore due to corrosion the caliper should be replaced with a new one. Do not try to remove a piston by levering it out or by using pliers or other grips.

11 Mark each piston and the caliper body to ensure that the pistons can be matched to their original bores on reassembly. Note that two sizes of piston are used in each caliper (see Specifications at the beginning of this Chapter).

12 Remove the dust seals and the piston seals from the piston bores using a soft wooden or plastic tool to avoid scratching the bores **(see illustrations)**. Discard the seals as new ones must be fitted on reassembly.

13 Clean the pistons and bores, paying attention to the seal grooves, with clean DOT 4 brake fluid. If compressed air is available, blow it through the fluid galleries in the caliper

to ensure they are clear (make sure it is filtered and unlubricated).

Caution: Do not, under any circumstances, use a petroleum-based solvent to clean brake parts.

14 Inspect the caliper bores and pistons for signs of corrosion, nicks and burrs and loss of plating. If surface defects are present, the pistons and/or the caliper assembly must be replaced with new ones. If the caliper is in poor condition, the other front caliper and the master cylinder should also be checked.

15 Lubricate the new piston seals with clean brake fluid and fit them in their grooves in the caliper bores **(see illustrations)**. Note that there are two sizes of bore in each caliper and care must therefore be taken to ensure that the correct size seals are fitted to the correct bores (see Specifications). The same applies when fitting the new dust seals and pistons.

16 Lubricate the new dust seals with clean brake fluid and fit them in their grooves in the caliper bores **(see illustration)**.

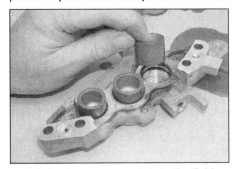

3.9 Apply compressed air to the fluid passage until the pistons are displaced

3.12a Remove the dust seals . . .

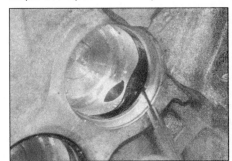

3.12b . . . and the piston seals and discard them

3.15a Lubricate the new seals with clean fluid

3.15b Fit the piston seal . . .

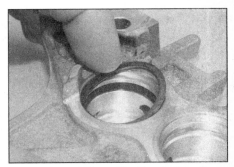

3.16 . . . followed by the dust seal

3.17a Lubricate each piston . . .

3.17b . . . then fit it into the bore . . .

3.17c . . . and push it all the way in

17 Lubricate the pistons with clean brake fluid and fit them, closed-end first, into the caliper bores, taking care not to displace the seals **(see illustration)**. Using your thumbs, push the pistons all the way in, making sure they enter the bore squarely.

18 Lubricate the new caliper body O-ring with clean brake fluid and fit it into the appropriate half of the caliper body **(see illustration)**. Join the two halves of the caliper body together, ensuring that the O-ring stays in place **(see illustration)**. Fit the joining bolts and tighten them evenly to the torque setting specified at the beginning of this Chapter **(see illustration)**. If it is not possible to tighten the bolts fully at this stage, tighten them as much as possible now and tighten them fully once the caliper has been installed on the machine.

Installation

19 If removed, install the brake pads (see Section 2).

20 Slide the caliper onto the brake disc, making sure the pads fit on each side of the disc **(see illustration 2.2b)**.

21 Install the caliper mounting bolts and tighten them to the torque setting specified at the beginning of this Chapter **(see illustration 2.12)**. If the calipers were overhauled and if not already done, tighten the caliper body joining bolts to the specified torque setting **(see illustration 3.5)**. If the pads were removed tighten the pad pin to the specified torque setting **(see illustration 2.13)**.

22 If removed, connect the brake hose to the caliper, using new sealing washers on each side of the banjo fitting. Align the fitting as noted on removal **(see illustration 3.3)**.

Tighten the banjo bolt to the specified torque setting.

23 If detached secure the brake hose in its holder on the front mudguard **(see illustration 3.2)**.

24 Top up the hydraulic reservoir with DOT 4 brake fluid (see *Pre-ride checks*) and bleed the system as described in Section 11. Check that there are no fluid leaks and test the operation of the brake before riding the motorcycle.

4 Front brake discs

Inspection

1 Inspect the surface of the disc for score marks and other damage. Light scratches are normal after use and won't affect brake operation, but deep grooves and heavy score marks will reduce braking efficiency and accelerate pad wear. If a disc is badly grooved it must be replaced with a new one.

2 The disc must not be allowed to wear down to a thickness less than the service limit as listed in this Chapter's Specifications. The minimum thickness is also stamped on the disc **(see illustration)**. Check the thickness of the disc with a micrometer and replace it with a new one if necessary.

3 To check if the disc is warped, position the bike on an auxiliary stand with the front wheel raised off the ground. Mount a dial

3.18a Fit new O-rings . . .

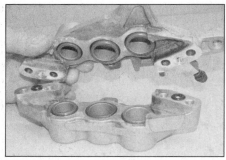

3.18b . . . then join the caliper halves . . .

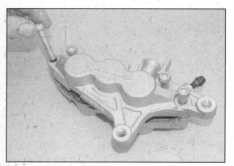

3.18c . . . install the bolts . . .

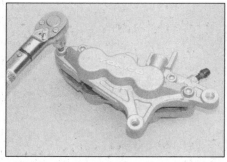

3.18d . . . and tighten them to the specified torque

4.2 The minimum thickness is marked on the disc

4.3 Checking disc runout with a dial gauge

4.5 The disc is secured by five bolts

5.1 Disconnect the brake light switch wiring connector

gauge to the fork leg, with the gauge plunger touching the surface of the disc about 10 mm from the outer edge **(see illustration)**. Rotate the wheel and watch the gauge needle, comparing the reading with the limit listed in the Specifications at the beginning of this Chapter. If the runout is greater than the service limit, check the wheel bearings for play (see Chapter 1). If the bearings are worn, install new ones (see Section 16) and repeat this check. If the disc runout is still excessive, a new pair of discs will have to be fitted.

Removal

4 Remove the wheel (see Section 14).
Caution: Don't lay the wheel down and allow it to rest on either disc – the disc could become warped. Set the wheel on wood blocks so the wheel rim supports the weight of the wheel.
5 If you are not replacing the disc with a new one, mark the relationship of the disc to the wheel, so it can be installed in the same position and on the same side as originally fitted. Unscrew the disc bolts, loosening them evenly and a little at a time in a criss-cross pattern to avoid distorting the disc, then remove the disc **(see illustration)**.

Installation

6 Before installing the disc, make sure there is no dirt or corrosion where the disc seats on the hub. If the disc does not sit flat when it is bolted down, it will appear to be warped when checked or when the front brake is used.
7 Install the disc on the wheel with its marked

side facing out, aligning the previously applied matchmarks (if you're reinstalling the original disc).
8 Clean the threads of the disc mounting bolts, then apply a suitable non-permanent thread locking compound. Install the bolts and tighten them evenly and a little at a time in a criss-cross pattern to the torque setting specified at the beginning of this Chapter. Clean the disc using acetone or brake system cleaner. If a new disc has been installed, remove any protective coating from its working surfaces.
9 Install the front wheel (see Section 14).
Caution: Always fit new brake pads when new discs are fitted.
10 Operate the brake lever several times to bring the pads into contact with the disc. Check the operation of the brake before riding the motorcycle.

---

5 Front brake master cylinder

![spanner symbol]

> ⚠ *Warning: If the brake master cylinder is in need of an overhaul all old brake fluid should be flushed from the system. Overhaul must be done in a spotlessly clean work area to avoid contamination and possible failure of the brake hydraulic system components. Do not, under any circumstances, use petroleum-based solvents to clean brake parts. Use clean DOT 4 brake fluid,*

dedicated brake cleaner or denatured alcohol only, as described. To prevent damage from spilled brake fluid, always cover paintwork when working on the braking system.

Removal

Note: *If the master cylinder is being overhauled (usually due to sticking or poor action, or fluid leaks) read through the entire procedure first and make sure that you have obtained all the new parts required, including some new DOT 4 brake fluid.*
1 Disconnect the wiring connector from the brake light switch **(see illustration)**.
2 If the master cylinder is just being displaced, ensure the fluid reservoir cover is secure. Unscrew the master cylinder clamp bolts and remove the back of the clamp, noting how it fits, then position the master cylinder and reservoir assembly clear of the handlebar **(see illustration)**. Ensure no strain is placed on the hydraulic hose. Keep the reservoir upright to prevent air entering the system.
3 If the master cylinder is being overhauled, remove the brake lever (see Chapter 5).
4 Unscrew the brake hose banjo bolt and detach the banjo union, noting its alignment with the master cylinder **(see illustration)**. Wrap Clingfilm and rag around the banjo union and secure the hose in an upright position to minimise fluid loss Discard the sealing washers as new ones must be fitted on reassembly.
5 Undo the reservoir cover screws **(see illustration)**.

5.2 Unscrew the clamp bolts (arrowed)

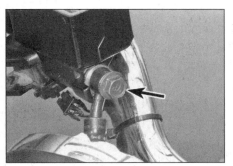

5.4 Unscrew the banjo bolt (arrowed)

5.5 Undo the cover screws

5.9 Remove the boot from the end of the master cylinder piston . . .

5.10a . . . then depress the piston and remove the circlip . . .

5.10b . . . then draw out the piston . . .

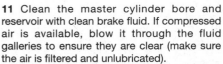

5.10c . . . and the spring

11 Clean the master cylinder bore and reservoir with clean brake fluid. If compressed air is available, blow it through the fluid galleries to ensure they are clear (make sure the air is filtered and unlubricated).
Caution: Do not, under any circumstances, use a petroleum-based solvent to clean brake parts.
12 Check the master cylinder bore for corrosion, scratches, nicks and score marks. If damage or wear is evident, the master cylinder must be replaced with a new one. If the master cylinder is in poor condition, then the calipers should be checked as well.
13 The dust boot, circlip, piston, cup, seal and spring are all included in the master cylinder rebuild kit. Use all of the new parts, regardless of the apparent condition of the old ones. Lubricate the master cylinder bore with new brake fluid.
14 Smear the cup and seal with new brake fluid. If the seal is not already on the piston, fit it into its groove so the wider end will fit into the master cylinder first **(see illustration)**. Fit the cup onto the narrow end of the spring **(see illustration)**. Fit the spring wide-end first into the master cylinder and push the cup in, making sure its lips do not turn inside out **(see illustration)**. Lubricate

6 Unscrew the master cylinder clamp bolts and remove the back of the clamp, noting how it fits, then lift the master cylinder and reservoir away from the handlebar **(see illustration 5.2)**.
7 Remove the reservoir cover, diaphragm plate and diaphragm. Drain the brake fluid from the master cylinder and reservoir into a suitable container. Wipe any remaining fluid out of the reservoir with a clean rag.
8 If required, undo the screw securing the brake light switch to the master cylinder and remove the switch.

Overhaul

9 Carefully remove the rubber boot from the master cylinder, noting how it locates in the groove in the outer end of the piston **(see illustration)**.
10 Depress the piston and use circlip pliers to remove the circlip, then slide out the piston assembly and the spring, noting how they fit **(see illustrations)**. If they are difficult to remove, apply low pressure compressed air to the brake fluid outlet. Lay the parts out in the proper order to prevent confusion during reassembly.

5.14a Make sure the cup is correctly installed on the piston

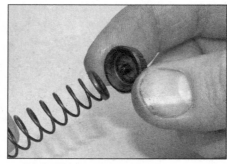

5.14b Fit the seal onto the end of the spring . . .

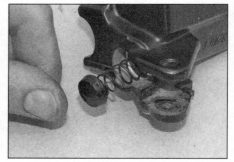

5.14c . . . then fit the spring into the master cylinder

5.14d Push the piston into the bore . . .

5.14e . . . then fit the circlip . . .

5.14f . . . and push the piston in and locate
the circlip in the groove

5.14g Fit the boot onto the pushrod . . .

5.14h . . . and locate its rim in the groove

the piston with clean DOT 4 brake fluid and slide it into the master cylinder and up against the cup and spring **(see illustration)**. Make sure the lips on the seal do not turn inside out. Depress the piston and fit the new circlip, making sure it locates properly in its groove **(see illustrations)**. Fit the rubber boot, making sure the lips are seated correctly in the master cylinder and in the groove around the piston **(see illustrations)**. Smear silicone grease onto the end of the piston.

15 Inspect the reservoir diaphragm and fit a new one it if it is damaged or deteriorated.

Installation

16 If removed, fit the brake light switch onto the bottom of the master cylinder, making sure the pin locates in the hole, and tighten the screw.

17 Attach the master cylinder to the handlebar, aligning the clamp joint with the punch mark on the underside of the handlebar, then fit the back of the clamp with its UP mark facing up **(see illustrations)**. Tighten the upper bolt to the torque setting specified at the beginning of this Chapter, followed by the lower bolt.

18 Connect the brake hose to the master

cylinder, using new sealing washers on each side of the banjo fitting **(see illustration)**. Align the hose as noted on removal **(see illustration 5.4)**. Tighten the banjo bolt to the torque setting specified at the beginning of this Chapter.

19 Install the brake lever (see Chapter 5).

20 Connect the brake light switch wiring **(see illustration 5.1)**.

21 Fill the fluid reservoir with new DOT 4 brake fluid (see *Pre-ride checks*). Refer to Section 11 and bleed the air from the system.

22 Check the operation of the brake before riding the motorcycle.

5.17b . . . and fit the clamp

5.18 Always use new sealing washers

5.17a Align the mating surface with the
punch mark (arrowed) . . .

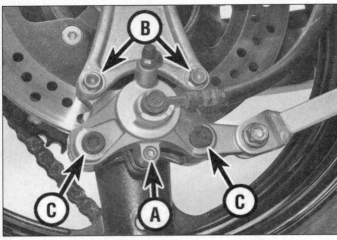

6.1 Pad retaining pin (A), caliper mounting bolts (B), caliper body joining bolts (C)

6.2 Unscrew the torque arm bolt nut

6 Rear brake pads

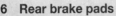

⚠️ **Warning: The dust created by the brake system may contain asbestos, which is harmful to your health. Never blow it out with compressed air and don't inhale any of it. An approved filtering mask should be worn when working on the brakes.**

1 Slacken the pad retaining pin **(see illustration)**.

6.3 Remove the bolts and slide the caliper down off the disc

2 Unscrew the nut on the bolt securing the brake torque arm to the caliper **(see illustration)**.

3 Unscrew the caliper mounting bolts, then withdraw the torque arm bolt and slide the caliper off the disc and the torque arm **(see illustration)**.

4 Unscrew and remove the pad pin, then remove the pad spring, noting how it fits, and remove the pads from the caliper **(see illustrations)**. **Note:** *Do not operate the brake pedal while the pads are out of the caliper.* If required remove the shim from the back of each pad, noting how they fit **(see illustration)** – note that new pads should come with new

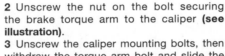

6.4a Withdraw the pad pin and remove the spring (arrowed) . . .

shims where applicable, but make sure they do, especially if fitting after-market pads, before discarding the old ones.

5 Inspect the surface of each pad for contamination and check that the friction material has not worn beyond its service limit (see Chapter 1, Section 10) **(see illustration)**. If any pad is worn down to, or beyond, the bottom of the groove, is fouled with oil or grease, or heavily scored or damaged, fit a new set of pads. **Note:** *It is not possible to degrease the friction material; if the pads are contaminated in any way they must be replaced with new ones.*

6 If the pads are in good condition clean them carefully, using a fine wire brush which is completely free of oil and grease to remove all traces of road dirt and corrosion. Using a pointed instrument, dig out any embedded particles of foreign matter. If required, spray with a dedicated brake cleaner to remove any dust.

7 Check the condition of the brake disc (see Section 8).

8 Remove all traces of corrosion from the pad pin and check it for wear and damage.

9 Clean around the exposed section of each piston to remove any dirt or debris that could cause the seals to be damaged. If new pads are being fitted, now push the pistons all the

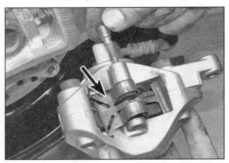

6.4b . . . and pads

6.4c Remove the shim from the back of each pad

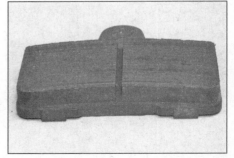

6.5 Check the pad material as described

6.9a Push the pistons in using one of the methods described

6.9b This is a commercially available piston pushing tool

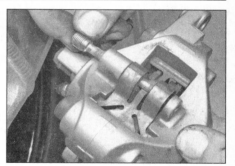

6.12 Make sure the pin seats over the centre leaf of the spring

way back into the caliper to create room for them; if the old pads are still serviceable push the pistons in a little way. To push the pads back use finger pressure or a piece of wood as leverage, or place the old pads back in the caliper and use a metal bar or a screwdriver inserted between them, or use grips and a piece of wood, rag or card to protect the caliper body **(see illustration)**. Alternatively obtain a proper piston-pushing tool from a good tool supplier **(see illustration)**. It may be necessary to remove the master cylinder reservoir cover and diaphragm and siphon out some fluid (see *Pre-ride checks*). If the pistons are difficult to push back, remove the bleed valve cap, then attach a length of clear hose to the bleed valve and place the open end in a suitable container, then open the valve and try again (see Section 11). Take great care not to draw any air into the system. If in doubt, bleed the brakes afterwards.

10 If either of the pistons appear seized, first block or hold the other piston using wood or a cable-tie, then apply the brake pedal and check whether the piston in question moves at all. If it moves out but can't be pushed back in the chances are there is some hidden corrosion stopping it. If it doesn't move at all, or to fully clean and inspect the pistons, disassemble the caliper and overhaul it (see Section 7).

11 Where applicable fit the shim onto the back of each pad **(see illustration 6.4c)**. Lightly smear the back of the pad backing material or shim and the edges of the backing material where it contacts the caliper body

with copper-based grease, making sure that none gets on the friction material. Also smear the pad pin.

12 Insert the pads into the caliper so that the friction material of each pad faces the disc **(see illustration 6.4b)**. Locate the pad spring and insert the pin, making sure it locates correctly through the spring and pads **(see illustration)**. Tighten the pin finger-tight.

13 Slide the caliper onto the disc and torque arm, making sure the pads locate correctly on each side **(see illustration 6.3)**. Install the caliper mounting bolts and tighten them finger-tight **(see illustration)**. Fit the torque arm bolt and tighten the nut to the torque setting specified at the beginning of the Chapter **(see illustration 6.2)**. Now tighten the caliper mounting bolts to the specified torque.

14 Tighten the pad pin to the torque setting specified at the beginning of this Chapter **(see illustration 6.1)**.

15 Operate the brake pedal until the pads contact with the disc. Check the level of fluid in the hydraulic reservoir and top-up if necessary (see *Pre-ride checks*).

16 Check the operation of the rear brake before riding the motorcycle.

7   Rear brake caliper

> ⚠ **Warning: If the caliper is in need of overhaul all old brake fluid should be flushed from the system. Also, the dust created by the brake**

system may contain asbestos, which is harmful to your health. Never blow it out with compressed air and do not inhale any of it. An approved filtering mask should be worn when working on the brakes. Overhaul must be done in a spotlessly clean work area to avoid contamination and possible failure of the brake hydraulic system components. Do not, under any circumstances, use petroleum-based solvents to clean brake parts. Use clean DOT 4 brake fluid, dedicated brake cleaner or denatured alcohol only, as described. To prevent damage from spilled brake fluid, always cover paintwork when working on the braking system.

Removal

Note: *If the caliper is being overhauled (usually due to sticking pistons or fluid leaks) read through the entire procedure first and make sure that you have obtained all the new parts required, including some new DOT 4 brake fluid.*

1 If the caliper is being overhauled, slacken the brake pad retaining pin **(see illustration 6.1)**. If the caliper is just being displaced the brake pads can be left in place.

2 If the caliper is being completely removed or overhauled, unscrew the brake hose banjo bolt and detach the banjo union, noting its alignment with the caliper **(see illustration)**. Wrap Clingfilm and rag around the banjo union and secure the hose in an upright position to minimise fluid loss. Discard the sealing washers, as new ones must be fitted on reassembly.

3 If the caliper body is to be split into its halves for overhaul, loosen the caliper body joining bolts and retighten them lightly **(see illustration 6.1)**.

4 Unscrew the nut on the bolt securing the brake torque arm to the caliper **(see illustration 6.2)**.

5 Unscrew the caliper mounting bolts, then withdraw the torque arm bolt and slide the caliper off the disc and the torque arm **(see illustration 6.3)**. If the caliper is just being displaced, secure it to the motorcycle with a cable-tie to avoid straining the brake hose. **Note:** *Do not operate the brake pedal while the caliper is off the disc. If the caliper is being overhauled, remove the brake pads (see Section 6).*

6.13 Locate the caliper and insert the bolts

7.2 Brake hose banjo bolt (arrowed)

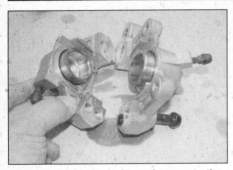

7.7a Unscrew the bolts and separate the halves

7.7b Discard the caliper O-ring

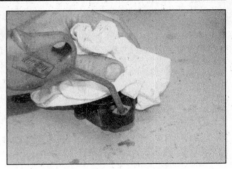

7.8a Apply the compressed air as described . . .

7.8b . . . until the piston is displaced

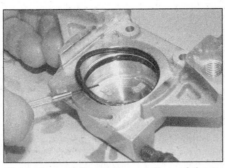

7.11 Remove the seals and discard them

7.14a Lubricate the new seals with clean fluid

Overhaul

6 Clean the exterior of the caliper with denatured alcohol or brake system cleaner. Have some clean rag ready to catch any spilled brake fluid.

7 Unscrew the caliper body joining bolts and separate the body halves, catching any residual fluid with the rag **(see illustration)**. Remove the caliper body O-ring from whichever body half it is in and discard it **(see illustration)** – fit a new one on reassembly.

8 Place a caliper half piston-up on the bench. Find a suitable bolt and thread it into the banjo bolt bore in the outer half. Get a wad of rag and/or block of wood and hold it against the piston as a cushion to protect your hand as the piston is forced out. Apply compressed air gradually and progressively, starting with a fairly low pressure, to the fluid passage on the

caliper joint and allow the piston to ease out of its bore, controlling it with hand pressure **(see illustrations)**. Repeat the procedure for the other caliper half.

9 If a piston is stuck in its bore due to corrosion the caliper should be replaced with a new one. Do not try to remove a piston by levering it out or by using pliers or other grips.

10 Mark each piston and the caliper body to ensure that the pistons can be matched to their original bores on reassembly.

11 Remove the dust seals and the piston seals from the piston bores using a soft wooden or plastic tool to avoid scratching the bores **(see illustration)**. Discard the seals as new ones must be fitted on reassembly.

12 Clean the pistons and bores, paying attention to the seal grooves, with clean DOT 4 brake fluid. If compressed air is available,

blow it through the fluid galleries in the caliper to ensure they are clear (make sure it is filtered and unlubricated).

Caution: Do not, under any circumstances, use a petroleum-based solvent to clean brake parts.

13 Inspect the caliper bores and pistons for signs of corrosion, nicks and burrs and loss of plating. If surface defects are present, the pistons and/or the caliper assembly must be replaced with new ones. If the caliper is in poor condition, the master cylinder should also be checked.

14 Lubricate the new piston seals with clean brake fluid and fit them in their grooves in the caliper bores **(see illustrations)**.

15 Lubricate the new dust seals with clean brake fluid and fit them in their grooves in the caliper bores **(see illustration)**.

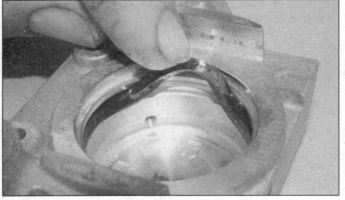

7.14b Fit the piston seal . . .

7.15 . . . followed by the dust seal

7.16a Lubricate each piston . . .

7.16b . . . then fit it into the bore and push it all the way in

7.17a Fit a new O-ring . . .

16 Lubricate the pistons with clean brake fluid and install them, closed-end first, into the caliper bores, taking care not to displace the seals. Using your thumbs, push the pistons all the way in, making sure they enter the bore squarely **(see illustrations)**.

17 Lubricate the new caliper body O-ring with clean brake fluid and fit it into the appropriate half of the caliper body **(see illustration)**. Join the two halves of the caliper body together, ensuring that the O-ring stays in place **(see illustration)**. Apply a suitable thread locking compound to the joining bolts and tighten them evenly to the torque setting specified at the beginning of this Chapter **(see illustration)**. If it is not possible to tighten the bolts fully at this stage, tighten them as much as possible now and tighten them fully once the caliper has been installed on the machine, but do not take long as the threadlock will set.

Installation

18 If removed, install the brake pads (see Section 6).

19 Slide the caliper onto the brake disc and torque arm, making sure the pads fit on each side of the disc **(see illustration 6.3)**.

20 Install the caliper mounting bolts and tighten them finger-tight **(see illustration 6.13)**. Fit the torque arm bolt and tighten the nut to the torque setting specified at the beginning of the Chapter **(see illustration 6.2)**. Now tighten the caliper mounting bolts to the specified torque.

21 If the caliper was overhauled and if not

already done, tighten the caliper body joining bolts to the specified torque setting **(see illustration 6.1)**. If the pads were removed tighten the pad pin to the specified torque setting.

22 If removed, connect the brake hose to the caliper, using new sealing washers on each side of the banjo fitting. Align the fitting as noted on removal **(see illustration 7.2)**. Tighten the banjo bolt to the specified torque setting.

23 Top up the hydraulic reservoir with DOT 4 brake fluid (see *Pre-ride checks*) and bleed the system as described in Section 11. Check that there are no fluid leaks and test the operation of the brake before riding the motorcycle.

8 Rear brake disc

Inspection

1 Refer to Section 4 of this Chapter, noting that the dial gauge should be attached to the swingarm.

Removal

2 Remove the wheel (see Section 15).
Caution: Don't lay the wheel down and allow it to rest on the disc or sprocket – they could become warped. Set the wheel on wood blocks so the wheel rim supports the weight of the wheel.

3 If you are not replacing the disc with a new one, mark the relationship of the disc to the wheel so it can be installed in the same position. Unscrew the disc retaining bolts, loosening them evenly and a little at a time in a criss-cross pattern to avoid distorting the disc, then remove the disc **(see illustration)**.

Installation

4 Before installing the disc, make sure there is no dirt or corrosion where the disc seats on the hub. If the disc does not sit flat when it is bolted down, it will appear to be warped when checked or when the rear brake is used.

5 Install the disc on the wheel with its marked side facing out, aligning the previously applied matchmarks (if you're reinstalling the original disc).

6 Clean the threads of the disc mounting bolts, then apply a suitable non-permanent thread locking compound. Install the bolts and tighten them evenly and a little at a time in a criss-cross pattern to the torque setting specified at the beginning of this Chapter. Clean the disc using acetone or brake system cleaner. If a new disc has been installed, remove any protective coating from its working surfaces and fit new brake pads.

7 Install the rear wheel (see Section 15).

8 Operate the brake pedal several times to bring the pads into contact with the disc. Check the operation of the brake before riding the motorcycle.

7.17b . . . then join the caliper halves . . .

7.17c . . . install the bolts and tighten them to the specified torque

8.3 Disc is secured by five bolts

9.1 Remove the split pin and washer (A) and withdraw the clevis pin (B)

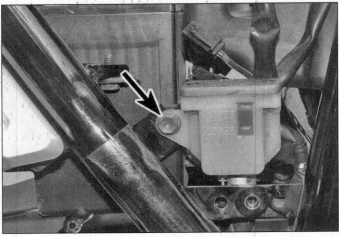

9.2 Reservoir mounting bolt (arrowed)

9 Rear brake master cylinder

Warning: If the brake master cylinder is in need of an overhaul all old brake fluid should be flushed from the system. Overhaul must be done in a spotlessly clean work area to avoid contamination and possible failure of the brake hydraulic system components. Do not, under any circumstances, use petroleum-based solvents to clean brake parts. Use clean DOT 4 brake fluid, dedicated brake cleaner or denatured alcohol only, as described. To prevent damage from spilled brake fluid, always cover paintwork when working on the braking system.

Removal

Note: If the master cylinder is being overhauled (usually due to sticking or poor action, or fluid leaks) read through the entire procedure first and make sure that you have obtained all the new parts required, including some new DOT 4 brake fluid.

1 Remove the split pin and washer from the clevis pin securing the master cylinder pushrod to the brake pedal **(see illustration)**. Withdraw the clevis pin and separate the pushrod from the pedal. Discard the split pin as a new one must be fitted on reassembly.

2 Remove the right-hand side panel (see Chapter 7). Undo the bolt securing the fluid reservoir to the frame and manoeuvre the reservoir down and out from behind the frame tube **(see illustration)**.

3 If the master cylinder is being completely removed or overhauled and not just displaced for swingarm removal undo the brake hose banjo bolt and detach the banjo union, noting its alignment with the master cylinder **(see illustration)**. Wrap Clingfilm and rag around the banjo union and secure the hose in an upright position to minimise fluid loss. Discard the sealing washers as new ones must be fitted on reassembly.

4 Unscrew the bolts securing the master cylinder to the footrest bracket and remove the master cylinder **(see illustration)**.

Overhaul

5 Undo the reservoir cover screws and remove the reservoir cover and diaphragm **(see illustration)**. Pour the brake fluid into a suitable container. Release the clip securing the reservoir hose to the union on the master

cylinder and detach the hose, being prepared to catch any residual fluid. Wipe any remaining fluid out of the reservoir with a clean rag. Release the circlip securing the fluid reservoir hose union and detach the union from the master cylinder. Discard the O-ring as a new one must be fitted on reassembly. Inspect the reservoir hose for cracks or splits and replace it with a new one if necessary.

6 Carefully remove the dust boot from the master cylinder to reveal the pushrod retaining circlip.

7 Depress the pushrod and use circlip pliers to remove the circlip. Slide out the pushrod,

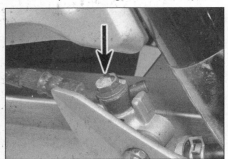

9.3 Brake hose banjo bolt (arrowed)

9.4 Master cylinder bolts (arrowed)

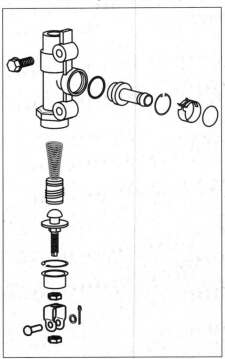

9.5 Rear brake master cylinder

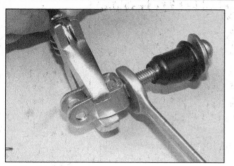

9.8 Hold the clevis to loosen the locknut

9.12a Make sure the seal is correctly fitted on the piston

9.12b Fit the cup onto the end of the spring, locating the peg in the hole

piston assembly and spring, noting how they fit. If they are difficult to remove, apply low pressure compressed air to the brake fluid outlet. Lay the parts out in the proper order to prevent confusion during reassembly.

8 If required, mark the position of the clevis locknut on the pushrod, then loosen the locknut and thread the clevis nut, clevis and locknut off the pushrod **(see illustration)**.

9 Clean the master cylinder and reservoir with clean DOT 4 brake fluid. If compressed air is available, blow it through the fluid galleries to ensure they are clear (make sure the air is filtered and unlubricated).

Caution: Do not, under any circumstances, use a petroleum-based solvent to clean brake parts.

10 Check the master cylinder bore for corrosion, scratches, nicks and score marks. If damage or wear is evident, the master cylinder must be replaced with a new one. If the master cylinder is in poor condition, then the caliper should be checked as well.

11 The dust boot, circlip, piston, seal, cup and spring are all included in the master cylinder rebuild kit. Use all of the new parts, regardless of the apparent condition of the old ones.

12 Smear the cup and seal with new brake fluid. If the seal is not already on the piston, fit it into its groove so the wider end will fit into the master cylinder first **(see illustration)**. Fit the cup onto the narrow end of the spring **(see illustration)**. Lubricate the master cylinder bore with new brake fluid.

13 Fit the clevis locknut, the clevis and the

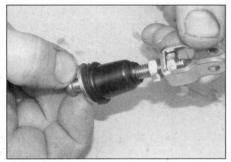

9.13 Thread the locknut and the clevis and its nut onto the pushrod

clevis nut onto the master cylinder pushrod end **(see illustration)**. Position the clevis as noted on removal, but leave the locknut finger-tight.

14 Fit the spring wide-end first into the master cylinder and push the cup in, making sure its lips do not turn inside out.

15 Lubricate the piston with clean brake fluid and slide it into the master cylinder and up against the cup and spring. Make sure the lips on the seal do not turn inside out.

16 Smear some silicone grease onto the rounded end of the pushrod and locate it against the end of the piston. Push the piston in using the pushrod until the washer is beyond the circlip groove, then fit the new circlip, making sure it locates properly.

17 Fit the rubber boot, making sure the lips are seated correctly in the master cylinder and around the pushrod.

18 Fit a new O-ring onto the fluid reservoir hose union, then press the union into the master cylinder and secure it with the circlip.

Installation

19 Locate the master cylinder on the inside of the footrest bracket, then fit the bolts and tighten them to the torque setting specified at the beginning of this Chapter **(see illustration 9.4)**.

20 Align the brake pedal with the master cylinder pushrod clevis and install the clevis pin **(see illustration 9.1)**. Fit the washer and a new split pin and bend the pin ends round the clevis pin. If the clevis position on the pushrod was disturbed during overhaul, check the brake pedal height (see Chapter 1, Section 10). Tighten the clevis locknut.

21 If detached, align the brake hose as noted on removal and connect the hose to the master cylinder, using a new sealing washer on each side of the banjo fitting **(see illustration 9.3)**. Tighten the banjo bolt to the torque setting specified at the beginning of this Chapter.

22 Fit the fluid reservoir onto the frame, making sure the pin on the back locates in the hole in the frame bracket **(see illustration 9.2)**. If detached connect the hose to the union on the master cylinder and secure it with the clip. Check that the hose is secured with a clip at the reservoir end as well. If the clips have weakened, use new ones.

23 Fill the fluid reservoir with new DOT 4 brake fluid (see *Pre-ride checks*). Refer to Section 11 and bleed the air from the system.

24 Check the operation of the brake carefully before riding the motorcycle.

10 Brake hoses and fittings

Inspection

1 Brake hose condition should be checked regularly and the hoses replaced with new ones at the specified interval (see Chapter 1).

2 Twist and flex the hoses while looking for cracks, bulges and seeping hydraulic fluid. Check extra carefully around the areas where the hoses connect with the banjo fittings, as these are common areas for hose failure.

3 Inspect the banjo fittings connected to the brake hoses. If the fittings are rusted, scratched or cracked, fit new hoses.

Removal and installation

4 The brake hoses have banjo fittings on each end. Cover the surrounding area with plenty of rag and unscrew the banjo bolt at each end of the hose, noting the alignment of the fitting with the master cylinder or brake caliper **(see illustrations 3.3, 5.4, 7.2 and 9.3)**. Free the hose from any clips or guides and remove it, noting its routing. Discard the sealing washers. **Note:** *Do not operate the brake lever or pedal while a brake hose is disconnected.*

5 Position the new hose, making sure it isn't twisted or otherwise strained, and ensure that it is correctly routed through any clips or guides and is clear of all moving components.

6 Check that the fittings align correctly, then install the banjo bolts, using new sealing washers on both sides of the fittings **(see illustration 5.18)**. Tighten the banjo bolts to the torque setting specified at the beginning of this Chapter.

7 Flush the old brake fluid from the system, refill with new DOT 4 brake fluid (see *Pre-ride checks*) and bleed the air from the system (see Section 11).

8 Check the operation of the brakes before riding the motorcycle.

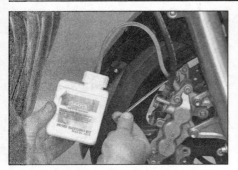

11.2 Set-up for bleeding the brakes

11.5a Front caliper bleed valve (arrowed)

11.5b Rear caliper bleed valves (arrowed)

11 Brake system bleeding and fluid change

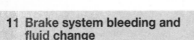

Note: *If required use a commercially available vacuum-type brake bleeding tool (see illustration 11.17). If bleeding the system using the conventional method does not work sufficiently well, it is advisable to obtain a bleeder and repeat the procedure detailed below, following the manufacturer's instructions for using the tool.*

Bleeding

1 Bleeding the brakes is simply the process of removing air from the brake fluid reservoir, the hose and the brake caliper. Bleeding is necessary whenever a brake system hydraulic connection is loosened, after a component or hose is replaced with a new one, or when the master cylinder or caliper is overhauled. Leaks in the system may also allow air to enter, but leaking brake fluid will reveal their presence and warn you of the need for repair.

2 To bleed the brakes, you will need some new DOT 4 brake fluid, a length of clear vinyl or plastic hose, a small container partially filled with clean brake fluid, some rags and a spanner to fit the brake caliper bleed valve **(see illustration).** Kits containing a hose with one-way valve fitted through the cap of a container are commercially available at little cost.

3 Cover the fuel tank and other painted components to prevent damage in the event that brake fluid is spilled.

4 Refer to 'Pre-ride checks' and remove the reservoir cover, diaphragm plate (front brake) and diaphragm and slowly pump the brake lever (front brake) or pedal (rear brake) a few times, until no air bubbles can be seen floating up from the holes in the bottom of the reservoir. This bleeds the air from the master cylinder end of the line. Temporarily refit the reservoir cover.

5 Pull the dust cap off the bleed valve **(see illustrations).** Attach one end of the clear vinyl or plastic hose to the bleed valve and submerge the other end in the clean brake fluid in the container **(see illustration 11.2).**
Note: *To avoid damaging the bleed valve during the procedure, loosen it and then tighten it temporarily with a ring spanner before attaching the hose. With the hose*

attached, the valve can then be opened and closed either with an open-ended spanner, or by leaving the ring spanner located on the valve and fitting the hose above it.

6 Check the fluid level in the reservoir. Do not allow the fluid level to drop below the lower mark during the procedure.

7 Carefully pump the brake lever or pedal three or four times and hold it in (front) or down (rear) while opening the bleed valve. When the valve is opened, brake fluid will flow out of the caliper into the clear tubing, and the lever will move to the handlebar, or the pedal will move down. If there is air in the system there will be air bubbles in the brake fluid coming out of the caliper.

8 Tighten the bleed valve, then release the brake lever or pedal gradually. Repeat the process, topping up the reservoir as required, until no air bubbles are visible in the brake fluid leaving the caliper, and the lever or pedal is firm when applied. On completion, disconnect the hose, then tighten the bleed valve to the torque setting specified at the beginning of this Chapter and fit the dust cap. When bleeding the rear brake, bleed both sides of the caliper – it has two bleed valves **(see illustration 11.5b).**

> **HAYNES HiNT** *If it is not possible to produce a firm feel to the lever or pedal, the fluid may be aerated. Let the brake fluid in the system stabilise for a few hours and then repeat the procedure when the tiny bubbles in the system have settled out.*

9 Top-up the reservoir, then fit the diaphragm, diaphragm plate (front brake) and cover (see Pre-ride checks). Wipe up any spilled brake fluid. Check the entire system for fluid leaks.
10 Check the operation of the brakes before riding the motorcycle.

Fluid change

11 Changing the brake fluid is a similar process to bleeding the brakes and requires the same materials plus a suitable tool for siphoning the fluid out of the reservoir. Also ensure that the container is large enough to take all the old fluid when it is flushed out of the system.
12 Follow Steps 3 and 5, then remove the reservoir cover, diaphragm plate (front brake)

and diaphragm. Carefully pump the brake lever or pedal three or four times and hold it in (front) or down (rear) while opening the caliper bleed valve. When the valve is opened, brake fluid will flow out of the caliper into the clear tubing, and the lever will move toward the handlebar, or the pedal will move down.
13 Tighten the bleed valve, then release the brake lever or pedal gradually. Keep the reservoir topped-up with new fluid to above the LOWER level at all times or air may enter the system and greatly increase the length of the task. Repeat the process until new fluid can be seen emerging from the caliper bleed valve. Repeat the process on the other front caliper if changing the front brake fluid.

> **HAYNES HiNT** *Old brake fluid is invariably much darker in colour than new fluid, making it easy to see when all old fluid has been expelled from the system.*

14 Disconnect the hose, then tighten the bleed valve to the specified torque setting and fit the dust cap.
15 Top-up the reservoir, then fit the diaphragm, diaphragm plate (front brake) and cover (see Pre-ride checks). Wipe up any spilled brake fluid. Check the entire system for fluid leaks.
16 Check the operation of the brakes before riding the motorcycle.

Draining the system for overhaul

17 Draining the brake fluid is again a similar process to bleeding the brakes. The quickest and easiest way is to use a commercially available vacuum-type brake bleeding tool **(see illustration)** – follow the manufacturer's

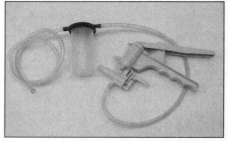

11.17 Vacuum pump to draw the fluid from or through the system

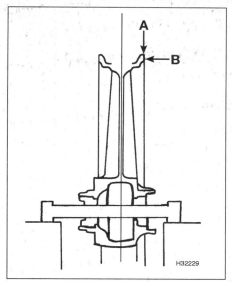

12.2 Check the wheel for radial (out-of-round) runout (A) and axial (side-to-side) runout (B)

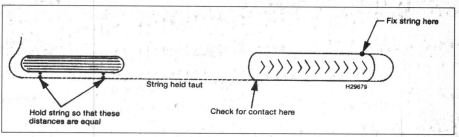

13.5 Wheel alignment check using string

instructions. Otherwise follow the procedure described above for changing the fluid, but quite simply do not put any new fluid into the reservoir – the system fills itself with air instead.

12 Wheel inspection and repair

1 Support the bike on its centrestand. Clean the wheels thoroughly to remove mud and dirt that may interfere with the inspection procedure or mask defects. Make a general check of the wheels (see Chapter 1) and tyres (see *Pre-ride checks*).

2 Attach a dial gauge to the fork or the swingarm and position its tip against the side of the wheel rim. Spin the wheel slowly and check the axial (side-to-side) runout of the rim **(see illustration)**.

3 In order to accurately check radial (out of round) runout with the dial gauge, remove the wheel from the machine, and the tyre from the wheel. With the axle clamped in a vice and the dial gauge positioned on the top of the rim, the wheel can be rotated to check the runout **(see illustration 12.2)**.

4 An easier, though slightly less accurate, method is to attach a stiff wire pointer to the fork leg or the swingarm and position the end a fraction of an inch from the wheel rim where the wheel and tyre join. If the wheel is true, the distance from the pointer to the rim will be constant as the wheel is rotated. **Note:** *If wheel runout is excessive, check the wheel bearings very carefully before renewing the wheel.*

5 The wheels should also be inspected for cracks, flat spots on the rim and other damage. Look very closely for dents in the area where

the tyre bead contacts the rim. Dents in this area may prevent complete sealing of the tyre against the rim, which leads to deflation of the tyre over a period of time. If damage is evident, or if runout in either direction is excessive, the wheel will have to be renewed. Never attempt to repair a damaged cast alloy wheel.

13 Wheel alignment check

1 Misalignment of the wheels due to a bent frame or forks can cause strange and possibly serious handling problems. If the frame or forks are at fault, repair by a frame specialist or renewal are the only options.

2 To check wheel alignment you will need an assistant, a length of string or a perfectly straight piece of wood and a ruler. A plumb bob or spirit level for checking that the wheels are vertical will also be required.

3 In order to make a proper check of the wheels it is necessary to support the bike on its centrestand. First ensure that the chain adjuster markings coincide on each side of the swingarm (see Chapter 1, Section 1). Next, measure the width of both tyres at their widest points. Subtract the smaller measurement from the larger measurement, then divide the difference by two. The result is the amount of offset that should exist between the front and rear tyres on both sides of the machine.

4 If a string is used, have your assistant hold one end of it about halfway between the floor and the rear axle, with the string touching the back edge of the rear tyre sidewall.

5 Run the other end of the string forward and pull it tight so that it is roughly parallel to the floor **(see illustration)**. Slowly bring the string into contact with the front edge of the rear tyre sidewall, then turn the front wheel until it is parallel with the string. Measure the distance from the front tyre sidewall to the string.

6 Repeat the procedure on the other side of the motorcycle. The distance from the front tyre sidewall to the string should be equal on both sides.

7 As previously mentioned, a perfectly straight length of wood or metal bar may be substituted for the string **(see illustration)**.

8 If the distance between the string and tyre is greater on one side, or if the rear wheel appears to be out of alignment, have your

machine checked by a Suzuki dealer or frame specialist.

9 If the front-to-back alignment is correct, the wheels still may be out of alignment vertically.

10 Using a plumb bob or spirit level, check the rear wheel to make sure it is vertical. To do this, hold the string of the plumb bob against the tyre upper sidewall and allow the weight to settle just off the floor. If the string touches both the upper and lower tyre sidewalls and is perfectly straight, the wheel is vertical. If it is not, adjust the stand until it is.

11 Once the rear wheel is vertical, check the front wheel in the same manner. If both wheels are not perfectly vertical, the frame and/or major suspension components are bent.

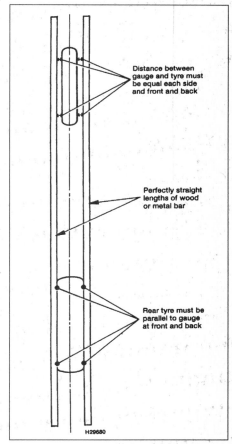

Distance between gauge and tyre must be equal each side and front and back

Perfectly straight lengths of wood or metal bar

Rear tyre must be parallel to gauge at front and back

13.7 Wheel alignment check using a straight-edge

14 Front wheel

Removal

Note: *All models require a 24 mm Hex key (Suzuki part No. 09900-17840, or commercially available equivalent) to unscrew and/or tighten the axle. If one is not available you can make a tool using suitable nuts and bolts* **(see illustration 14.3c)**.

1 Put the bike on its centrestand on level ground and elevate the front wheel using a jack under the engine, with a piece of wood between them to spread the load. Make sure the bike is secure.

2 Displace the front brake calipers (see Section 3). **Note:** *Do not operate the brake lever while the calipers are off the disc.*

3 Loosen the axle clamp bolts on the bottom of the right-hand fork **(see illustration)**. Support the wheel, then unscrew the axle and withdraw it from the right-hand side, then lower the wheel and remove it from between the forks **(see illustrations)**.

4 If required, loosen the pinch bolts on the bottom of the left-hand fork and withdraw the axle nut **(see illustration)**.

Caution: Don't lay the wheel down and allow it to rest on either disc – the disc could become warped. Set the wheel on wood blocks so the wheel rim supports the weight of the wheel.

5 Clean the axle, and the axle nut if removed, and remove any corrosion using steel wool. Check the axle is straight by rolling it on a flat surface such as a piece of plate glass. If available, place the axle in V-blocks and check for runout using a dial gauge. If the axle is bent or the runout exceeds the limit specified at the beginning of this Chapter, replace it with a new one.

6 Wipe any old grease off the bearing seals and check the condition of the seals and the wheel bearings (see Section 16).

Installation

7 If removed, fit the axle nut into the bottom of the left-hand fork and push it in so that its

14.3a Loosen the clamp bolts (arrowed) . . .

14.3c . . . using a nut and bolt tool as shown if necessary

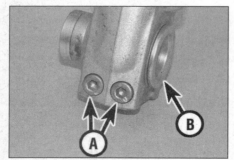

14.4 Loosen the clamp bolts (A) and remove the axle nut (B) if required

flanged rim is pressed against the outside of the fork **(see illustration 14.4)**. Tighten the clamp bolts to the torque setting specified at the beginning of this Chapter, making sure the nut remains pressed against the fork.

8 Manoeuvre the wheel into position between the forks, making sure the directional arrow is pointing in the normal direction of rotation **(see illustration)**. Apply a thin coat of grease to the axle and to the lips of the bearing seals.

9 Lift the wheel and slide the axle through from the right-hand side, and thread it into the axle nut **(see illustration 14.3d)**. Push the wheel to the left so that the inner end of the axle nut locates in the bearing seal, then tighten the axle finger-tight.

10 Install the brake calipers (see Section 3), then tighten the axle to the specified torque setting **(see illustration)**.

11 Move the motorcycle off the stand, apply

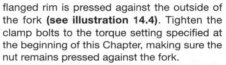

14.8 Make sure the wheel is the right way round

the front brake and pump the front forks a few times to settle all components in position.

12 Tighten the axle clamp bolts on the right-hand fork to the specified torque setting **(see illustration 14.3a)**.

13 Check the operation of the front brake before riding the motorcycle.

15 Rear wheel

Removal

1 Support the motorcycle on its centrestand. Displace the rear brake caliper (see Section 7). **Note:** *Do not operate the brake pedal while the caliper is off the disc.*

2 Slacken the drive chain (see Chapter 1).

3 Unscrew the axle nut from the left-hand end of the axle and remove the washer and the

14.3b . . . then unscrew the axle . . .

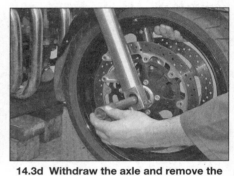

14.3d Withdraw the axle and remove the wheel

14.10 Tighten the axle to the correct torque setting

15.3 Remove the axle nut, the washer, and the adjuster block (arrowed)

15.4a Support the wheel and withdraw the axle

15.4b Remove the caliper bracket . . .

chain adjuster block, noting how it fits **(see illustration)**.

4 Support the wheel and withdraw the axle with the right-hand adjuster block, then lower the wheel **(see illustration)**. Remove the caliper bracket and the spacer from the right-hand side **(see illustrations)**.

5 Disengage the chain from the sprocket then draw the wheel back and remove it **(see illustration)**.

6 Remove the spacer from the left-hand side **(see illustration)**. Remove the chain adjuster block from the axle.

Caution: Don't lay the wheel down and allow it to rest on the disc or the sprocket – they could become warped. Set the wheel on wood blocks so the wheel rim supports the weight of the wheel. Do not operate the brake pedal with the wheel removed.

7 Clean the axle and remove any corrosion using steel wool. Check the axle is straight by rolling it on a flat surface such as a piece of plate glass. If available, place the axle in V-blocks and check for runout using a dial gauge. If the axle is bent or the runout exceeds the limit specified at the beginning of this Chapter, renew it.

8 Wipe all old grease off the bearing seal in the sprocket coupling and check the condition of the seal and the wheel bearings (see Section 16).

Installation

9 Apply a thin coat of grease to the lips of the sprocket coupling seal, to the inside and the faces of the axle spacers and the caliper

15.4c . . . and the spacer

bracket, and to the axle. Fit the spacer into the seal in the left-hand side of the hub **(see illustration 15.6)**. Slide the right-hand chain adjuster block onto the axle with the raised sections facing the axle head.

10 Manoeuvre the wheel into position between the ends of the swingarm and fit the drive chain around the sprocket **(see illustration 15.5)**.

11 Fit the spacer into the right-hand side, then locate the caliper bracket between the spacer and the swingarm **(see illustrations 15.4c and b)**.

12 Lift the wheel into position, making sure the caliper bracket and spacers stay in place and the bracket is correctly aligned with the wheel and the swingarm, and slide the axle through from the right-hand side **(see illustration 15.4a)**.

15.5 Disengage the chain from the sprocket and remove the wheel

13 Locate the right-hand chain adjuster block in the swingarm with the raised edges vertical and the thicker one to the front, and locate the flats on the axle head between the raised edges **(see illustration)**. Check that everything is correctly aligned, then fit the left-hand adjuster block with its raised edge vertical and to the front **(see illustration)**. Fit the washer and the axle nut and tighten the nut finger-tight **(see illustration 15.3)**.

14 Adjust the chain slack as described in Chapter 1.

15 Tighten the axle nut to the torque setting specified at the beginning of this Chapter.

16 Install the brake caliper (see Section 7). Operate the brake pedal several times to bring the pads into contact with the disc. Check the operation of the brake before riding the motorcycle.

15.6 Remove the spacer

15.13a Make sure the right-hand adjuster block is the correct way round and the axle head locates correctly

15.13b Make sure the left-hand adjuster block is the correct way round

16.2 Lever out the bearing seals

16 Wheel bearing renewal

Caution: Don't lay the wheel down and allow it to rest on the disc or the sprocket – they could become warped. Set the wheel on wood blocks so the wheel rim/tyre supports the weight of the wheel, or keep the wheel upright. Don't operate either brake with the wheel removed.

Note: *Always renew the wheel bearings in sets, never individually. Avoid using a high pressure cleaner on the wheel bearing area.*

Front wheel bearings

1 Remove the front wheel (see Section 14).
2 Lever out the bearing seal from each side

16.7 Using a socket to drive the bearing in

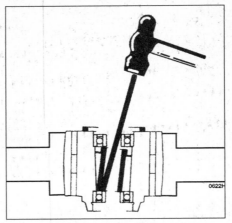

16.4a Move the spacer aside to expose the bearing inner race . . .

of the hub using a seal hook or a flat-bladed screwdriver **(see illustration)**. Take care not to damage the hub. Discard the seals as new ones must be fitted on reassembly.

3 Inspect the bearings – check that the inner race turns smoothly and that the outer race is a tight fit in the hub (see *Tools and Workshop Tips (Section 5)* in the Reference Section). **Note:** *Suzuki recommends that the bearings are not removed unless they are going to be replaced with new ones.*

4 If the bearings are worn, remove the left-hand bearing first. Place the wheel on the blocks so the left-hand side faces upwards and use an internal expanding puller with slide-hammer attachment to pull the bearing out of the hub **(see illustrations 16.13a and b)**. Alternatively the bearing can be drifted out using a suitable punch inserted through the wheel from the opposite side – move the bearing spacer to one side to reveal the inner race on which the drift can be located **(see illustrations)**. Use a drift with a shaped end for better purchase if necessary, and move the spacer and drift round to drive the bearing out evenly and squarely. After removing the left-hand bearing the spacer which fits between the bearings can be removed.

5 With the spacer removed it is easier to drive

16.4b . . . then drive the bearing out

out the right-hand bearing, again by passing a drift through the opposite side of the hub. Note that a piece of tubing or a proper bearing driver the same diameter as the inner race can be used in place of the drift.

6 Thoroughly clean the hub area of the wheel with a suitable solvent and inspect the bearing housings for scoring and wear. If the housings are damaged, consult a Suzuki dealer before reassembling the wheel.

7 The new bearings can be installed in the hub using a drawbolt arrangement or by using a bearing driver or suitable socket (see *Tools and Workshop Tips*) **(see illustration)**. Ensure that the drawbolt washer or driver (as applicable) bears only on the outer race and does not contact the bearing housing.

8 Install the left-hand bearing first, with its marked (sealed) side facing outwards. Ensure the bearing is fitted squarely and all the way into its housing until it seats. When seated turn the wheel over, install the bearing spacer and drive the other new bearing into its housing, noting that it will seat against the bearing spacer.

9 Apply a smear of grease to the new seals, then press them into the hub **(see illustration)**. Level the seals with the rim of the hub with a small block of wood **(see illustration)**.

10 Clean the brake discs using acetone or brake system cleaner, then install the wheel (see Section 14).

Rear wheel bearings

11 Remove the wheel (see Section 15). Lift

16.9a Press the seal into place . . .

16.9b . . . setting it flush with the rim

16.11a Lift the sprocket coupling off the wheel . . .

16.11b . . . and remove the spacer

16.13a Locate the curved bottom edge of the puller in the gap between the bearing and the spacer then expand the ends to lock it in place . . .

the sprocket coupling out of the hub, and remove the spacer that fits between them from the coupling **(see illustrations)**.

12 Inspect the bearings in both sides of the hub – check that the inner race turns smoothly and that the outer race is a tight fit in the hub (see *Tools and Workshop Tips (Section 5)* in the *Reference* section). **Note:** *Suzuki recommends that the bearings are not removed unless they are going to be renewed.*

13 If the bearings are worn, remove the left-hand bearing first. Place the wheel on the blocks so the left-hand side faces upwards and use an internal expanding puller with slide-hammer attachment to pull the bearing out of the hub **(see illustrations)**. Alternatively insert a suitable drift through the wheel hub from the opposite side and drive the bearing out. Move the bearing spacer to one side to reveal the inner race on which the drift can be located **(see illustrations 16.4a and b)**. Use a drift with a shaped end for better purchase if necessary, and move the spacer and drift round to drive the bearing out evenly and squarely. After removing the left-hand bearing the spacer which fits between the bearings can be removed.

14 With the spacer removed it is easier to drive out the right-hand bearing, again by passing a drift through the opposite side of the hub. Note that a piece of tubing or a proper bearing driver the same diameter as the inner race can be used in place of the drift.

15 Thoroughly clean the hub area of the

wheel with a suitable solvent and inspect the bearing housings for scoring and wear. If the housings are damaged, consult a Suzuki dealer before reassembling the wheel.

16 The new bearings can be installed in the hub using a drawbolt arrangement or by using a bearing driver or suitable socket (see *Tools and Workshop Tips*) **(see illustration 16.7)**. Ensure that the drawbolt washer or driver (as applicable) bears only on the outer race and does not contact the bearing housing.

17 Install the right-hand bearing first, with the marked (sealed) side facing outwards. Ensure the bearing is fitted squarely and all the way into its housing until it seats. When seated turn the wheel over, install the bearing spacer and then the other new bearing, noting that it will seat on the bearing spacer.

18 Clean the brake disc using acetone or brake system cleaner. Fit the spacer into the sprocket coupling bearing **(see illustration 16.11b)**. Check the sprocket coupling/rubber dampers (see Section 20), then fit the sprocket coupling onto the wheel **(see illustration 16.11a)**. Install the wheel (see Section 15).

Sprocket coupling bearing

19 Remove the wheel (see Section 15). Lift the sprocket coupling out of the hub, and remove the spacer that fits between them from the coupling **(see illustrations 16.11a and b)**.

20 Lever out the bearing seal on the outside of the coupling using a seal hook or a flat-bladed screwdriver **(see illustration)**. Take care not to damage the rim of the coupling. Discard the seal as a new one should be fitted on reassembly.

21 Inspect the bearing – check that the inner race turns smoothly and that the outer race is a tight fit in the coupling (see *Tools and Workshop Tips (Section 5)* in the Reference Section). **Note:** *Suzuki recommends that the bearing is not removed unless it is going to be replaced with a new one.*

22 Support the coupling on blocks of wood, sprocket side down, and drive the bearing out from the inside using a bearing driver or socket on the inner race **(see illustration)**.

23 Thoroughly clean the bearing housing with a suitable solvent and inspect it for scoring and wear. If the housing is damaged, consult a Suzuki dealer before reassembling the wheel.

24 The new bearing can be installed in the coupling using a drawbolt arrangement or by using a bearing driver or suitable socket (see *Tools and Workshop Tips*). Ensure that the drawbolt washer or driver (as applicable) bears only on the outer race and does not contact the bearing housing. Ensure the bearing is fitted squarely and all the way into its housing until it seats.

25 Apply a smear of grease to the new seal, then press it into the coupling, using a bearing driver or suitable socket. Level the seal with

16.13b . . . then use the slide-hammer to jar the bearing out

16.20 Lever out the bearing seal

16.22 Drive the bearing out from the inside

16.25 Press the seal into place and set it flush with the rim

the rim of the coupling with a small block of wood **(see illustration)**.

26 Fit the spacer into the bearing **(see illustration 16.11b)**.

27 Check the sprocket coupling/rubber dampers (see Section 20), then fit the sprocket coupling onto the wheel **(see illustration 16.11a)**. Install the wheel (see Section 15).

17 Tyres

General information

1 The wheels fitted to all models are designed to take tubeless tyres only. Tyre sizes are given in the Specifications at the beginning of this chapter.

2 Refer to *Pre-ride checks* listed at the beginning of this manual for tyre maintenance.

Fitting new tyres

3 When selecting new tyres, refer to the tyre information in the Owner's Handbook. Ensure that front and rear tyre types are compatible, the correct size and correct speed rating; if necessary seek advice from a Suzuki dealer or tyre fitting specialist **(see illustration)**.

4 It is recommended that tyres are fitted by a motorcycle tyre specialist rather than attempted in the home workshop. This is because the force required to break the seal between the wheel rim and tyre bead is substantial, and is usually beyond the capabilities of an individual working with normal tyre levers. Additionally, the specialist will be able to balance the wheels after tyre fitting.

5 Note that punctured tubeless tyres can in some cases be repaired. Repairs must be carried out by a motorcycle tyre fitting specialist. Suzuki advise that a repaired tyre should not be used at speeds above 50 mph (80 kmh) for the first 24 hours, and not above 80 mph (130 kmh) thereafter.

18 Drive chain

⚠️ *Warning: NEVER install a drive chain which uses a clip-type (split) master link. ONLY use the correct tools to secure the riveted soft link – if you do not have access to such tools or do not have the skill to operate them correctly, have the chain installed by a Suzuki dealer.*

Cleaning

1 Refer to Chapter 1, Section 1, for details of routine cleaning with the chain installed on the sprockets.

2 If the chain is extremely dirty remove it from the motorcycle and soak it in paraffin (kerosene) for approximately five or six minutes, then clean it using a soft brush.

Caution: Don't use gasoline (petrol), solvent or other cleaning fluids which might damage its internal sealing properties. Don't use high-pressure water. Remove the chain, wipe it off, then blow dry it with compressed air immediately. The entire process shouldn't take longer than ten minutes – if it does, the O-rings in the chain rollers could be damaged.

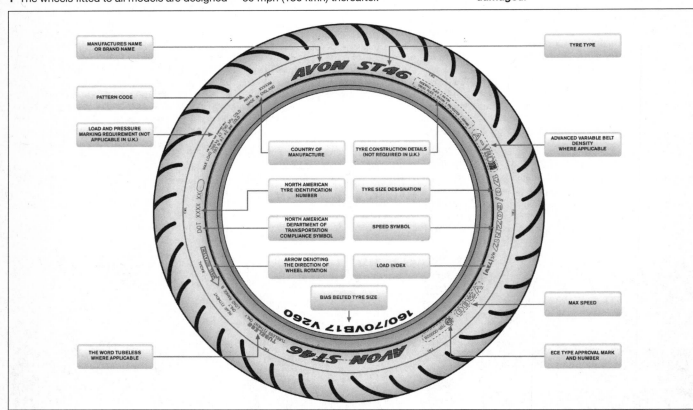

17.3 Common tyre sidewall markings

19.1 Undo the pinch bolt (arrowed) and slide the arm off the shaft

Removal without splitting the chain

3 Remove the front sprocket cover (see Section 19).

4 Remove the swingarm (see Chapter 5).

5 Slip the chain off the front sprocket and remove it.

6 Installation is the reverse of removal. On completion adjust and lubricate the chain following the procedures described in Chapter 1.

Splitting the chain at the soft link

7 Follow the procedure in Section 8 of Tools and Workshop Tips in the Reference section at the end of this manual for information on how to break and rejoin the chain at its soft link. Note that it is essential to have the correct tool for this job and to use a new soft link when rejoining the chain.

19 Sprockets

Note: *Always renew the engine and rear wheel sprockets as a set, together with the drive chain.*

Front sprocket cover

1 Make an alignment mark between the slit in the gearchange linkage arm clamp and the end of the gearchange shaft, then unscrew the pinch bolt and slide the arm off the shaft **(see illustration)**.

19.6 Undo the bolt (arrowed) and remove the speed sensor rotor

19.2 Undo the bolts and remove the cover

2 Undo the bolts securing the sprocket cover to the crankcase and remove the cover **(see illustration)**.

3 Installation is the reverse of removal. Align the gearchange linkage arm correctly with the shaft **(see illustration 19.1)**.

Front sprocket

Removal

4 Remove the front sprocket cover (Steps 1 and 2).

5 Unscrew the clutch release cylinder housing bolts and detach the assembly from the engine, then support or tie it clear of the sprocket **(see illustration)**. Note the dowels and remove them if they are loose – they could be in either the housing or the engine **(see illustration 19.13a)**. Withdraw the pushrod **(see illustration)**.

6 Have an assistant apply the rear brake, then undo the bolt securing the speed sensor rotor and remove the rotor **(see illustration)**.

19.5b ... then displace the housing ...

19.7 Unscrew the nut (arrowed) and remove the washer

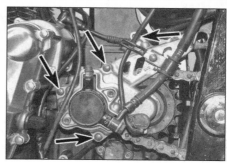

19.5a Unscrew the bolts (arrowed) ...

7 Apply the rear brake hard and slacken the front sprocket nut, then remove the nut and washer **(see illustration)**. The sprocket nut is of the self-locking type. If the locking device is no longer effective, discard the nut and fit a new one on reassembly.

8 Fully slacken the drive chain (see Chapter 1). If the sprocket is to be reused mark its outer face so it can be installed the same way round. Lift the chain off the sprocket and slide the sprocket off the shaft **(see illustration)**.

Installation

9 Slide the sprocket onto the shaft and fit the chain around it **(see illustration 19.8)**; if the original sprocket is being refitted ensure it is installed the same way around as on removal according to the mark made. Adjust the chain (see Chapter 1).

10 Clean the threads of the output shaft, then apply thread locking compound to the

19.5c ... and withdraw the pushrod

19.8 Slide the sprocket off the gearbox shaft

19.10 Fit the nut with its washer

19.11 Fit the rotor and tighten the bolt

19.13a Make sure the dowels (arrowed) are in place

threads. Fit the washer and sprocket nut **(see illustration)**. Have an assistant apply the rear brake, then tighten the nut to the torque setting specified at the beginning of this Chapter.

11 Fit the speed sensor rotor and rotor bolt **(see illustration)**. Apply the rear brake and tighten the bolt to the specified torque setting.

12 Lubricate the clutch pushrod with molybdenum disulphide oil (a 50/50 mixture of molybdenum disulphide grease and engine oil) then slide it through the seal and into the engine **(see illustration 19.5c)**. Wipe the outer end of the pushrod clean and smear some silicon grease onto it.

13 Clean the speed sensor tip on the inside of the clutch release cylinder housing. Make sure the housing dowels are fitted in either the housing or the engine **(see illustration)**. Fit the housing onto the engine, locating the pushrod in its hole, and tighten the bolts **(see illustration)**.

14 Install the front sprocket cover (Step 3).

Rear sprocket

Removal

15 Remove the rear wheel (see Chapter 6).
Caution: Don't lay the wheel down on the disc as it could become warped. Lay the wheel rim/tyre on wooden blocks so that

the disc is off the ground. Don't operate the brake pedal with the wheel removed.

16 Undo the sprocket nuts then lift the sprocket off the sprocket coupling, noting which way round it fits **(see illustration)**. If required, pull the sprocket coupling out of the hub and check the condition of the rubber dampers (see Section 20).

17 The sprocket nuts are the self-locking type. If the locking device is no longer effective, discard the nuts and fit new ones on reassembly.

Installation

18 If removed, fit the rubber dampers and sprocket coupling into the hub (see Section 20).

19 Fit the sprocket onto the coupling and install the sprocket nuts. If the original sprocket is being refitted ensure it is installed the same way around as on removal – the stamped side should face outwards. Tighten the nuts evenly to the torque setting specified at the beginning of this Chapter.

20 Install the rear wheel (see Chapter 6).

20 Rear sprocket coupling/ rubber dampers

1 Remove the wheel (see Section 15).

Check for any rotational freeplay between the sprocket coupling and the rear wheel. The coupling should be a good fit between the dampers – if there is freeplay the damper segments have compressed and should be replaced with a new set.

2 Lift the sprocket coupling out of the hub, and remove the spacer that fits between them from the coupling **(see illustrations 16.11a and b)**.

Caution: Don't lay the wheel down on the disc as it could become warped. Lay the wheel rim/tyre on wooden blocks so that the disc is off the ground. Don't operate the brake pedal with the wheel removed.

3 Check the coupling for cracks and damage. Also check the sprocket studs for damage and ensure they are secure in the coupling.

4 Lift the rubber dampers from the hub and check them for cracks, hardening and general deterioration **(see illustration)**. Replace the rubber dampers with a new set if necessary.

5 Checking and renewal procedures for the coupling bearing are described in Section 16.

6 Ensure the rubber dampers are correctly located in the hub.

7 Fit the spacer into the coupling bearing, then press the coupling firmly into the hub **(see illustrations 16.11b and a)**.

8 Install the rear wheel (see Section 15).

19.13b Make sure the pushrod locates in the hole (arrowed)

19.16 The sprocket is secured by five nuts

20.4 Remove the dampers and check them

Chapter 7
Bodywork

Contents

Degrees of difficulty

Easy, suitable for novice with little experience	**Fairly easy,** suitable for beginner with some experience	**Fairly difficult,** suitable for competent DIY mechanic	**Difficult,** suitable for experienced DIY mechanic	**Very difficult,** suitable for expert DIY or professional

1 General information

In the case of damage to the seat cowling, mudguard or side panels, it is usually necessary to remove the broken component and replace it with a new (or used) one. Note, however, that some companies specialise in 'plastic welding' and there are a number of bodywork repair kits now available for motorcycles.

When attempting to remove any body panel, first study it closely, noting any fasteners and associated fittings, to be sure of returning everything to its correct place on installation. Once the evident fasteners have been removed, try to remove the panel as described but DO NOT FORCE IT – if it will not release, check that all fasteners have been removed and try again.

When installing a body panel, first study it closely, noting any fasteners and associated fittings removed with it, to be sure of returning everything to its correct place. Check that all fasteners are in good condition, including the trim clips and damping/rubber mounts;

replace any faulty fasteners with new ones before the panel is reassembled. Check also that all mounting brackets are straight and repair them or replace them with new ones if necessary before attempting to install the panel.

Tighten the fasteners securely, but be careful not to overtighten any of them or the panel may break (not always immediately) due to the uneven stress.

2 Seat

1 Insert the ignition key into the seat lock located under the left-hand side of the seat cowling, and turn it clockwise to unlock the seat **(see illustration)**. Draw the seat up and back to disengage the tabs at the front and sides, then remove the seat.

2 Installation is the reverse of removal, noting the following:

● Make sure the seat tabs are properly located under the tank bracket at the front and under the hook on each side **(see illustration)**.

● Press down on the back of the seat to engage the lock.

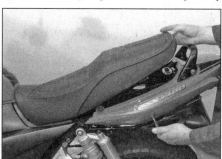

2.1 Turn the key to unlock the seat, then lift the back of the seat and remove it

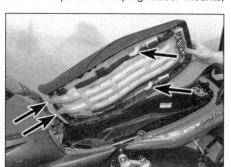

2.2 Make sure the four tabs (arrowed) locate correctly

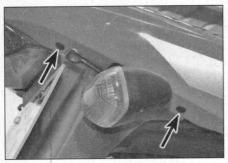

3.2a Remove the trim clips (arrowed) . . .

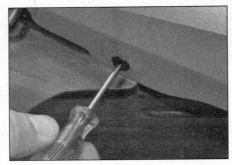

3.2b . . . push the centre pin in . . .

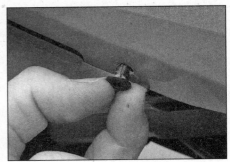

3.2c . . . then draw the clip out

3.3 Undo the screw (arrowed) on each side

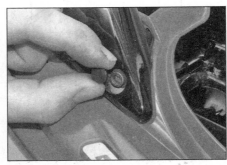

3.4a Remove the blanking caps . . .

3.4b . . . then unscrew the bolts and remove the rail

3.5 Disconnect the wiring connector

3 Seat cowling

Removal

1 Remove the seat (see Section 2).
2 Release the two trim clips on each side – push the centre pin into the body of the clip then draw the clip out of the panel **(see illustrations)**.
3 Undo the screw on each side of the seat cowling at the front **(see illustration)**.
4 Remove the blanking caps from the passenger grab-rail bolts **(see illustration)**. Unscrew the bolts and remove the rail **(see illustration)**. Note the washers fitted with the bungee hook bolts, and the spacers and rubber grommets fitted in the seat cowling, and remove them if loose or if required.
5 Displace the seat cowling to the rear and disconnect the tail light wiring connector **(see illustration)**.
6 Lift the cowling off and release the seat lock cable **(see illustrations)**.

Installation

7 Installation is the reverse of removal. To fit the trim clips, first push the centre pin out

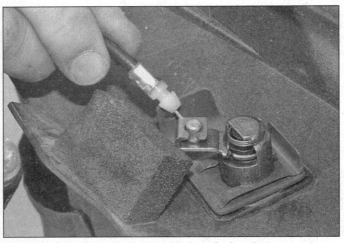

3.6a Free the outer cable from its bracket . . .

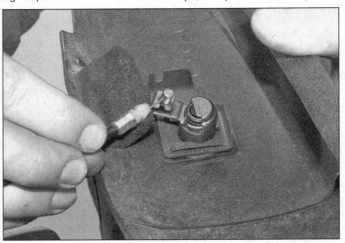

3.6b . . . and inner cable from the lock arm

3.7a Reset the clip by pushing the centre pin back out

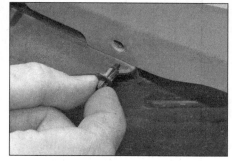

3.7b Fit the clip into its hole . . .

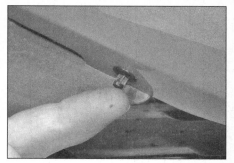

3.7c . . . then push the centre pin in so it is flush

so that its head extends from the body **(see illustration)**. Now fit the clip into its hole, then push the centre pin in so that it is flush with the body **(see illustrations)**. The clip should now be locked in place. Check the operation of the tail/brake light before riding the motorcycle.

4 Mirrors

1 Slacken the locknut on the bottom slightly so it is free of the master cylinder **(see illustration)**.
2 Unscrew the complete mirror from the master cylinder **(see illustrations)**.
3 Installation is the reverse of removal – thread the mirror into the master cylinder until the locknut almost contacts it, then position the mirror as required and tighten the locknut onto the master cylinder.

5 Side panels

1 Remove the seat (see Section 2).

4.1 Slacken the locknut . . .

4.2 . . . then unscrew the mirror

2 Undo the screw at the bottom of the panel **(see illustration)**.
3 Carefully pull the panel away to release the four pegs from the grommets **(see illustrations)**.
4 Separate the upper and lower panel sections if required by undoing the two screws **(see illustration)**.
5 Installation is the reverse of removal. Make sure each peg engages correctly with its grommet – lubricate the grommets to make installation and future removal easier if required.

5.2 Undo the screw (arrowed) . . .

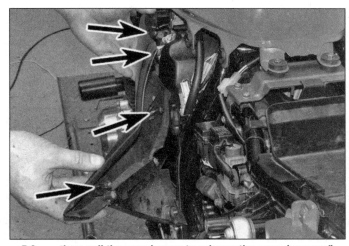

5.3 . . . then pull the panel away to release the pegs (arrowed) from their grommets

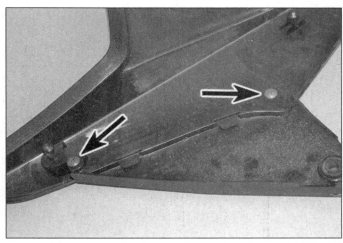

5.4 Undo the screws (arrowed) to separate the sections

6.2a Unscrew the bolts (arrowed) on each side . . .

6.2b . . . noting how the brake hose holders fit . . .

6.3 . . . then position the fork as shown and lower the mudguard

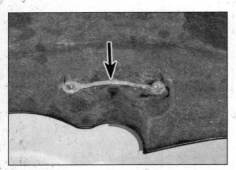

6.4 Make sure each set plate (arrowed) is fitted

6 Front mudguard

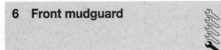

1 Remove the front wheel (see Chapter 6).
2 Unscrew the two bolts on each side and remove the brake hose holders from between the fork and rear mounts **(see illustrations)**.

3 Turn the left-hand fork outer tube 90° so that the axle nut faces back and the caliper mounting lugs face out, then lower the mudguard and remove it from between the bottom of the forks **(see illustration)**.
4 Installation is the reverse of removal. Make sure each set plate for the bolts is securely in place on the inside of the mudguard **(see illustration)**.

Chapter 8
Electrical system

Contents

Degrees of difficulty

Easy, suitable for novice with little experience	**Fairly easy,** suitable for beginner with some experience	**Fairly difficult,** suitable for competent DIY mechanic	**Difficult,** suitable for experienced DIY mechanic	**Very difficult,** suitable for expert DIY or professional

Specifications

Battery
Type FTX14-BS
Capacity 12V, 12Ah

Charging system
Battery current leakage . . . . 3 mA (max)
Alternator stator coil resistance . . . . 0.2 to 1.0 ohms
Alternator output
   Regulated voltage output. . . . . 14.0 to 15.5V @ 5000 rpm
   Unregulated voltage output (no-load). . . . . min. 60V AC @ 5000 rpm

Starter system
Starter relay resistance. . . . . 3.0 to 5.0 ohms

Fuses
Main 30A
Head-Hi (High beam and high beam LED in instrument cluster). 10A
Head-Lo (Low beam). 10A
Fuel/Meter (ECM, speedometer, fuel pump and fuel injectors). 10A
Ignition (ECM, CMP sensor, fuel pump relay,
   starter relay and ignition coils. . . . . 15A (10A K4 onwards)
Signal (sidelight, brake and tail lights, turn signals, horns,
   tachometer, instrument and warning lights) 15A
Fan (oil cooling fan) 10A

Bulbs

Headlight 60/55W H4
Sidelight 5W
Brake/tail light . . . . 21/5W x 2
Turn signal lights. 21W
Instrument and warning lights . . . . LED

Torque settings

Alternator rotor bolt . . . . 160 Nm
Alternator cover bolts. . . . . 11 Nm
Alternator stator and wiring clamp bolts . . . . 10 Nm
Oil hose union bolts . . . . 10 Nm
Oil pressure switch. . . . . 14 Nm
Timing rotor cover bolts . . . . 11 Nm

1 General information

All models have a 12-volt electrical system charged by a three-phase alternator with a separate regulator/rectifier.

The regulator maintains the charging system output within the specified range to prevent overcharging, and the rectifier converts the ac (alternating current) output of the alternator to dc (direct current) to power the lights and other components and to charge the battery. The alternator rotor is mounted on the left-hand end of the crankshaft.

The starter motor is mounted behind the cylinders. The starting system includes the motor, the battery, the relay, the clutch switch, gear position sensor and sidestand switch. If the engine kill switch is in the RUN position and the ignition (main) switch is ON, the starter relay allows the starter motor to operate if the transmission is in neutral (neutral light on) and the clutch lever is pulled in or, if the transmission is in gear, the side-stand is up and the clutch lever is pulled in.

Note: *Keep in mind that electrical parts, once purchased, cannot be returned. To avoid unnecessary expense, make very sure the faulty component has been positively identified before buying a replacement part.*

2 Electrical system fault finding

⚠ *Warning: To prevent the risk of short circuits, the ignition switch must always be OFF and the battery negative (–) terminal should be disconnected before any of the bike's other electrical components are disturbed. Don't forget to reconnect the terminal securely once work is finished or if battery power is needed for circuit testing.*

1 A typical electrical circuit consists of an electrical component, the switches, relays, etc, related to that component and the wiring and connectors that link the component to the battery and the frame.

2 Before tackling any troublesome electrical circuit, first study the wiring diagram thoroughly to get a complete picture of what makes up that individual circuit. Trouble spots, for instance, can often be narrowed down by noting if other components related to that circuit are operating properly or not. If several components or circuits fail at one time, chances are the fault lies either in the fuse or in the common earth (ground) connection, as several circuits are often routed through the same fuse and earth (ground) connections.

3 Electrical problems often stem from simple causes, such as loose or corroded connections or a blown fuse. Prior to any electrical fault finding, always visually check the condition of the fuse, wires and connections in the problem circuit. Intermittent failures can be especially frustrating, since you can't always duplicate the failure when it's convenient to test. In such situations, a good practice is to clean all connections in the affected circuit, whether or not they appear to be good – where possible use a dedicated electrical cleaning spray along with sandpaper, wire wool or other abrasive material to remove corrosion, and a dedicated electrical protection spray to prevent further problems. All of the connections and wires should also be wiggled to check for looseness which can cause intermittent failure.

4 If you don't have a multimeter it is highly advisable to obtain one – they are not expensive and will enable a full range of electrical tests to be made. Go for a modern digital one with LCD display as they are easier to use. A continuity tester and/or test light are useful for certain electrical checks as an alternative, though are limited in their usefulness compared to a multimeter **(see illustrations)**.

Continuity checks

5 The term continuity describes the uninterrupted flow of electricity through an electrical circuit. Continuity can be checked with a multimeter set either to its continuity

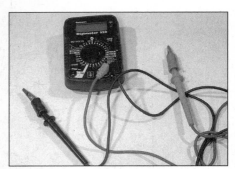

2.4a A digital multimeter can be used for all electrical tests

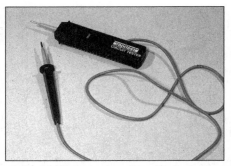

2.4b A battery-powered continuity tester

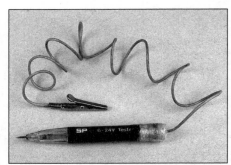

2.4c A simple test light is useful for voltage tests

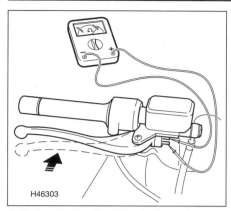

2.10 Continuity should be indicated across switch terminals when lever is operated

function (a beep is emitted when continuity is found), or to the resistance (ohms / Ω) function, or with a dedicated continuity tester. Both instruments are powered by an internal battery, therefore the checks are made with the ignition OFF. As a safety precaution, always disconnect the battery negative (–) lead before making continuity checks, particularly if ignition switch checks are being made.

6 If using a multimeter, select the continuity function if it has one, or the resistance (ohms) function. Touch the meter probes together and check that a beep is emitted or the meter reads zero, which indicates continuity. If there is no continuity there will be no beep or the meter will show infinite resistance. After using the meter, always switch it OFF to conserve its battery.

7 A continuity tester can be used in the same way – its light should come on or it should beep to indicate continuity in the switch ON position, but should be off or silent in the OFF position.

8 Note that the polarity of the test probes doesn't matter for continuity checks, although care should be taken to follow specific test procedures if a diode or solid-state component is being checked.

Switch continuity checks

9 If a switch is at fault, trace its wiring to the wiring connectors. Separate the connectors and inspect them for security and condition. A build-up of dirt or corrosion here will most

likely be the cause of the problem – clean up and apply a water dispersant such as WD40, or alternatively use a dedicated contact cleaner and protection spray.

10 If using a multimeter, select the continuity function if it has one, or the resistance (ohms) function, and connect its probes to the terminals in the connector **(see illustration)**. Simple ON/OFF type switches, such as brake light switches, only have two wires whereas combination switches, like the handlebar switches, have many wires. Study the wiring diagram to ensure that you are connecting to the correct pair of wires. Continuity should be indicated with the switch ON and no continuity with it OFF.

Wiring continuity checks

11 Many electrical faults are caused by damaged wiring, often due to incorrect routing or chaffing on frame components. Loose, wet or corroded wire connectors can also be the cause of electrical problems.

12 A continuity check can be made on a single length of wire by disconnecting it at each end and connecting the meter or continuity tester probes to each end of the wire **(see illustration)**. Continuity (low or no resistance – 0 ohms) should be indicated if the wire is good. If no continuity (high resistance) is shown, suspect a broken wire.

13 To check for continuity to earth in any earth wire connect one probe of your meter or tester to the earth wire terminal in the connector and the other to the frame, engine, or battery earth (–) terminal. Continuity (low or no resistance – 0 ohms) should be indicated if the wire is good. If no continuity (high resistance) is shown, suspect a broken wire or corroded or loose earth point (see below).

Voltage checks

14 A voltage check can determine whether power is reaching a component. Use a multimeter set to the dc voltage scale, or a test light. The test light is the cheaper component, but the meter has the advantage of being able to give a voltage reading.

15 Connect the meter or test light in parallel, i.e. across the load **(see illustration)**.

16 First identify the relevant wiring circuit by referring to the wiring diagram at the end of this manual. If other electrical components

share the same power supply (i.e. are fed from the same fuse), take note whether they are working correctly – this is useful information in deciding where to start checking the circuit.

17 If using a meter, check first that the meter leads are plugged into the correct terminals on the meter (red to positive (+), black to negative (–). Set the meter to the dc volts function, where necessary at a range suitable for the battery voltage – 0 to 20 vdc. Connect the meter red probe (+) to the power supply wire and the black probe to a good metal earth (ground) on the motorcycle's frame or directly to the battery negative terminal. Battery voltage should be shown on the meter with the ignition switch, and if necessary any other relevant switch, ON.

18 If using a test light, connect its positive (+) probe to the power supply terminal and its negative (–) probe to a good earth (ground) on the motorcycle's frame. With the switch, and if necessary any other relevant switch, ON, the test light should illuminate.

19 If no voltage is indicated, work back towards the fuse continuing to check for voltage. When you reach a point where there is voltage, you know the problem lies between that point and your last check point.

Earth (ground) checks

20 Earth connections are made either directly to the engine or frame (such as the gear position sensor, oil pressure switch etc. which only have a positive feed) or by a separate wire into the earth circuit of the wiring harness. Alternatively a short earth wire is sometimes run from the component directly to the motorcycle's frame.

21 Corrosion is a common cause of a poor earth connection, as is a loose earth terminal fastener.

22 If total or multiple component failure is experienced, check the security of the main earth lead from the negative (–) terminal of the battery, the earth lead bolted to the engine, and the main earth point(s) on the frame. If corroded, dismantle the connection and clean all surfaces back to bare metal. Remake the connection and prevent further corrosion from forming by smearing battery terminal grease over the connection.

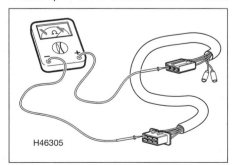

2.12 Wiring continuity check. Connect the meter probes across each end of the same wire

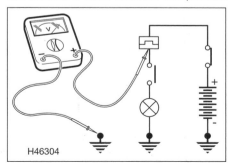

2.15 Voltage check. Connect the meter positive probe to the component and the negative probe to earth

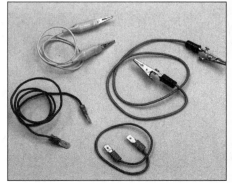

2.23 A selection of insulated jumper wires

3.1 Remove the storage tray, noting how it locates

3.2a Disconnect the negative lead first . . .

3.2b . . . then the positive lead . . .

23 To check the earthing of a component, use an insulated jumper wire to temporarily bypass its earth connection **(see illustration)** – connect one end of the jumper wire to the earth terminal or metal body of the component and the other end to the motorcycle's frame. If the circuit works with the jumper wire installed, the earth circuit is faulty.

24 To check an earth wire first check for corroded or loose connections, then check the wiring for continuity (Step 13) between each connector in the circuit in turn, and then to its earth point, to locate the break.

3 Battery removal, installation, inspection and maintenance

Caution: Be extremely careful when handling or working around the battery. The electrolyte is very caustic and an explosive gas (hydrogen) is given off when the battery is charging.

Removal and installation

1 Make sure the ignition is turned OFF. Remove the seat (see Chapter 7). Unclip and remove the storage tray **(see illustration)**.

2 Unscrew the negative (–) terminal bolt first and disconnect the lead from the battery **(see illustration)**. Lift up the red insulating cover to access the positive (+) terminal, then unscrew the bolt and disconnect the lead **(see illustration)**. Lift the battery from the bike **(see illustration)**.

3 On installation, clean the battery terminals and lead ends with a soft wire brush, blunt knife, sandpaper or steel wool. Reconnect the leads, connecting the positive (+) terminal first and the negative (–) last.

Battery corrosion can be kept to a minimum by applying a layer of battery terminal grease or petroleum jelly (Vaseline) to the terminals after the leads have been connected. DO NOT use a mineral based grease.

4 Fit the storage tray, making sure it locates correctly **(see illustration)**. Install the seat (see Chapter 7).

Inspection and maintenance

5 The battery is of the maintenance-free (sealed) type, therefore requiring no regular maintenance. However, the following checks should still be regularly performed.

6 Check the battery terminals and leads for tightness and corrosion. If corrosion is evident, clean the terminals as described in Step 3.

7 The battery case should be kept clean to prevent current leakage, which can discharge the battery over a period of time (especially when it sits unused). Wash the outside of the case with a solution of baking soda and water. Rinse the battery thoroughly, then dry it.

8 Look for cracks in the case and replace the battery with a new one if any are found. If acid has been spilled on the frame or battery box,

neutralise it with a baking soda and water solution, dry it thoroughly, then touch up any damaged paint.

9 If the motorcycle sits unused for long periods of time, disconnect the leads from the battery terminals, negative (–) terminal first. Refer to Section 4 and charge the battery once every month to six weeks.

10 The condition of the battery can be assessed by measuring the voltage at the battery terminals. Connect the voltmeter positive (+) probe to the battery positive (+) terminal and the negative (–) probe to the battery negative (–) terminal **(see illustration)**. When fully charged there should be more than 12.5 volts present. If the voltage falls below 12.0 volts remove the battery and recharge it (see Section 4).

4 Battery charging

Caution: Be extremely careful when handling or working around the battery. The electrolyte is very caustic and an explosive gas (hydrogen) is given off when the battery is charging.

1 Make sure the battery charger is suitable for charging a 12 volt battery.

2 Remove the battery (see Section 3). Connect the charger to the battery, making sure that the positive (+ve) lead on the charger is connected to the positive (+) terminal on the battery, and the negative (–) lead is connected

3.2c . . . and lift the battery out

3.4 Make sure each side tab locates over the rim of the rear mudguard

3.10 Measuring battery voltage

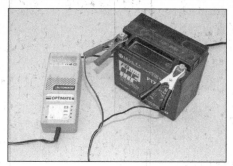

4.2 Charging the battery using the Optimate battery charger

to the negative (–) terminal **(see illustration)**.

3 Suzuki recommend that the battery is charged at a rate of 1.4 amps for 5 to 10 hours. Exceeding this figure can cause the battery to overheat, buckling the plates and rendering it useless. If a normal domestic charger is used check that after a possible initial peak, the charge rate falls to a safe level **(see illustration)**. If the battery becomes hot during charging **stop**. Further charging will cause damage. **Note:** *In emergencies the battery can be charged at a maximum rate of 6.0 amps for a period of 1 hour. However, this is not recommended and the low amp charge is by far the safer method of charging the battery.*

4 After charging, allow the battery to stand for 30 minutes, then measure its terminal voltage (see Section 3). If the voltage is below 12.5 volts, charge the battery again and repeat the voltage measuring process. If the voltage is

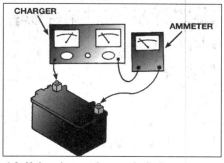

4.3 If the charger has no built-in ammeter, connect one in series as shown. DO NOT connect the ammeter between the battery terminals or it will be ruined

still low, the battery is failing and should be replaced with a new one.

5 If the recharged battery discharges rapidly when left disconnected, it is likely that an internal short caused by physical damage or sulphation has occurred. A new battery will be required. A good battery will tend to lose its charge at about 1% per day.

6 Install the battery (see Section 3).

7 If the motorcycle is unused for long periods of time, charge the battery once every month to six weeks and leave it disconnected.

5 Fuses

1 The electrical system is protected by fuses of different ratings. The main fuse is in the starter

relay, and the circuit fuses are housed in the fusebox, both of which are behind the left-hand side panel **(see illustration)** – remove the side panel for access (see Chapter 7).

2 To access the main fuse, remove the starter relay cover **(see illustration)**. To access the circuit fuses, undo the screw securing the fusebox lid and lift the lid **(see illustrations)** – the location, rating and designation of each is marked inside the lid, and the circuits and components protected by each fuse are listed in the Specifications at the beginning of the Chapter.

3 The fuses can be removed and checked visually. If you can't pull the fuse out with your fingertips, use a pair of needle-nose pliers **(see illustration)**. A blown fuse is easily identified by a break in the element **(see illustration)**. Each fuse is clearly marked with its rating and must only be replaced with a fuse of the correct rating. A spare fuse of each rating is supplied, with the spare main fuse housed under the starter relay and the others housed in the fusebox. If a spare fuse is used, always replace it with a new one so that a spare of each rating is carried on the bike at all times.

⚠️ **Warning: Never put in a fuse of a higher rating or bridge the terminals with any other substitute, however temporary it may be. Serious damage may be done to the circuit, or a fire may start.**

4 If a fuse blows, be sure to check the wiring circuit very carefully for evidence of a short-circuit. Look for bare wires and chafed,

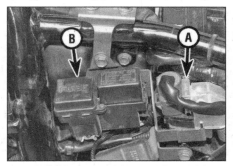

5.1 Starter relay (A) and fusebox (B)

5.2a Remove the relay cover to access the main fuse (arrowed)

5.2b Undo the screw (arrowed) . . .

5.2c . . . and lift the fusebox lid to access the circuit fuses

5.3a Remove the fuse to check it

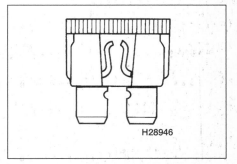

H28946

5.3b A blown fuse can be identified by a break in the element

melted or burned insulation. If a new fuse is fitted before the cause is located, it will probably blow immediately.

5 Occasionally a fuse will blow or cause an open-circuit for no obvious reason. Corrosion of the fuse ends and fusebox terminals may occur and cause poor fuse contact. If this happens, remove the corrosion with a wire brush or wire wool, then spray the fuse ends and terminals with electrical contact cleaner.

6 Lighting system check

1 The battery provides power for operation of the headlight, tail light, brake light and instrument cluster lights. If none of the lights operate, always check battery voltage before proceeding. Low battery voltage indicates either a faulty battery or a defective charging system. Refer to Section 3 for battery checks and Section 28 for charging system tests. Also, check the condition of the fuses (see Section 5). When checking for a blown filament in a bulb, it is advisable to back up a visual check with a continuity test of the filament as it is not always apparent that a bulb has blown. When testing for continuity, remember that on tail light and turn signal bulbs it is often the metal body of the bulb that is the earth (ground).

Headlight

2 If the headlight fails to work, first check the bulb and the bulb terminals, and the wiring connector (see Section 7), and then the headlight HI beam or LO beam fuse (see Section 5). Next check for battery voltage at the headlight wiring connector with a test light or multimeter. Refer to *Wiring Diagrams* at the end of this Chapter, then connect the negative (–) probe of the multimeter to earth (ground) and the positive (+) probe to first the high beam connector terminal (yellow wire) and then the low beam connector terminal (white wire) with the ignition switch ON, and on K2/K3 Europe models with the light switch ON. Don't forget to select either high or low beam at the dimmer switch while conducting this test.

3 If no voltage is indicated at either terminal, check the wiring between the headlight connector, HI/LO switch, light switch (K2/K3 Europe models), and the ignition switch, then check the switches themselves.

4 If voltage is indicated, check for continuity between the black/white wire terminal and earth (ground). If there is no continuity, check the earth (ground) circuit for a broken or poor connection.

Sidelight

5 If the sidelight fails to work, first check the bulb, the bulb terminals in the bulbholder, and the wiring connector (see Section 7), then the signal fuse (see Section 5). Next check for voltage on the supply side of the sidelight wiring connector (brown wire), with the ignition switch in the ON (and light switch ON – K2/K3 Europe models) and PARK positions.

6 If no voltage is indicated, check the wiring between the connector and the light switch (where fitted), the ignition switch, then between the ignition switch and the fuses.

7 If voltage is indicated, check for continuity between the black/white wire terminal and earth (ground). If there is no continuity, check the earth (ground) circuit for a broken or poor connection.

Tail light

8 If a tail light fails to work, first check the bulb and the bulb terminals in the bulbholder, and if both lights fail check the wiring connector (see Section 9), then the signal fuse (see Section 5). Next check for voltage at each bulbholder (brown wire) with the ignition switch in the ON (and light switch ON – K2/K3 Europe models) and PARK positions.

9 If no voltage is indicated, check the wiring between the connector and the light switch (where fitted), the ignition switch, then check the switch(es).

10 If voltage is indicated, check for continuity between the black/white wire terminal and earth (ground). If there is no continuity, check the earth (ground) circuit for a broken or poor connection.

Brake light

11 If a brake light fails to work, first check bulb and the bulb terminals in the bulbholder, and if both lights fail check the wiring connector (see Section 9), then the signal fuse (see Section 5). Next check for battery voltage on the supply side of the tail light wiring connector (white/black wire), with the brake lever pulled in or the pedal depressed.

12 If no voltage is indicated, check the wiring between the connector, the brake light switches and the ignition switch, then check the brake light switches (see Section 14).

13 If voltage is indicated, check for continuity between the black/white wire terminal and earth (ground). If there is no continuity, check the earth (ground) circuit for a broken or poor connection.

Turn signal lights

14 If one light fails to work, check the bulb and the bulb terminal first, then the wiring connector (see Section 11). If none of the turn signals work, first check the signal fuse.

15 If the fuse is good, see Section 13 for the turn signal circuit check.

Instrument cluster and warning lights

16 The instrument cluster and warning lights are LEDs. If an LED fails, and a fault cannot be traced anywhere else in the system, a new instrument cluster will have to be fitted (see Section 15).

7 Headlight bulb and sidelight bulb

Note: *The headlight bulbs are of the quartz-halogen type. Do not touch the bulb glass as skin acids will shorten the bulb's service life. If the bulb is accidentally touched, it should be wiped carefully with a rag soaked in methylated spirit and dried before fitting.*

Headlight bulb

1 Undo the screw on each side of the headlight, then carefully draw the beam unit out of the shell, bottom first, noting how it locates at the top **(see illustrations).**

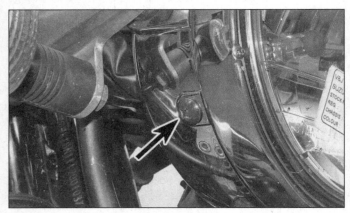

7.1a Undo the screw (arrowed) on each side . . .

7.1b . . . and displace the beam unit

7.2a Disconnect the wiring connector . . .

7.2b . . . and remove the rubber cover

7.3a Release the retaining clip . . .

7.3b . . . and withdraw the bulb

7.5 Fit the cover with the TOP mark at the top

7.6 Make sure the tab on the top of the beam unit locates behind the retainer

2 Disconnect the headlight wiring connector and remove the rubber cover, noting how it fits **(see illustrations)**.

3 Release the bulb retaining clip, noting how it fits, then remove the bulb **(see illustrations)**.

4 Fit the bulb into the headlight, bearing in mind the information in the **Note** above, making sure it locates correctly, and secure it in position with the retaining clip.

5 Check that the contacts inside the connector are clean and free from corrosion. Fit the rubber cover, making sure it is correctly seated and with the 'TOP' mark at the top **(see illustration)**. Connect the wiring connector **(see illustration 7.2a)**.

6 Locate the top of the beam unit in the shell, then push the base in and secure it with the screws **(see illustration)**.

7 Check the operation of the headlight.

 HAYNES HiNT *Always use a paper towel or dry cloth when handling a new bulb to prevent injury if the bulb should break and to increase bulb life.*

Sidelight bulb

8 Undo the screw on each side of the headlight, then carefully draw the beam unit out of the shell, bottom first, and noting how it locates at the top **(see illustrations 7.1a and b)**.

9 Pull the bulbholder out of the headlight, then carefully pull the bulb out of the holder **(see illustrations)**.

10 Check that the contacts inside the bulbholder are clean and free from corrosion. Fit the new bulb in the bulbholder, then fit the holder into its socket in the headlight.

11 Locate the top of the beam unit in the

shell, then push the base in and secure it with the screws **(see illustration 7.6)**.

12 Check the operation of the sidelight.

8 Headlight

Removal
Beam unit

1 Undo the screw on each side of the headlight, then carefully draw the beam unit out of the shell, bottom first, noting how it locates at the top **(see illustration 7.1a and b)**.

2 Disconnect the headlight wiring connector **(see illustration 7.2a)** and the sidelight wiring connector and remove the beam unit **(see illustration)**.

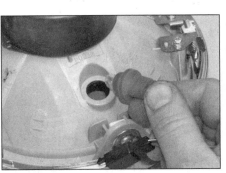

7.9a Pull the bulbholder out . . .

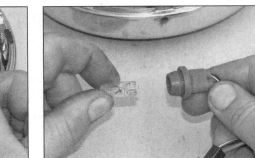

7.9b . . . then remove the bulb

8.2 Disconnect the wiring connectors and remove the beam unit

8.3 Undo the screws (arrowed) and lift the beam unit out of the rim

8.6 Unscrew the bolts (arrowed)

3 If required separate the beam unit from the rim by undoing the horizontal adjuster screw, noting how it fits, and the top and bottom mounting screws (see illustration).

Shell

4 Remove the beam unit (Steps 1 and 2).
5 Release the wiring clamp on each side of the shell, then disconnect all the wiring connectors (see illustration).
6 Unscrew the brake hose splitter bolts on the underside of the bottom yoke to free the headlight adjuster bracket (see illustration).
7 Unscrew the nut and withdraw the bolt on each side, noting the wiring clamps and washers (see illustration). Remove the shell from between the brackets and feed the wiring through the holes in the back of the shell, noting what goes where (see illustration). Note the collar fitted into the rubber bushes on each side.
8 If required unscrew the bolts securing the

8.9a Make sure the wiring is correctly routed

8.5 Release the wiring clamps and disconnect the wiring connectors

8.7a Unscrew the nuts and remove the wiring clamps, bolts and washers . . .

bracket and detach it from the holder (see illustration).

Installation

9 Installation is the reverse of removal, noting the following:

8.7b . . . then displace the shell and draw all the wiring out

8.9b Locate the bracket between the yoke and the splitter

● Make sure the wiring is correctly routed – the main loom, the left-hand turn signal wiring, and where fitted the immobiliser wiring, feed through the left-hand hole, and the handlebar switch, ignition switch, right-hand turn signal and instrument wiring feed through the right-hand hole.
● Do not tighten the shell nuts until the adjuster bracket is bolted to the underside of the bottom yoke with the brake hose splitter (see illustration).
● Check the operation of the headlight and sidelight.
● Check the headlight aim (see below).

Headlight aim

Note: *An improperly adjusted headlight may cause problems for oncoming traffic or provide poor, unsafe illumination of the road ahead. Before adjusting the headlight aim, be sure to consult with local traffic laws and regulations – for UK models refer to MOT Test Checks in the Reference section at the back of this manual.*

10 The headlight beam can adjusted both horizontally and vertically. Before making any adjustment, check that the tyre pressures are correct and the suspension is adjusted as required. Make any adjustments to the headlight aim with the machine on level ground, with the fuel tank half full and with an assistant sitting on the seat. If the bike is usually ridden with a passenger, have a second assistant to do this. Adjust the beam horizontally first, then vertically.

11 Horizontal adjustment is made by turning the adjuster screw on the right-hand side of the beam unit rim (see illustration). Turn the

8.8 Unscrew the bolts and detach each bracket from its holder

8.11 Horizontal adjustment screw (arrowed)

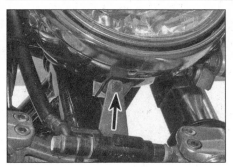

8.12 Vertical adjustment screw (arrowed)

9.1 Remove the toolkit

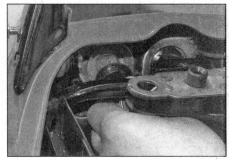

9.2 Turn the bulbholder anti-clockwise and draw it out

screw clockwise to move the beam to the left, and anti-clockwise to move the beam to the right.

12 Vertical adjustment is made by turning the adjuster screw on the underside of the headlight shell **(see illustration)**. Turn the screw clockwise to move the beam up, and anti-clockwise to move the beam down.

9 Tail and brake light bulbs

1 Remove the seat (see Chapter 7). Remove the tool kit **(see illustration)**.
2 Turn the relevant bulbholder anti-clockwise to release it from the tail light **(see illustration)**.
3 Push the bulb in and twist it anti-clockwise to release it **(see illustration)**.

4 Check the terminals for corrosion and clean them if necessary.
5 Line up the pins of the new bulb with the slots in the holder, then push the bulb in and turn it clockwise until it locks into place.
6 Fit the bulbholder into the tail light, aligning the tab with the slot, and turn it clockwise to secure it.
7 Check the operation of the bulb, replace the tool kit then install the seat (see Chapter 7).

10 Tail light assembly

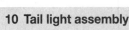

1 Remove the seat cowling (see Chapter 7).
2 Undo the four screws and carefully withdraw the tail light assembly from the seat cowling **(see illustration)**.
3 Installation is the reverse of removal.

11 Turn signal bulbs

1 Undo the screw securing the turn signal in its housing and draw it out, noting how it fits **(see illustrations)**.
2 Turn the bulbholder anti-clockwise to release it from the lens **(see illustration)**.
3 Push the bulb in and twist it anti-clockwise to release it **(see illustration)**.
4 Check the terminals for corrosion and clean them if necessary.
5 Line up the pins of the new bulb with the slots in the holder, then push the bulb in and turn it clockwise until it locks into place.
6 Fit the bulbholder into the lens, aligning the tabs with the slots, and turn it clockwise to secure it.

9.3 Push in and twist the bulb to remove it

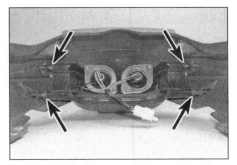

10.2 Undo the screws (arrowed) and remove the tail light

11.1a Undo the screw . . .

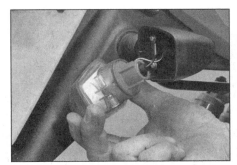

11.1b . . . and remove the turn signal

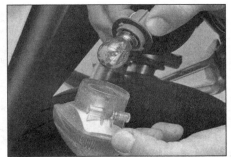

11.2 Release the bulbholder . . .

11.3 . . . and remove the bulb

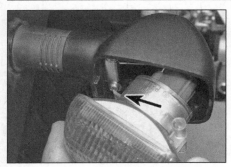

11.7 Make sure the tab (arrowed) locates correctly

7 Fit the turn signal into the housing, locating the tab behind the bar, then fit the screw **(see illustration)**.

HAYNES HiNT *If the socket contacts are dirty or corroded, scrape them clean and spray with electrical contact cleaner before a new bulb is installed.*

12 Turn signal assemblies

Front

1 Remove the headlight beam unit (see Section 8).
2 Disconnect the relevant turn signal wiring connector **(see illustration)**. Feed the wiring out the back of the shell.
3 Undo the nut securing the turn signal to the headlight bracket and remove it, taking care not to snag the wiring as you draw it through **(see illustration)**.
4 Installation is the reverse of removal. Check the operation of the turn signals.

Rear

5 Remove the seat (see Chapter 7). Remove the tool kit **(see illustration 9.1)**.
6 Disconnect the relevant turn signal wiring connector **(see illustration)**. Feed the wiring down to the turn signal.

13.3 Turn signal/sidestand relay (arrowed)

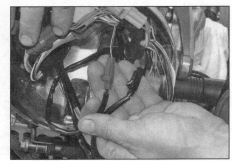

12.2 Disconnect the relevant wiring connector and feed the wiring out . . .

12.6 Disconnect the relevant wiring connector (arrowed) and feed the wiring out . . .

7 Undo the nut and remove the washer securing the turn signal assembly on the inside of the mudguard, then withdraw the signal assembly from the mudguard, noting the spacer **(see illustration)**. Take care not to snag the wiring as you pull it through.
8 Installation is the reverse of removal. Check the operation of the turn signals.

13 Turn signal circuit check

1 Most turn signal problems are the result of a blown bulb or corroded socket. This is especially true when the turn signals function

13.4 Pull the relay off its connector and check the left-hand outer terminal (arrowed) for voltage

12.3 . . . then unscrew the nut (arrowed)

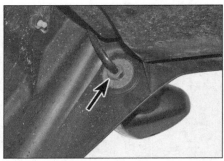

12.7 . . . then unscrew the nut (arrowed)

properly in one direction, but not in the other. Check the bulbs and the sockets (see Section 11) and the wiring connectors. Also, check the signal fuse (see Section 5) and the switch (see Section 19).
2 The battery provides power for operation of the turn signal lights, so if they do not operate, also check the battery voltage. Low battery voltage indicates either a faulty battery or a defective charging system. Refer to Section 3 for battery checks and Section 28 for charging system tests.
3 If all the above are good, check the integral turn signal/sidestand relay **(see illustration)** – remove the left-hand side panel to access it (see Chapter 7).
4 Make sure the ignition is OFF. Pull the relay off its connector **(see illustration)**. Turn the ignition ON, then connect the positive (+) probe of a voltmeter to the orange/green or brown (according to model) wire terminal (the left-hand terminal in the outer row of three) in the relay connector and the negative (–) probe to a good earth (ground) and check for battery voltage. Turn the ignition OFF.
5 If there is no voltage, check the wiring from the connector to the ignition switch via the fuse for continuity.
6 If there is voltage, check for continuity in the light blue wire to the turn signal switch, then check for continuity in the wiring from the switch to the turn signals. If the wiring is good, replace the relay with a new one.

14 Brake light switches

Check

1 Before checking the switches, check the brake light circuit (see Section 6, Step 11).
2 The front brake light switch is mounted on the underside of the brake master cylinder. Disconnect the wiring connector from the switch **(see illustration)**. Using a continuity tester, connect the probes to the terminals of the switch. With the brake lever at rest, there should be no continuity. With the brake lever applied, there should be continuity. If the switch does not behave as described, replace it with a new one.
3 The rear brake light switch is mounted on the inside of the frame, next to the brake fluid reservoir. Remove the right-hand side panel to access it (see Chapter 7). Lift the boot off the switch and disconnect the wiring connector **(see illustration)**. Using a continuity tester, connect the probes to the terminals on the switch. With the brake pedal at rest, there should be no continuity. With the brake pedal applied, there should be continuity. If the switch does not behave as described, replace it with a new one.
4 If the switches are good, check for voltage at the black/red wire terminal (front brake switch) or the orange/green wire terminal (rear brake switch) on the connector with the ignition switch ON – there should be battery voltage. If there's no voltage present, check the wiring between the switch and the ignition switch (see the *Wiring Diagrams* at the end of this Chapter). If there is voltage, check the wiring and connectors between the switch and the brake light bulbs.

Removal and installation

Front brake switch

5 The switch is mounted on the underside of the brake master cylinder. Disconnect the wiring connector from the switch **(see illustration 14.2)**.

14.2 Disconnect the wiring connector

14.6 Undo the screw (arrowed) and remove the switch

6 Undo the screw securing the switch to the bottom of the master cylinder and remove the switch **(see illustration)**.
7 Installation is the reverse of removal. The switch isn't adjustable.

Rear brake switch

8 The switch is mounted on the inside of the frame on the right-hand side above the swingarm pivot. Remove the right-hand side panel to access it (see Chapter 7). Lift the boot off the switch and disconnect the wiring connector **(see illustration 14.3)**.
9 Detach the lower end of the switch spring from the brake pedal, then hold the adjusting nut and unscrew and remove the switch **(see illustration)**.
10 Installation is the reverse of removal. Make sure the spring locates in its groove in

14.3 Pull the wiring connector off the top of the switch (arrowed)

14.9 Unhook the bottom end of the spring (arrowed)

the lug. Make sure the brake light is activated just before the rear brake pedal takes effect. If adjustment is necessary, hold the switch and turn the adjusting nut until the brake light is activated as required.

15 Instrument cluster removal and installation

Removal

1 Remove the headlight beam unit and displace the shell – you only need to disconnect and feed out the blue instrument cluster wiring connectors **(see illustrations)**, and the shell can dangle by the rest of the wiring, but remove the shell completely if you

15.1a Disconnect the instrument wiring connectors . . .

15.1b . . . and draw them out the back

prefer (see Section 8). Release the wiring from any ties.

2 Undo the instrument cowl screws and remove the cowl **(see illustrations)**.

3 Unscrew the nuts securing the instrument cluster, then pull the cluster off to free the peg from the grommet **(see illustrations)**.

Installation

4 Installation is the reverse of removal. Check the condition of the grommets and fit new ones if they are damaged or deteriorated.

16 Instrument check

Note: *The tachometer, LCD display and LEDs are integral with the instrument cluster printed circuit board (PCB) – separate components for the PCB are not available, but the PCB is available separately from the cover and housing.*

Function check

1 When the ignition is switched ON the LEDs should all come on briefly and the instrument needles should swing round fully then return to zero.

2 If this does not happen first check the fuses (see Section 5), then remove the headlight beam unit (Section 8) and check the instrument wiring connectors **(see illustration 15.1a)**. If all appears good check for battery voltage at the red wire terminal in the loom side of the 6-pin wiring connector with the ignition ON. If there is no voltage check the wire for continuity to the fusebox, and if that is good check the red/white wire from the fusebox to the starter relay and the main fuse. Similarly check for voltage at the orange/green wire in the 10-pin wiring connector, then if necessary check the wire for continuity to the fusebox, and if that is good check the orange wire from the fusebox to the ignition switch, then check the switch and its wiring connector. Otherwise

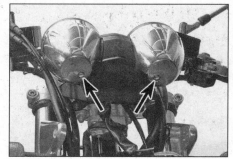

15.2a Undo the screws (arrowed) . . .

15.2b . . . and remove the cowl

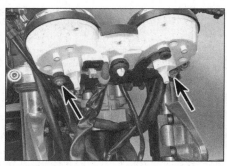

15.3a Unscrew the nuts (arrowed) . . .

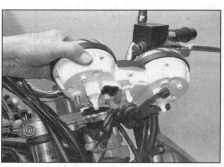

15.3b . . . and lift the cluster off its bracket

take the motorcycle to a Suzuki dealer for assessment.

3 In cold temperatures it is possible that the needles may not return to zero after their initial swing round the dial when the ignition is switched on. If this is the case, hold the right-hand (reset) button down, then turn the ignition ON and between 3 and five seconds after that release the button and press it twice quickly – this should reset the needle(s). If not take the motorcycle to a Suzuki dealer for assessment.

Speedometer and speed sensor

Check

4 If the speedometer, odometer or trip

meter fail to work, remove the front sprocket cover (see Chapter 6, Section 19) and the left-hand side panel to access the speed sensor, mounted in the clutch release cylinder housing. Unscrew its bolt, withdraw the sensor and make sure the head is clean **(see illustration)**. Also check the wiring up to its black connector and the connector itself, then check the orange/red and pink/black wires between the connector and the instrument cluster for continuity, and check for continuity to earth in the black/white wire – refer to Section 2 for details **(see illustration)**. Next displace the clutch release cylinder and check the condition of the speed sensor rotor. If all

16.4a Speed sensor bolt (arrowed)

16.4b Speed sensor wiring connector (arrowed)

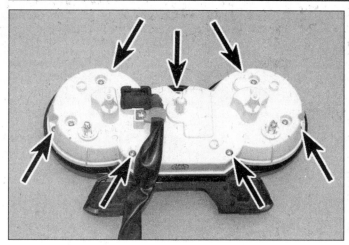

16.6a Undo the screws (arrowed) . . .

16.6b . . . and remove the front cover

appears good take the motorcycle to a Suzuki dealer for assessment. Special equipment is needed to check the operation of the speedometer and the speed sensor.

Removal and installation

5 Remove the instrument cluster (see Section 15). The instruments, LCD display and printed circuit board (PCB) come as an assembly, while all other parts of the instrument cluster are available separately.

6 Undo the screws on the back of the instrument cluster to free the front cover **(see illustrations)**. Note the sealing ring in the groove in the rear cover.

7 Undo the warning light panel screws and remove the panel **(see illustrations)**.

8 Remove the blanking plug from the rear cover, then undo the wiring clamp screw **(see illustration)**.

9 Undo the instrument and PCB screws and carefully lift the assembly out of the rear cover, noting how the PCB locates on the two pegs, and drawing the wiring through the hole **(see illustrations)**. Disconnect the wiring connectors from the back of the PCB **(see illustration)**.

10 Reassemble the instrument cluster in a reverse order. Make sure the PCB locates

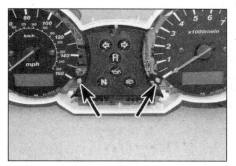

16.7a Undo the screws (arrowed) . . .

16.7b . . . and remove the panel

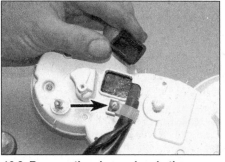

16.8 Remove the plug and undo the screw (arrowed)

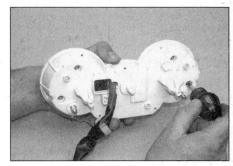

16.9a Undo the screws . . .

16.9b . . . then lift the PCB off the pegs (arrowed) . . .

16.9c . . . and draw the wiring through

16.9d Disconnect the wiring connectors

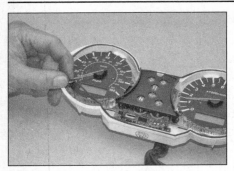

16.10 Make sure the sealing ring is not kinked or twisted

correctly on the two pegs (see illustration 16.9b). Make sure the sealing ring is seated correctly in its groove (see illustration).

11 To remove the speed sensor, mounted in the clutch release cylinder housing, remove the front sprocket cover (see Chapter 6, Section 19) and the left-hand side panel. Trace the wiring from the sensor and disconnect it at the connector (see illustration 16.4b). Free the wiring from any clips and feed it down to the sensor, noting its routing. Unscrew the bolt securing the sensor and withdraw it (see illustration 16.4a). On installation make sure the head of the sensor is clean.

12 Refer to Chapter 6, Section 19, for removal and installation of the sensor rotor.

Tachometer

Check

13 Suzuki provides no data for testing the tachometer. If the tachometer fails to work, take the motorcycle to a Suzuki dealer for assessment.

Removal and installation

14 See Steps 5 to 10.

Fuel gauge and clock

Check

15 When the ignition is switched ON the low fuel warning LED will come on, then either extinguish or flash according to the level of fuel in the tank. The low fuel warning LED will flash when the volume of fuel in the tank drops below 6.0 litres. The fuel level is

also indicated by the number of segments displaced between E and F on the display. When only one segment is displayed the level has dropped to 6.0 litres. When this segment flashes the level has dropped to 1.75 litres.

16 If the display does not function, check the wiring from the base of the fuel tank to the instrument cluster for continuity (see *Wiring Diagrams* at the end of this Chapter). Also check the operation of the fuel level sensor (see Chapter 4, Section 6).

17 If the fuel level warning LED and/or the LCD display is faulty the instrument and PCB assembly must be replaced with a new one.

Removal and installation

18 See Steps 5 to 10.

LEDs

Check

19 If all LEDs fail simultaneously refer to Steps 1 to 3.

20 If one of the individual LEDs fails, first check the component(s), wiring and connectors relevant to its function and the circuit between them to the instrument cluster, referring to the Wiring Diagrams. Refer to Section 6 for the headlight circuit, Section 13 for the turn signal circuit, Section 17 for the oil pressure switch circuit and Section 21 for the gear position sensor circuit.

21 If the LED itself is faulty the instrument and PCB assembly must be replaced with a new one.

Removal and installation

22 See Steps 5 to 10.

17 Oil pressure switch

Check

1 The oil pressure switch is screwed into the right-hand side of the crankcase. When the ignition is first turned ON and before the engine is started, the oil warning LED should come on. When the engine is started it should extinguish.

2 If the LED does not come on, turn the ignition OFF. Remove the timing rotor cover to access the switch (see Step 5).

3 Undo the screw and detach the wiring connector from the switch (see illustration 17.6a). Turn the ignition ON and earth (ground) the wiring connector on the crankcase – the warning LED should come on. If the LED does not come on, check for voltage at the wiring connector, and if there is none check the wire between the oil pressure switch and instrument cluster for continuity. If there is voltage, touch the connector to the terminal on the switch and check that the LED comes on. If not, the switch must be assumed faulty and a new one must be fitted. If there was no voltage but there is continuity in the wire to the instrument cluster the LED could be faulty (see Section 16).

4 If the LED comes on when the engine is running, and this is not due to low oil level or low oil pressure, disconnect the oil pressure switch wiring connector (see Step 4), then turn the ignition ON; the LED should be out. If it is on, the wire between the switch and instrument cluster must be earthed (grounded) at some point.

Removal and installation

5 Drain the engine oil (see Chapter 1). Unscrew the timing rotor cover bolts, noting the sealing washer fitted with the top bolt and remove the cover (see illustration). Discard the gasket as new one must be fitted on reassembly.

6 Undo the screw and detach the wiring connector from the switch (see illustration). Unscrew the switch and withdraw it from the crankcase (see illustration).

7 Apply a suitable sealant (Suzuki-Bond 1207B or equivalent) to the threads near the switch body, then thread the switch into the crankcase and tighten it to the torque setting specified at the beginning of this Chapter.

8 Attach the wiring connector and tighten the screw.

9 Apply a suitable sealant (Suzuki Bond 1207B or equivalent) to the CKP sensor wiring grommet and to the crankcase joints (see

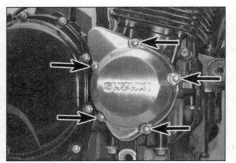

17.5 Unscrew the bolts (arrowed) and remove the cover

17.6a Undo the screw and detach the wire

17.6b Oil pressure switch (arrowed)

17.9a Apply some sealant to the grommet (arrowed) and crankcase joints . . .

17.9b . . . then fit the cover using a new gasket

18.1 Disconnect the green wiring connector

illustration). Install the timing rotor cover using a new gasket and tighten the bolts to the torque setting specified at the beginning of the chapter, not forgetting the sealing washer with the top bolt **(see illustration)**.

10 Fill the engine with the correct type and quantity of oil (see Chapter 1 and *Pre-ride checks*). Start the engine and check the function of the switch and LED.

18 Ignition switch

> ⚠ **Warning: To prevent the risk of short circuits, disconnect the battery negative (–) lead before making any ignition switch checks.**

Check

1 Remove the headlight beam unit (see Section 8). Trace the wiring from the ignition switch and disconnect it at the green connector **(see illustration)**.

2 Using an ohmmeter or a continuity tester, check the continuity of the connector terminal pairs (see the *Wiring Diagrams* at the end of this Chapter). Continuity should exist between the terminals connected by a solid line in the switch box diagram when the switch is in the indicated position (see *Wiring Diagrams* at the end of this Chapter).

3 If the switch fails any of the tests, replace it with a new one.

Removal and installation

Note: *The bolts used to secure the ignition switch to the top yoke are of a special security Torx type which have a raised pip in their centre **(see illustration 18.6b)**. Ensure that you have the necessary Torx bit to undo them.*

4 Remove the instrument cluster (see Section 15).

5 If you haven't removed the headlight shell completely trace the wiring from the ignition switch and disconnect it at the green connector **(see illustration 18.1)**. On K5 models onward also disconnect the immobiliser black/white wiring connector. Free the wiring from its guide and feed it out of the back of the shell to the switch.

6 Undo the special Torx bolts used to mount the ignition switch to the underside of the top yoke and remove the switch **(see illustrations)**.

7 If required remove the immobiliser receiver from the top of the yoke by undoing its two bolts.

8 Installation is the reverse of removal, noting the following:

● Apply a suitable non-permanent thread locking compound to the switch mounting bolts.

● Make sure the wiring is correctly routed and securely connected – the switch wiring feeds through the right-hand hole in the headlight shell, and the immobiliser wiring through the left-hand hole (see Section 8).

19 Handlebar switch check

1 Generally speaking, the switches are reliable and trouble-free. Most troubles, when they do occur, are caused by dirty or corroded contacts, but wear and breakage of internal parts is a possibility that should not be overlooked. If breakage does occur, the entire switch and related wiring harness will have to be renewed, since individual parts are not available.

2 The switches can be checked for continuity using an ohmmeter or a continuity test light. Always disconnect the battery negative (–) lead (see Section 3), which will prevent the possibility of a short circuit, before making the checks.

3 Remove the headlight beam unit (see Section 8). Trace the wiring from the switch in question and disconnect it – the connector for the right-hand switches is black and that for the left-hand switches is yellow **(see illustration)**.

4 Check for continuity between the terminals of the connector on the switch side, with the switch in the various positions (i.e. switch OFF – no continuity, switch ON – continuity) – see the switch boxes in the *Wiring Diagrams* at the end of this Chapter.

5 If the continuity check indicates a problem exists, remove the switch (see Section 20) and spray the switch contacts with electrical

18.6a Ignition switch is secured by two special Torx bolts (arrowed) . . .

18.6b . . . that require a special Torx bit to unscrew them

19.3 Disconnect the relevant switch wiring connector

19.5 Clean the contacts and check the terminals

20.3a Undo the housing screws . . .

20.3b . . . and detach the switch assembly from the handlebar

contact cleaner **(see illustration)**. If they are accessible, the contacts can be scraped clean with a knife or polished with crocus cloth. Check all terminals are tight. If switch components are damaged or broken, it will be obvious when the switch is disassembled.

20 Handlebar switch removal and installation

Removal

1 If the switch is to be removed from the bike, rather than just displaced from the handlebar, remove the headlight beam unit (see Section 8). Trace the wiring harness of the switch in question and disconnect it – the connector for the right-hand switches is black and that for the left-hand switches is yellow **(see illustration 19.3)**. Free the wiring from its clamps and ties and feed it out of the back of the shell to the switch, noting its routing.
2 Disconnect the front brake light switch wiring connector or the clutch switch wiring connectors as required **(see illustration 14.2 or 23.2)**.
3 Undo the housing screws and detach the halves from the handlebar **(see illustrations)**.

Installation

4 Installation is the reverse of removal. Make sure the locating pin in the upper half of the

housing fits into the hole in the top of the handlebar **(see illustration 20.3b)**.

21 Gear position sensor

Note: *The neutral LED in the instrument cluster is activated by the gear position (GP) sensor which is part of the fuel injection system. For full details of the GP sensor see Chapter 4, Section 10.*

Check

1 Remove the left-hand side panel (see Chapter 7). Trace the wiring from the GP sensor on the lower left-hand side of the engine and disconnect it at the white connector **(see illustration)**. Make sure the transmission is in neutral, then turn the ignition ON. With the connector disconnected, the neutral LED should be out. If not, the wire between the connector and instrument cluster must be earthed (grounded) at some point.
2 If the neutral LED doesn't come on with the transmission in neutral, refer to the *Wiring Diagrams* at the end of this Chapter and check the blue/black wire from the instrument cluster to the diodes for continuity (see Section 22 to access the diodes), then check the blue wire from the diodes to the gear position sensor for continuity. Check the diodes as described in

the next section. Check the black/white wire for continuity to earth.
3 Also check that when in neutral there is continuity between the blue and black/white wire terminals on the switch side of the connector, and no continuity when a gear is selected. If not, and the wiring is good, the switch is faulty.
4 If the fuel injection system self-diagnostic function indicates a fault in the GP sensor, refer to Chapter 4 and check the sensor output voltage.

Removal and installation

5 Refer to Chapter 4, Section 10.

22 Sidestand switch, relay and diodes

Sidestand switch

1 The sidestand switch is mounted on the sidestand bracket. The switch incorporates a diode and is part of the safety circuit which prevents or stops the engine running if the transmission is in gear whilst the sidestand is down, and prevents the engine from starting if the transmission is in gear unless the sidestand is up and the clutch lever is pulled in.
2 Remove the left-hand side panel (see Chapter 7). Trace the wiring from the switch and disconnect it at the connector **(see illustration)**.
3 Check the operation of the switch using a multimeter with a diode test function, and set it to the diode function. Connect the meter positive (+) probe to the green wire terminal on the switch side of the connector and the negative (−) to the black/white wire terminal. With the sidestand up there should be 0.4 to 0.6 V between the terminals, with the stand down there should be more than 1.4 V (the actual amount corresponding to the battery voltage of the multimeter).
4 If the switch does not perform as expected, check that the fault is not caused by a sticking switch plunger due to the ingress of road dirt; spray the switch with a water dispersant

21.1 Gear position sensor wiring connector (arrowed)

22.2 Sidestand switch wiring connector (arrowed)

22.4 Check the operation of the switch plunger

aerosol **(see illustration)**. If the switch still does not work it is defective and must be replaced with a new one.

5 If the switch is good, check the sidestand relay (Steps 11 to 13) and the other diodes (Steps 14 to 16). Also check the wiring between the various components (see *Wiring Diagrams* at the end of this Chapter).

6 To remove the switch, first remove the front sprocket cover (see Chapter 6), then disconnect the switch wiring (see Step 2). Feed the wiring back to the switch noting its routing and freeing it from any clips or ties.

7 Unscrew the bolts securing the switch and remove it **(see illustration)**.

8 Fit the new switch onto the bracket, then apply a suitable non-permanent thread locking compound to the bolt threads and tighten them.

9 Make sure the wiring is correctly routed up to the connector and retained by clips and ties. Reconnect the wiring connector.

10 Install the sprocket cover and side panel.

Sidestand relay

11 Remove the left-hand side panel (see Chapter 7).

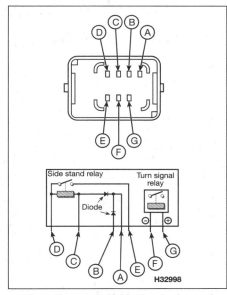

22.12 Turn signal/sidestand relay and diode terminal identification

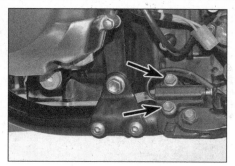

22.7 Switch is secured by two bolts (arrowed)

12 Pull the relay off its connector **(see illustration 13.4)**. Using an ohmmeter or continuity tester, check for continuity between the D and E terminals on the relay **(see illustration)**. There should be no continuity (infinite resistance).

13 Now use jumper wires to connect the positive (+) terminal of a 12V battery to the D terminal on the relay and the negative (–) battery terminal to the C relay terminal, and again check for continuity between the D and E terminals. There should be continuity (zero resistance). If there is no continuity, fit a new relay.

Diodes

14 The diodes are integral with the sidestand/turn signal relay. Access the relay (see Step 11) and pull it off its connector **(see illustration 13.4)**.

15 Using a multimeter with a diode test function, and set to the diode function, connect the meter positive (+) probe to the C terminal and the negative (–) to the A wire terminal **(see illustration 22.12)**. There should be 0.4 to 0.6 V between the terminals. Now reverse the probes. There should be more than 1.4 V (the actual amount corresponding to the battery voltage of the multimeter). Repeat the tests between B terminal and A terminal. The same results should be achieved. If it doesn't behave as stated, install a new diode/turn signal relay/sidestand relay unit.

16 If the diodes are good, check the other components in the starter interlock circuit (clutch switch, gear position sensor, sidestand switch) as described in the relevant sections

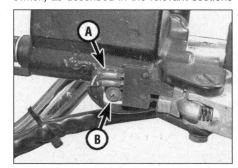

23.2 Clutch switch wiring connectors (A) and mounting screw (B)

of this Chapter. If all components are good, check the wiring between the various components (see *Wiring diagrams* at the end of this book).

23 Clutch switch

Check

1 The clutch switch is situated on the front of the clutch master cylinder. The switch is part of the starter interlock circuit and the lever must be pulled in (switch on) to allow the engine to be started.

2 To check the switch, disconnect the wiring connectors **(see illustration)**. Connect the probes of an ohmmeter or a continuity test light to the two switch terminals. With the clutch lever pulled in, there should be continuity (zero resistance). With the clutch lever out, there should be no continuity (infinite resistance).

3 If the switch is good, check the other components in the starter circuit as described in the relevant sections of this Chapter. If all components are good, check the wiring between the various components (see the *Wiring Diagrams* at the end of this Chapter).

Removal and installation

4 Disconnect the wiring connectors from the clutch switch **(see illustration 23.2)**. Undo the screw securing the switch to the master cylinder and remove it, noting how it locates.

5 Installation is the reverse of removal. The switch isn't adjustable.

24 Horns

Check

1 A horn is mounted on each side of the frame at the front of the fuel tank.

2 Disconnect the wiring connectors from the horn being tested **(see illustration)**. Using jumper wires, apply battery voltage directly to the terminals on the horn. If the horn sounds,

24.2 Disconnect the wiring connectors (arrowed) from the horn

24.4 Horn mounting bolt (arrowed)

25.3a Remove the relay cover

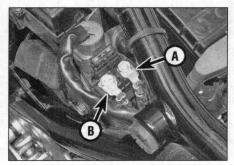

25.3b Starter motor lead (A) and battery lead (B)

check the switch (see Section 19) and the wiring between the switch and the horn (see the *Wiring Diagrams* at the end of this Chapter).

3 If the horn doesn't sound, install a new one.

Removal and installation

4 Disconnect the wiring connectors from the horn, then undo the mounting bolt and remove the horn from the bike **(see illustration)**.

5 Install the horn, making sure the one marked L is on the left, and that marked R is on the right, and tighten the mounting bolt. Connect the wiring connectors and test the operation of the horn.

25.4 Disconnect the starter relay wiring connector and check for battery voltage as described

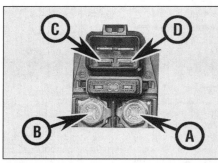

25.6a Starter relay terminal identification

---

25 Starter relay

Check

1 If the starter circuit is faulty, first check the main and ignition fuses (see Section 5).

2 Disconnect the battery negative (–) lead (see Section 3). Remove the left-hand side panel (see Chapter 7).

3 Remove the relay cover **(see illustration)**. Undo the bolt securing the starter motor lead (black lead, right-hand bolt) to its terminal on the relay and disconnect the lead, then position the lead away from the terminal **(see illustration)**. Reconnect the battery negative (–) lead. With the ignition ON, the engine kill

switch in the RUN position, the transmission in neutral and the clutch lever pulled in, press the starter switch. The relay should be heard to click. Turn the ignition OFF.

4 If the relay doesn't click, disconnect the relay wiring connector **(see illustration)**. Insert the positive (+) probe of a voltmeter into the C terminal in the connector and the negative (–) probe into the D terminal **(see illustration 25.6a)**. Check for battery voltage with the ignition ON, kill switch in the RUN position, clutch lever pulled in and starter switch pressed. If no voltage is present, check the terminals in the wiring connector, the wiring (see *Wiring Diagrams* at the end of this Chapter) and the other components in the starter interlock circuit as described in the relevant sections of this Chapter.

5 If there is voltage present, test the relay.

Ensure the ignition is OFF and disconnect the battery negative (–) lead. Undo the bolts securing the starter motor and battery leads to the relay, noting where they fit, and remove the relay **(see illustration 25.3b)**.

6 Set a multimeter to the ohms scale and connect it across the relay's starter motor and battery lead terminals (A and B) **(see illustration)**. Use jumper wires to connect the positive (+) terminal of a 12V battery to the C terminal on the relay and the negative (–) battery terminal to the D relay terminal **(see illustration)**. The relay should be heard to click and there should be continuity (zero resistance) shown on the meter. Disconnect the battery. **Note:** *Do not apply battery voltage to the relay for more than 5 seconds to avoid damaging the relay coil.*

7 Now use the multimeter set to the ohms scale to measure the resistance between the relay's C and D terminals and compare the result with the Specifications at the beginning of this Chapter **(see illustration)**. If the result of either test is not as specified, the relay is faulty and must be replaced with a new one.

Removal and installation

8 Disconnect the battery negative (–) lead (see Section 3). Remove the left-hand side panel (see Chapter 7).

9 Remove the relay cover **(see illustration 25.3a)**. Undo the bolts securing the starter motor and battery leads to the relay, noting where they fit **(see illustration 25.3b)**. Disconnect the relay wiring connector and remove the relay **(see illustration 25.4)**.

25.6b Set-up for checking the starter relay for continuity

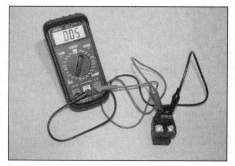

25.7 Measuring the starter relay resistance

26.2a Unscrew the bolts (arrowed) and detach the hose from the crankcase . . .

26.2b . . . and from the left-hand side of the valve cover

26.3 Displace the boot, unscrew the nut and disconnect the lead

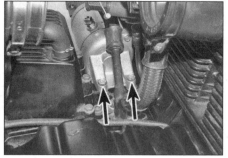

26.4 Unscrew the two bolts (arrowed) . . .

26.5 . . . and manoeuvre the starter motor out

26.6 Fit a new O-ring

10 Installation is the reverse of removal. Make sure the terminal bolts are tight – the starter motor lead (black) connects to the inner terminal, and the battery lead (red) to the outer.

26 Starter motor removal and installation

Removal

1 Disconnect the battery negative (–) lead (see Section 3). Remove the fuel tank (see Chapter 4).
2 Unscrew the two bolts securing the oil hose union to the crankcase behind the cylinder block (see illustration). Also unscrew the two bolts securing the oil hose union to the rear of the valve cover on the left-hand side (see illustration). Discard the O-rings as new ones must be used.
3 Pull back the rubber boot on the starter motor terminal, then undo the nut securing the lead and disconnect it (see illustration).
4 Undo the two bolts securing the starter motor to the crankcase (see illustration).
5 Slide the starter motor out of the crankcase and remove it from the machine (see illustration). Remove the O-ring on the end of the starter motor and discard it as a new one must be fitted on reassembly (see illustration 26.6).

Installation

6 Fit a new O-ring on the end of the starter motor, making sure it is seated in its groove (see illustration). Apply a smear of engine oil or grease to the O-ring.
7 Manoeuvre the motor into position and slide it into the crankcase (see illustration 26.5). Ensure that the starter motor teeth mesh correctly with those of the starter idle/reduction gear.
8 Install and tighten the bolts (see illustration 26.4).
9 Connect the starter lead to the terminal and secure it with the nut (see illustration 26.3). Fit the rubber boot.
10 Fit the oil hose unions onto the valve cover and crankcase, using new O-rings smeared with grease (see illustrations 26.2b and a). Tighten the union bolts to the specified torque setting.
11 Install the fuel tank and connect the battery lead.

27 Starter motor overhaul

Disassembly

1 Remove the starter motor (see Section 26).
2 Note the alignment marks between the main housing and the front and rear covers, or make your own if they aren't clear (see illustration).
3 Unscrew the two long bolts and withdraw them from the starter motor (see illustration).

27.2 Note the alignment marks . . .

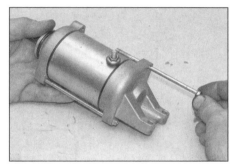

27.3 . . . then unscrew and remove the long bolts

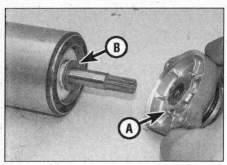

27.4 Remove the front cover, the tabbed washer (A) fitted on it, and the washer and shims (B) on the shaft

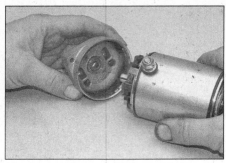

27.5 Remove the rear cover

4 Remove the front cover **(see illustration)**. Remove the insulating washer and shim(s) from the front end of the armature shaft and the tabbed washer from inside the front cover, noting how it fits.

5 Remove the rear cover **(see illustration)**. Remove the shims from the armature shaft **(see illustration 27.20a)**.

6 Draw the armature out of the main housing, noting that it is held by the attraction of the magnets **(see illustration)**.

7 Draw the brushes out of their housings. Check for continuity between each insulated brush and the terminal bolt **(see illustration)**. There should be continuity (zero resistance). Check for continuity between the un-insulated brushes and the brush plate **(see illustration)**. There should be continuity (zero resistance). Check for continuity between the terminal bolt

and the housing. There should be no continuity (infinite resistance). If any of the results are not as they should be see Step 10.

8 Remove the brush plate, noting how the insulated brush wires route through the cut-outs **(see illustration 27.17)**.

9 Noting the correct fitted location of each component, unscrew the terminal nut and remove it along with its washer, insulating washers and O-ring **(see illustrations 27.16g and e)**. Withdraw the terminal then remove the insulated brush holder, the insulator piece and the brush plate seat **(see illustrations 27.16d, c, b and a)**.

Inspection

10 The parts of the starter motor that are most likely to require attention are the brushes. Suzuki give no specifications for the minimum length of the brushes, however if they are obviously worn, cracked, chipped, or

otherwise damaged, or any of the continuity test results in Step 7 were not as they should be, a new set of brushes must be fitted – the insulated brushes, holder and terminal bolt assembly come as one set but this does not include the O-ring which must be obtained separately, and the brush plate along with the other brushes come as another set but does not include the brush springs, so remove them from the old brush plate beforehand. If in doubt as to what you need seek the advice of your parts dealer.

11 Inspect the commutator bars on the armature for scoring, scratches and discoloration. The commutator can be cleaned and polished with crocus cloth, do not use sandpaper or emery paper. After cleaning, wipe away any residue with a cloth soaked in electrical system cleaner or denatured alcohol. Check that the insulation mica between each bar is below the level of the bars **(see illustration)**. If not, carefully scrape some away.

12 Using an ohmmeter or a continuity tester, check for continuity between the commutator bars **(see illustration)**. Continuity (zero resistance) should exist between each bar and all of the others. Also, check for continuity between the commutator bars and the armature shaft **(see illustration)**. There should be no continuity (infinite resistance) between the commutator and the shaft. If the checks indicate otherwise, the armature is defective.

13 Check the front end of the armature shaft for worn, cracked, chipped and broken teeth. If the shaft is damaged or worn, fit a new armature.

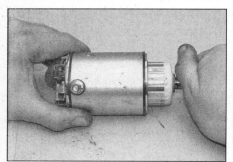

27.6 Carefully draw the armature out

27.7a Checking for continuity between the terminal bolt and the insulated brushes . . .

27.7b . . . and between the un-insulated brushes and the plate

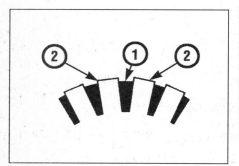

27.11 Make sure the insulating mica (1) is below the commutator bars (2)

27.12a Checking for continuity between the commutator bars

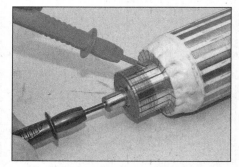

27.12b There should be no continuity between the commutator bars and the armature shaft

14 Check the bearing and oil seal in the front cover and the bush in the rear cover for wear and damage **(see illustrations)**. Individual components are not available; fit new covers if necessary.

15 Check the terminal insulating washers and O-ring, brush plate seat and insulator piece for signs of deterioration and replace them with new ones if necessary. Likewise replace the main housing sealing rings with new ones if necessary **(see illustration)**.

Reassembly

16 Fit the brush plate seat into the housing, then fit the insulator piece and the insulated brush holder **(see illustrations)**. Fit the terminal bolt through, then fit the small O-ring onto it and locate it between the base of the bolt and the housing **(see illustrations)**. Fit

27.14a Check the bearing and seal . . .

27.14b . . . and the bush (arrowed)

the insulating washers over the terminal, then fit the standard washer and the nut and tighten the nut **(see illustration)**.

17 Fit the brush plate assembly onto the housing, fitting the insulated brush wires

into their cut-outs and locating the tab in its cut-out **(see illustration)**. At this point repeat the continuity tests in Step 7 to make sure everything is correctly fitted.

18 Push the brushes fully into their housings

27.15 Make sure the housing sealing rings are in good condition and seat correctly

27.16a Fit the brush plate seat . . .

27.16b . . . then the insulator piece . . .

27.16c . . . and the brush holder

27.16d Insert the terminal bolt . . .

27.16e . . . then fit the O-ring onto it . . .

27.16f . . . and fit it between the bolt and the housing to insulate them

27.16g Fit the washers and nut as shown

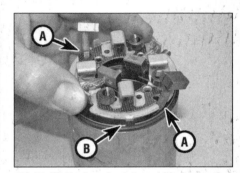

27.17 Fit the brush plate, making sure the insulated wires (A) and tab (B) locate in the cut-outs

27.18a Slide each brush into its housing . . .

27.18b . . . then lift the brush spring onto the top of the brush to hold it in place . . .

then locate the spring ends onto the protruding outer ends of the brushes so they are held in the retracted position to allow the armature to be fitted **(see illustrations)**.

19 Fit the armature into the main housing and brush plate **(see illustration)**. Note that the armature will be forcefully drawn into the housing by the magnets – take care not to trap your fingers between them. Place each spring back onto the end of its brush so the brushes are now pressed against the commutator bars **(see illustrations)**.

27.18c . . . so that all brushes are out of the way of the armature

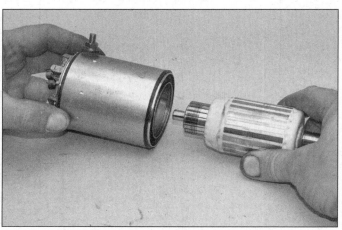

27.19a Carefully slide the armature into the housing and brush plate . . .

27.19b . . . then move the brush springs off the top of each brush . . .

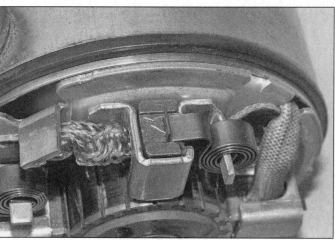

27.19c . . . and locate them against the back so they are pressed onto the commutator

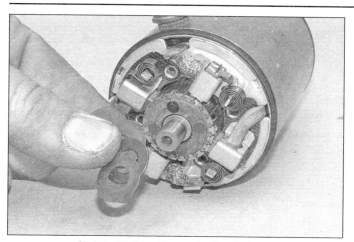

27.20a Fit the shims onto the shaft . . .

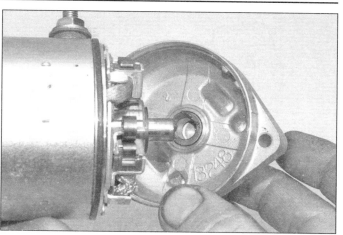

27.20b . . . then fit the rear cover, making sure the tab locates between the ribs

27.21a Fit the shims onto the shaft . . .

20 Fit the shims onto the rear of the armature shaft **(see illustration)**. Apply a smear of molybdenum disulphide grease to the shaft and fit the rear cover, aligning the marks and locating the tab on the brush plate between the ribs in the cover **(see illustration)**.
21 Fit the shims and insulating washer onto the front of the armature shaft **(see illustration)**. Apply a smear of grease to

the lips of the front cover oil seal and fit the special washer into the cover, making sure its tabs locate correctly **(see illustration)**. Fit the cover, aligning the marks made on removal **(see illustration 27.2)**.
22 Apply a suitable non-permanent thread lock to the threads of the long bolts then fit the bolts and tighten them **(see illustration 27.3)**.
23 Install the starter motor (see Section 26).

28 Charging system testing

1 If the performance of the charging system is suspect, the system as a whole should be checked first, followed by testing of the individual components. **Note:** *Before beginning the checks, make sure the battery is fully charged and that all system connections are clean and tight.*
2 Checking the output of the charging system

and the performance of the various components within the charging system requires the use of a multimeter (with voltage, current and resistance checking facilities). If a multimeter is not available, the job of checking the charging system should be left to a Suzuki dealer.
3 When making the checks, follow the procedures carefully to prevent incorrect connections or short circuits resulting in irreparable damage to electrical system components.

Leakage test

Caution: Always connect an ammeter in series, never in parallel with the battery, otherwise it will be damaged. Do not turn the ignition ON or operate the starter motor when the ammeter is connected – a sudden surge in current will blow the meter's fuse.
4 Disconnect the battery negative (–) lead (see Section 3).
5 Set the multimeter to the Amps function and connect its negative (–) probe to the battery negative (–) terminal, and positive (+) probe to the disconnected negative (–) lead

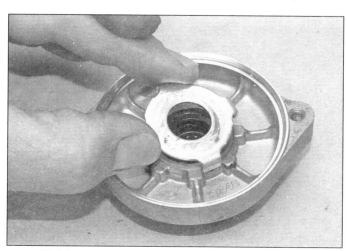

27.21b . . . and the tabbed washer onto the cover . . .

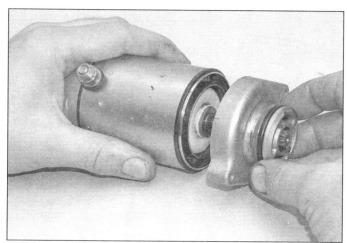

27.21c . . . then fit the cover

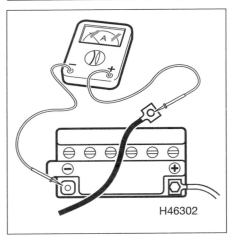

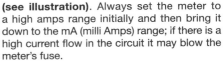

28.5 Checking the charging system leakage rate. Connect the meter as shown

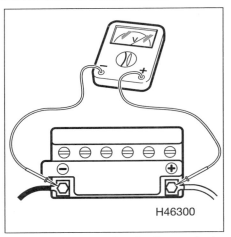

28.9 Checking regulated voltage output

Clues to a faulty regulator are constantly blowing bulbs, with brightness varying considerably with engine speed, and battery overheating.

(see illustration). Always set the meter to a high amps range initially and then bring it down to the mA (milli Amps) range; if there is a high current flow in the circuit it may blow the meter's fuse.

6 Battery current leakage should not exceed the maximum limit (see Specifications). If a higher leakage rate is shown there is a short circuit in the wiring, although if an immobiliser or alarm is fitted, its current draw should be taken into account. Disconnect the meter and reconnect the battery negative (–) lead.

7 If leakage is indicated, refer to *Wiring Diagrams* at the end of this Chapter to systematically disconnect individual electrical components and repeat the test until the source is identified.

Output test

8 Remove the seat (see Chapter 7). Unclip and remove the storage tray **(see illustration 3.1)**. Start the engine and warm it up.
9 To check the regulated (DC) voltage output, allow the engine to idle with the headlight main

beam (HI) turned ON. Connect a multimeter set to the 0-20 volts DC scale across the terminals of the battery **(see illustration)**. Connect the positive (+) meter probe to battery positive (+) terminal and the negative (–) meter probe to battery negative (–) terminal.
10 Slowly increase the engine speed to 5000 rpm and note the reading obtained. Compare the result with the Specification at the beginning of this Chapter. If the regulated voltage output is outside the specification, check the alternator and the regulator (see Sections 29 and 30).
11 To check the unregulated voltage output, remove the front sprocket cover (see Chapter 6). Disconnect the alternator wiring connector **(see illustration 29.1)**. Start the engine and increase the engine speed to 5000 rpm, then using a multimeter set to 0-250 volts AC range, connect the meter probes to one pair of terminals at a time on the alternator side of the wiring connector **(see illustration)**. Make a note of the three readings obtained.
12 Compare the result with the Specification at the beginning of this Chapter. If the

unregulated voltage output is outside the specification, check the alternator and the regulator (see Sections 29 and 30).

29 Alternator

Check

1 Remove the front sprocket cover (see Chapter 6). Disconnect the alternator wiring connector **(see illustration)**.
2 Using a multimeter set to the ohms scale, connect the meter probes to one pair of terminals at a time on the alternator side of the wiring connector and measure the resistance between the terminals. Make a note of the three readings obtained. Now check for continuity between each terminal and ground (earth).
3 If the stator coil windings are in good condition the three readings should be within the range shown in the Specifications at the beginning of this Chapter and there should be no continuity (infinite resistance) between any of the terminals and earth. If not, the alternator stator coil assembly is faulty and should be renewed. **Note:** *Before condemning the stator coils, check the fault is not due to damaged wiring between the connector and coils.*

Removal

4 Drain the engine oil (see Chapter 1).
5 Remove the front sprocket cover (see Chapter 6). Disconnect the alternator wiring connector **(see illustration 29.1)**.
6 Unscrew the alternator cover bolts, noting the position of those with sealing washers, and

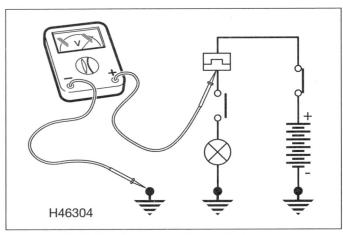

28.11 Checking unregulated voltage output

29.1 Disconnect the wiring connector

29.6 Unscrew the bolts (arrowed), noting those with sealing washers (A)

29.7 Withdraw the shaft and remove the gear

29.8 Hold the rotor and unscrew the bolt

29.9 Hold the rotor and turn the puller until the rotor is displaced

29.10a Remove the driven gear from the starter clutch . . .

remove the cover **(see illustration)**. Discard the gasket as a new one must be fitted on reassembly. Remove the dowels from either the cover or the crankcase if they are loose.

7 Withdraw the idle/reduction gear shaft and remove the gear **(see illustration)**.

8 To remove the rotor bolt it is necessary to stop the crankshaft from turning – a large spanner can be applied to the two flats machined into the boss in the rotor to do this. With the rotor held unscrew and remove the bolt **(see illustration)**.

9 To remove the rotor from the crankshaft taper it is necessary to use a rotor puller. Suzuki produces a service tool (Pt. No. 09930-30450) to do this, or alternatively there are commercially available equivalents. Thread the rotor puller fully into the centre of the rotor. Hold the rotor as before to stop it turning, then turn the puller clockwise until the rotor is free of the crankshaft taper **(see illustration)**. Remove the puller from the rotor.

10 Withdraw the starter driven gear from the starter clutch on the back of the rotor (if it appears stuck, rotate it anti-clockwise as you withdraw it to free it from the sprags), or slide it off the crankshaft if it did not come with it **(see illustrations)**. If required detach the starter clutch from the rotor (see Chapter 2).

11 To remove the stator from the cover, unscrew the bolts securing the stator, and the bolt securing the wiring clamp, then remove the assembly, noting how the wiring grommet fits **(see illustration)**.

29.10b . . . or from the shaft

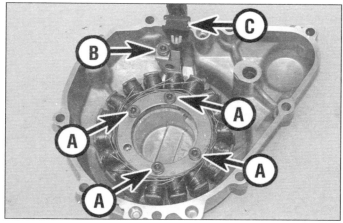

29.11 Unscrew the stator bolts (A) and the wiring clamp bolt (B) and free the grommet (C)

29.13 Lubricate the inner flat section of the shaft with oil

29.14 Slide the rotor onto the shaft . . .

29.15a . . . then fit the bolt with its washer . . .

29.15b . . . and tighten it to the specified torque

29.17a Smear some sealant across the joints . . .

29.17b . . . and onto the grommet

29.17c Install the dowels (arrowed) and a new cover gasket . . .

Installation

12 Apply a suitable sealant to the stator wiring grommet, then fit the stator into the cover, aligning the grommet with the cut-out in the cover **(see illustration 29.11)**. Install the stator and wiring clamp bolts and tighten them to the specified torque setting.

13 Lubricate the flat inner section of the crankshaft end with oil **(see illustration)**. Slide the starter driven gear onto the shaft **(see illustration 29.10b)**.

14 Clean the tapered end of the crankshaft and the corresponding mating surface on the inside of the rotor with a suitable solvent. Make sure that no metal objects have attached themselves to the magnet on the inside of the rotor, then slide the rotor onto the shaft and the starter driven gear, holding the gear and turning the rotor clockwise as you do to spread the starter clutch sprags and allow it to enter **(see illustration)**.

15 Fit the rotor bolt with its washer and tighten it to the torque setting specified at the beginning of this Chapter, using the method employed on removal to prevent the rotor turning **(see illustrations)**.

16 Lubricate the idle/reduction gear shaft with oil. Position the idle/reduction gear then slide the shaft through and into its bore in the crankcase **(see illustration 29.7)**.

29.17d . . . then fit the cover

29.17e Fit new sealing washers with the two bolts

30.1 Regulator/rectifier wiring connector (A) and its bolts (B)

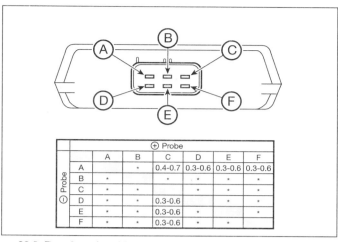

30.2 Regulator/rectifier test data and terminal identification

		⊕ Probe					
		A	B	C	D	E	F
⊖ Probe	A		*	0.4-0.7	0.3-0.6	0.3-0.6	0.3-0.6
	B	*		*	*	*	*
	C	*	*			*	*
	D	*	*	0.3-0.6		*	*
	E	*	*	0.3-0.6	*		*
	F	*	*	0.3-0.6	*	*	

17 Apply a suitable sealant across the crankcase joints and to the wiring grommet in the cover **(see illustrations)**. If removed, fit the dowels into the crankcase, then fit a new gasket, locating it on the dowels **(see illustration)**. Fit the cover onto the dowels **(see illustration)**. Fit new sealing washers on the upper front and lower rear cover bolts **(see illustration)**. Tighten the bolts evenly in a criss-cross pattern to the specified torque setting.

18 Reconnect the alternator wiring connector **(see illustration 29.1)**. Install the front sprocket cover (see Chapter 6).

19 Replenish the engine oil (see Chapter 1 and *Pre-ride checks*).

30 Regulator/rectifier

Check

1 The regulator/rectifier is mounted on the rear mudguard between the back of the engine and the battery **(see illustration)**. Due to its location it is much easier to test it when it has been removed, rather than trying to do it in situ (see Steps 4 to 6).

2 Using a multimeter set to diode test, measure the voltage between the various terminals on the regulator/rectifier side of the wiring connector as shown in the table **(see illustration)**. **Note:** *Depending on the multimeter used for the test, the results may vary from the specified figures. However, as long as the variance is constant, the test will give an indication of the condition of the regulator/rectifier. If the readings do not compare closely with those shown in the table, have the regulator/rectifier tested by a Suzuki dealer.*

3 If the regulator/rectifier appears to be good, check the wiring between the battery, regulator/rectifier and alternator, and the wiring connectors (see *Wiring Diagrams* at the end of this Chapter).

Removal and installation

4 The regulator/rectifier is mounted on the rear mudguard between the back of the engine and the battery **(see illustration 30.1)**. Access to it is tricky and how you remove it will depend on the your dexterity and the tools you have available.

5 First locate it visually and assess whether you can remove it by accessing it from under the bike and/or from each side – remove each side panel (see Chapter 7), then unscrew the bolt securing the rear brake fluid reservoir and move it aside **(see illustration)**. Access the wiring connector from underneath the bike, and access the bolts from each side, or from underneath if you prefer. Disconnect the wiring connector, then unscrew the two bolts, noting the wiring clamp, and remove the regulator/rectifier **(see illustration 30.1)**.

6 If access is too difficult remove the seat cowling (see Chapter 7), the battery (see Section 3), and the ECM (see Chapter 4). Disconnect the rear turn signal wiring connectors **(see illustration 12.6)**. Unscrew the rear mudguard bolts, one at the front and one at the back on each side, then move the rear mudguard back **(see illustrations)**. Disconnect the regulator/rectifier wiring connector, then unscrew the two bolts and remove it **(see illustration 30.1)**.

7 Install it in a reverse of the removal procedure.

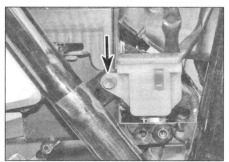

30.5 Unscrew the bolt (arrowed) and displace the reservoir

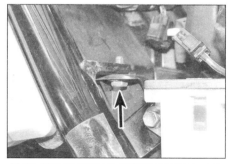

30.6a Unscrew the bolt (arrowed) on each side at the front . . .

30.6b . . . and at the back

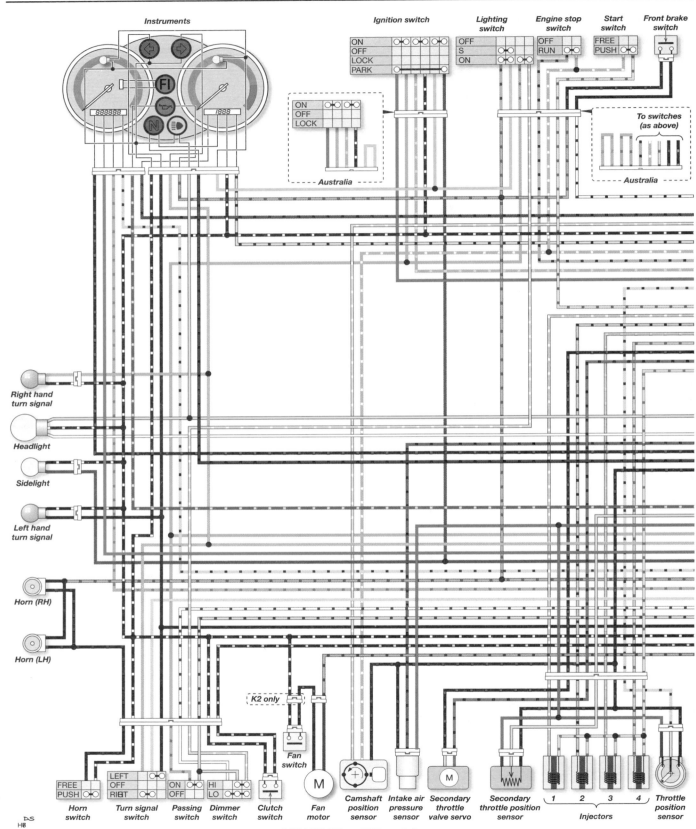

GSX1400 K2 and K3 models

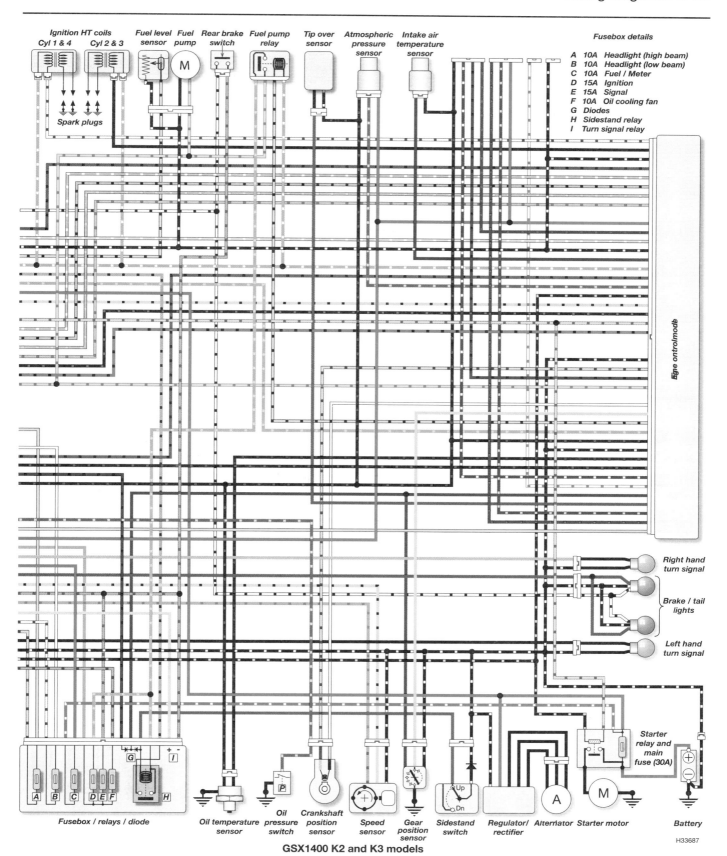

Ignition HT coils Cyl 1 & 4 Cyl 2 & 3
Spark plugs
Fuel level sensor
Fuel pump
Rear brake switch
Fuel pump relay
Tip over sensor
Atmospheric pressure sensor
Intake air temperature sensor

Fusebox details

A 10A Headlight (high beam)
B 10A Headlight (low beam)
C 10A Fuel / Meter
D 15A Ignition
E 15A Signal
F 10A Oil cooling fan
G Diodes
H Sidestand relay
I Turn signal relay

Engine control mode

Right hand turn signal
Brake / tail lights
Left hand turn signal

Starter relay and main fuse (30A)

Fusebox / relays / diode
Oil temperature sensor
Oil pressure switch
Crankshaft position sensor
Speed sensor
Gear position sensor
Sidestand switch
Regulator/ rectifier
Alternator
Starter motor
Battery

GSX1400 K2 and K3 models

H33687

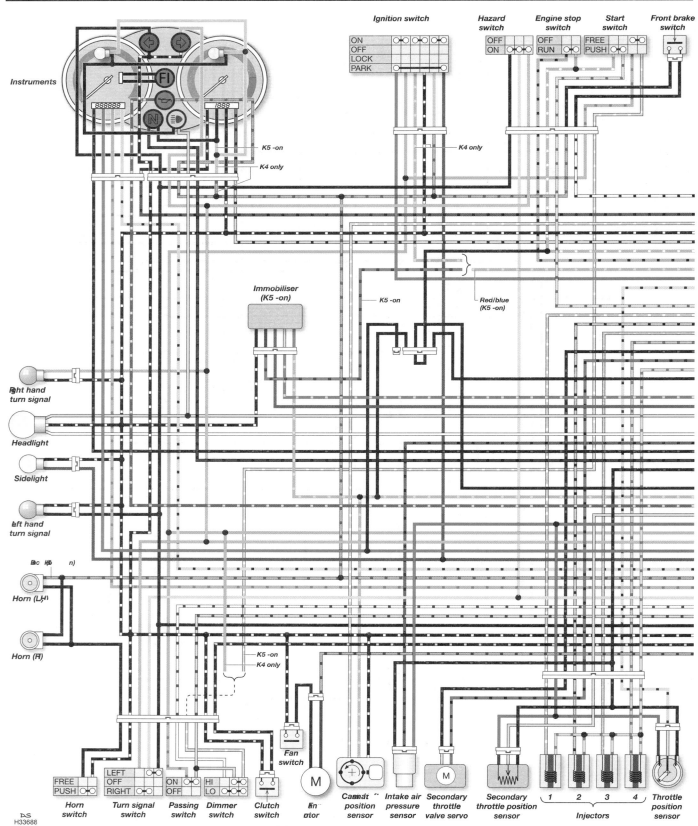

GSX1400 K4 models onward

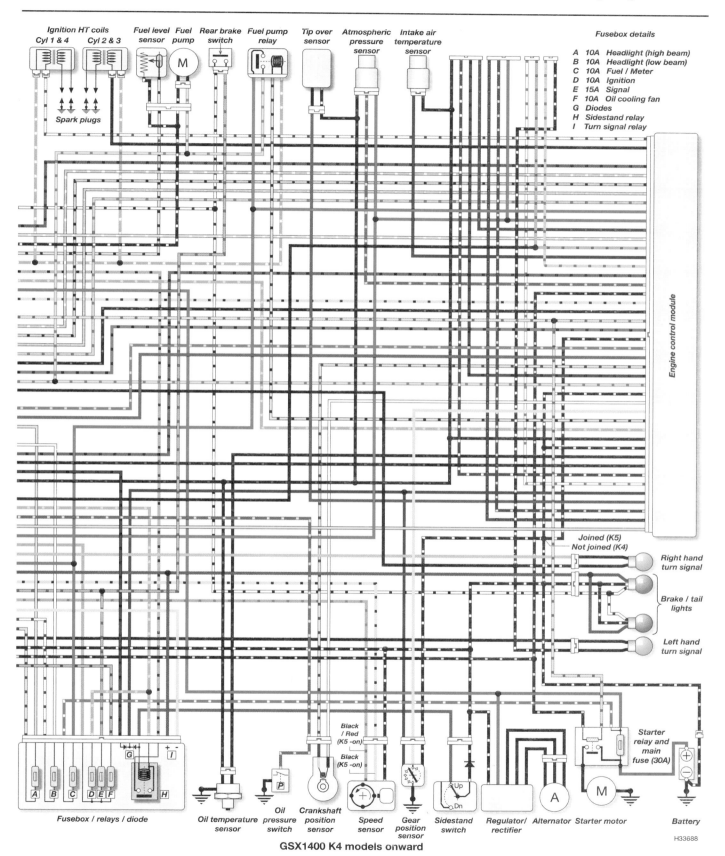

Ignition HT coils
Cyl 1 & 4   Cyl 2 & 3

Spark plugs

Fuel level sensor
Fuel pump
Rear brake switch
Fuel pump relay
Tip over sensor
Atmospheric pressure sensor
Intake air temperature sensor

Fusebox details

A 10A Headlight (high beam)
B 10A Headlight (low beam)
C 10A Fuel / Meter
D 10A Ignition
E 15A Signal
F 10A Oil cooling fan
G Diodes
H Sidestand relay
I Turn signal relay

Engine control module

Joined (K5)
Not joined (K4)

Right hand turn signal

Brake / tail lights

Left hand turn signal

Starter relay and main fuse (30A)

Black / Red (K5 -on)

Black (K5 -on)

G   + I

A B C D E F H

Fusebox / relays / diode

Oil temperature sensor

Oil pressure switch

Crankshaft position sensor

Speed sensor

Gear position sensor

Up

Dn

Sidestand switch

Regulator/ rectifier

A
Alternator

M
Starter motor

Battery

GSX1400 K4 models onward

H33688

Notes

Reference

Tools and Workshop Tips   REF•2

- Building up a tool kit and equipping your workshop ● Using tools ● Understanding bearing, seal, fastener and chain sizes and markings ● Repair techniques

Security   REF•20

- Locks and chains ● U-locks ● Disc locks ● Alarms and immobilisers ● Security marking systems ● Tips on how to prevent bike theft

Lubricants and fluids   REF•23

- Engine oils ● Transmission (gear) oils ● Coolant/anti-freeze ● Fork oils and suspension fluids ● Brake/clutch fluids ● Spray lubes, degreasers and solvents

Conversion Factors   REF•26

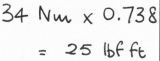

34 Nm x 0.738

= 25 lbf ft

- Formulae for conversion of the metric (SI) units used throughout the manual into Imperial measures

MOT Test Checks   REF•27

- A guide to the UK MOT test ● Which items are tested ● How to prepare your motorcycle for the test and perform a pre-test check

Storage   REF•32

- How to prepare your motorcycle for going into storage and protect essential systems ● How to get the motorcycle back on the road

Fault Finding   REF•35

- Common faults and their likely causes ● Links to main chapters for testing or repair procedures

Technical Terms Explained   REF•46

- Component names, technical terms and common abbreviations explained

Index   REF•50

Buying tools

A toolkit is a fundamental requirement for servicing and repairing a motorcycle. Although there will be an initial expense in building up enough tools for servicing, this will soon be offset by the savings made by doing the job yourself. As experience and confidence grow, additional tools can be added to enable the repair and overhaul of the motorcycle. Many of the specialist tools are expensive and not often used so it may be preferable to hire them, or for a group of friends or motorcycle club to join in the purchase.

As a rule, it is better to buy more expensive, good quality tools. Cheaper tools are likely to wear out faster and need to be renewed more often, nullifying the original saving.

Warning: To avoid the risk of a poor quality tool breaking in use, causing injury or damage to the component being worked on, always aim to purchase tools which meet the relevant national safety standards.

The following lists of tools do not represent the manufacturer's service tools, but serve as a guide to help the owner decide which tools are needed for this level of work. In addition, items such as an electric drill, hacksaw, files, soldering iron and a workbench equipped with a vice, may be needed. Although not classed as tools, a selection of bolts, screws, nuts, washers and pieces of tubing always come in useful.

For more information about tools, refer to the Haynes *Motorcycle Workshop Practice Techbook* (Bk. No. 3470).

Manufacturer's service tools

Inevitably certain tasks require the use of a service tool. Where possible an alternative tool or method of approach is recommended, but sometimes there is no option if personal injury or damage to the component is to be avoided. Where required, service tools are referred to in the relevant procedure.

Service tools can usually only be purchased from a motorcycle dealer and are identified by a part number. Some of the commonly-used tools, such as rotor pullers, are available in aftermarket form from mail-order motorcycle tool and accessory suppliers.

Maintenance and minor repair tools

1 Set of flat-bladed screwdrivers
2 Set of Phillips head screwdrivers
3 Combination open-end and ring spanners
4 Socket set (3/8 inch or 1/2 inch drive)
5 Set of Allen keys or bits

6 Set of Torx keys or bits
7 Pliers, cutters and self-locking grips (Mole grips)
8 Adjustable spanners
9 C-spanners
10 Tread depth gauge and tyre pressure gauge

11 Cable oiler clamp
12 Feeler gauges
13 Spark plug gap measuring tool
14 Spark plug spanner or deep plug sockets
15 Wire brush and emery paper

16 Calibrated syringe, measuring vessel and funnel
17 Oil filter adapters
18 Oil drainer can or tray
19 Pump type oil can
20 Grease gun

21 Straight-edge and steel rule
22 Continuity tester
23 Battery charger
24 Hydrometer (for battery specific gravity check)
25 Anti-freeze tester (for liquid-cooled engines)

Repair and overhaul tools

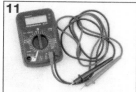

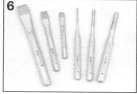
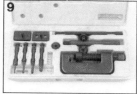

1 Torque wrench
  (small and mid-ranges)
2 Conventional, plastic or
  soft-faced hammers
3 Impact driver set

4 Vernier gauge
5 Circlip pliers (internal and
  external, or combination)
6 Set of cold chisels
  and punches

7 Selection of pullers
8 Breaker bars
9 Chain breaking/
  riveting tool set

10 Wire stripper and
   crimper tool
11 Multimeter (measures
   amps, volts and ohms)
12 Stroboscope (for
   dynamic timing checks)

13 Hose clamp
   (wingnut type shown)
14 Clutch holding tool
15 One-man brake/clutch
   bleeder kit

Specialist tools

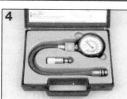

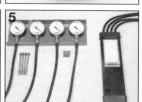
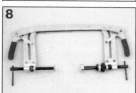
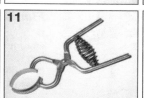

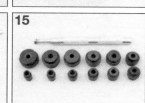
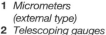

1 Micrometers
  (external type)
2 Telescoping gauges
3 Dial gauge

4 Cylinder
  compression gauge
5 Vacuum gauges (left) or
  manometer (right)
6 Oil pressure gauge

7 Plastigauge kit
8 Valve spring compressor
  (4-stroke engines)
9 Piston pin drawbolt tool

10 Piston ring removal and
   installation tool
11 Piston ring clamp
12 Cylinder bore hone
   (stone type shown)

13 Stud extractor
14 Screw extractor set
15 Bearing driver set

1 Workshop equipment and facilities

The workbench

● Work is made much easier by raising the bike up on a ramp - components are much more accessible if raised to waist level. The hydraulic or pneumatic types seen in the dealer's workshop are a sound investment if you undertake a lot of repairs or overhauls **(see illustration 1.1)**.

1.1 Hydraulic motorcycle ramp

● If raised off ground level, the bike must be supported on the ramp to avoid it falling. Most ramps incorporate a front wheel locating clamp which can be adjusted to suit different diameter wheels. When tightening the clamp, take care not to mark the wheel rim or damage the tyre - use wood blocks on each side to prevent this.
● Secure the bike to the ramp using tie-downs **(see illustration 1.2)**. If the bike has only a sidestand, and hence leans at a dangerous angle when raised, support the bike on an auxiliary stand.

1.2 Tie-downs are used around the passenger footrests to secure the bike

● Auxiliary (paddock) stands are widely available from mail order companies or motorcycle dealers and attach either to the wheel axle or swingarm pivot **(see illustration 1.3)**. If the motorcycle has a centrestand, you can support it under the crankcase to prevent it toppling whilst either wheel is removed **(see illustration 1.4)**.

1.3 This auxiliary stand attaches to the swingarm pivot

1.4 Always use a block of wood between the engine and jack head when supporting the engine in this way

Fumes and fire

● Refer to the Safety first! page at the beginning of the manual for full details. Make sure your workshop is equipped with a fire extinguisher suitable for fuel-related fires (Class B fire - flammable liquids) - it is not sufficient to have a water-filled extinguisher.
● Always ensure adequate ventilation is available. Unless an exhaust gas extraction system is available for use, ensure that the engine is run outside of the workshop.
● If working on the fuel system, make sure the workshop is ventilated to avoid a build-up of fumes. This applies equally to fume build-up when charging a battery. Do not smoke or allow anyone else to smoke in the workshop.

Fluids

● If you need to drain fuel from the tank, store it in an approved container marked as suitable for the storage of petrol (gasoline) **(see illustration 1.5)**. Do not store fuel in glass jars or bottles.

1.5 Use an approved can only for storing petrol (gasoline)

● Use proprietary engine degreasers or solvents which have a high flash-point, such as paraffin (kerosene), for cleaning off oil, grease and dirt - never use petrol (gasoline) for cleaning. Wear rubber gloves when handling solvent and engine degreaser. The fumes from certain solvents can be dangerous - always work in a well-ventilated area.

Dust, eye and hand protection

● Protect your lungs from inhalation of dust particles by wearing a filtering mask over the nose and mouth. Many frictional materials still contain asbestos which is dangerous to your health. Protect your eyes from spouts of liquid and sprung components by wearing a pair of protective goggles **(see illustration 1.6)**.

1.6 A fire extinguisher, goggles, mask and protective gloves should be at hand in the workshop

● Protect your hands from contact with solvents, fuel and oils by wearing rubber gloves. Alternatively apply a barrier cream to your hands before starting work. If handling hot components or fluids, wear suitable gloves to protect your hands from scalding and burns.

What to do with old fluids

● Old cleaning solvent, fuel, coolant and oils should not be poured down domestic drains or onto the ground. Package the fluid up in old oil containers, label it accordingly, and take it to a garage or disposal facility. Contact your local authority for location of such sites or ring the oil care hotline.

OIL CARE
FOLLOW THE CODE

OIL BANK LINE
0800 66 33 66
www.oilbankline.org.uk

Note: It is antisocial and illegal to dump oil down the drain. To find the location of your local oil recycling bank, call this number free.

In the USA, note that any oil supplier must accept used oil for recycling.

2 Fasteners -
screws, bolts and nuts

Fastener types and applications

Bolts and screws

● Fastener head types are either of hexagonal, Torx or splined design, with internal and external versions of each type **(see illustrations 2.1 and 2.2)**; splined head fasteners are not in common use on motorcycles. The conventional slotted or Phillips head design is used for certain screws. Bolt or screw length is always measured from the underside of the head to the end of the item **(see illustration 2.11)**.

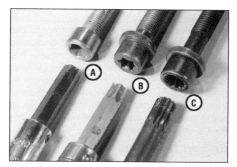

2.1 Internal hexagon/Allen (A), Torx (B) and splined (C) fasteners, with corresponding bits

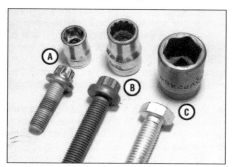

2.2 External Torx (A), splined (B) and hexagon (C) fasteners, with corresponding sockets

● Certain fasteners on the motorcycle have a tensile marking on their heads, the higher the marking the stronger the fastener. High tensile fasteners generally carry a 10 or higher marking. Never replace a high tensile fastener with one of a lower tensile strength.

Washers **(see illustration 2.3)**

● Plain washers are used between a fastener head and a component to prevent damage to the component or to spread the load when torque is applied. Plain washers can also be used as spacers or shims in certain assemblies. Copper or aluminium plain washers are often used as sealing washers on drain plugs.

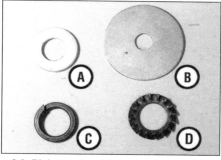

2.3 Plain washer (A), penny washer (B), spring washer (C) and serrated washer (D)

● The split-ring spring washer works by applying axial tension between the fastener head and component. If flattened, it is fatigued and must be renewed. If a plain (flat) washer is used on the fastener, position the spring washer between the fastener and the plain washer.

● Serrated star type washers dig into the fastener and component faces, preventing loosening. They are often used on electrical earth (ground) connections to the frame.

● Cone type washers (sometimes called Belleville) are conical and when tightened apply axial tension between the fastener head and component. They must be installed with the dished side against the component and often carry an OUTSIDE marking on their outer face. If flattened, they are fatigued and must be renewed.

● Tab washers are used to lock plain nuts or bolts on a shaft. A portion of the tab washer is bent up hard against one flat of the nut or bolt to prevent it loosening. Due to the tab washer being deformed in use, a new tab washer should be used every time it is disturbed.

● Wave washers are used to take up endfloat on a shaft. They provide light springing and prevent excessive side-to-side play of a component. Can be found on rocker arm shafts.

Nuts and split pins

● Conventional plain nuts are usually six-sided **(see illustration 2.4)**. They are sized by thread diameter and pitch. High tensile nuts carry a number on one end to denote their tensile strength.

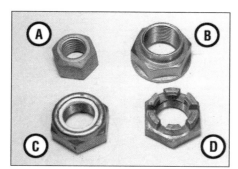

2.4 Plain nut (A), shouldered locknut (B), nylon insert nut (C) and castellated nut (D)

● Self-locking nuts either have a nylon insert, or two spring metal tabs, or a shoulder which is staked into a groove in the shaft - their advantage over conventional plain nuts is a resistance to loosening due to vibration. The nylon insert type can be used a number of times, but must be renewed when the friction of the nylon insert is reduced, ie when the nut spins freely on the shaft. The spring tab type can be reused unless the tabs are damaged. The shouldered type must be renewed every time it is disturbed.

● Split pins (cotter pins) are used to lock a castellated nut to a shaft or to prevent slackening of a plain nut. Common applications are wheel axles and brake torque arms. Because the split pin arms are deformed to lock around the nut a new split pin must always be used on installation - always fit the correct size split pin which will fit snugly in the shaft hole. Make sure the split pin arms are correctly located around the nut **(see illustrations 2.5 and 2.6)**.

2.5 Bend split pin (cotter pin) arms as shown (arrows) to secure a castellated nut

2.6 Bend split pin (cotter pin) arms as shown to secure a plain nut

Caution: If the castellated nut slots do not align with the shaft hole after tightening to the torque setting, tighten the nut until the next slot aligns with the hole - never slacken the nut to align its slot.

● R-pins (shaped like the letter R), or slip pins as they are sometimes called, are sprung and can be reused if they are otherwise in good condition. Always install R-pins with their closed end facing forwards **(see illustration 2.7)**.

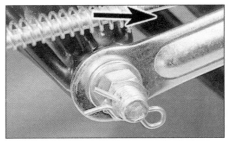

2.7 Correct fitting of R-pin. Arrow indicates forward direction

Circlips (see illustration 2.8)

● Circlips (sometimes called snap-rings) are used to retain components on a shaft or in a housing and have corresponding external or internal ears to permit removal. Parallel-sided (machined) circlips can be installed either way round in their groove, whereas stamped circlips (which have a chamfered edge on one face) must be installed with the chamfer facing away from the direction of thrust load **(see illustration 2.9)**.

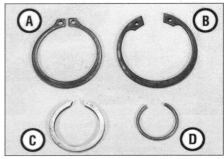

2.8 External stamped circlip (A), internal stamped circlip (B), machined circlip (C) and wire circlip (D)

● Always use circlip pliers to remove and install circlips; expand or compress them just enough to remove them. After installation, rotate the circlip in its groove to ensure it is securely seated. If installing a circlip on a splined shaft, always align its opening with a shaft channel to ensure the circlip ends are well supported and unlikely to catch **(see illustration 2.10)**.

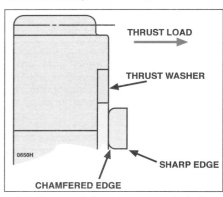

2.9 Correct fitting of a stamped circlip

THRUST LOAD
THRUST WASHER
SHARP EDGE
CHAMFERED EDGE
0650H

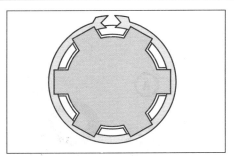

2.10 Align circlip opening with shaft channel

● Circlips can wear due to the thrust of components and become loose in their grooves, with the subsequent danger of becoming dislodged in operation. For this reason, renewal is advised every time a circlip is disturbed.

● Wire circlips are commonly used as piston pin retaining clips. If a removal tang is provided, long-nosed pliers can be used to dislodge them, otherwise careful use of a small flat-bladed screwdriver is necessary. Wire circlips should be renewed every time they are disturbed.

Thread diameter and pitch

● Diameter of a male thread (screw, bolt or stud) is the outside diameter of the threaded portion **(see illustration 2.11)**. Most motorcycle manufacturers use the ISO (International Standards Organisation) metric system expressed in millimetres, eg M6 refers to a 6 mm diameter thread. Sizing is the same for nuts, except that the thread diameter is measured across the valleys of the nut.

● Pitch is the distance between the peaks of the thread **(see illustration 2.11)**. It is expressed in millimetres, thus a common bolt size may be expressed as 6.0 x 1.0 mm (6 mm thread diameter and 1 mm pitch). Generally pitch increases in proportion to thread diameter, although there are always exceptions.

● Thread diameter and pitch are related for conventional fastener applications and the accompanying table can be used as a guide. Additionally, the AF (Across Flats), spanner or socket size dimension of the bolt or nut **(see illustration 2.11)** is linked to thread and pitch specification. Thread pitch can be measured with a thread gauge **(see illustration 2.12)**.

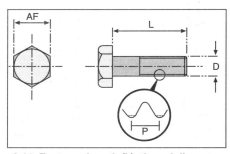

2.11 Fastener length (L), thread diameter (D), thread pitch (P) and head size (AF)

AF
L
D
P

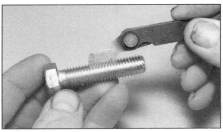

2.12 Using a thread gauge to measure pitch

AF size	Thread diameter x pitch (mm)
8 mm	M5 x 0.8
8 mm	M6 x 1.0
10 mm	M6 x 1.0
12 mm	M8 x 1.25
14 mm	M10 x 1.25
17 mm	M12 x 1.25

● The threads of most fasteners are of the right-hand type, ie they are turned clockwise to tighten and anti-clockwise to loosen. The reverse situation applies to left-hand thread fasteners, which are turned anti-clockwise to tighten and clockwise to loosen. Left-hand threads are used where rotation of a component might loosen a conventional right-hand thread fastener.

Seized fasteners

● Corrosion of external fasteners due to water or reaction between two dissimilar metals can occur over a period of time. It will build up sooner in wet conditions or in countries where salt is used on the roads during the winter. If a fastener is severely corroded it is likely that normal methods of removal will fail and result in its head being ruined. When you attempt removal, the fastener thread should be heard to crack free and unscrew easily - if it doesn't, stop there before damaging something.

● A smart tap on the head of the fastener will often succeed in breaking free corrosion which has occurred in the threads **(see illustration 2.13)**.

● An aerosol penetrating fluid (such as WD-40) applied the night beforehand may work its way down into the thread and ease removal. Depending on the location, you may be able to make up a Plasticine well around the fastener head and fill it with penetrating fluid.

2.13 A sharp tap on the head of a fastener will often break free a corroded thread

● If you are working on an engine internal component, corrosion will most likely not be a problem due to the well lubricated environment. However, components can be very tight and an impact driver is a useful tool in freeing them (see illustration 2.14).

2.14 Using an impact driver to free a fastener

● Where corrosion has occurred between dissimilar metals (eg steel and aluminium alloy), the application of heat to the fastener head will create a disproportionate expansion rate between the two metals and break the seizure caused by the corrosion. Whether heat can be applied depends on the location of the fastener - any surrounding components likely to be damaged must first be removed (see illustration 2.15). Heat can be applied using a paint stripper heat gun or clothes iron, or by immersing the component in boiling water - wear protective gloves to prevent scalding or burns to the hands.

2.15 Using heat to free a seized fastener

● As a last resort, it is possible to use a hammer and cold chisel to work the fastener head unscrewed (see illustration 2.16). This will damage the fastener, but more importantly extreme care must be taken not to damage the surrounding component.

Caution: Remember that the component being secured is generally of more value than the bolt, nut or screw - when the fastener is freed, do not unscrew it with force, instead work the fastener back and forth when resistance is felt to prevent thread damage.

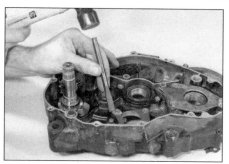

2.16 Using a hammer and chisel to free a seized fastener

Broken fasteners and damaged heads

● If the shank of a broken bolt or screw is accessible you can grip it with self-locking grips. The knurled wheel type stud extractor tool or self-gripping stud puller tool is particularly useful for removing the long studs which screw into the cylinder mouth surface of the crankcase or bolts and screws from which the head has broken off (see illustration 2.17). Studs can also be removed by locking two nuts together on the threaded end of the stud and using a spanner on the lower nut (see illustration 2.18).

2.17 Using a stud extractor tool to remove a broken crankcase stud

2.18 Two nuts can be locked together to unscrew a stud from a component

● A bolt or screw which has broken off below or level with the casing must be extracted using a screw extractor set. Centre punch the fastener to centralise the drill bit, then drill a hole in the fastener (see illustration 2.19). Select a drill bit which is approximately half to three-quarters the

2.19 When using a screw extractor, first drill a hole in the fastener . . .

diameter of the fastener and drill to a depth which will accommodate the extractor. Use the largest size extractor possible, but avoid leaving too small a wall thickness otherwise the extractor will merely force the fastener walls outwards wedging it in the casing thread.

● If a spiral type extractor is used, thread it anti-clockwise into the fastener. As it is screwed in, it will grip the fastener and unscrew it from the casing (see illustration 2.20).

2.20 . . . then thread the extractor anti-clockwise into the fastener

● If a taper type extractor is used, tap it into the fastener so that it is firmly wedged in place. Unscrew the extractor (anti-clockwise) to draw the fastener out.

⚠ *Warning: Stud extractors are very hard and may break off in the fastener if care is not taken - ask an engineer about spark erosion if this happens.*

● Alternatively, the broken bolt/screw can be drilled out and the hole retapped for an oversize bolt/screw or a diamond-section thread insert. It is essential that the drilling is carried out squarely and to the correct depth, otherwise the casing may be ruined - if in doubt, entrust the work to an engineer.

● Bolts and nuts with rounded corners cause the correct size spanner or socket to slip when force is applied. Of the types of spanner/socket available always use a six-point type rather than an eight or twelve-point type - better grip

2.21 Comparison of surface drive ring spanner (left) with 12-point type (right)

is obtained. Surface drive spanners grip the middle of the hex flats, rather than the corners, and are thus good in cases of damaged heads **(see illustration 2.21)**.

● Slotted-head or Phillips-head screws are often damaged by the use of the wrong size screwdriver. Allen-head and Torx-head screws are much less likely to sustain damage. If enough of the screw head is exposed you can use a hacksaw to cut a slot in its head and then use a conventional flat-bladed screwdriver to remove it. Alternatively use a hammer and cold chisel to tap the head of the fastener around to slacken it. Always replace damaged fasteners with new ones, preferably Torx or Allen-head type.

HAYNES
HiNT

A dab of valve grinding compound between the screw head and screwdriver tip will often give a good grip.

Thread repair

● Threads (particularly those in aluminium alloy components) can be damaged by overtightening, being assembled with dirt in the threads, or from a component working loose and vibrating. Eventually the thread will fail completely, and it will be impossible to tighten the fastener.

● If a thread is damaged or clogged with old locking compound it can be renovated with a thread repair tool (thread chaser) **(see illustrations 2.22 and 2.23)**; special thread

2.22 A thread repair tool being used to correct an internal thread

2.23 A thread repair tool being used to correct an external thread

chasers are available for spark plug hole threads. The tool will not cut a new thread, but clean and true the original thread. Make sure that you use the correct diameter and pitch tool. Similarly, external threads can be cleaned up with a die or a thread restorer file **(see illustration 2.24)**.

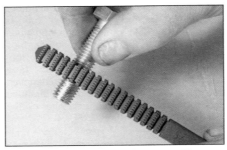

2.24 Using a thread restorer file

● It is possible to drill out the old thread and retap the component to the next thread size. This will work where there is enough surrounding material and a new bolt or screw can be obtained. Sometimes, however, this is not possible - such as where the bolt/screw passes through another component which must also be suitably modified, also in cases where a spark plug or oil drain plug cannot be obtained in a larger diameter thread size.

● The diamond-section thread insert (often known by its popular trade name of Heli-Coil) is a simple and effective method of renewing the thread and retaining the original size. A kit can be purchased which contains the tap, insert and installing tool **(see illustration 2.25)**. Drill out the damaged thread with the size drill specified **(see illustration 2.26)**. Carefully retap the thread **(see illustration 2.27)**. Install the

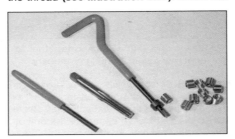

2.25 Obtain a thread insert kit to suit the thread diameter and pitch required

2.26 To install a thread insert, first drill out the original thread . . .

2.27 . . . tap a new thread . . .

2.28 . . . fit insert on the installing tool . . .

2.29 . . . and thread into the component . . .

2.30 . . . break off the tang when complete

insert on the installing tool and thread it slowly into place using a light downward pressure **(see illustrations 2.28 and 2.29)**. When positioned between a 1/4 and 1/2 turn below the surface withdraw the installing tool and use the break-off tool to press down on the tang, breaking it off **(see illustration 2.30)**.

● There are epoxy thread repair kits on the market which can rebuild stripped internal threads, although this repair should not be used on high load-bearing components.

Thread locking and sealing compounds

● Locking compounds are used in locations where the fastener is prone to loosening due to vibration or on important safety-related items which might cause loss of control of the motorcycle if they fail. It is also used where important fasteners cannot be secured by other means such as lockwashers or split pins.

● Before applying locking compound, make sure that the threads (internal and external) are clean and dry with all old compound removed. Select a compound to suit the component being secured - a non-permanent general locking and sealing type is suitable for most applications, but a high strength type is needed for permanent fixing of studs in castings. Apply a drop or two of the compound to the first few threads of the fastener, then thread it into place and tighten to the specified torque. Do not apply excessive thread locking compound otherwise the thread may be damaged on subsequent removal.

● Certain fasteners are impregnated with a dry film type coating of locking compound on their threads. Always renew this type of fastener if disturbed.

● Anti-seize compounds, such as copper-based greases, can be applied to protect threads from seizure due to extreme heat and corrosion. A common instance is spark plug threads and exhaust system fasteners.

3 Measuring tools and gauges

Feeler gauges

● Feeler gauges (or blades) are used for measuring small gaps and clearances **(see illustration 3.1)**. They can also be used to measure endfloat (sideplay) of a component on a shaft where access is not possible with a dial gauge.

● Feeler gauge sets should be treated with care and not bent or damaged. They are etched with their size on one face. Keep them clean and very lightly oiled to prevent corrosion build-up.

3.1 Feeler gauges are used for measuring small gaps and clearances - thickness is marked on one face of gauge

● When measuring a clearance, select a gauge which is a light sliding fit between the two components. You may need to use two gauges together to measure the clearance accurately.

Micrometers

● A micrometer is a precision tool capable of measuring to 0.01 or 0.001 of a millimetre. It should always be stored in its case and not in the general toolbox. It must be kept clean and never dropped, otherwise its frame or measuring anvils could be distorted resulting in inaccurate readings.

● External micrometers are used for measuring outside diameters of components and have many more applications than internal micrometers. Micrometers are available in different size ranges, eg 0 to 25 mm, 25 to 50 mm, and upwards in 25 mm steps; some large micrometers have interchangeable anvils to allow a range of measurements to be taken. Generally the largest precision measurement you are likely to take on a motorcycle is the piston diameter.

● Internal micrometers (or bore micrometers) are used for measuring inside diameters, such as valve guides and cylinder bores. Telescoping gauges and small hole gauges are used in conjunction with an external micrometer, whereas the more expensive internal micrometers have their own measuring device.

External micrometer

Note: *The conventional analogue type instrument is described. Although much easier to read, digital micrometers are considerably more expensive.*

● Always check the calibration of the micrometer before use. With the anvils closed (0 to 25 mm type) or set over a test gauge (for

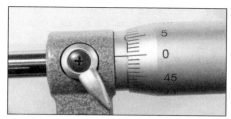

3.2 Check micrometer calibration before use

the larger types) the scale should read zero **(see illustration 3.2)**; make sure that the anvils (and test piece) are clean first. Any discrepancy can be adjusted by referring to the instructions supplied with the tool. Remember that the micrometer is a precision measuring tool - don't force the anvils closed, use the ratchet (4) on the end of the micrometer to close it. In this way, a measured force is always applied.

● To use, first make sure that the item being measured is clean. Place the anvil of the micrometer (1) against the item and use the thimble (2) to bring the spindle (3) lightly into contact with the other side of the item **(see illustration 3.3)**. Don't tighten the thimble down because this will damage the micrometer - instead use the ratchet (4) on the end of the micrometer. The ratchet mechanism applies a measured force preventing damage to the instrument.

● The micrometer is read by referring to the linear scale on the sleeve and the annular scale on the thimble. Read off the sleeve first to obtain the base measurement, then add the fine measurement from the thimble to obtain the overall reading. The linear scale on the sleeve represents the measuring range of the micrometer (eg 0 to 25 mm). The annular scale

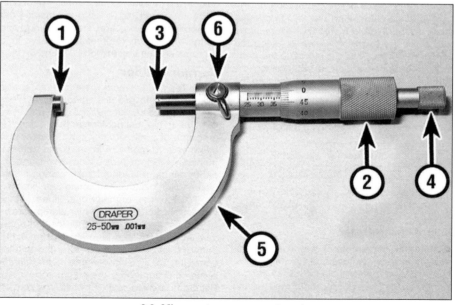

3.3 Micrometer component parts

1 Anvil	3 Spindle	5 Frame
2 Thimble	4 Ratchet	6 Locking lever

on the thimble will be in graduations of 0.01 mm (or as marked on the frame) - one full revolution of the thimble will move 0.5 mm on the linear scale. Take the reading where the datum line on the sleeve intersects the thimble's scale. Always position the eye directly above the scale otherwise an inaccurate reading will result.

In the example shown the item measures 2.95 mm **(see illustration 3.4)**:

Linear scale	2.00 mm
Linear scale	0.50 mm
Annular scale	0.45 mm
Total figure	**2.95 mm**

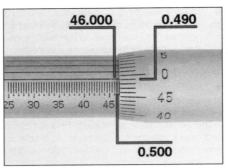

3.5 **Micrometer reading of 46.99 mm on linear and annular scales . . .**

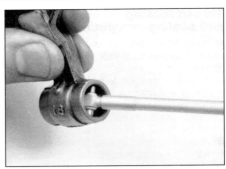

3.7 **Expand the telescoping gauge in the bore, lock its position . . .**

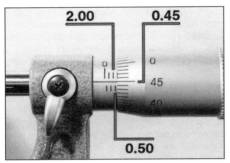

3.4 **Micrometer reading of 2.95 mm**

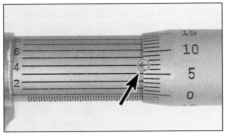

3.6 **. . . and 0.004 mm on vernier scale**

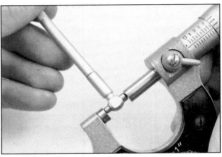

3.8 **. . . then measure the gauge with a micrometer**

Most micrometers have a locking lever (6) on the frame to hold the setting in place, allowing the item to be removed from the micrometer.
● Some micrometers have a vernier scale on their sleeve, providing an even finer measurement to be taken, in 0.001 increments of a millimetre. Take the sleeve and thimble measurement as described above, then check which graduation on the vernier scale aligns with that of the annular scale on the thimble **Note:** *The eye must be perpendicular to the scale when taking the vernier reading - if necessary rotate the body of the micrometer to ensure this.* Multiply the vernier scale figure by 0.001 and add it to the base and fine measurement figures.

In the example shown the item measures 46.994 mm **(see illustrations 3.5 and 3.6)**:

Linear scale (base)	46.000 mm
Linear scale (base)	00.500 mm
Annular scale (fine)	00.490 mm
Vernier scale	00.004 mm
Total figure	**46.994 mm**

Internal micrometer

● Internal micrometers are available for measuring bore diameters, but are expensive and unlikely to be available for home use. It is suggested that a set of telescoping gauges and small hole gauges, both of which must be used with an external micrometer, will suffice for taking internal measurements on a motorcycle.
● Telescoping gauges can be used to

measure internal diameters of components. Select a gauge with the correct size range, make sure its ends are clean and insert it into the bore. Expand the gauge, then lock its position and withdraw it from the bore **(see illustration 3.7)**. Measure across the gauge ends with a micrometer **(see illustration 3.8)**.
● Very small diameter bores (such as valve guides) are measured with a small hole gauge. Once adjusted to a slip-fit inside the component, its position is locked and the gauge withdrawn for measurement with a micrometer **(see illustrations 3.9 and 3.10)**.

Vernier caliper

Note: *The conventional linear and dial gauge type instruments are described. Digital types are easier to read, but are far more expensive.*
● The vernier caliper does not provide the precision of a micrometer, but is versatile in being able to measure internal and external diameters. Some types also incorporate a depth gauge. It is ideal for measuring clutch plate friction material and spring free lengths.
● To use the conventional linear scale vernier, slacken off the vernier clamp screws (1) and set its jaws over (2), or inside (3), the item to be measured **(see illustration 3.11)**. Slide the jaw into contact, using the thumb-wheel (4) for fine movement of the sliding scale (5) then tighten the clamp screws (1). Read off the main scale (6) where the zero on the sliding scale (5) intersects it, taking the whole number to the left of the zero; this provides the base measurement. View along the sliding scale and select the division which

3.9 **Expand the small hole gauge in the bore, lock its position . . .**

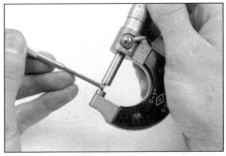

3.10 **. . . then measure the gauge with a micrometer**

lines up exactly with any of the divisions on the main scale, noting that the divisions usually represents 0.02 of a millimetre. Add this fine measurement to the base measurement to obtain the total reading.

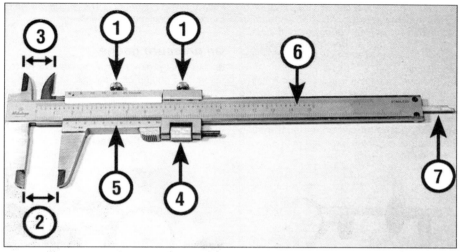

3.11 Vernier component parts (linear gauge)

1 Clamp screws	3 Internal jaws	5 Sliding scale	7 Depth gauge
2 External jaws	4 Thumbwheel	6 Main scale	

In the example shown the item measures 55.92 mm **(see illustration 3.12)**:

Base measurement	55.00 mm
Fine measurement	00.92 mm
Total figure	**55.92 mm**

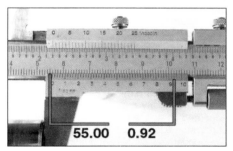

3.12 Vernier gauge reading of 55.92 mm

● Some vernier calipers are equipped with a dial gauge for fine measurement. Before use, check that the jaws are clean, then close them fully and check that the dial gauge reads zero. If necessary adjust the gauge ring accordingly. Slacken the vernier clamp screw (1) and set its jaws over (2), or inside (3), the item to be measured **(see illustration 3.13)**. Slide the jaws into contact, using the thumbwheel (4) for fine movement. Read off the main scale (5) where the edge of the sliding scale (6) intersects it, taking the whole number to the left of the zero; this provides the base measurement. Read off the needle position on the dial gauge (7) scale to provide the fine measurement; each division represents 0.05 of a millimetre. Add this fine measurement to the base measurement to obtain the total reading.

In the example shown the item measures 55.95 mm **(see illustration 3.14)**:

Base measurement	55.00 mm
Fine measurement	00.95 mm
Total figure	**55.95 mm**

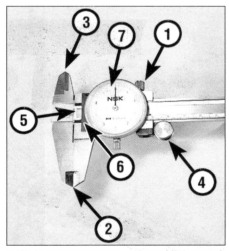

3.13 Vernier component parts (dial gauge)

1 Clamp screw	5 Main scale
2 External jaws	6 Sliding scale
3 Internal jaws	7 Dial gauge
4 Thumbwheel	

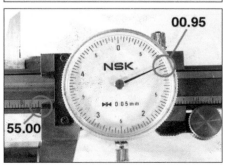

3.14 Vernier gauge reading of 55.95 mm

Plastigauge

● Plastigauge is a plastic material which can be compressed between two surfaces to measure the oil clearance between them. The width of the compressed Plastigauge is measured against a calibrated scale to determine the clearance.

● Common uses of Plastigauge are for measuring the clearance between crankshaft journal and main bearing inserts, between crankshaft journal and big-end bearing inserts, and between camshaft and bearing surfaces. The following example describes big-end oil clearance measurement.

● Handle the Plastigauge material carefully to prevent distortion. Using a sharp knife, cut a length which corresponds with the width of the bearing being measured and place it carefully across the journal so that it is parallel with the shaft **(see illustration 3.15)**. Carefully install both bearing shells and the connecting rod. Without rotating the rod on the journal tighten its bolts or nuts (as applicable) to the specified torque. The connecting rod and bearings are then disassembled and the crushed Plastigauge examined.

3.15 Plastigauge placed across shaft journal

● Using the scale provided in the Plastigauge kit, measure the width of the material to determine the oil clearance **(see illustration 3.16)**. Always remove all traces of Plastigauge after use using your fingernails.

Caution: Arriving at the correct clearance demands that the assembly is torqued correctly, according to the settings and sequence (where applicable) provided by the motorcycle manufacturer.

3.16 Measuring the width of the crushed Plastigauge

Dial gauge or DTI (Dial Test Indicator)

● A dial gauge can be used to accurately measure small amounts of movement. Typical uses are measuring shaft runout or shaft endfloat (sideplay) and setting piston position for ignition timing on two-strokes. A dial gauge set usually comes with a range of different probes and adapters and mounting equipment.

● The gauge needle must point to zero when at rest. Rotate the ring around its periphery to zero the gauge.

● Check that the gauge is capable of reading the extent of movement in the work. Most gauges have a small dial set in the face which records whole millimetres of movement as well as the fine scale around the face periphery which is calibrated in 0.01 mm divisions. Read off the small dial first to obtain the base measurement, then add the measurement from the fine scale to obtain the total reading.

In the example shown the gauge reads 1.48 mm **(see illustration 3.17)**:

Base measurement	1.00 mm
Fine measurement	0.48 mm
Total figure	**1.48 mm**

3.17 Dial gauge reading of 1.48 mm

● If measuring shaft runout, the shaft must be supported in vee-blocks and the gauge mounted on a stand perpendicular to the shaft. Rest the tip of the gauge against the centre of the shaft and rotate the shaft slowly whilst watching the gauge reading **(see illustration 3.18)**. Take several measurements along the length of the shaft and record the

3.18 Using a dial gauge to measure shaft runout

maximum gauge reading as the amount of runout in the shaft. **Note:** *The reading obtained will be total runout at that point - some manufacturers specify that the runout figure is halved to compare with their specified runout limit.*

● Endfloat (sideplay) measurement requires that the gauge is mounted securely to the surrounding component with its probe touching the end of the shaft. Using hand pressure, push and pull on the shaft noting the maximum endfloat recorded on the gauge **(see illustration 3.19)**.

3.19 Using a dial gauge to measure shaft endfloat

● A dial gauge with suitable adapters can be used to determine piston position BTDC on two-stroke engines for the purposes of ignition timing. The gauge, adapter and suitable length probe are installed in the place of the spark plug and the gauge zeroed at TDC. If the piston position is specified as 1.14 mm BTDC, rotate the engine back to 2.00 mm BTDC, then slowly forwards to 1.14 mm BTDC.

Cylinder compression gauges

● A compression gauge is used for measuring cylinder compression. Either the rubber-cone type or the threaded adapter type can be used. The latter is preferred to ensure a perfect seal against the cylinder head. A 0 to 300 psi (0 to 20 Bar) type gauge (for petrol/gasoline engines) will be suitable for motorcycles.

● The spark plug is removed and the gauge either held hard against the cylinder head (cone type) or the gauge adapter screwed into the cylinder head (threaded type) **(see illustration 3.20)**. Cylinder compression is measured with the engine turning over, but not running - carry out the compression test as described in

3.20 Using a rubber-cone type cylinder compression gauge

Fault Finding Equipment. The gauge will hold the reading until manually released.

Oil pressure gauge

● An oil pressure gauge is used for measuring engine oil pressure. Most gauges come with a set of adapters to fit the thread of the take-off point **(see illustration 3.21)**. If the take-off point specified by the motorcycle manufacturer is an external oil pipe union, make sure that the specified replacement union is used to prevent oil starvation.

3.21 Oil pressure gauge and take-off point adapter (arrow)

● Oil pressure is measured with the engine running (at a specific rpm) and often the manufacturer will specify pressure limits for a cold and hot engine.

Straight-edge and surface plate

● If checking the gasket face of a component for warpage, place a steel rule or precision straight-edge across the gasket face and measure any gap between the straight-edge and component with feeler gauges **(see illustration 3.22)**. Check diagonally across the component and between mounting holes **(see illustration 3.23)**.

3.22 Use a straight-edge and feeler gauges to check for warpage

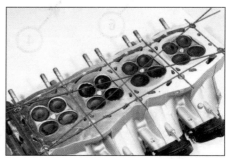

3.23 Check for warpage in these directions

● Checking individual components for warpage, such as clutch plain (metal) plates, requires a perfectly flat plate or piece or plate glass and feeler gauges.

4 Torque and leverage

What is torque?

● Torque describes the twisting force about a shaft. The amount of torque applied is determined by the distance from the centre of the shaft to the end of the lever and the amount of force being applied to the end of the lever; distance multiplied by force equals torque.

● The manufacturer applies a measured torque to a bolt or nut to ensure that it will not slacken in use and to hold two components securely together without movement in the joint. The actual torque setting depends on the thread size, bolt or nut material and the composition of the components being held.

● Too little torque may cause the fastener to loosen due to vibration, whereas too much torque will distort the joint faces of the component or cause the fastener to shear off. Always stick to the specified torque setting.

Using a torque wrench

● Check the calibration of the torque wrench and make sure it has a suitable range for the job. Torque wrenches are available in Nm (Newton-metres), kgf m (kilograms-force metre), lbf ft (pounds-feet), lbf in (inch-pounds). Do not confuse lbf ft with lbf in.

● Adjust the tool to the desired torque on the scale (see illustration 4.1). If your torque wrench is not calibrated in the units specified, carefully convert the figure (see Conversion Factors). A manufacturer sometimes gives a torque setting as a range (8 to 10 Nm) rather than a single figure - in this case set the tool midway between the two settings. The same torque may be expressed as 9 Nm ± 1 Nm. Some torque wrenches have a method of locking the setting so that it isn't inadvertently altered during use.

4.1 Set the torque wrench index mark to the setting required, in this case 12 Nm

● Install the bolts/nuts in their correct location and secure them lightly. Their threads must be clean and free of any old locking compound. Unless specified the threads and flange should be dry - oiled threads are necessary in certain circumstances and the manufacturer will take this into account in the specified torque figure. Similarly, the manufacturer may also specify the application of thread-locking compound.

● Tighten the fasteners in the specified sequence until the torque wrench clicks, indicating that the torque setting has been reached. Apply the torque again to double-check the setting. Where different thread diameter fasteners secure the component, as a rule tighten the larger diameter ones first.

● When the torque wrench has been finished with, release the lock (where applicable) and fully back off its setting to zero - do not leave the torque wrench tensioned. Also, do not use a torque wrench for slackening a fastener.

Angle-tightening

● Manufacturers often specify a figure in degrees for final tightening of a fastener. This usually follows tightening to a specific torque setting.

● A degree disc can be set and attached to the socket (see illustration 4.2) or a protractor can be used to mark the angle of movement on the bolt/nut head and the surrounding casting (see illustration 4.3).

4.2 Angle tightening can be accomplished with a torque-angle gauge . . .

4.3 . . . or by marking the angle on the surrounding component

Loosening sequences

● Where more than one bolt/nut secures a component, loosen each fastener evenly a little at a time. In this way, not all the stress of the joint is held by one fastener and the components are not likely to distort.

● If a tightening sequence is provided, work in the REVERSE of this, but if not, work from the outside in, in a criss-cross sequence (see illustration 4.4).

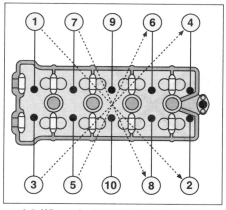

4.4 When slackening, work from the outside inwards

Tightening sequences

● If a component is held by more than one fastener it is important that the retaining bolts/nuts are tightened evenly to prevent uneven stress build-up and distortion of sealing faces. This is especially important on high-compression joints such as the cylinder head.

● A sequence is usually provided by the manufacturer, either in a diagram or actually marked in the casting. If not, always start in the centre and work outwards in a criss-cross pattern (see illustration 4.5). Start off by securing all bolts/nuts finger-tight, then set the torque wrench and tighten each fastener by a small amount in sequence until the final torque is reached. By following this practice,

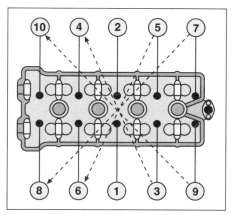

4.5 When tightening, work from the inside outwards

the joint will be held evenly and will not be distorted. Important joints, such as the cylinder head and big-end fasteners often have two- or three-stage torque settings.

Applying leverage

● Use tools at the correct angle. Position a socket wrench or spanner on the bolt/nut so that you pull it towards you when loosening. If this can't be done, push the spanner without curling your fingers around it **(see illustration 4.6)** - the spanner may slip or the fastener loosen suddenly, resulting in your fingers being crushed against a component.

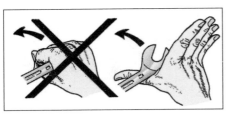

4.6 If you can't pull on the spanner to loosen a fastener, push with your hand open

● Additional leverage is gained by extending the length of the lever. The best way to do this is to use a breaker bar instead of the regular length tool, or to slip a length of tubing over the end of the spanner or socket wrench.
● If additional leverage will not work, the fastener head is either damaged or firmly corroded in place (see *Fasteners*).

5 Bearings

Bearing removal and installation

Drivers and sockets

● Before removing a bearing, always inspect the casing to see which way it must be driven out - some casings will have retaining plates or a cast step. Also check for any identifying markings on the bearing and if installed to a certain depth, measure this at this stage. Some roller bearings are sealed on one side - take note of the original fitted position.
● Bearings can be driven out of a casing using a bearing driver tool (with the correct size head) or a socket of the correct diameter. Select the driver head or socket so that it contacts the outer race of the bearing, not the balls/rollers or inner race. Always support the casing around the bearing housing with wood blocks, otherwise there is a risk of fracture. The bearing is driven out with a few blows on the driver or socket from a heavy mallet. Unless access is severely restricted (as with wheel bearings), a pin-punch is not recommended unless it is moved around the bearing to keep it square in its housing.

● The same equipment can be used to install bearings. Make sure the bearing housing is supported on wood blocks and line up the bearing in its housing. Fit the bearing as noted on removal - generally they are installed with their marked side facing outwards. Tap the bearing squarely into its housing using a driver or socket which bears only on the bearing's outer race - contact with the bearing balls/rollers or inner race will destroy it **(see illustrations 5.1 and 5.2)**.
● Check that the bearing inner race and balls/rollers rotate freely.

5.1 Using a bearing driver against the bearing's outer race

5.2 Using a large socket against the bearing's outer race

Pullers and slide-hammers

● Where a bearing is pressed on a shaft a puller will be required to extract it **(see illustration 5.3)**. Make sure that the puller clamp or legs fit securely behind the bearing and are unlikely to slip out. If pulling a bearing

5.3 This bearing puller clamps behind the bearing and pressure is applied to the shaft end to draw the bearing off

off a gear shaft for example, you may have to locate the puller behind a gear pinion if there is no access to the race and draw the gear pinion off the shaft as well **(see illustration 5.4)**.

> **Caution: Ensure that the puller's centre bolt locates securely against the end of the shaft and will not slip when pressure is applied. Also ensure that puller does not damage the shaft end.**

5.4 Where no access is available to the rear of the bearing, it is sometimes possible to draw off the adjacent component

● Operate the puller so that its centre bolt exerts pressure on the shaft end and draws the bearing off the shaft.
● When installing the bearing on the shaft, tap only on the bearing's inner race - contact with the balls/rollers or outer race with destroy the bearing. Use a socket or length of tubing as a drift which fits over the shaft end **(see illustration 5.5)**.

5.5 When installing a bearing on a shaft use a piece of tubing which bears only on the bearing's inner race

● Where a bearing locates in a blind hole in a casing, it cannot be driven or pulled out as described above. A slide-hammer with knife-edged bearing puller attachment will be required. The puller attachment passes through the bearing and when tightened expands to fit firmly behind the bearing **(see illustration 5.6)**. By operating the slide-hammer part of the tool the bearing is jarred out of its housing **(see illustration 5.7)**.
● It is possible, if the bearing is of reasonable weight, for it to drop out of its housing if the casing is heated as described opposite. If this

5.6 Expand the bearing puller so that it locks behind the bearing . . .

5.7 . . . attach the slide hammer to the bearing puller

method is attempted, first prepare a work surface which will enable the casing to be tapped face down to help dislodge the bearing - a wood surface is ideal since it will not damage the casing's gasket surface. Wearing protective gloves, tap the heated casing several times against the work surface to dislodge the bearing under its own weight (see illustration 5.8).

5.8 Tapping a casing face down on wood blocks can often dislodge a bearing

● Bearings can be installed in blind holes using the driver or socket method described above.

Drawbolts

● Where a bearing or bush is set in the eye of a component, such as a suspension linkage arm or connecting rod small-end, removal by drift may damage the component. Furthermore, a rubber bushing in a shock absorber eye cannot successfully be driven out of position. If access is available to a engineering press, the task is straightforward. If not, a drawbolt can be fabricated to extract the bearing or bush.

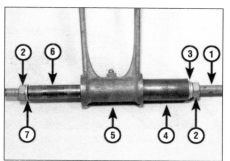

5.9 Drawbolt component parts assembled on a suspension arm

1 Bolt or length of threaded bar
2 Nuts
3 Washer (external diameter greater than tubing internal diameter)
4 Tubing (internal diameter sufficient to accommodate bearing)
5 Suspension arm with bearing
6 Tubing (external diameter slightly smaller than bearing)
7 Washer (external diameter slightly smaller than bearing)

5.10 Drawing the bearing out of the suspension arm

● To extract the bearing/bush you will need a long bolt with nut (or piece of threaded bar with two nuts), a piece of tubing which has an internal diameter larger than the bearing/bush, another piece of tubing which has an external diameter slightly smaller than the bearing/bush, and a selection of washers (see illustrations 5.9 and 5.10). Note that the pieces of tubing must be of the same length, or longer, than the bearing/bush.
● The same kit (without the pieces of tubing) can be used to draw the new bearing/bush back into place (see illustration 5.11).

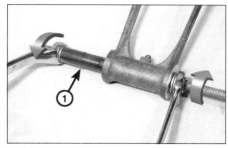

5.11 Installing a new bearing (1) in the suspension arm

Temperature change

● If the bearing's outer race is a tight fit in the casing, the aluminium casing can be heated to release its grip on the bearing. Aluminium will expand at a greater rate than the steel bearing outer race. There are several ways to do this, but avoid any localised extreme heat (such as a blow torch) - aluminium alloy has a low melting point.
● Approved methods of heating a casing are using a domestic oven (heated to 100°C) or immersing the casing in boiling water (see illustration 5.12). Low temperature range localised heat sources such as a paint stripper heat gun or clothes iron can also be used (see illustration 5.13). Alternatively, soak a rag in boiling water, wring it out and wrap it around the bearing housing.

> ⚠ **Warning: All of these methods require care in use to prevent scalding and burns to the hands. Wear protective gloves when handling hot components.**

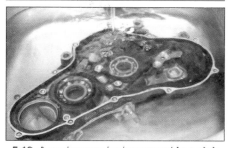

5.12 A casing can be immersed in a sink of boiling water to aid bearing removal

5.13 Using a localised heat source to aid bearing removal

● If heating the whole casing note that plastic components, such as the neutral switch, may suffer - remove them beforehand.
● After heating, remove the bearing as described above. You may find that the expansion is sufficient for the bearing to fall out of the casing under its own weight or with a light tap on the driver or socket.
● If necessary, the casing can be heated to aid bearing installation, and this is sometimes the recommended procedure if the motorcycle manufacturer has designed the housing and bearing fit with this intention.

● Installation of bearings can be eased by placing them in a freezer the night before installation. The steel bearing will contract slightly, allowing easy insertion in its housing. This is often useful when installing steering head outer races in the frame.

Bearing types and markings

● Plain shell bearings, ball bearings, needle roller bearings and tapered roller bearings will all be found on motorcycles **(see illustrations 5.14 and 5.15)**. The ball and roller types are usually caged between an inner and outer race, but uncaged variations may be found.

5.14 Shell bearings are either plain or grooved. They are usually identified by colour code (arrow)

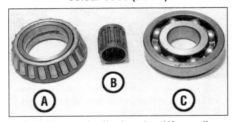

5.15 Tapered roller bearing (A), needle roller bearing (B) and ball journal bearing (C)

● Shell bearings (often called inserts) are usually found at the crankshaft main and connecting rod big-end where they are good at coping with high loads. They are made of a phosphor-bronze material and are impregnated with self-lubricating properties.

● Ball bearings and needle roller bearings consist of a steel inner and outer race with the balls or rollers between the races. They require constant lubrication by oil or grease and are good at coping with axial loads. Taper roller bearings consist of rollers set in a tapered cage set on the inner race; the outer race is separate. They are good at coping with axial loads and prevent movement along the shaft - a typical application is in the steering head.

● Bearing manufacturers produce bearings to ISO size standards and stamp one face of the bearing to indicate its internal and external diameter, load capacity and type **(see illustration 5.16)**.

● Metal bushes are usually of phosphor-bronze material. Rubber bushes are used in suspension mounting eyes. Fibre bushes have also been used in suspension pivots.

5.16 Typical bearing marking

Bearing fault finding

● If a bearing outer race has spun in its housing, the housing material will be damaged. You can use a bearing locking compound to bond the outer race in place if damage is not too severe.

● Shell bearings will fail due to damage of their working surface, as a result of lack of lubrication, corrosion or abrasive particles in the oil **(see illustration 5.17)**. Small particles of dirt in the oil may embed in the bearing material whereas larger particles will score the bearing and shaft journal. If a number of short journeys are made, insufficient heat will be generated to drive off condensation which has built up on the bearings.

5.17 Typical bearing failures

● Ball and roller bearings will fail due to lack of lubrication or damage to the balls or rollers. Tapered-roller bearings can be damaged by overloading them. Unless the bearing is sealed on both sides, wash it in paraffin (kerosene) to remove all old grease then allow it to dry. Make a visual inspection looking to dented balls or rollers, damaged cages and worn or pitted races **(see illustration 5.18)**.

● A ball bearing can be checked for wear by listening to it when spun. Apply a film of light oil to the bearing and hold it close to the ear - hold the outer race with one hand and spin the inner

5.18 Example of ball journal bearing with damaged balls and cages

5.19 Hold outer race and listen to inner race when spun

race with the other hand **(see illustration 5.19)**. The bearing should be almost silent when spun; if it grates or rattles it is worn.

6 Oil seals

Oil seal removal and installation

● Oil seals should be renewed every time a component is dismantled. This is because the seal lips will become set to the sealing surface and will not necessarily reseal.

● Oil seals can be prised out of position using a large flat-bladed screwdriver **(see illustration 6.1)**. In the case of crankcase seals, check first that the seal is not lipped on the inside, preventing its removal with the crankcases joined.

6.1 Prise out oil seals with a large flat-bladed screwdriver

● New seals are usually installed with their marked face (containing the seal reference code) outwards and the spring side towards the fluid being retained. In certain cases, such as a two-stroke engine crankshaft seal, a double lipped seal may be used due to there being fluid or gas on each side of the joint.

● Use a bearing driver or socket which bears only on the outer hard edge of the seal to install it in the casing - tapping on the inner edge will damage the sealing lip.

Oil seal types and markings

● Oil seals are usually of the single-lipped type. Double-lipped seals are found where a liquid or gas is on both sides of the joint.
● Oil seals can harden and lose their sealing ability if the motorcycle has been in storage for a long period - renewal is the only solution.
● Oil seal manufacturers also conform to the ISO markings for seal size - these are moulded into the outer face of the seal (see illustration 6.2).

6.2 These oil seal markings indicate inside diameter, outside diameter and seal thickness

7 Gaskets and sealants

Types of gasket and sealant

● Gaskets are used to seal the mating surfaces between components and keep lubricants, fluids, vacuum or pressure contained within the assembly. Aluminium gaskets are sometimes found at the cylinder joints, but most gaskets are paper-based. If the mating surfaces of the components being joined are undamaged the gasket can be installed dry, although a dab of sealant or grease will be useful to hold it in place during assembly.
● RTV (Room Temperature Vulcanising) silicone rubber sealants cure when exposed to moisture in the atmosphere. These sealants are good at filling pits or irregular gasket faces, but will tend to be forced out of the joint under very high torque. They can be used to replace a paper gasket, but first make sure that the width of the paper gasket is not essential to the shimming of internal components. RTV sealants should not be used on components containing petrol (gasoline).
● Non-hardening, semi-hardening and hard setting liquid gasket compounds can be used with a gasket or between a metal-to-metal joint. Select the sealant to suit the application: universal non-hardening sealant can be used on virtually all joints; semi-hardening on joint faces which are rough or damaged; hard setting sealant on joints which require a permanent bond and are subjected to high temperature and pressure. **Note:** *Check first if the paper gasket has a bead of sealant*

impregnated in its surface before applying additional sealant.
● When choosing a sealant, make sure it is suitable for the application, particularly if being applied in a high-temperature area or in the vicinity of fuel. Certain manufacturers produce sealants in either clear, silver or black colours to match the finish of the engine. This has a particular application on motorcycles where much of the engine is exposed.
● Do not over-apply sealant. That which is squeezed out on the outside of the joint can be wiped off, whereas an excess of sealant on the inside can break off and clog oilways.

Breaking a sealed joint

● Age, heat, pressure and the use of hard setting sealant can cause two components to stick together so tightly that they are difficult to separate using finger pressure alone. Do not resort to using levers unless there is a pry point provided for this purpose (see illustration 7.1) or else the gasket surfaces will be damaged.
● Use a soft-faced hammer (see illustration 7.2) or a wood block and conventional hammer to strike the component near the mating surface. Avoid hammering against cast extremities since they may break off. If this method fails, try using a wood wedge between the two components.

Caution: If the joint will not separate, double-check that you have removed all the fasteners.

7.1 If a pry point is provided, apply gently pressure with a flat-bladed screwdriver

7.2 Tap around the joint with a soft-faced mallet if necessary - don't strike cooling fins

Removal of old gasket and sealant

● Paper gaskets will most likely come away complete, leaving only a few traces stuck on

Most components have one or two hollow locating dowels between the two gasket faces. If a dowel cannot be removed, do not resort to gripping it with pliers - it will almost certainly be distorted. Install a close-fitting socket or Phillips screwdriver into the dowel and then grip the outer edge of the dowel to free it.

the sealing faces of the components. It is imperative that all traces are removed to ensure correct sealing of the new gasket.
● Very carefully scrape all traces of gasket away making sure that the sealing surfaces are not gouged or scored by the scraper (see illustrations 7.3, 7.4 and 7.5). Stubborn deposits can be removed by spraying with an aerosol gasket remover. Final preparation of

7.3 Paper gaskets can be scraped off with a gasket scraper tool . . .

7.4 . . . a knife blade . . .

7.5 . . . or a household scraper

7.6 Fine abrasive paper is wrapped around a flat file to clean up the gasket face

7.7 A kitchen scourer can be used on stubborn deposits

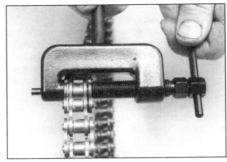

8.1 Tighten the chain breaker to push the pin out of the link . . .

8.2 . . . withdraw the pin, remove the tool . . .

8.3 . . . and separate the chain link

8.4 Insert the new soft link, with O-rings, through the chain ends . . .

8.5 . . . install the O-rings over the pin ends . . .

8.6 . . . followed by the sideplate

the gasket surface can be made with very fine abrasive paper or a plastic kitchen scourer **(see illustrations 7.6 and 7.7)**.

● Old sealant can be scraped or peeled off components, depending on the type originally used. Note that gasket removal compounds are available to avoid scraping the components clean; make sure the gasket remover suits the type of sealant used.

8 Chains

Breaking and joining final drive chains

● Drive chains for all but small bikes are continuous and do not have a clip-type connecting link. The chain must be broken using a chain breaker tool and the new chain securely riveted together using a new soft rivet-type link. Never use a clip-type connecting link instead of a rivet-type link, except in an emergency. Various chain breaking and riveting tools are available, either as separate tools or combined as illustrated in the accompanying photographs - read the instructions supplied with the tool carefully.

> ⚠ **Warning: The need to rivet the new link pins correctly cannot be overstressed - loss of control of the motorcycle is very likely to result if the chain breaks in use.**

● Rotate the chain and look for the soft link. The soft link pins look like they have been

deeply centre-punched instead of peened over like all the other pins **(see illustration 8.9)** and its sideplate may be a different colour. Position the soft link midway between the sprockets and assemble the chain breaker tool over one of the soft link pins **(see illustration 8.1)**. Operate the tool to push the pin out through the chain **(see illustration 8.2)**. On an O-ring chain, remove the O-rings **(see illustration 8.3)**. Carry out the same procedure on the other soft link pin.

> **Caution: Certain soft link pins (particularly on the larger chains) may require their ends to be filed or ground off before they can be pressed out using the tool.**

● Check that you have the correct size and strength (standard or heavy duty) new soft link - do not reuse the old link. Look for the size marking on the chain sideplates **(see illustration 8.10)**.

● Position the chain ends so that they are engaged over the rear sprocket. On an O-ring

chain, install a new O-ring over each pin of the link and insert the link through the two chain ends **(see illustration 8.4)**. Install a new O-ring over the end of each pin, followed by the sideplate (with the chain manufacturer's marking facing outwards) **(see illustrations 8.5 and 8.6)**. On an unsealed chain, insert the link through the two chain ends, then install the sideplate with the chain manufacturer's marking facing outwards.

● Note that it may not be possible to install the sideplate using finger pressure alone. If using a joining tool, assemble it so that the plates of the tool clamp the link and press the sideplate over the pins **(see illustration 8.7)**. Otherwise, use two small sockets placed over

8.7 Push the sideplate into position using a clamp

8.8 Assemble the chain riveting tool over one pin at a time and tighten it fully

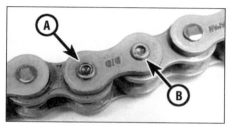

8.9 Pin end correctly riveted (A), pin end unriveted (B)

the rivet ends and two pieces of the wood between a G-clamp. Operate the clamp to press the sideplate over the pins.

● Assemble the joining tool over one pin (following the maker's instructions) and tighten the tool down to spread the pin end securely **(see illustrations 8.8 and 8.9)**. Do the same on the other pin.

> ⚠ **Warning: Check that the pin ends are secure and that there is no danger of the sideplate coming loose. If the pin ends are cracked the soft link must be renewed.**

Final drive chain sizing

● Chains are sized using a three digit number, followed by a suffix to denote the chain type **(see illustration 8.10)**. Chain type is either standard or heavy duty (thicker sideplates), and also unsealed or O-ring/X-ring type.

● The first digit of the number relates to the pitch of the chain, ie the distance from the centre of one pin to the centre of the next pin **(see illustration 8.11)**. Pitch is expressed in eighths of an inch, as follows:

8.10 Typical chain size and type marking

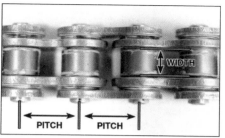

8.11 Chain dimensions

| Sizes commencing with a 4 (eg 428) have a pitch of 1/2 inch (12.7 mm) |
| Sizes commencing with a 5 (eg 520) have a pitch of 5/8 inch (15.9 mm) |
| Sizes commencing with a 6 (eg 630) have a pitch of 3/4 inch (19.1 mm) |

● The second and third digits of the chain size relate to the width of the rollers, again in imperial units, eg the 525 shown has 5/16 inch (7.94 mm) rollers **(see illustration 8.11)**.

9 Hoses

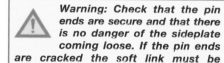

Clamping to prevent flow

● Small-bore flexible hoses can be clamped to prevent fluid flow whilst a component is worked on. Whichever method is used, ensure that the hose material is not permanently distorted or damaged by the clamp.

a) A brake hose clamp available from auto accessory shops **(see illustration 9.1)**.
b) A wingnut type hose clamp **(see illustration 9.2)**.

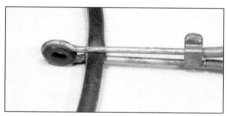

9.1 Hoses can be clamped with an automotive brake hose clamp . . .

9.2 . . . a wingnut type hose clamp . . .

c) Two sockets placed each side of the hose and held with straight-jawed self-locking grips **(see illustration 9.3)**.
d) Thick card each side of the hose held between straight-jawed self-locking grips **(see illustration 9.4)**.

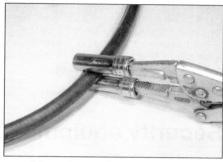

9.3 . . . two sockets and a pair of self-locking grips . . .

9.4 . . . or thick card and self-locking grips

Freeing and fitting hoses

● Always make sure the hose clamp is moved well clear of the hose end. Grip the hose with your hand and rotate it whilst pulling it off the union. If the hose has hardened due to age and will not move, slit it with a sharp knife and peel its ends off the union **(see illustration 9.5)**.

● Resist the temptation to use grease or soap on the unions to aid installation; although it helps the hose slip over the union it will equally aid the escape of fluid from the joint. It is preferable to soften the hose ends in hot water and wet the inside surface of the hose with water or a fluid which will evaporate.

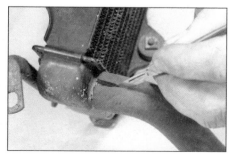

9.5 Cutting a coolant hose free with a sharp knife

Introduction

In less time than it takes to read this introduction, a thief could steal your motorcycle. Returning only to find your bike has gone is one of the worst feelings in the world. Even if the motorcycle is insured against theft, once you've got over the initial shock, you will have the inconvenience of dealing with the police and your insurance company.

The motorcycle is an easy target for the professional thief and the joyrider alike and the official figures on motorcycle theft make for depressing reading; on average a motorcycle is stolen every 16 minutes in the UK!

Motorcycle thefts fall into two categories, those stolen 'to order' and those taken by opportunists. The thief stealing to order will be on the look out for a specific make and model and will go to extraordinary lengths to obtain that motorcycle. The opportunist thief on the other hand will look for easy targets which can be stolen with the minimum of effort and risk.

Whilst it is never going to be possible to make your machine 100% secure, it is estimated that around half of all stolen motorcycles are taken by opportunist thieves. Remember that the opportunist thief is always on the look out for the easy option: if there are two similar motorcycles parked side-by-side, they will target the one with the lowest level of security. By taking a few precautions, you can reduce the chances of your motorcycle being stolen.

Security equipment

There are many specialised motorcycle security devices available and the following text summarises their applications and their good and bad points.

Once you have decided on the type of security equipment which best suits your needs, we recommended that you read one of the many equipment tests regularly carried

Ensure the lock and chain you buy is of good quality and long enough to shackle your bike to a solid object

out by the motorcycle press. These tests compare the products from all the major manufacturers and give impartial ratings on their effectiveness, value-for-money and ease of use.

No one item of security equipment can provide complete protection. It is highly recommended that two or more of the items described below are combined to increase the security of your motorcycle (a lock and chain plus an alarm system is just about ideal). The more security measures fitted to the bike, the less likely it is to be stolen.

Lock and chain

Pros: *Very flexible to use; can be used to secure the motorcycle to almost any immovable object. On some locks and chains, the lock can be used on its own as a disc lock (see below).*

Cons: *Can be very heavy and awkward to carry on the motorcycle, although some types* will be supplied with a carry bag which can be strapped to the pillion seat.

● Heavy-duty chains and locks are an excellent security measure **(see illustration 1)**. Whenever the motorcycle is parked, use the lock and chain to secure the machine to a solid, immovable object such as a post or railings. This will prevent the machine from being ridden away or being lifted into the back of a van.

● When fitting the chain, always ensure the chain is routed around the motorcycle frame or swingarm **(see illustrations 2 and 3)**. Never merely pass the chain around one of the wheel rims; a thief may unbolt the wheel and lift the rest of the machine into a van, leaving you with just the wheel! Try to avoid having excess chain free, thus making it difficult to use cutting tools, and keep the chain and lock off the ground to prevent thieves attacking it with a cold chisel. Position the lock so that its lock barrel is facing downwards; this will make it harder for the thief to attack the lock mechanism.

Pass the chain through the bike's frame, rather than just through a wheel . . .

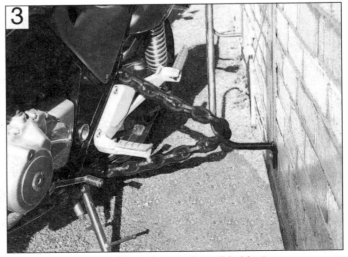

. . . and loop it around a solid object

U-locks

Pros: *Highly effective deterrent which can be used to secure the bike to a post or railings. Most U-locks come with a carrier which allows the lock to be easily carried on the bike.*

Cons: *Not as flexible to use as a lock and chain.*

● These are solid locks which are similar in use to a lock and chain. U-locks are lighter than a lock and chain but not so flexible to use. The length and shape of the lock shackle limit the objects to which the bike can be secured **(see illustration 4)**.

Disc locks

Pros: *Small, light and very easy to carry; most can be stored underneath the seat.*

Cons: *Does not prevent the motorcycle being lifted into a van. Can be very embarrassing if you*

U-locks can be used to secure the bike to a solid object – ensure you purchase one which is long enough

forget to remove the lock before attempting to ride off!

● Disc locks are designed to be attached to the front brake disc. The lock passes through one of the holes in the disc and prevents the wheel rotating by jamming against the fork/brake caliper **(see illustration 5)**. Some are equipped with an alarm siren which sounds if the disc lock is moved; this not only acts as a theft deterrent but also as a handy reminder if you try to move the bike with the lock still fitted.

● Combining the disc lock with a length of cable which can be looped around a post or railings provides an additional measure of security **(see illustration 6)**.

Alarms and immobilisers

Pros: *Once installed it is completely hassle-free to use. If the system is 'Thatcham' or 'Sold Secure-approved', insurance companies may give you a discount.*

Cons: *Can be expensive to buy and complex to install. No system will prevent the motorcycle from being lifted into a van and taken away.*

● Electronic alarms and immobilisers are available to suit a variety of budgets. There are three different types of system available: pure alarms, pure immobilisers, and the more expensive systems which are combined alarm/immobilisers **(see illustration 7)**.
● An alarm system is designed to emit an audible warning if the motorcycle is being tampered with.
● An immobiliser prevents the motorcycle being started and ridden away by disabling its electrical systems.
● When purchasing an alarm/immobiliser system, check the cost of installing the system unless you are able to do it yourself. If the motorcycle is not used regularly, another consideration is the current drain of the system. All alarm/immobiliser systems are powered by the motorcycle's battery; purchasing a system with a very low current drain could prevent the battery losing its charge whilst the motorcycle is not being used.

A typical disc lock attached through one of the holes in the disc

A disc lock combined with a security cable provides additional protection

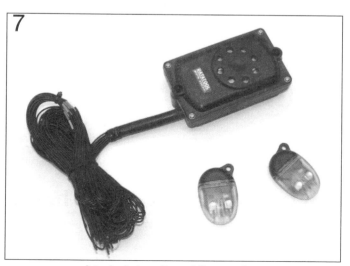

A typical alarm/immobiliser system

8

Indelible markings can be applied to most areas of the bike – always apply the manufacturer's sticker to warn off thieves

9

Chemically-etched code numbers can be applied to main body panels . . .

10

. . . again, always ensure that the kit manufacturer's sticker is applied in a prominent position

Security marking kits

Pros: *Very cheap and effective deterrent. Many insurance companies will give you a discount on your insurance premium if a recognised security marking kit is used on your motorcycle.*

Cons: *Does not prevent the motorcycle being stolen by joyriders.*

● There are many different types of security marking kits available. The idea is to mark as many parts of the motorcycle as possible with a unique security number **(see illustrations 8, 9 and 10)**. A form will be included with the kit to register your personal details and those of the motorcycle with the kit manufacturer. This register is made available to the police to help them trace the rightful owner of any motorcycle or components which they recover should all other forms of identification have been removed. Always apply the warning stickers provided with the kit to deter thieves.

Ground anchors, wheel clamps and security posts

Pros: *An excellent form of security which will deter all but the most determined of thieves.*

Cons: *Awkward to install and can be expensive.*

● Whilst the motorcycle is at home, it is a good idea to attach it securely to the floor or a solid wall, even if it is kept in a securely locked garage. Various types of ground anchors, security posts and wheel clamps are available for this purpose **(see illustration 11)**. These security devices are either bolted to a solid concrete or brick structure or can be cemented into the ground.

11

Permanent ground anchors provide an excellent level of security when the bike is at home

Security at home

A high percentage of motorcycle thefts are from the owner's home. Here are some things to consider whenever your motorcycle is at home:

✔ Where possible, always keep the motorcycle in a securely locked garage. Never rely solely on the standard lock on the garage door, these are usual hopelessly inadequate. Fit an additional locking mechanism to the door and consider having the garage alarmed. A security light, activated by a movement sensor, is also a good investment.

✔ Always secure the motorcycle to the ground or a wall, even if it is inside a securely locked garage.

✔ Do not regularly leave the motorcycle outside your home, try to keep it out of sight wherever possible. If a garage is not available, fit a motorcycle cover over the bike to disguise its true identity.

✔ It is not uncommon for thieves to follow a motorcyclist home to find out where the bike is kept. They will then return at a later date. Be aware of this whenever you are returning

home on your motorcycle. If you suspect you are being followed, do not return home, instead ride to a garage or shop and stop as a precaution.

✔ When selling a motorcycle, do not provide your home address or the location where the bike is normally kept. Arrange to meet the buyer at a location away from your home. Thieves have been known to pose as potential buyers to find out where motorcycles are kept and then return later to steal them.

Security away from the home

As well as fitting security equipment to your motorcycle here are a few general rules to follow whenever you park your motorcycle.

✔ Park in a busy, public place.
✔ Use car parks which incorporate security features, such as CCTV.

✔ At night, park in a well-lit area, preferably directly underneath a street light.
✔ Engage the steering lock.
✔ Secure the motorcycle to a solid, immovable object such as a post or railings with an additional lock. If this is not possible,

secure the bike to a friend's motorcycle. Some public parking places provide security loops for motorcycles.

✔ Never leave your helmet or luggage attached to the motorcycle. Take them with you at all times.

Lubricants and fluids

A wide range of lubricants, fluids and cleaning agents is available for motor-cycles. This is a guide as to what is available, its applications and properties.

Four-stroke engine oil

● Engine oil is without doubt the most important component of any four-stroke engine. Modern motorcycle engines place a lot of demands on their oil and choosing the right type is essential. Using an unsuitable oil will lead to an increased rate of engine wear and could result in serious engine damage. Before purchasing oil, always check the recommended oil specification given by the manufacturer. The manufacturer will state a recommended 'type or classification' and also a specific 'viscosity' range for engine oil.

● The oil 'type or classification' is identified by its API (American Petroleum Institute) rating. The API rating will be in the form of two letters, e.g. SG. The S identifies the oil as being suitable for use in a petrol (gasoline) engine (S stands for spark ignition) and the second letter, ranging from A to J, identifies the oil's performance rating. The later this letter, the higher the specification of the oil; for example API SG oil exceeds the requirements of API SF oil. **Note:** *On some oils there may also be a second rating consisting of another two letters, the first letter being C, e.g. API SF/CD. This rating indicates the oil is also suitable for use in a diesel engines (the C stands for compression ignition) and is thus of no relevance for motorcycle use.*

● The 'viscosity' of the oil is identified by its SAE (Society of Automotive Engineers) rating. All modern engines require multigrade oils and the SAE rating will consist of two numbers, the first followed by a W, e.g. 10W/40. The first number indicates the viscosity rating of the oil at low temperatures (W stands for winter – tested at –20°C) and the second number represents the viscosity of the oil at high temperatures (tested at 100°C). The lower the number, the thinner the oil. For example an oil with an SAE 10W/40 rating will give better cold starting and running than an SAE 15W/40 oil.

● As well as ensuring the 'type' and 'viscosity' of the oil match the recommendations, another consideration to make when buying engine oil is whether to purchase a standard mineral-based oil, a semi-synthetic oil (also known as a synthetic blend or synthetic-based oil) or a fully-synthetic oil. Although all oils will have a similar rating and viscosity, their cost will vary considerably; mineral-based oils are the cheapest, the fully-synthetic oils the most expensive with the semi-synthetic oils falling somewhere in-between. This decision is very much up to the owner, but it should be noted that modern synthetic oils have far better lubricating and cleaning qualities than traditional mineral-based oils and tend to retain these properties for far longer. Bearing in mind the operating conditions inside a modern, high-revving motorcycle engine it is highly recommended that a fully synthetic oil is used. The extra expense at each service could save you money in the long term by preventing premature engine wear.

● As a final note always ensure that the oil is specifically designed for use in motorcycle engines. Engine oils designed primarily for use in car engines sometimes contain additives or friction modifiers which could cause clutch slip on a motorcycle fitted with a wet-clutch.

Two-stroke engine oil

● Modern two-stroke engines, with their high power outputs, place high demands on their oil. If engine seizure is to be avoided it is essential that a high-quality oil is used. Two-stroke oils differ hugely from four-stroke oils. The oil lubricates only the crankshaft and piston(s) (the transmission has its own lubricating oil) and is used on a total-loss basis where it is burnt completely during the combustion process.

● The Japanese have recently introduced a classification system for two-stroke oils, the JASO rating. This rating is in the form of two letters, either FA, FB or FC – FA is the lowest classification and FC the highest. Ensure the oil being used meets or exceeds the recommended rating specified by the manufacturer.

● As well as ensuring the oil rating matches the recommendation, another consideration to make when buying engine oil is whether to purchase a standard mineral-based oil, a semi-synthetic oil (also known as a synthetic blend or synthetic-based oil) or a fully-synthetic oil. The cost of each type of oil varies considerably; mineral-based oils are the cheapest, the fully-synthetic oils the most expensive with the semi-synthetic oils falling somewhere in-between. This decision is very much up to the owner, but it should be noted that modern synthetic oils have far better lubricating properties and burn cleaner than traditional mineral-based oils. It is therefore recommended that a fully synthetic oil is used. The extra expense could save you money in the long term by preventing premature engine wear, engine performance will be improved, carbon deposits and exhaust smoke will be reduced.

● Always ensure that the oil is specifically designed for use in an injector system. Many high quality two-stroke oils are designed for competition use and need to be pre-mixed with fuel. These oils are of a much higher viscosity and are not designed to flow through the injector pumps used on road-going two-stroke motorcycles.

Transmission (gear) oil

● On a two-stroke engine, the transmission and clutch are lubricated by their own separate oil bath which must be changed in accordance with the Maintenance Schedule.
● Although the engine and transmission units of most four-strokes use a common lubrication supply, there are some exceptions where the engine and gearbox have separate oil reservoirs and a dry clutch is used.
● Motorcycle manufacturers will either recommend a monograde transmission oil or a four-stroke multigrade engine oil to lubricate the transmission.
● Transmission oils, or gear oils as they are often called, are designed specifically for use in transmission systems. The viscosity of these oils is represented by an SAE number, but the scale of measurement applied is different to that used to grade engine oils. As a rough guide a SAE90 gear oil will be of the same viscosity as an SAE50 engine oil.

Shaft drive oil

● On models equipped with shaft final drive, the shaft drive gears are will have their own oil supply. The manufacturer will state a recommended 'type or classification' and also a specific 'viscosity' range in the same manner as for four-stroke engine oil.
● Gear oil classification is given by the number which follows the API GL (GL standing for gear lubricant) rating, the higher the number, the higher the specification of the oil, e.g. API GL5 oil is a higher specification than API GL4 oil. Ensure the oil meets or

exceeds the classification specified and is of the correct viscosity. The viscosity of gear oils is also represented by an SAE number but the scale of measurement used is different to that used to grade engine oils. As a rough guide an SAE90 gear oil will be of the same viscosity as an SAE50 engine oil.
● If the use of an EP (Extreme Pressure) gear oil is specified, ensure the oil purchased is suitable.

Fork oil and suspension fluid

● Conventional telescopic front forks are hydraulic and require fork oil to work. To ensure the forks function correctly, the fork oil must be changed in accordance with the Maintenance Schedule.
● Fork oil is available in a variety of viscosities, identified by their SAE rating; fork oil ratings vary from light (SAE 5) to heavy (SAE 30). When purchasing fork oil, ensure the viscosity rating matches that specified by the manufacturer.
● Some lubricant manufacturers also produce a range of high-quality suspension fluids which are very similar to fork oil but are designed mainly for competition use. These fluids may have a different viscosity rating system which is not to be confused with the SAE rating of normal fork oil. Refer to the manufacturer's instructions if in any doubt.

Brake and clutch fluid

● All disc brake systems and some clutch systems are hydraulically operated. To ensure correct operation, the hydraulic fluid must be changed in accordance with the Maintenance Schedule.
● Brake and clutch fluid is classified by its DOT rating with most motorcycle manufacturers specifying DOT 3 or 4 fluid. Both fluid types are glycol-based and can be mixed together without adverse effect; DOT 4 fluid exceeds the requirements of DOT 3

fluid. Although it is safe to use DOT 4 fluid in a system designed for use with DOT 3 fluid, never use DOT 3 fluid in a system which specifies the use of DOT 4 as this will adversely affect the system's performance. The type required for the system will be marked on the fluid reservoir cap.
● Some manufacturers also produce a DOT 5 hydraulic fluid. DOT 5 hydraulic fluid is silicone-based and is not compatible with the glycol-based DOT 3 and 4 fluids. Never mix DOT 5 fluid with DOT 3 or 4 fluid as this will seriously affect the performance of the hydraulic system.

Coolant/antifreeze

● When purchasing coolant/antifreeze, always ensure it is suitable for use in an aluminium engine and contains corrosion inhibitors to prevent possible blockages of the internal coolant passages of the system. As a general rule, most coolants are designed to be used neat and should not be diluted whereas antifreeze can be mixed with distilled water to provide a coolant solution of the required strength. Refer to the manufacturer's instructions on the bottle.
● Ensure the coolant is changed in accordance with the Maintenance Schedule.

Chain lube

● Chain lube is an aerosol-type spray lubricant specifically designed for use on motorcycle final drive chains. Chain lube has two functions, to minimise friction between the final drive chain and sprockets and to prevent corrosion of the chain. Regular use of a good-quality chain lube will extend the life of the drive chain and sprockets and thus maximise the power being transmitted from the transmission to the rear wheel.
● When using chain lube, always allow some time for the solvents in the lube to evaporate before riding the motorcycle. This will minimise the amount of lube which will

'fling' off from the chain when the motorcycle is used. If the motorcycle is equipped with an 'O-ring' chain, ensure the chain lube is labelled as being suitable for use on 'O-ring' chains.

Degreasers and solvents

● There are many different types of solvents and degreasers available to remove the grime and grease which accumulate around the motorcycle during normal use. Degreasers and solvents are usually available as an aerosol-type spray or as a liquid which you apply with a brush. Always closely follow the manufacturer's instructions and wear eye protection during use. Be aware that many solvents are flammable and may give off noxious fumes; take adequate precautions when using them (see Safety First!).

● For general cleaning, use one of the many solvents or degreasers available from most motorcycle accessory shops. These solvents are usually applied then left for a certain time before being washed off with water.

Brake cleaner is a solvent specifically designed to remove all traces of oil, grease and dust from braking system components. Brake cleaner is designed to evaporate quickly and leaves behind no residue.

Carburettor cleaner is an aerosol-type solvent specifically designed to clear carburettor blockages and break down the hard deposits and gum often found inside carburettors during overhaul.

Contact cleaner is an aerosol-type solvent designed for cleaning electrical components. The cleaner will remove all traces of oil and dirt from components such as switch contacts or fouled spark plugs and then dry, leaving behind no residue.

Gasket remover is an aerosol-type solvent designed for removing stubborn gaskets from engine components during overhaul. Gasket remover will minimise the amount of scraping required to remove the gasket and therefore reduce the risk of damage to the mating surface.

Spray lubricants

● Aerosol-based spray lubricants are widely available and are excellent for lubricating lever pivots and exposed cables and switches. Try to use a lubricant which is of the dry-film type as the fluid evaporates, leaving behind a dry-film of lubricant. Lubricants which leave behind an oily residue will attract dust and dirt which will increase the rate of wear of the cable/lever.

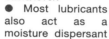

● Most lubricants also act as a moisture dispersant and a penetrating fluid. This means they can also be used to 'dry out' electrical components such as wiring connectors or switches as well as helping to free seized fasteners.

Greases

● Grease is used to lubricate many of the pivot-points. A good-quality multi-purpose grease is suitable for most applications but some manufacturers will specify the use of specialist greases for use on components such as swingarm and suspension linkage bushes. These specialist greases can be purchased from most motorcycle (or car) accessory shops; commonly specified types include molybdenum disulphide grease, lithium-based grease, graphite-based grease, silicone-based grease and high-temperature copper-based grease.

Gasket sealing compounds

● Gasket sealing compounds can be used in conjunction with gaskets, to improve their sealing capabilities, or on their own to seal metal-to-metal joints. Depending on their type, sealing compounds either set hard or stay relatively soft and pliable.

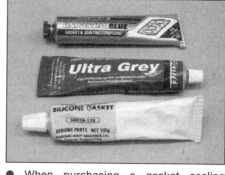

● When purchasing a gasket sealing compound, ensure that it is designed specifically for use on an internal combustion engine. General multi-purpose sealants available from DIY stores may appear visibly similar but they are not designed to withstand the extreme heat or contact with fuel and oil encountered when used on an engine (see 'Tools and Workshop Tips' for further information).

Thread locking compound

● Thread locking compounds are used to secure certain threaded fasteners in position to prevent them from loosening due to vibration. Thread locking compounds can be purchased from most motorcycle (and car) accessory shops. Ensure the threads of the both components are completely clean and dry before sparingly applying the locking compound (see 'Tools and Workshop Tips' for further information).

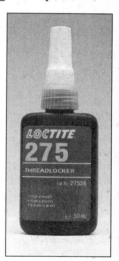

Fuel additives

● Fuel additives which protect and clean the fuel system components are widely available. These additives are designed to remove all traces of deposits that build up on the carburettors/injectors and prevent wear, helping the fuel system to operate more efficiently. If a fuel additive is being used, check that it is suitable for use with your motorcycle, especially if your motorcycle is equipped with a catalytic converter.

● Octane boosters are also available. These additives are designed to improve the performance of highly-tuned engines being run on normal pump-fuel and are of no real use on standard motorcycles.

Conversion factors

Length (distance)

Inches (in)	x 25.4	= Millimetres (mm)	x 0.0394	= Inches (in)
Feet (ft)	x 0.305	= Metres (m)	x 3.281	= Feet (ft)
Miles	x 1.609	= Kilometres (km)	x 0.621	= Miles

Volume (capacity)

Cubic inches (cu in; in³)	x 16.387	= Cubic centimetres (cc; cm³)	x 0.061	= Cubic inches (cu in; in³)
Imperial pints (Imp pt)	x 0.568	= Litres (l)	x 1.76	= Imperial pints (Imp pt)
Imperial quarts (Imp qt)	x 1.137	= Litres (l)	x 0.88	= Imperial quarts (Imp qt)
Imperial quarts (Imp qt)	x 1.201	= US quarts (US qt)	x 0.833	= Imperial quarts (Imp qt)
US quarts (US qt)	x 0.946	= Litres (l)	x 1.057	= US quarts (US qt)
Imperial gallons (Imp gal)	x 4.546	= Litres (l)	x 0.22	= Imperial gallons (Imp gal)
Imperial gallons (Imp gal)	x 1.201	= US gallons (US gal)	x 0.833	= Imperial gallons (Imp gal)
US gallons (US gal)	x 3.785	= Litres (l)	x 0.264	= US gallons (US gal)

Mass (weight)

Ounces (oz)	x 28.35	= Grams (g)	x 0.035	= Ounces (oz)
Pounds (lb)	x 0.454	= Kilograms (kg)	x 2.205	= Pounds (lb)

Force

Ounces-force (ozf; oz)	x 0.278	= Newtons (N)	x 3.6	= Ounces-force (ozf; oz)
Pounds-force (lbf; lb)	x 4.448	= Newtons (N)	x 0.225	= Pounds-force (lbf; lb)
Newtons (N)	x 0.1	= Kilograms-force (kgf; kg)	x 9.81	= Newtons (N)

Pressure

Pounds-force per square inch (psi; lbf/in²; lb/in²)	x 0.070	= Kilograms-force per square centimetre (kgf/cm²; kg/cm²)	x 14.223	= Pounds-force per square inch (psi; lbf/in²; lb/in²)
Pounds-force per square inch (psi; lbf/in²; lb/in²)	x 0.068	= Atmospheres (atm)	x 14.696	= Pounds-force per square inch (psi; lbf/in²; lb/in²)
Pounds-force per square inch (psi; lbf/in²; lb/in²)	x 0.069	= Bars	x 14.5	= Pounds-force per square inch (psi; lbf/in²; lb/in²)
Pounds-force per square inch (psi; lbf/in²; lb/in²)	x 6.895	= Kilopascals (kPa)	x 0.145	= Pounds-force per square inch (psi; lbf/in²; lb/in²)
Kilopascals (kPa)	x 0.01	= Kilograms-force per square centimetre (kgf/cm²; kg/cm²)	x 98.1	= Kilopascals (kPa)
Millibar (mbar)	x 100	= Pascals (Pa)	x 0.01	= Millibar (mbar)
Millibar (mbar)	x 0.0145	= Pounds-force per square inch (psi; lbf/in²; lb/in²)	x 68.947	= Millibar (mbar)
Millibar (mbar)	x 0.75	= Millimetres of mercury (mmHg)	x 1.333	= Millibar (mbar)
Millibar (mbar)	x 0.401	= Inches of water (inH₂O)	x 2.491	= Millibar (mbar)
Millimetres of mercury (mmHg)	x 0.535	= Inches of water (inH₂O)	x 1.868	= Millimetres of mercury (mmHg)
Inches of water (inH₂O)	x 0.036	= Pounds-force per square inch (psi; lbf/in²; lb/in²)	x 27.68	= Inches of water (inH₂O)

Torque (moment of force)

Pounds-force inches (lbf in; lb in)	x 1.152	= Kilograms-force centimetre (kgf cm; kg cm)	x 0.868	= Pounds-force inches (lbf in; lb in)
Pounds-force inches (lbf in; lb in)	x 0.113	= Newton metres (Nm)	x 8.85	= Pounds-force inches (lbf in; lb in)
Pounds-force inches (lbf in; lb in)	x 0.083	= Pounds-force feet (lbf ft; lb ft)	x 12	= Pounds-force inches (lbf in; lb in)
Pounds-force feet (lbf ft; lb ft)	x 0.138	= Kilograms-force metres (kgf m; kg m)	x 7.233	= Pounds-force feet (lbf ft; lb ft)
Pounds-force feet (lbf ft; lb ft)	x 1.356	= Newton metres (Nm)	x 0.738	= Pounds-force feet (lbf ft; lb ft)
Newton metres (Nm)	x 0.102	= Kilograms-force metres (kgf m; kg m)	x 9.804	= Newton metres (Nm)

Power

Horsepower (hp)	x 745.7	= Watts (W)	x 0.0013	= Horsepower (hp)

Velocity (speed)

Miles per hour (miles/hr; mph)	x 1.609	= Kilometres per hour (km/hr; kph)	x 0.621	= Miles per hour (miles/hr; mph)

Fuel consumption*

Miles per gallon (mpg)	x 0.354	= Kilometres per litre (km/l)	x 2.825	= Miles per gallon (mpg)

Temperature

Degrees Fahrenheit = (°C x 1.8) + 32   Degrees Celsius (Degrees Centigrade; °C) = (°F - 32) x 0.56

It is common practice to convert from miles per gallon (mpg) to litres/100 kilometres (l/100km), where mpg x l/100 km = 282

About the MOT Test

In the UK, all vehicles more than three years old are subject to an annual test to ensure that they meet minimum safety requirements. A current test certificate must be issued before a machine can be used on public roads, and is required before a road fund licence can be issued. Riding without a current test certificate will also invalidate your insurance.

For most owners, the MOT test is an annual cause for anxiety, and this is largely due to owners not being sure what needs to be checked prior to submitting the motorcycle for testing. The simple answer is that a fully roadworthy motorcycle will have no difficulty in passing the test.

This is a guide to getting your motorcycle through the MOT test. Obviously it will not be possible to examine the motorcycle to the same standard as the professional MOT tester, particularly in view of the equipment required for some of the checks. However, working through the following procedures will enable you to identify any problem areas before submitting the motorcycle for the test.

It has only been possible to summarise the test requirements here, based on the regulations in force at the time of printing. Test standards are becoming increasingly stringent, although there are some exemptions for older vehicles. More information about the MOT test can be obtained from the TSO publications, *How Safe is your Motorcycle* and *The MOT Inspection Manual for Motorcycle Testing*.

Many of the checks require that one of the wheels is raised off the ground. If the motorcycle doesn't have a centre stand, note that an auxiliary stand will be required. Additionally, the help of an assistant may prove useful.

Certain exceptions apply to machines under 50 cc, machines without a lighting system, and Classic bikes - if in doubt about any of the requirements listed below seek confirmation from an MOT tester prior to submitting the motorcycle for the test.

Check that the frame number is clearly visible.

Electrical System

Lights, turn signals, horn and reflector

✔ With the ignition on, check the operation of the following electrical components. **Note:** *The electrical components on certain small-capacity machines are powered by the generator, requiring that the engine is run for this check.*

a) *Headlight and tail light. Check that both illuminate in the low and high beam switch positions.*

b) *Position lights. Check that the front position (or sidelight) and tail light illuminate in this switch position.*

c) *Turn signals. Check that all flash at the correct rate, and that the warning light(s) function correctly. Check that the turn signal switch works correctly.*

d) *Hazard warning system (where fitted). Check that all four turn signals flash in this switch position.*

e) *Brake stop light. Check that the light comes on when the front and rear brakes are independently applied. Models first used on or after 1st April 1986 must have a brake light switch on each brake.*

f) *Horn. Check that the sound is continuous and of reasonable volume.*

✔ Check that there is a red reflector on the rear of the machine, either mounted separately or as part of the tail light lens.

✔ Check the condition of the headlight, tail light and turn signal lenses.

Headlight beam height

✔ The MOT tester will perform a headlight beam height check using specialised beam setting equipment **(see illustration 1)**. This equipment will not be available to the home mechanic, but if you suspect that the headlight is incorrectly set or may have been maladjusted in the past, you can perform a rough test as follows.

✔ Position the bike in a straight line facing a brick wall. The bike must be off its stand, upright and with a rider seated. Measure the height from the ground to the centre of the headlight and mark a horizontal line on the wall at this height. Position the motorcycle 3.8 metres from the wall and draw a vertical

Headlight beam height checking equipment

line up the wall central to the centreline of the motorcycle. Switch to dipped beam and check that the beam pattern falls slightly lower than the horizontal line and to the left of the vertical line **(see illustration 2)**.

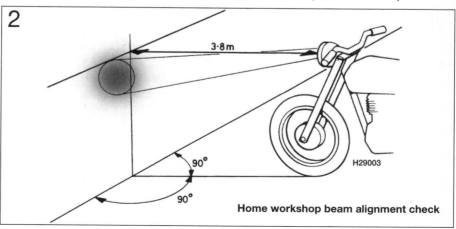

3·8 m

90°

90°

H29003

Home workshop beam alignment check

Exhaust System and Final Drive

Exhaust

✔ Check that the exhaust mountings are secure and that the system does not foul any of the rear suspension components.
✔ Start the motorcycle. When the revs are increased, check that the exhaust is neither holed nor leaking from any of its joints. On a linked system, check that the collector box is not leaking due to corrosion.

✔ Note that the exhaust decibel level ("loudness" of the exhaust) is assessed at the discretion of the tester. If the motorcycle was first used on or after 1st January 1985 the silencer must carry the BSAU 193 stamp, or a marking relating to its make and model, or be of OE (original equipment) manufacture. If the silencer is marked NOT FOR ROAD USE, RACING USE ONLY or similar, it will fail the MOT.

Final drive

✔ On chain or belt drive machines, check that the chain/belt is in good condition and does not have excessive slack. Also check that the sprocket is securely mounted on the rear wheel hub. Check that the chain/belt guard is in place.
✔ On shaft drive bikes, check for oil leaking from the drive unit and fouling the rear tyre.

Steering and Suspension

Steering

✔ With the front wheel raised off the ground, rotate the steering from lock to lock. The handlebar or switches must not contact the fuel tank or be close enough to trap the rider's hand. Problems can be caused by damaged lock stops on the lower yoke and frame, or by the fitting of non-standard handlebars.
✔ When performing the lock to lock check, also ensure that the steering moves freely without drag or notchiness. Steering movement can be impaired by poorly routed cables, or by overtight head bearings or worn bearings. The tester will perform a check of the steering head bearing lower race by mounting the front wheel on a surface plate, then performing a lock to

lock check with the weight of the machine on the lower bearing (see illustration 3).
✔ Grasp the fork sliders (lower legs) and attempt to push and pull on the forks (see

Front wheel mounted on a surface plate for steering head bearing lower race check

illustration 4). Any play in the steering head bearings will be felt. Note that in extreme cases, wear of the front fork bushes can be misinterpreted for head bearing play.
✔ Check that the handlebars are securely mounted.
✔ Check that the handlebar grip rubbers are secure. They should by bonded to the bar left end and to the throttle cable pulley on the right end.

Front suspension

✔ With the motorcycle off the stand, hold the front brake on and pump the front forks up and down (see illustration 5). Check that they are adequately damped.

Checking the steering head bearings for freeplay

Hold the front brake on and pump the front forks up and down to check operation

Inspect the area around the fork dust seal for oil
leakage (arrow)

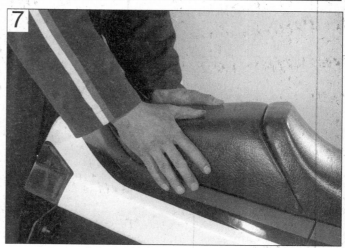

Bounce the rear of the motorcycle to check rear
suspension operation

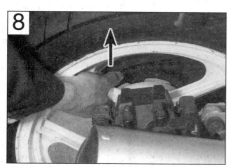

Checking for rear suspension linkage play

✔ Inspect the area above and around the
front fork oil seals **(see illustration 6)**. There
should be no sign of oil on the fork tube
(stanchion) nor leaking down the slider (lower
leg). On models so equipped, check that there
is no oil leaking from the anti-dive units.

✔ On models with swingarm front
suspension, check that there is no freeplay in
the linkage when moved from side to side.

Rear suspension

✔ With the motorcycle off the stand and an
assistant supporting the motorcycle by its
handlebars, bounce the rear suspension **(see
illustration 7)**. Check that the suspension
components do not foul on any of the cycle
parts and check that the shock absorber(s)
provide adequate damping.

✔ Visually inspect the shock absorber(s) and
check that there is no sign of oil leakage from
its damper. This is somewhat restricted on
certain single shock models due to the
location of the shock absorber.

✔ With the rear wheel raised off the
ground, grasp the wheel at the highest point
and attempt to pull it up **(see illustration 8)**.
Any play in the swingarm pivot or suspension
linkage bearings will be felt as movement.
Note: *Do not confuse play with actual
suspension movement.* Failure to lubricate
suspension linkage bearings can lead to
bearing failure **(see illustration 9)**.

✔ With the rear wheel raised off the ground,
grasp the swingarm ends and attempt to
move the swingarm from side to side and
forwards and backwards - any play indicates
wear of the swingarm pivot bearings **(see
illustration 10)**.

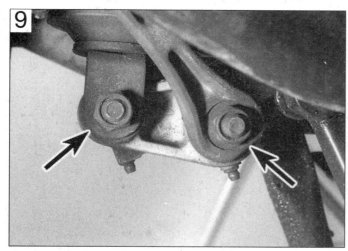

Worn suspension linkage pivots (arrows) are usually the cause of
play in the rear suspension

Grasp the swingarm at the ends to check for play in its pivot
bearings

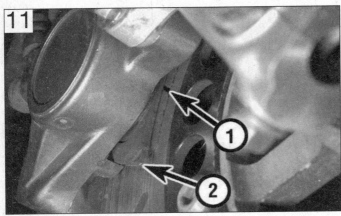

Brake pad wear can usually be viewed without removing the caliper. Most pads have wear indicator grooves (1) and some also have indicator tangs (2)

On drum brakes, check the angle of the operating lever with the brake fully applied. Most drum brakes have a wear indicator pointer and scale.

Brakes, Wheels and Tyres

Brakes

✔ With the wheel raised off the ground, apply the brake then free it off, and check that the wheel is about to revolve freely without brake drag.

✔ On disc brakes, examine the disc itself. Check that it is securely mounted and not cracked.

✔ On disc brakes, view the pad material through the caliper mouth and check that the pads are not worn down beyond the limit (see illustration 11).

✔ On drum brakes, check that when the brake is applied the angle between the operating lever and cable or rod is not too great (see illustration 12). Check also that the operating lever doesn't foul any other components.

✔ On disc brakes, examine the flexible hoses from top to bottom. Have an assistant hold the brake on so that the fluid in the hose is under pressure, and check that there is no sign of fluid leakage, bulges or cracking. If there are any metal brake pipes or unions, check that these are free from corrosion and damage. Where a brake-linked anti-dive system is fitted, check the hoses to the anti-dive in a similar manner.

✔ Check that the rear brake torque arm is secure and that its fasteners are secured by self-locking nuts or castellated nuts with split-pins or R-pins (see illustration 13).

✔ On models with ABS, check that the self-check warning light in the instrument panel works.

✔ The MOT tester will perform a test of the motorcycle's braking efficiency based on a calculation of rider and motorcycle weight. Although this cannot be carried out at home, you can at least ensure that the braking systems are properly maintained. For hydraulic disc brakes, check the fluid level, lever/pedal feel (bleed of air if its spongy) and pad material. For drum brakes, check adjustment, cable or rod operation and shoe lining thickness.

Wheels and tyres

✔ Check the wheel condition. Cast wheels should be free from cracks and if of the built-up design, all fasteners should be secure. Spoked wheels should be checked for broken, corroded, loose or bent spokes.

✔ With the wheel raised off the ground, spin the wheel and visually check that the tyre and wheel run true. Check that the tyre does not foul the suspension or mudguards.

✔ With the wheel raised off the ground, grasp the wheel and attempt to move it about the axle (spindle) (see illustration 14). Any play felt here indicates wheel bearing failure.

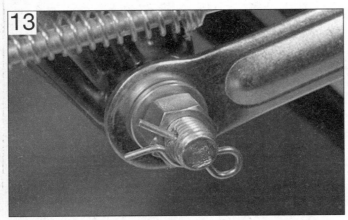

Brake torque arm must be properly secured at both ends

Check for wheel bearing play by trying to move the wheel about the axle (spindle)

Checking the tyre tread depth

Tyre direction of rotation arrow can be found on tyre sidewall

Castellated type wheel axle (spindle) nut must be secured by a split pin or R-pin

Two straightedges are used to check wheel alignment

✔ Check the tyre tread depth, tread condition and sidewall condition **(see illustration 15)**.

✔ Check the tyre type. Front and rear tyre types must be compatible and be suitable for road use. Tyres marked NOT FOR ROAD USE, COMPETITION USE ONLY or similar, will fail the MOT.

✔ If the tyre sidewall carries a direction of rotation arrow, this must be pointing in the direction of normal wheel rotation **(see illustration 16)**.

✔ Check that the wheel axle (spindle) nuts (where applicable) are properly secured. A self-locking nut or castellated nut with a split-pin or R-pin can be used **(see illustration 17)**.

✔ Wheel alignment is checked with the motorcycle off the stand and a rider seated. With the front wheel pointing straight ahead, two perfectly straight lengths of metal or wood and placed against the sidewalls of both tyres **(see illustration 18)**. The gap each side of the front tyre must be equidistant on both sides. Incorrect wheel alignment may be due to a cocked rear wheel (often as the result of poor chain adjustment) or in extreme cases, a bent frame.

General checks and condition

✔ Check the security of all major fasteners, bodypanels, seat, fairings (where fitted) and mudguards.

✔ Check that the rider and pillion footrests, handlebar levers and brake pedal are securely mounted.

✔ Check for corrosion on the frame or any load-bearing components. If severe, this may affect the structure, particularly under stress.

Sidecars

A motorcycle fitted with a sidecar requires additional checks relating to the stability of the machine and security of attachment and swivel joints, plus specific wheel alignment (toe-in) requirements. Additionally, tyre and lighting requirements differ from conventional motorcycle use. Owners are advised to check MOT test requirements with an official test centre.

Preparing for storage

Before you start

If repairs or an overhaul is needed, see that this is carried out now rather than left until you want to ride the bike again.

Give the bike a good wash and scrub all dirt from its underside. Make sure the bike dries completely before preparing for storage.

Engine

● Remove the spark plug(s) and lubricate the cylinder bores with approximately a teaspoon of motor oil using a spout-type oil can (see illustration 1). Reinstall the spark plug(s). Crank the engine over a couple of times to coat the piston rings and bores with oil. If the bike has a kickstart, use this to turn the engine over. If not, flick the kill switch to the OFF position and crank the engine over on the starter (see illustration 2). If the nature on the ignition system prevents the starter operating with the kill switch in the OFF position,

remove the spark plugs and fit them back in their caps; ensure that the plugs are earthed (grounded) against the cylinder head when the starter is operated (see illustration 3).

⚠️ **Warning: It is important that the plugs are earthed (grounded) away from the spark plug holes otherwise there is a risk of atomised fuel from the cylinders igniting.**

HAYNES HINT *On a single cylinder four-stroke engine, you can seal the combustion chamber completely by positioning the piston at TDC on the compression stroke.*

● Drain the carburettor(s) otherwise there is a risk of jets becoming blocked by gum deposits from the fuel (see illustration 4).

● If the bike is going into long-term storage, consider adding a fuel stabiliser to the fuel in the tank. If the tank is drained completely, corrosion of its internal surfaces may occur if left unprotected for a long period. The tank can be treated with a rust preventative especially for this purpose. Alternatively, remove the tank and pour half a litre of motor oil into it, install the filler cap and shake the tank to coat its internals with oil before draining off the excess. The same effect can also be achieved by spraying WD40 or a similar water-dispersant around the inside of the tank via its flexible nozzle.

● Make sure the cooling system contains the correct mix of antifreeze. Antifreeze also contains important corrosion inhibitors.

● The air intakes and exhaust can be sealed off by covering or plugging the openings. Ensure that you do not seal in any condensation; run the engine until it is hot,

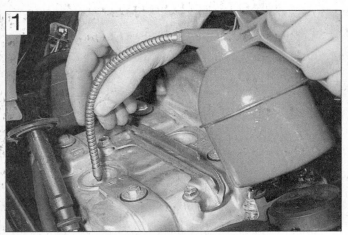

Squirt a drop of motor oil into each cylinder

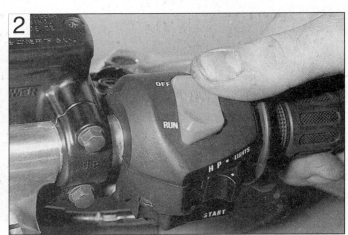

Flick the kill switch to OFF . . .

. . . and ensure that the metal bodies of the plugs (arrows) are earthed against the cylinder head

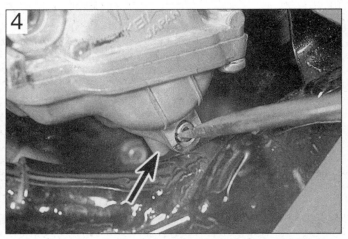

Connect a hose to the carburettor float chamber drain stub (arrow) and unscrew the drain screw

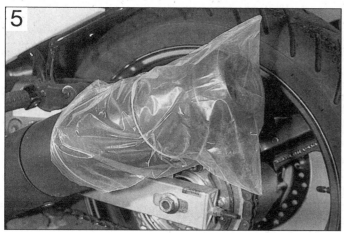

Exhausts can be sealed off with a plastic bag

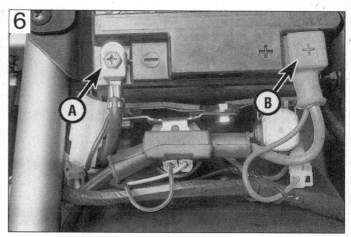

Disconnect the negative lead (A) first, followed by the positive lead (B)

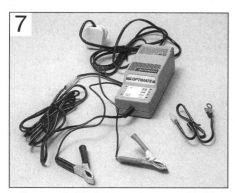

Use a suitable battery charger - this kit also assess battery condition

then switch off and allow to cool. Tape a piece of thick plastic over the silencer end(s) **(see illustration 5)**. Note that some advocate pouring a tablespoon of motor oil into the silencer(s) before sealing them off.

Battery

● Remove it from the bike - in extreme cases of cold the battery may freeze and crack its case **(see illustration 6)**.

● Check the electrolyte level and top up if necessary (conventional refillable batteries). Clean the terminals.
● Store the battery off the motorcycle and away from any sources of fire. Position a wooden block under the battery if it is to sit on the ground.
● Give the battery a trickle charge for a few hours every month **(see illustration 7)**.

Tyres

● Place the bike on its centrestand or an auxiliary stand which will support the motorcycle in an upright position. Position wood blocks under the tyres to keep them off the ground and to provide insulation from damp. If the bike is being put into long-term storage, ideally both tyres should be off the ground; not only will this protect the tyres, but will also ensure that no load is placed on the steering head or wheel bearings.
● Deflate each tyre by 5 to 10 psi, no more or the beads may unseat from the rim, making subsequent inflation difficult on tubeless tyres.

Pivots and controls

● Lubricate all lever, pedal, stand and footrest pivot points. If grease nipples are fitted to the rear suspension components, apply lubricant to the pivots.
● Lubricate all control cables.

Cycle components

● Apply a wax protectant to all painted and plastic components. Wipe off any excess, but don't polish to a shine. Where fitted, clean the screen with soap and water.
● Coat metal parts with Vaseline (petroleum jelly). When applying this to the fork tubes, do not compress the forks otherwise the seals will rot from contact with the Vaseline.
● Apply a vinyl cleaner to the seat.

Storage conditions

● Aim to store the bike in a shed or garage which does not leak and is free from damp.
● Drape an old blanket or bedspread over the bike to protect it from dust and direct contact with sunlight (which will fade paint). This also hides the bike from prying eyes. Beware of tight-fitting plastic covers which may allow condensation to form and settle on the bike.

Getting back on the road

Engine and transmission

● Change the oil and replace the oil filter. If this was done prior to storage, check that the oil hasn't emulsified - a thick whitish substance which occurs through condensation.
● Remove the spark plugs. Using a spout-type oil can, squirt a few drops of oil into the cylinder(s). This will provide initial lubrication as the piston rings and bores comes back into contact. Service the spark plugs, or fit new ones, and install them in the engine.

● Check that the clutch isn't stuck on. The plates can stick together if left standing for some time, preventing clutch operation. Engage a gear and try rocking the bike back and forth with the clutch lever held against the handlebar. If this doesn't work on cable-operated clutches, hold the clutch lever back against the handlebar with a strong elastic band or cable tie for a couple of hours **(see illustration 8)**.
● If the air intakes or silencer end(s) were blocked off, remove the bung or cover used.
● If the fuel tank was coated with a rust

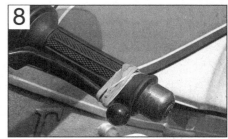

Hold clutch lever back against the handlebar with elastic bands or a cable tie

preventative, oil or a stabiliser added to the fuel, drain and flush the tank and dispose of the fuel sensibly. If no action was taken with the fuel tank prior to storage, it is advised that the old fuel is disposed of since it will go off over a period of time. Refill the fuel tank with fresh fuel.

Frame and running gear

● Oil all pivot points and cables.
● Check the tyre pressures. They will definitely need inflating if pressures were reduced for storage.
● Lubricate the final drive chain (where applicable).
● Remove any protective coating applied to the fork tubes (stanchions) since this may well destroy the fork seals. If the fork tubes weren't protected and have picked up rust spots, remove them with very fine abrasive paper and refinish with metal polish.
● Check that both brakes operate correctly. Apply each brake hard and check that it's not possible to move the motorcycle forwards, then check that the brake frees off again once released. Brake caliper pistons can stick due to corrosion around the piston head, or on the sliding caliper types, due to corrosion of the slider pins. If the brake doesn't free after repeated operation, take the caliper off for examination. Similarly drum brakes can stick due to a seized operating cam, cable or rod linkage.
● If the motorcycle has been in long-term storage, renew the brake fluid and clutch fluid (where applicable).
● Depending on where the bike has been stored, the wiring, cables and hoses may have been nibbled by rodents. Make a visual check and investigate disturbed wiring loom tape.

Battery

● If the battery has been previously removal and given top up charges it can simply be reconnected. Remember to connect the positive cable first and the negative cable last.
● On conventional refillable batteries, if the battery has not received any attention, remove it from the motorcycle and check its electrolyte level. Top up if necessary then charge the battery. If the battery fails to hold a charge and a visual checks show heavy white sulphation of the plates, the battery is probably defective and must be renewed. This is particularly likely if the battery is old. Confirm battery condition with a specific gravity check.
● On sealed (MF) batteries, if the battery has not received any attention, remove it from the motorcycle and charge it according to the information on the battery case - if the battery fails to hold a charge it must be renewed.

Starting procedure

● If a kickstart is fitted, turn the engine over a couple of times with the ignition OFF to distribute oil around the engine. If no kickstart is fitted, flick the engine kill switch OFF and the ignition ON and crank the engine over a couple of times to work oil around the upper cylinder components. If the nature of the ignition system is such that the starter won't work with the kill switch OFF, remove the spark plugs, fit them back into their caps and earth (ground) their bodies on the cylinder head. Reinstall the spark plugs afterwards.
● Switch the kill switch to RUN, operate the choke and start the engine. If the engine won't start don't continue cranking the engine - not only will this flatten the battery, but the starter motor will overheat. Switch the ignition off and try again later. If the engine refuses to start, go through the fault finding procedures in this manual. **Note:** *If the bike has been in storage for a long time, old fuel or a carburettor blockage may be the problem. Gum deposits in carburettors can block jets - if a carburettor cleaner doesn't prove successful the carburettors must be dismantled for cleaning.*

● Once the engine has started, check that the lights, turn signals and horn work properly.

● Treat the bike gently for the first ride and check all fluid levels on completion. Settle the bike back into the maintenance schedule.

This Section provides an easy reference-guide to the more common faults that are likely to afflict your machine. Obviously, the opportunities are almost limitless for faults to occur as a result of obscure failures, and to try and cover all eventualities would require a book. Indeed, a number have been written on the subject.

Successful troubleshooting is not a mysterious 'black art' but the application of a bit of knowledge combined with a systematic and logical approach to the problem. Approach any troubleshooting by first accurately identifying the symptom and then checking through the list of possible causes, starting with the simplest or most obvious and progressing in stages to the most complex.

Take nothing for granted, but above all apply liberal quantities of common sense.

The main symptom of a fault is given in the text as a major heading below which are listed the various systems or areas which may contain the fault. Details of each possible cause for a fault and the remedial action to be taken are given, in brief, in the paragraphs below each heading. Further information should be sought in the relevant Chapter.

1 Engine doesn't start or is difficult to start

- [ ] Starter motor doesn't rotate
- [ ] Starter motor rotates but engine does not turn over
- [ ] Starter works but engine won't turn over (seized)
- [ ] No fuel flow
- [ ] Engine flooded
- [ ] No spark or weak spark
- [ ] Compression low
- [ ] Stalls after starting
- [ ] Rough idle

2 Poor running at low speed

- [ ] Spark weak
- [ ] Fuel/air mixture incorrect
- [ ] Compression low
- [ ] Poor acceleration

3 Poor running or no power at high speed

- [ ] Firing incorrect
- [ ] Fuel/air mixture incorrect
- [ ] Compression low
- [ ] Knocking or pinking
- [ ] Miscellaneous causes

4 Overheating

- [ ] Engine overheats
- [ ] Firing incorrect
- [ ] Fuel/air mixture incorrect
- [ ] Compression too high
- [ ] Engine load excessive
- [ ] Lubrication inadequate
- [ ] Miscellaneous causes

5 Clutch problems

- [ ] Clutch slipping
- [ ] Clutch not disengaging completely

6 Gearchanging problems

- [ ] Doesn't go into gear, or lever doesn't return
- [ ] Jumps out of gear
- [ ] Overselects

7 Abnormal engine noise

- [ ] Knocking or pinking
- [ ] Piston slap or rattling
- [ ] Valve noise
- [ ] Other noise

8 Abnormal driveline noise

- [ ] Clutch noise
- [ ] Transmission noise
- [ ] Final drive noise

9 Abnormal frame and suspension noise

- [ ] Front end noise
- [ ] Shock absorber noise
- [ ] Brake noise

10 Oil pressure warning light comes on

- [ ] Engine lubrication system
- [ ] Electrical system

11 Excessive exhaust smoke

- [ ] White smoke
- [ ] Black smoke
- [ ] Brown smoke

12 Poor handling or stability

- [ ] Handlebar hard to turn
- [ ] Handlebar shakes or vibrates excessively
- [ ] Handlebar pulls to one side
- [ ] Poor shock absorbing qualities

13 Braking problems

- [ ] Brakes are spongy, don't hold
- [ ] Brake lever or pedal pulsates
- [ ] Brakes drag

14 Electrical problems

- [ ] Battery dead or weak
- [ ] Battery overcharged

1 Engine doesn't start or is difficult to start

Starter motor doesn't rotate

☐ Engine kill switch OFF.
☐ Fuse blown. Check main fuse and ignition circuit fuse (Chapter 8).
☐ Battery voltage low. Check and recharge battery (Chapter 8).
☐ Starter motor defective. Make sure the wiring to the starter is secure. Make sure the starter relay clicks when the start button is pushed. If the relay clicks, then the fault is in the wiring or motor (see Chapter 8).
☐ Starter switch not contacting. The contacts could be wet, corroded or dirty. Disassemble and clean the switch (Chapter 8).
☐ Wiring open or shorted. Check all wiring connections and harnesses to make sure that they are dry, tight and not corroded. Also check for broken or frayed wires that can cause a short to ground (earth) (see *Wiring diagrams*, Chapter 8).
☐ Ignition switch defective. Check the switch and renew it if it is defective (see Chapter 8).
☐ Engine stop switch defective. Check for wet, dirty or corroded contacts. Clean or renew the switch as necessary (see Chapter 8).
☐ Faulty gear position sensor, sidestand switch or clutch switch. Check the wiring to each switch and the switch itself (see Chapter 8).
☐ Faulty sidestand relay or diode (Chapter 8).
☐ Fuel injection system shutdown due to system fault (Chapter 4).

Starter motor rotates but engine does not turn over

☐ Starter clutch defective. Inspect and repair or renew (see Chapter 2).
☐ Damaged idle/reduction or starter gears. Inspect and renew the damaged parts (see Chapter 2).

Starter works but engine won't turn over (seized)

☐ Seized engine caused by one or more internally damaged components. Failure due to wear, abuse or lack of lubrication. Damage can include seized valves, followers, camshafts, pistons, crankshaft, connecting rod bearings, or transmission gears or bearings. Refer to Chapter 2 for engine disassembly.

No fuel flow

☐ No fuel in tank.
☐ Fuel tank breather hose obstructed.
☐ Fuel pump faulty, or the fuel filter is blocked (see Chapter 4).
☐ Fuel hose clogged. Remove the fuel hose and carefully blow through it. Check the fuel filter for damage.
☐ Fuel rail or injector clogged. For all of the injectors to be clogged, either a very bad batch of fuel with an unusual additive has been used, or some other foreign material has entered the tank. Check the fuel filter. In some cases, if a machine has been unused for several months, the fuel turns to a varnish-like liquid which can cause an injector needle to stick to its seat. Drain the tank and fuel system (Chapter 4).

Engine flooded

☐ Injector needle valve worn or stuck open. A piece of dirt, rust or other debris can cause the needle to seat improperly, causing excess fuel to be admitted to the throttle body. In this case, the injector should be cleaned and the needle and seat inspected (see Chapter 4). If the needle and seat are worn, then the leaking will persist and the parts should be renewed.
☐ Starting technique incorrect. Under normal circumstances (i.e. if all the components of the fuel injection system are good) the machine should start with the throttle closed.

No spark or weak spark

☐ Ignition switch OFF.
☐ Fuse blown. Check ignition circuit fuse (Chapter 8).
☐ Battery voltage low. Check and recharge the battery as necessary (Chapter 8).
☐ Spark plug caps not making good contact. Make sure that the caps fit snugly over the plug ends.
☐ Spark plugs dirty, defective or worn out. Locate reason for fouled plugs using spark plug condition chart on the inside back cover and follow the plug maintenance procedures (see Chapter 1).
☐ Incorrect spark plugs. Wrong type or heat range. Check and install correct plugs (see Chapter 1).
☐ Ignition HT coil or spark plug cap defective. Test and renew if necessary (Chapter 4).
☐ Fuel injection system shutdown due to system fault (Chapter 4).
☐ Camshaft position (CMP) sensor defective (see Chapter 4).
☐ Crankshaft position (CKP) sensor defective (see Chapter 4).
☐ Engine control module (ECM) defective (see Chapter 4).
☐ Wiring shorted or broken between:
   a) *Ignition switch and engine stop switch (or blown fuse)*
   b) *ECM and engine stop switch*
   c) *ECM and HT ignition coil*
   d) *ECM and CKP sensor*
☐ Make sure that all wiring connections are clean, dry and tight. Look for chafed and broken wires (see Chapters 4 and 8).

Compression low

☐ Spark plugs loose. Remove the plugs and inspect their threads. Reinstall and tighten securely (see Chapter 1).
☐ Cylinder head not sufficiently tightened down. If a cylinder head is suspected of being loose, then there's a chance that the gasket or head is damaged if the problem has persisted for any length of time. The head bolts should be tightened to the proper torque and in the correct sequence (Chapter 2).
☐ Improper valve clearance. This means that the valve is not closing completely and compression pressure is leaking past the valve. Check and adjust the valve clearances (Chapter 1).
☐ Cylinder and/or piston worn. Excessive wear will cause compression pressure to leak past the rings. This is usually accompanied by worn rings as well. A top-end overhaul is necessary (Chapter 2).
☐ Piston rings worn, weak, broken, or sticking. Broken or sticking piston rings usually indicate a lubrication or fuelling problem that causes excess carbon deposits to form on the pistons and rings. Top-end overhaul is necessary (Chapter 2).
☐ Piston ring-to-groove clearance excessive. This is caused by excessive wear of the piston ring lands. Piston renewal is necessary (Chapter 2).
☐ Cylinder head gasket damaged. If a head is allowed to become loose, or if excessive carbon build-up on the piston crown and combustion chamber causes extremely high compression, the head gasket may leak. Retorquing the head is not always sufficient to restore the seal, so gasket renewal is necessary (Chapter 2).
☐ Cylinder head warped. This is caused by overheating or improperly tightened head bolts. Machine shop resurfacing or head renewal is necessary (Chapter 2).
☐ Valve spring broken or weak. Caused by component failure or wear; the springs must be renewed (Chapter 2).
☐ Valve not seating properly. This is caused by a bent valve (from over-revving or improper valve adjustment), burned valve or seat (improper fuelling) or an accumulation of carbon deposits on the seat. The valves must be cleaned and/or renewed and the seats serviced (Chapter 2).

1 Engine doesn't start or is difficult to start (continued)

Stalls after starting

- ☐ Faulty fast idle system. Check the operation of the fast idle mechanism (see Chapter 4).
- ☐ Engine idle speed incorrect. Turn idle adjusting screw until the engine idles at the specified rpm (Chapter 1).
- ☐ Ignition malfunction (see Chapter 4).
- ☐ Fuel injection system malfunction (see Chapter 4).
- ☐ Fuel contaminated. The fuel can be contaminated with either dirt or water, or can change chemically if the machine has been unused for several months. Drain the tank and fuel system (Chapter 4).
- ☐ Intake air leak. Check for loose throttle body-to-intake manifold connections, loose or damaged PAIR vacuum hose or missing vacuum gauge blanking caps (Chapter 4).

Rough idle

- ☐ Idle speed incorrect (see Chapter 1).
- ☐ Ignition fault (see Chapter 4).
- ☐ Throttle valves not synchronised. Adjust them with vacuum gauge or manometer set as described in Chapter 1.
- ☐ Fuel injection system malfunction (see Chapter 4).
- ☐ Fuel contaminated. The fuel can be contaminated with either dirt or water, or can change chemically if the machine has been unused for several months. Drain the tank and the fuel system (Chapter 4).
- ☐ Intake air leak. Check for loose throttle body-to-intake manifold connections, loose or damaged PAIR vacuum hose or missing vacuum gauge blanking caps (Chapter 4).
- ☐ Air filter clogged. Clean or renew the air filter element (Chapter 1).

2 Poor running at low speeds

Spark weak

- ☐ Battery voltage low. Check and recharge battery (see Chapter 8).
- ☐ Spark plug caps not making good contact. Make sure that the caps fit snugly over the plug ends.
- ☐ Spark plugs dirty, defective or worn out. Locate reason for fouled plugs using spark plug condition chart on the inside back cover and follow the plug maintenance procedures (see Chapter 1).
- ☐ Incorrect spark plugs. Wrong type or heat range. Check and install correct plugs (see Chapter 1).
- ☐ Ignition HT coil or spark plug cap defective. Test and renew if necessary (see Chapter 4).

Fuel/air mixture incorrect

- ☐ Fuel tank breather hose obstructed.
- ☐ Fuel pump faulty, or the fuel filter is blocked (see Chapter 4).
- ☐ Fuel hose clogged. Remove the fuel hose and carefully blow through it. Check the fuel filter for damage.
- ☐ Fuel rail or injector clogged. For all of the injectors to be clogged, either a very bad batch of fuel with an unusual additive has been used, or some other foreign material has entered the tank. Check the fuel filter. In some cases, if a machine has been unused for several months, the fuel turns to a varnish-like liquid which can cause an injector needle to stick to its seat. Drain the tank and fuel system (Chapter 4).
- ☐ Intake air leak. Check for loose throttle body-to-intake manifold connections, loose or damaged PAIR vacuum hose or missing vacuum gauge blanking caps (Chapter 4).
- ☐ Air filter clogged. Renew the air filter element (Chapter 1).

Compression low

- ☐ Spark plugs loose. Remove the plugs and inspect their threads. Reinstall and tighten securely (see Chapter 1).
- ☐ Cylinder head not sufficiently tightened down. If a cylinder head is suspected of being loose, then there's a chance that the gasket or head is damaged if the problem has persisted for any length of time. The head bolts should be tightened to the proper torque and in the correct sequence (Chapter 2).
- ☐ Improper valve clearance. This means that the valve is not closing completely and compression pressure is leaking past the valve.

☐ Check and adjust the valve clearances (Chapter 1).
- ☐ Cylinder and/or piston worn. Excessive wear will cause compression pressure to leak past the rings. This is usually accompanied by worn rings as well. A top-end overhaul is necessary (Chapter 2).
- ☐ Piston rings worn, weak, broken, or sticking. Broken or sticking piston rings usually indicate a lubrication or fuelling problem that causes excess carbon deposits to form on the pistons and rings. Top-end overhaul is necessary (Chapter 2).
- ☐ Piston ring-to-groove clearance excessive. This is caused by excessive wear of the piston ring lands. Piston renewal is necessary (Chapter 2).
- ☐ Cylinder head gasket damaged. If the head is allowed to become loose, or if excessive carbon build-up on the piston crown and combustion chamber causes extremely high compression, the head gasket may leak. Retorquing the head is not always sufficient to restore the seal, so gasket renewal is necessary (Chapter 2).
- ☐ Cylinder head warped. This is caused by overheating or improperly tightened head bolts. Machine shop resurfacing or head renewal is necessary (Chapter 2).
- ☐ Valve spring broken or weak. Caused by component failure or wear; the springs must be renewed (Chapter 2).
- ☐ Valve not seating properly. This is caused by a bent valve (from over-revving or improper valve adjustment), burned valve or seat (improper fuelling) or an accumulation of carbon deposits on the seat (from fuelling or lubrication problems). The valves must be cleaned and/or renewed and the seats serviced (Chapter 2).

Poor acceleration

- ☐ Timing not advancing. The crankshaft position sensor (CKP) or the engine control module (ECM) may be defective (see Chapter 4). If so, they must be renewed.
- ☐ Throttle valves not synchronised. Adjust them with a vacuum gauge set or manometer (see Chapter 1).
- ☐ Engine oil viscosity too high. Using a heavier oil than that recommended in Chapter 1 can damage the oil pump or lubrication system and cause drag on the engine.
- ☐ Brakes dragging. Usually caused by debris which has entered the brake caliper piston seals, or from a warped disc or bent axle (see Chapter 6).

3 Poor running or no power at high speed

Firing incorrect

☐ Spark plug caps not making good contact. Make sure that the caps fit snugly over the plug ends and that the wiring is secure.

☐ Spark plugs dirty, defective or worn out. Locate reason for fouled plugs using spark plug condition chart on the inside back cover and follow the plug maintenance procedures (see Chapter 1).

☐ Incorrect spark plugs. Wrong type or heat range. Check and install correct plugs (see Chapter 1).

☐ Ignition HT coil or spark plug cap defective. Test and renew if necessary (see Chapter 4).

☐ Faulty ECM (engine control module) (see Chapter 4.

Fuel/air mixture incorrect

☐ Fuel tank breather hose obstructed.

☐ Fuel pump faulty, or the fuel filter is blocked (see Chapter 4).

☐ Fuel hose clogged. Remove the fuel hose and carefully blow through it. Check the fuel filter for damage.

☐ Fuel rail or injector clogged. For all of the injectors to be clogged, either a very bad batch of fuel with an unusual additive has been used, or some other foreign material has entered the tank. Check the fuel filter. In some cases, if a machine has been unused for several months, the fuel turns to a varnish-like liquid which can cause an injector needle to stick to its seat. Drain the tank and fuel system (Chapter 4).

☐ Intake air leak. Check for loose throttle body-to-intake manifold connections, loose or damaged PAIR vacuum hose or missing vacuum gauge blanking caps (Chapter 4).

☐ Air filter clogged. Renew the air filter element (Chapter 1).

Compression low

☐ Spark plugs loose. Remove the plugs and inspect their threads. Reinstall and tighten securely (see Chapter 1).

☐ Cylinder head not sufficiently tightened down. If a cylinder head is suspected of being loose, then there's a chance that the gasket or head is damaged if the problem has persisted for any length of time. The head bolts should be tightened to the proper torque and in the correct sequence (Chapter 2).

☐ Improper valve clearance. This means that the valve is not closing completely and compression pressure is leaking past the valve. Check and adjust the valve clearances (Chapter 1).

☐ Cylinder and/or piston worn. Excessive wear will cause compression pressure to leak past the rings. This is usually accompanied by worn rings as well. A top-end overhaul is necessary (Chapter 2).

☐ Piston rings worn, weak, broken, or sticking. Broken or sticking piston rings usually indicate a lubrication or fuelling problem that causes excess carbon deposits to form on the pistons and rings. Top-end overhaul is necessary (Chapter 2).

☐ Piston ring-to-groove clearance excessive. This is caused by excessive wear of the piston ring lands. Piston renewal is necessary (Chapter 2).

☐ Cylinder head gasket damaged. If a head is allowed to become loose, or if excessive carbon build-up on the piston crown and combustion chamber causes extremely high compression, the head gasket may leak. Retorquing the head is not always sufficient to restore the seal, so gasket renewal is necessary (Chapter 2).

☐ Cylinder head warped. This is caused by overheating or improperly tightened head bolts. Machine shop resurfacing or head renewal is necessary (Chapter 2).

☐ Valve spring broken or weak. Caused by component failure or wear; the springs must be renewed (Chapter 2).

☐ Valve not seating properly. This is caused by a bent valve (from over-revving or improper valve adjustment), burned valve or seat (improper fuelling) or an accumulation of carbon deposits on the seat (from fuelling or lubrication problems). The valves must be cleaned and/or renewed and the seats serviced (Chapter 2).

Knocking or pinking

☐ Carbon build-up in combustion chamber. Use of a fuel additive that will dissolve the adhesive bonding the carbon particles to the piston crown and chamber is the easiest way to remove the build-up. Otherwise, the cylinder head will have to be removed and decarbonised (Chapter 2).

☐ Incorrect or poor quality fuel. Old or improper grades of fuel can cause detonation. This causes the piston to rattle, thus the knocking or pinking sound. Drain old fuel and always use the recommended fuel grade.

☐ Spark plug heat range incorrect. Uncontrolled detonation indicates the plug heat range is too hot. The plug in effect becomes a glow plug, raising cylinder temperatures. Install the proper heat range plug (Chapter 1).

☐ Improper air/fuel mixture. This will cause the cylinders to run hot, which leads to detonation. A blockage in the fuel system or an air leak can cause this imbalance (see Chapter 4).

Miscellaneous causes

☐ Throttle valve doesn't open fully. Adjust the throttle twistgrip freeplay (see Chapter 1).

☐ Clutch slipping due loose or worn clutch components (see Chapter 2).

☐ Timing not advancing. The crankshaft position sensor (CKP) or the engine control module (ECM) may be defective (see Chapter 4). If so, they must be renewed.

☐ Engine oil viscosity too high. Using a heavier oil than the one recommended in Chapter 1 can damage the oil pump or lubrication system and cause drag on the engine.

☐ Brakes dragging. Usually caused by debris which has entered the brake caliper piston seals, or from a warped disc or bent axle (see Chapter 6).

4 Overheating

Engine overheats

- [ ] Engine oil level low. Check and add oil (see *Pre-ride checks*).
- [ ] Oil pump defective. Remove the pump and check the components (see Chapter 3).
- [ ] Clogged or damaged oil cooler fins (see Chapter 3).
- [ ] Faulty oil cooler fan or fan switch (see Chapter 3).

Firing incorrect

- [ ] Wrongly connected ignition HT coil wiring or spark plug cap.
- [ ] Spark plugs dirty, defective or worn out. Locate reason for fouled plugs using spark plug condition chart on the inside back cover and follow the plug maintenance procedures (see Chapter 1).
- [ ] Incorrect spark plugs. Wrong type or heat range. Check and install correct plugs (see Chapter 1).
- [ ] Ignition HT coil or spark plug cap defective. Test and renew if necessary (see Chapter 5).
- [ ] Faulty ECM (engine control module) (see Chapter 4).

Fuel/air mixture incorrect

- [ ] Fuel tank breather hose obstructed.
- [ ] Fuel pump faulty, or the fuel filter is blocked (see Chapter 4).
- [ ] Fuel hose clogged. Remove the fuel hose and carefully blow through it. Check the fuel filter for damage.
- [ ] Fuel rail or injector clogged. For all of the injectors to be clogged, either a very bad batch of fuel with an unusual additive has been used, or some other foreign material has entered the tank. Check the fuel filter. In some cases, if a machine has been unused for several months, the fuel turns to a varnish-like liquid which can cause an injector needle to stick to its seat. Drain the tank and fuel system (Chapter 4).
- [ ] Intake air leak. Check for loose throttle body-to-intake manifold connections, loose or damaged PAIR vacuum hose or missing vacuum gauge blanking caps (Chapter 4).
- [ ] Air filter clogged. Renew the air filter element (Chapter 1).

Compression too high

- [ ] Carbon build-up in combustion chamber. Use of a fuel additive that will dissolve the adhesive bonding the carbon particles to the piston crown and chamber is the easiest way to remove the build-up. Otherwise, the cylinder head will have to be removed and decarbonised (Chapter 2).
- [ ] Improperly machined head surface or installation of incorrect gasket during engine assembly.

Engine load excessive

- [ ] Clutch slipping due loose or worn clutch components (see Chapter 2).
- [ ] Engine oil level too high. Too much oil will cause pressurisation of the crankcase and inefficient engine operation. Drain to proper level (see *Pre-ride checks*).
- [ ] Engine oil viscosity too high. Using a heavier oil than the one recommended in Chapter 1 can damage the oil pump or lubrication system as well as cause drag on the engine.
- [ ] Brakes dragging. Usually caused by debris which has entered the brake caliper piston seals, or from a warped disc or bent axle (see Chapter 6).

Lubrication inadequate

- [ ] Engine oil level too low. Friction caused by intermittent lack of lubrication or from oil that is overworked can cause overheating. The oil provides a definite cooling function in the engine. Check the oil level (see *Pre-ride checks*).
- [ ] Low engine oil pressure. Check the pressure (see Chapter 2).
- [ ] Blocked oil filter or oil cooler (see Chapter 2).
- [ ] Poor quality engine oil or incorrect viscosity or type. Oil is rated not only according to viscosity but also according to type. Some oils are not rated high enough for use in this engine. Change to the correct oil (see *Pre-ride checks*).

Miscellaneous causes

- [ ] Modification to exhaust system. Most aftermarket exhaust systems cause the engine to run leaner, which make them run hotter. When installing an accessory exhaust system, check with the manufacturer/supplier if adjustments are required.

5   Clutch problems

Clutch slipping

- ☐ Clutch master or release cylinder faulty (Chapter 4).
- ☐ Friction plates worn or warped. Overhaul the clutch assembly (Chapter 2).
- ☐ Plain plates warped (Chapter 2).
- ☐ Use of an engine oil designed for car engines, i.e. it contains friction modifiers. Change to a dedicated motorcycle engine oil.
- ☐ Clutch springs broken or weak. Old or heat-damaged (from slipping clutch) springs should be replaced with new ones (Chapter 2).
- ☐ Clutch release mechanism defective. Replace any defective parts (Chapter 2).
- ☐ Clutch centre or housing unevenly worn. This causes improper engagement of the plates. Renew the damaged or worn parts (Chapter 2).

Clutch not disengaging completely

- ☐ Clutch master or release cylinder faulty, or system requires bleeding (Chapter 4).
- ☐ Clutch plates warped or damaged. This will cause clutch drag, which in turn will cause the machine to creep. Overhaul the clutch assembly (Chapter 2).
- ☐ Clutch spring tension uneven. Usually caused by a sagged or broken spring. Check and renew the springs as a set (Chapter 2).
- ☐ Engine oil deteriorated. Old, thin, worn out oil will not provide proper lubrication for the plates, causing the clutch to drag. Renew the oil and filter (Chapter 1).
- ☐ Engine oil viscosity too high. Using a heavier oil than recommended in Chapter 1 can cause the plates to stick together, putting a drag on the engine. Change to the correct weight oil (see Pre-ride checks).
- ☐ Clutch needle bearing or spacer seized on gearbox input shaft. Lack of lubrication, severe wear or damage can cause these components to seize on the shaft. Overhaul of the clutch, and perhaps transmission, may be necessary to repair the damage (Chapter 2).
- ☐ Clutch release mechanism defective (Chapter 2).
- ☐ Loose clutch centre nut. Causes housing and centre misalignment putting a drag on the engine. Engagement adjustment continually varies. Overhaul the clutch assembly (Chapter 2).

6 Gearchanging problems

Doesn't go into gear or lever doesn't return

- ☐ Clutch not disengaging (see above).
- ☐ Gearchange mechanism stopper arm spring weak or broken, or arm roller broken or worn. Renew the spring or arm (see Chapter 2).
- ☐ Selector fork(s) bent, worn or seized. Overhaul the transmission (see Chapter 2).
- ☐ Gear(s) stuck on shaft. Most often caused by a lack of lubrication or excessive wear in transmission bearings and bushes. Overhaul the transmission (see Chapter 2).
- ☐ Selector drum binding. Caused by lubrication failure or excessive wear. Renew the drum and bearing (see Chapter 2).
- ☐ Gearchange mechanism return spring weak or broken (see Chapter 2).
- ☐ Gearchange linkage arm broken. Splines stripped out of arm or shaft, caused by a loose linkage arm pinch bolt or from dropping the machine (see Chapter 2).

Jumps out of gear

- ☐ Selector fork(s) worn (see Chapter 2).
- ☐ Selector fork groove(s) in selector drum worn (see Chapter 2).
- ☐ Gear pinion dogs or dog slots worn or damaged. The gear pinions should be inspected and renewed. No attempt should be made to repair the worn parts.

Overselects

- ☐ Gearchange mechanism stopper arm spring weak or broken, or arm roller broken or worn. Renew the spring or arm (see Chapter 2).
- ☐ Gearchange mechanism return spring weak or broken (see Chapter 2).

7 Abnormal engine noise

Knocking or pinking

☐ Carbon build-up in combustion chamber. Use of a fuel additive that will dissolve the adhesive bonding the carbon particles to the piston crown and chamber is the easiest way to remove the build-up. Otherwise, the cylinder head will have to be removed and decarbonised (Chapter 2).

☐ Incorrect or poor quality fuel. Old or improper grades of fuel can cause detonation. This causes the piston to rattle, thus the knocking or pinking sound. Drain old fuel and always use the recommended fuel grade.

☐ Spark plug heat range incorrect. Uncontrolled detonation indicates the plug heat range is too hot. The plug in effect becomes a glow plug, raising cylinder temperatures. Install the proper heat range plug (Chapter 1).

☐ Improper air/fuel mixture. This will cause the cylinders to run hot, which leads to detonation. A blockage in the fuel system or an air leak can cause this imbalance (see Chapter 4).

Piston slap or rattling

☐ Cylinder-to-piston clearance excessive. Cylinder and/or piston worn, usually accompanied by worn rings as well. A top-end overhaul is necessary (see Chapter 2).

☐ Piston ring(s) worn, broken or sticking. Overhaul the top-end (see Chapter 2).

☐ Piston pin, piston pin bore or connecting rod small-end worn from high mileage or seized due to lack of lubrication (see Chapter 2).

☐ Piston seizure damage. Usually from lack of lubrication or overheating. Renew the pistons and cylinder block, as necessary (see Chapter 2).

☐ Connecting rod big-end clearance excessive. Caused by excessive wear or lack of lubrication. Renew worn parts.

☐ Connecting rod bent. Caused by over-revving, trying to start a badly flooded engine or from ingesting a foreign object into the combustion chamber. Renew the damaged parts (Chapter 2).

Valve noise

☐ Incorrect valve clearances – check and adjust (see Chapter 1).

☐ Valve spring broken or weak. Check and renew weak valve springs (see Chapter 2).

☐ Camshaft or camshaft journals in the cylinder head worn or damaged. Lubrication failure at high rpm is usually the cause of damage due to insufficient oil or failure to change the oil at the recommended intervals. Since there are no replaceable bearings in the head, the head itself will have to be renewed (see Chapter 2).

Other noise

☐ Cylinder head gasket leaking. Check around the joint for blowing with the engine running.

☐ Exhaust pipe leaking at cylinder head connection. Caused by incorrect fit of pipe(s), loose exhaust flange or damaged gasket. All exhaust system fasteners should be tightened evenly and carefully to avoid leaks (see Chapter 4).

☐ Crankshaft runout excessive. Caused by a bent crankshaft (from over-revving) or damage from an upper cylinder component failure. Can also be attributed to dropping the machine on either of the crankshaft ends.

☐ Engine mounting bolts loose – ensure all the bolts are tightened to the specified torque settings (see Chapter 2).

☐ Crankshaft bearings worn (see Chapter 2).

☐ Cam chain rattle, due to worn chain or defective tensioner. Also worn chain tensioner/guide blades (see Chapter 2).

8 Abnormal driveline noise

Clutch noise

- [ ] Clutch housing/friction plate clearance excessive (Chapter 2).
- [ ] Wear between the clutch housing splines and input shaft splines (Chapter 2).
- [ ] Worn release bearing (Chapter 2).

Transmission noise

- [ ] Bearings worn. Also includes the possibility that the shafts are worn. Overhaul the transmission (Chapter 2).
- [ ] Gears worn or chipped (Chapter 2).
- [ ] Metal chips jammed in gear teeth. Probably pieces from a broken clutch, gear or selector mechanism that were picked up by the gears. This will cause early bearing failure (Chapter 2).
- [ ] Engine oil level too low. Causes a howl from transmission. Also affects engine power and clutch operation (see *Pre-ride checks*).

Final drive noise

- [ ] Chain not adjusted properly (Chapter 1).
- [ ] Front or rear sprocket loose. Tighten fasteners (Chapter 6).
- [ ] Sprockets and/or chain worn. Renew sprockets and chain (Chapter 6).
- [ ] Rear sprocket warped. Renew sprocket (Chapter 6).
- [ ] Rubber dampers in rear wheel sprocket coupling worn (Chapter 6).

9 Abnormal frame and suspension noise

Front end noise

- [ ] Low oil level or improper viscosity oil in forks. This can sound like spurting and is usually accompanied by irregular fork action (Chapter 5).
- [ ] Spring weak or broken. Makes a clicking or scraping sound. Fork oil, when drained, will have a lot of metal particles in it (Chapter 5).
- [ ] Steering head bearings loose or damaged. Clicks when braking. Check and adjust or renew as necessary (Chapters 1 and 5).
- [ ] Fork yoke clamp bolts loose – ensure all the bolts are tightened to the specified torque (Chapter 5).
- [ ] Forks bent. Good possibility if machine has been dropped. Renew forks (Chapter 5).
- [ ] Front axle or axle pinch bolts loose. Tighten them to the specified torque (Chapter 6).
- [ ] Loose or worn wheel bearings. Check and renew as needed (Chapters 1 and 6).

Shock absorber noise

- [ ] Fluid level incorrect. Indicates a leak caused by defective seal. Shock will be covered with oil. Renew shocks (as a pair) or seek advice on repair from a suspension specialist (Chapter 5).
- [ ] Defective shock absorber with internal damage. This is in the body of the shock and can't be remedied. The shocks must be renewed (as a pair) or rebuilt (Chapter 5).
- [ ] Bent or damaged shock body. Renew the shocks as a pair (Chapter 5).

Brake noise

- [ ] Squeal caused by dust on brake pads. Usually found in combination with glazed pads. Clean using brake cleaning solvent (Chapter 6).
- [ ] Pads glazed. Caused by excessive heat from prolonged hard use or from contamination. DO NOT use sandpaper, emery cloth, carborundum cloth or any other abrasive to roughen the pad surfaces as abrasives will stay in the pad material and damage the disc. A very fine flat file can be used, but pad renewal is suggested as a cure (Chapter 6).
- [ ] Contamination of brake pads. Oil or brake fluid can cause the brake pads to chatter or squeal. Fit new pads. Identify the cause of the contamination, especially check the caliper piston seals for leaking fluid. Clean disc thoroughly with brake system cleaner (Chapter 6).
- [ ] Disc warped. Can cause a chattering, clicking or intermittent squeal. Usually accompanied by a pulsating lever and uneven braking. Renew the disc (Chapter 6).
- [ ] Loose or worn wheel bearings. Check and renew as needed (Chapters 1 and 6).

10 Oil pressure warning light comes on

Engine lubrication system

☐ Engine oil level low. Inspect for leak or other problem causing low oil level and add recommended oil (see *Pre-ride checks*).

☐ Engine oil pump defective, blocked oil strainer gauze or failed pressure regulator. Carry out an oil pressure check (Chapter 2).

☐ Engine oil viscosity too low. Very old, thin oil or an improper weight of oil used in the engine. Change to correct oil (see *Pre-ride checks*).

☐ Camshaft or crankshaft journals worn. Excessive wear causing drop in oil pressure. Abnormal wear could be caused by oil starvation at high rpm from low oil level or improper weight or type of oil.

Electrical system

☐ Oil pressure switch defective. Check the switch according to the procedure in Chapter 8. Renew it if it is defective.

☐ Oil pressure warning LED or symbol defective. Check for pinched, shorted, disconnected or damaged wiring (Chapter 8).

11 Excessive exhaust smoke

White smoke

☐ Piston rings worn or broken, causing oil from the crankcase to be pulled past the piston into the combustion chamber. Renew the rings (Chapter 2).

☐ Cylinders worn or scored. Caused by overheating or oil starvation. Install a new cylinder block (Chapter 2).

☐ Valve oil seal damaged or worn. Renew oil seals (Chapter 2).

☐ Valve guide worn. Perform a complete valve job (Chapter 2).

☐ Engine oil level too high, which causes the oil to be forced past the rings. Drain oil to the proper level (see *Pre-ride checks*).

☐ Head gasket broken between oil return and cylinder. Causes oil to be pulled into the combustion chamber. Renew the head gasket and check the head for warpage (Chapter 2).

☐ Abnormal crankcase pressurisation which forces oil past the rings, usually caused by a clogged breather.

Black smoke

☐ Air filter clogged. Clean or renew the element (Chapter 1).

☐ Fuel injection system malfunction (Chapter 4).

Brown smoke

☐ Air filter poorly sealed or not installed (Chapter 1).

☐ Fuel injection system malfunction (Chapter 4).

12 Poor handling or stability

Handlebar hard to turn

☐ Steering head bearing adjuster nut too tight. Check adjustment as described in Chapter 1.

☐ Bearings damaged. Roughness can be felt as the bars are turned from side-to-side. Renew bearings (Chapter 5).

☐ Races dented or worn. Denting results from wear in only one position (e.g., straight-ahead), from a collision or hitting a pothole or from dropping the machine. Renew bearings (Chapter 5).

☐ Steering stem lubrication inadequate. Causes are grease getting hard from age or being washed out by high pressure car washes. Disassemble steering head and repack bearings (Chapter 5).

☐ Steering stem bent. Caused by a collision, hitting a pothole or by dropping the machine. Renew damaged part. Don't try to straighten the steering stem (Chapter 5).

☐ Front tyre air pressure too low (see *Pre-ride checks*).

Handlebar shakes or vibrates excessively

☐ Tyres worn or out of balance.

☐ Swingarm bearings worn. Renew worn bearings (Chapter 5).

☐ Wheel rim(s) warped or damaged. Inspect wheels for runout (Chapter 6).

☐ Wheel bearings worn. Worn front or rear wheel bearings can cause poor tracking. Worn front bearings will cause wobble (Chapters 1 and 6).

☐ Fork yoke clamp bolts or handlebar clamp bolts loose. Tighten them to the specified torque (Chapter 5).

☐ Engine mounting bolts loose. Will cause excessive vibration with increased engine rpm – ensure all the bolts are tightened to the specified torque settings (see Chapter 2).

Machine pulls to one side

☐ Frame bent. Definitely suspect this if the machine has been dropped. May or may not be accompanied by cracking near the steering head, swingarm mountings or engine mountings. Renew the frame (Chapter 5).

☐ Wheels out of alignment. Caused by incorrect chain adjustment procedure (Chapter 1), or by improper location of axle spacers or from bent steering stem or frame (Chapter 5).

☐ Forks bent. Disassemble the forks and renew the damaged parts (Chapter 5).

☐ Swingarm bent or twisted. Renew the arm (Chapter 5).

☐ Fork oil level uneven. Check and add or drain as necessary (Chapter 5).

Poor shock absorbing qualities

☐ Too hard:
  a) Suspension settings incorrect.
  b) Fork oil level excessive (Chapter 5).
  c) Fork oil viscosity too high. Use a lighter oil (see the Specifications in Chapter 5).
  d) Fork inner tube bent. Causes a harsh, sticking feeling (Chapter 5).
  e) Fork internal damage (Chapter 5).
  f) Shock shaft or body bent or damaged (Chapter 5).
  g) Shock internal damage.
  h) Tyre pressure too high (see Pre-ride checks).

☐ Too soft:
  a) Suspension settings incorrect.
  b) Fork oil level too low (Chapter 5).
  c) Fork oil viscosity too light (Chapter 5).
  d) Fork springs weak or broken (Chapter 5).
  e) Fork or shock oil leaking (Chapter 5).
  f) Shock internal damage (Chapter 5).

13 Braking problems

Brakes are spongy, don't hold

- [ ] Low brake fluid level (see *Pre-ride checks*).
- [ ] Air in hydraulic system. Caused by inattention to master cylinder fluid level or by leakage. Locate problem and bleed brakes (Chapter 6).
- [ ] Pad or disc worn (Chapters 1 and 6).
- [ ] Contaminated pads. Caused by contamination with oil, grease, brake fluid, etc. Fit new pads. Identify the cause of the contamination, especially check the caliper piston seals for leaking fluid. Clean disc thoroughly with brake system cleaner (Chapter 6).
- [ ] Brake fluid deteriorated. Fluid is old or contaminated. Drain system, replenish with new fluid and bleed the system (Chapter 6).
- [ ] Master cylinder internal seals worn or damaged causing fluid to bypass (Chapter 6).
- [ ] Master cylinder bore scratched by foreign material or broken spring. Repair or renew master cylinder (Chapter 6).
- [ ] Disc warped. Renew disc (Chapter 6).

Brake lever or pedal pulsates

- [ ] Disc warped. Renew disc (Chapter 6).
- [ ] Axle bent. Renew axle (Chapter 6).
- [ ] Brake caliper bolts loose – tighten the bolts to the specified torque (Chapter 6).
- [ ] Wheel warped or otherwise damaged (Chapter 6).
- [ ] Wheel bearings damaged or worn (Chapters 1 and 6).

Brakes drag

- [ ] Master cylinder piston seized. Caused by wear or damage to piston or cylinder bore (Chapter 6).
- [ ] Lever balky or stuck. Check pivot and lubricate (Chapter 6).
- [ ] Brake caliper piston seized in bore. Caused by corrosion or ingestion of dirt past deteriorated seal (Chapter 6).
- [ ] Brake pad damaged. Pad material separated from backing plate. Usually caused by faulty manufacturing process or from contact with chemicals. Renew pads (Chapter 6).
- [ ] Pads improperly installed (Chapter 6).
- [ ] Brake caliper incorrectly installed (Chapter 6).

14 Electrical problems

Battery dead or weak

- [ ] Battery faulty. Caused by sulphated plates which are shorted through sedimentation. Confirm with battery condition check (Chapter 8).
- [ ] Broken battery terminal making only occasional contact.
- [ ] Battery leads making poor contact (Chapter 8).
- [ ] Load excessive. Caused by addition of high wattage lights or other electrical accessories.
- [ ] Ignition switch defective. Switch either earths internally or fails to shut off system. Renew the switch (Chapter 8).
- [ ] Regulator/rectifier defective (Chapter 8).
- [ ] Alternator stator coil open or shorted (Chapter 8).
- [ ] Charging system fault. Check for excessive current leakage (Chapter 8).
- [ ] Wiring faulty. Wiring earthed or connections loose in ignition, charging or lighting circuits (Chapter 8).

Battery overcharged

- [ ] Regulator/rectifier defective. Overcharging is noticed when battery gets excessively warm (Chapter 8).
- [ ] Battery faulty. Confirm with battery condition check (Chapter 8).
- [ ] Battery amperage too low, wrong type or size of battery. Install manufacturer's specified amp-hour battery to handle charging load (Chapter 8).

A

ABS (Anti-lock braking system) A system, usually electronically controlled, that senses incipient wheel lockup during braking and relieves hydraulic pressure at wheel which is about to skid.

Aftermarket Components suitable for the motorcycle, but not produced by the motorcycle manufacturer.

Allen key A hexagonal wrench which fits into a recessed hexagonal hole.

Alternating current (ac) Current produced by an alternator. Requires converting to direct current by a rectifier for charging purposes.

Alternator Converts mechanical energy from the engine into electrical energy to charge the battery and power the electrical system.

Ampere (amp) A unit of measurement for the flow of electrical current. Current = Volts ÷ Ohms.

Ampere-hour (Ah) Measure of battery capacity.

Angle-tightening A torque expressed in degrees. Often follows a conventional tightening torque for cylinder head or main bearing fasteners **(see illustration)**.

Angle-tightening cylinder head bolts

Antifreeze A substance (usually ethylene glycol) mixed with water, and added to the cooling system, to prevent freezing of the coolant in winter. Antifreeze also contains chemicals to inhibit corrosion and the formation of rust and other deposits that would tend to clog the radiator and coolant passages and reduce cooling efficiency.

Anti-dive System attached to the fork lower leg (slider) to prevent fork dive when braking hard.

Anti-seize compound A coating that reduces the risk of seizing on fasteners that are subjected to high temperatures, such as exhaust clamp bolts and nuts.

API American Petroleum Institute. A quality standard for 4-stroke motor oils.

Asbestos A natural fibrous mineral with great heat resistance, commonly used in the composition of brake friction materials. Asbestos is a health hazard and the dust created by brake systems should never be inhaled or ingested.

ATF Automatic Transmission Fluid. Often used in front forks.

ATU Automatic Timing Unit. Mechanical device for advancing the ignition timing on early engines.

ATV All Terrain Vehicle. Often called a Quad.

Axial play Side-to-side movement.

Axle A shaft on which a wheel revolves. Also known as a spindle.

B

Backlash The amount of movement between meshed components when one component is held still. Usually applies to gear teeth.

Ball bearing A bearing consisting of a hardened inner and outer race with hardened steel balls between the two races.

Bearings Used between two working surfaces to prevent wear of the components and a build-up of heat. Four types of bearing are commonly used on motorcycles: plain shell bearings, ball bearings, tapered roller bearings and needle roller bearings.

Bevel gears Used to turn the drive through 90°. Typical applications are shaft final drive and camshaft drive **(see illustration)**.

Bevel gears are used to turn the drive through 90°

BHP Brake Horsepower. The British measurement for engine power output. Power output is now usually expressed in kilowatts (kW).

Bias-belted tyre Similar construction to radial tyre, but with outer belt running at an angle to the wheel rim.

Big-end bearing The bearing in the end of the connecting rod that's attached to the crankshaft.

Bleeding The process of removing air from an hydraulic system via a bleed nipple or bleed screw.

Bottom-end A description of an engine's crankcase components and all components contained there-in.

BTDC Before Top Dead Centre in terms of piston position. Ignition timing is often expressed in terms of degrees or millimetres BTDC.

Bush A cylindrical metal or rubber component used between two moving parts.

Burr Rough edge left on a component after machining or as a result of excessive wear.

C

Cam chain The chain which takes drive from the crankshaft to the camshaft(s).

Canister The main component in an evaporative emission control system (California market only); contains activated charcoal granules to trap vapours from the fuel system rather than allowing them to vent to the atmosphere.

Castellated Resembling the parapets along the top of a castle wall. For example, a castellated wheel axle or spindle nut.

Catalytic converter A device in the exhaust system of some machines which converts certain pollutants in the exhaust gases into less harmful substances.

Charging system Description of the components which charge the battery, ie the alternator, rectifier and regulator.

Circlip A ring-shaped clip used to prevent endwise movement of cylindrical parts and shafts. An internal circlip is installed in a groove in a housing; an external circlip fits into a groove on the outside of a cylindrical piece such as a shaft. Also known as a snap-ring.

Clearance The amount of space between two parts. For example, between a piston and a cylinder, between a bearing and a journal, etc.

Coil spring A spiral of elastic steel found in various sizes throughout a vehicle, for example as a springing medium in the suspension and in the valve train.

Compression Reduction in volume, and increase in pressure and temperature, of a gas, caused by squeezing it into a smaller space.

Compression damping Controls the speed the suspension compresses when hitting a bump.

Compression ratio The relationship between cylinder volume when the piston is at top dead centre and cylinder volume when the piston is at bottom dead centre.

Continuity The uninterrupted path in the flow of electricity. Little or no measurable resistance.

Continuity tester Self-powered bleeper or test light which indicates continuity.

Cp Candlepower. Bulb rating commonly found on US motorcycles.

Crossply tyre Tyre plies arranged in a criss-cross pattern. Usually four or six plies used, hence 4PR or 6PR in tyre size codes.

Cush drive Rubber damper segments fitted between the rear wheel and final drive sprocket to absorb transmission shocks **(see illustration)**.

Cush drive rubbers dampen out transmission shocks

D

Degree disc Calibrated disc for measuring piston position. Expressed in degrees.

Dial gauge Clock-type gauge with adapters for measuring runout and piston position. Expressed in mm or inches.

Diaphragm The rubber membrane in a master cylinder or carburettor which seals the upper chamber.

Diaphragm spring A single sprung plate often used in clutches.

Direct current (dc) Current produced by a dc generator.

Decarbonisation The process of removing carbon deposits - typically from the combustion chamber, valves and exhaust port/system.

Detonation Destructive and damaging explosion of fuel/air mixture in combustion chamber instead of controlled burning.

Diode An electrical valve which only allows current to flow in one direction. Commonly used in rectifiers and starter interlock systems.

Disc valve (or rotary valve) A induction system used on some two-stroke engines.

Double-overhead camshaft (DOHC) An engine that uses two overhead camshafts, one for the intake valves and one for the exhaust valves.

Drivebelt A toothed belt used to transmit drive to the rear wheel on some motorcycles. A drivebelt has also been used to drive the camshafts. Drivebelts are usually made of Kevlar.

Driveshaft Any shaft used to transmit motion. Commonly used when referring to the final driveshaft on shaft drive motorcycles.

E

Earth return The return path of an electrical circuit, utilising the motorcycle's frame.

ECU (Electronic Control Unit) A computer which controls (for instance) an ignition system, or an anti-lock braking system.

EGO Exhaust Gas Oxygen sensor. Sometimes called a Lambda sensor.

Electrolyte The fluid in a lead-acid battery.

EMS (Engine Management System) A computer controlled system which manages the fuel injection and the ignition systems in an integrated fashion.

Endfloat The amount of lengthways movement between two parts. As applied to a crankshaft, the distance that the crankshaft can move side-to-side in the crankcase.

Endless chain A chain having no joining link. Common use for cam chains and final drive chains.

EP (Extreme Pressure) Oil type used in locations where high loads are applied, such as between gear teeth.

Evaporative emission control system Describes a charcoal filled canister which stores fuel vapours from the tank rather than allowing them to vent to the atmosphere. Usually only fitted to California models and referred to as an EVAP system.

Expansion chamber Section of two-stroke engine exhaust system so designed to improve engine efficiency and boost power.

F

Feeler blade or gauge A thin strip or blade of hardened steel, ground to an exact thickness, used to check or measure clearances between parts.

Final drive Description of the drive from the transmission to the rear wheel. Usually by chain or shaft, but sometimes by belt.

Firing order The order in which the engine cylinders fire, or deliver their power strokes, beginning with the number one cylinder.

Flooding Term used to describe a high fuel level in the carburettor float chambers, leading to fuel overflow. Also refers to excess fuel in the combustion chamber due to incorrect starting technique.

Free length The no-load state of a component when measured. Clutch, valve and fork spring lengths are measured at rest, without any preload.

Freeplay The amount of travel before any action takes place. The looseness in a linkage, or an assembly of parts, between the initial application of force and actual movement. For example, the distance the rear brake pedal moves before the rear brake is actuated.

Fuel injection The fuel/air mixture is metered electronically and directed into the engine intake ports (indirect injection) or into the cylinders (direct injection). Sensors supply information on engine speed and conditions.

Fuel/air mixture The charge of fuel and air going into the engine. See **Stoichiometric ratio**.

Fuse An electrical device which protects a circuit against accidental overload. The typical fuse contains a soft piece of metal which is calibrated to melt at a predetermined current flow (expressed as amps) and break the circuit.

G

Gap The distance the spark must travel in jumping from the centre electrode to the side electrode in a spark plug. Also refers to the distance between the ignition rotor and the pickup coil in an electronic ignition system.

Gasket Any thin, soft material - usually cork, cardboard, asbestos or soft metal - installed between two metal surfaces to ensure a good seal. For instance, the cylinder head gasket seals the joint between the block and the cylinder head.

Gauge An instrument panel display used to monitor engine conditions. A gauge with a movable pointer on a dial or a fixed scale is an analogue gauge. A gauge with a numerical readout is called a digital gauge.

Gear ratios The drive ratio of a pair of gears in a gearbox, calculated on their number of teeth.

Glaze-busting see **Honing**

Grinding Process for renovating the valve face and valve seat contact area in the cylinder head.

Gudgeon pin The shaft which connects the connecting rod small-end with the piston. Often called a piston pin or wrist pin.

H

Helical gears Gear teeth are slightly curved and produce less gear noise that straight-cut gears. Often used for primary drives.

Installing a Helicoil thread insert in a cylinder head

Helicoil A thread insert repair system. Commonly used as a repair for stripped spark plug threads **(see illustration)**.

Honing A process used to break down the glaze on a cylinder bore (also called glaze-busting). Can also be carried out to roughen a rebored cylinder to aid ring bedding-in.

HT (High Tension) Description of the electrical circuit from the secondary winding of the ignition coil to the spark plug.

Hydraulic A liquid filled system used to transmit pressure from one component to another. Common uses on motorcycles are brakes and clutches.

Hydrometer An instrument for measuring the specific gravity of a lead-acid battery.

Hygroscopic Water absorbing. In motorcycle applications, braking efficiency will be reduced if DOT 3 or 4 hydraulic fluid absorbs water from the air - care must be taken to keep new brake fluid in tightly sealed containers.

I

lbf ft Pounds-force feet. An imperial unit of torque. Sometimes written as ft-lbs.

lbf in Pound-force inch. An imperial unit of torque, applied to components where a very low torque is required. Sometimes written as in-lbs.

IC Abbreviation for Integrated Circuit.

Ignition advance Means of increasing the timing of the spark at higher engine speeds. Done by mechanical means (ATU) on early engines or electronically by the ignition control unit on later engines.

Ignition timing The moment at which the spark plug fires, expressed in the number of crankshaft degrees before the piston reaches the top of its stroke, or in the number of millimetres before the piston reaches the top of its stroke.

Infinity (∞) Description of an open-circuit electrical state, where no continuity exists.

Inverted forks (upside down forks) The sliders or lower legs are held in the yokes and the fork tubes or stanchions are connected to the wheel axle (spindle). Less unsprung weight and stiffer construction than conventional forks.

J

JASO Quality standard for 2-stroke oils.

Joule The unit of electrical energy.

Journal The bearing surface of a shaft.

K

Kickstart Mechanical means of turning the engine over for starting purposes. Only usually fitted to mopeds, small capacity motorcycles and off-road motorcycles.

Kill switch Handebar-mounted switch for emergency ignition cut-out. Cuts the ignition circuit on all models, and additionally prevent starter motor operation on others.

km Symbol for kilometre.

kmh Abbreviation for kilometres per hour.

L

Lambda (λ) sensor A sensor fitted in the exhaust system to measure the exhaust gas oxygen content (excess air factor).

Lapping see **Grinding**.
LCD Abbreviation for Liquid Crystal Display.
LED Abbreviation for Light Emitting Diode.
Liner A steel cylinder liner inserted in a aluminium alloy cylinder block.
Locknut A nut used to lock an adjustment nut, or other threaded component, in place.
Lockstops The lugs on the lower triple clamp (yoke) which abut those on the frame, preventing handlebar-to-fuel tank contact.
Lockwasher A form of washer designed to prevent an attaching nut from working loose.
LT Low Tension Description of the electrical circuit from the power supply to the primary winding of the ignition coil.

M

Main bearings The bearings between the crankshaft and crankcase.
Maintenance-free (MF) battery A sealed battery which cannot be topped up.
Manometer Mercury-filled calibrated tubes used to measure intake tract vacuum. Used to synchronise carburettors on multi-cylinder engines.
Micrometer A precision measuring instrument that measures component outside diameters **(see illustration)**.

Tappet shims are measured with a micrometer

MON (Motor Octane Number) A measure of a fuel's resistance to knock.
Monograde oil An oil with a single viscosity, eg SAE80W.
Monoshock A single suspension unit linking the swingarm or suspension linkage to the frame.
mph Abbreviation for miles per hour.
Multigrade oil Having a wide viscosity range (eg 10W40). The W stands for Winter, thus the viscosity ranges from SAE10 when cold to SAE40 when hot.
Multimeter An electrical test instrument with the capability to measure voltage, current and resistance. Some meters also incorporate a continuity tester and buzzer.

N

Needle roller bearing Inner race of caged needle rollers and hardened outer race. Examples of uncaged needle rollers can be found on some engines. Commonly used in rear suspension applications and in two-stroke engines.
Nm Newton metres.
NOx Oxides of Nitrogen. A common toxic pollutant emitted by petrol engines at higher temperatures.

O

Octane The measure of a fuel's resistance to knock.
OE (Original Equipment) Relates to components fitted to a motorcycle as standard or replacement parts supplied by the motorcycle manufacturer.
Ohm The unit of electrical resistance. Ohms = Volts ÷ Current.
Ohmmeter An instrument for measuring electrical resistance.
Oil cooler System for diverting engine oil outside of the engine to a radiator for cooling purposes.
Oil injection A system of two-stroke engine lubrication where oil is pump-fed to the engine in accordance with throttle position.
Open-circuit An electrical condition where there is a break in the flow of electricity - no continuity (high resistance).
O-ring A type of sealing ring made of a special rubber-like material; in use, the O-ring is compressed into a groove to provide the sealing action.
Oversize (OS) Term used for piston and ring size options fitted to a rebored cylinder.
Overhead cam (sohc) engine An engine with single camshaft located on top of the cylinder head.
Overhead valve (ohv) engine An engine with the valves located in the cylinder head, but with the camshaft located in the engine block or crankcase.
Oxygen sensor A device installed in the exhaust system which senses the oxygen content in the exhaust and converts this information into an electric current. Also called a Lambda sensor.

P

Plastigauge A thin strip of plastic thread, available in different sizes, used for measuring clearances. For example, a strip of Plastigauge is laid across a bearing journal. The parts are assembled and dismantled; the width of the crushed strip indicates the clearance between journal and bearing.
Polarity Either negative or positive earth (ground), determined by which battery lead is connected to the frame (earth return). Modern motorcycles are usually negative earth.
Pre-ignition A situation where the fuel/air mixture ignites before the spark plug fires. Often due to a hot spot in the combustion chamber caused by carbon build-up. Engine has a tendency to 'run-on'.
Pre-load (suspension) The amount a spring is compressed when in the unloaded state. Preload can be applied by gas, spacer or mechanical adjuster.
Premix The method of engine lubrication on older two-stroke engines. Engine oil is mixed with the petrol in the fuel tank in a specific ratio. The fuel/oil mix is sometimes referred to as "petroil".
Primary drive Description of the drive from the crankshaft to the clutch. Usually by gear or chain.
PS Pfedestärke - a German interpretation of BHP.
PSI Pounds-force per square inch. Imperial measurement of tyre pressure and cylinder pressure measurement.
PTFE Polytetrafluroethylene. A low friction substance.

Pulse secondary air injection system A process of promoting the burning of excess fuel present in the exhaust gases by routing fresh air into the exhaust ports.

Q

Quartz halogen bulb Tungsten filament surrounded by a halogen gas. Typically used for the headlight **(see illustration)**.

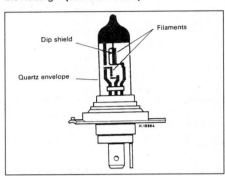

Quartz halogen headlight bulb construction

R

Rack-and-pinion A pinion gear on the end of a shaft that mates with a rack (think of a geared wheel opened up and laid flat). Sometimes used in clutch operating systems.
Radial play Up and down movement about a shaft.
Radial ply tyres Tyre plies run across the tyre (from bead to bead) and around the circumference of the tyre. Less resistant to tread distortion than other tyre types.
Radiator A liquid-to-air heat transfer device designed to reduce the temperature of the coolant in a liquid cooled engine.
Rake A feature of steering geometry - the angle of the steering head in relation to the vertical **(see illustration)**.

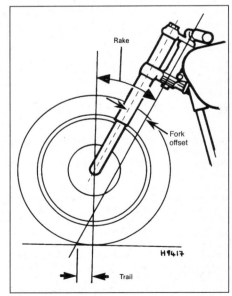

Steering geometry

Rebore Providing a new working surface to the cylinder bore by boring out the old surface. Necessitates the use of oversize piston and rings.

Rebound damping A means of controlling the oscillation of a suspension unit spring after it has been compressed. Resists the spring's natural tendency to bounce back after being compressed.

Rectifier Device for converting the ac output of an alternator into dc for battery charging.

Reed valve An induction system commonly used on two-stroke engines.

Regulator Device for maintaining the charging voltage from the generator or alternator within a specified range.

Relay A electrical device used to switch heavy current on and off by using a low current auxiliary circuit.

Resistance Measured in ohms. An electrical component's ability to pass electrical current.

RON (Research Octane Number) A measure of a fuel's resistance to knock.

rpm revolutions per minute.

Runout The amount of wobble (in-and-out movement) of a wheel or shaft as it's rotated. The amount a shaft rotates 'out-of-true'. The out-of-round condition of a rotating part.

S

SAE (Society of Automotive Engineers) A standard for the viscosity of a fluid.

Sealant A liquid or paste used to prevent leakage at a joint. Sometimes used in conjunction with a gasket.

Service limit Term for the point where a component is no longer useable and must be renewed.

Shaft drive A method of transmitting drive from the transmission to the rear wheel.

Shell bearings Plain bearings consisting of two shell halves. Most often used as big-end and main bearings in a four-stroke engine. Often called bearing inserts.

Shim Thin spacer, commonly used to adjust the clearance or relative positions between two parts. For example, shims inserted into or under tappets or followers to control valve clearances. Clearance is adjusted by changing the thickness of the shim.

Short-circuit An electrical condition where current shorts to earth (ground) bypassing the circuit components.

Skimming Process to correct warpage or repair a damaged surface, eg on brake discs or drums.

Slide-hammer A special puller that screws into or hooks onto a component such as a shaft or bearing; a heavy sliding handle on the shaft bottoms against the end of the shaft to knock the component free.

Small-end bearing The bearing in the upper end of the connecting rod at its joint with the gudgeon pin.

Spalling Damage to camshaft lobes or bearing journals shown as pitting of the working surface.

Specific gravity (SG) The state of charge of the electrolyte in a lead-acid battery. A measure of the electrolyte's density compared with water.

Straight-cut gears Common type gear used on gearbox shafts and for oil pump and water pump drives.

Stanchion The inner sliding part of the front forks, held by the yokes. Often called a fork tube.

Stoichiometric ratio The optimum chemical air/fuel ratio for a petrol engine, said to be 14.7 parts of air to 1 part of fuel.

Sulphuric acid The liquid (electrolyte) used in a lead-acid battery. Poisonous and extremely corrosive.

Surface grinding (lapping) Process to correct a warped gasket face, commonly used on cylinder heads.

T

Tapered-roller bearing Tapered inner race of caged needle rollers and separate tapered outer race. Examples of taper roller bearings can be found on steering heads.

Tappet A cylindrical component which transmits motion from the cam to the valve stem, either directly or via a pushrod and rocker arm. Also called a cam follower.

TCS Traction Control System. An electronically-controlled system which senses wheel spin and reduces engine speed accordingly.

TDC Top Dead Centre denotes that the piston is at its highest point in the cylinder.

Thread-locking compound Solution applied to fastener threads to prevent slackening. Select type to suit application.

Thrust washer A washer positioned between two moving components on a shaft. For example, between gear pinions on gearshaft.

Timing chain See **Cam Chain.**

Timing light Stroboscopic lamp for carrying out ignition timing checks with the engine running.

Top-end A description of an engine's cylinder block, head and valve gear components.

Torque Turning or twisting force about a shaft.

Torque setting A prescribed tightness specified by the motorcycle manufacturer to ensure that the bolt or nut is secured correctly. Undertightening can result in the bolt or nut coming loose or a surface not being sealed. Overtightening can result in stripped threads, distortion or damage to the component being retained.

Torx key A six-point wrench.

Tracer A stripe of a second colour applied to a wire insulator to distinguish that wire from another one with the same colour insulator. For example, Br/W is often used to denote a brown insulator with a white tracer.

Trail A feature of steering geometry. Distance from the steering head axis to the tyre's central contact point.

Triple clamps The cast components which extend from the steering head and support the fork stanchions or tubes. Often called fork yokes.

Turbocharger A centrifugal device, driven by exhaust gases, that pressurises the intake air. Normally used to increase the power output from a given engine displacement.

TWI Abbreviation for Tyre Wear Indicator. Indicates the location of the tread depth indicator bars on tyres.

U

Universal joint or U-joint (UJ) A double-pivoted connection for transmitting power from a driving to a driven shaft through an angle. Typically found in shaft drive assemblies.

Unsprung weight Anything not supported by the bike's suspension (ie the wheel, tyres, brakes, final drive and bottom (moving) part of the suspension).

V

Vacuum gauges Clock-type gauges for measuring intake tract vacuum. Used for carburettor synchronisation on multi-cylinder engines.

Valve A device through which the flow of liquid, gas or vacuum may be stopped, started or regulated by a moveable part that opens, shuts or partially obstructs one or more ports or passageways. The intake and exhaust valves in the cylinder head are of the poppet type.

Valve clearance The clearance between the valve tip (the end of the valve stem) and the rocker arm or tappet/follower. The valve clearance is measured when the valve is closed. The correct clearance is important - if too small the valve won't close fully and will burn out, whereas if too large noisy operation will result.

Valve lift The amount a valve is lifted off its seat by the camshaft lobe.

Valve timing The exact setting for the opening and closing of the valves in relation to piston position.

Vernier caliper A precision measuring instrument that measures inside and outside dimensions. Not quite as accurate as a micrometer, but more convenient.

VIN Vehicle Identification Number. Term for the bike's engine and frame numbers.

Viscosity The thickness of a liquid or its resistance to flow.

Volt A unit for expressing electrical "pressure" in a circuit. Volts = current x ohms.

W

Water pump A mechanically-driven device for moving coolant around the engine.

Watt A unit for expressing electrical power. Watts = volts x current.

Wear limit see **Service limit**

Wet liner A liquid-cooled engine design where the pistons run in liners which are directly surrounded by coolant **(see illustration).**

Wet liner arrangement

Wheelbase Distance from the centre of the front wheel to the centre of the rear wheel.

Wiring harness or loom Describes the electrical wires running the length of the motorcycle and enclosed in tape or plastic sheathing. Wiring coming off the main harness is usually referred to as a sub harness.

Woodruff key A key of semi-circular or square section used to locate a gear to a shaft. Often used to locate the alternator rotor on the crankshaft.

Wrist pin Another name for gudgeon or piston pin.

Note: *References throughout this index are in the form - "Chapter number" • "Page number"*

Haynes Motorcycle Manuals – The Complete List

Title	Book No
APRILIA RS50 (99 - 06) & RS125 (93 - 06)	4298
Aprilia RSV1000 Mille (98 - 03)	♦ 4255
BMW 2-valve Twins (70 - 96)	♦ 0249
BMW K100 & 75 2-valve Models (83 - 96)	♦ 1373
BMW R850, 1100 & 1150 4-valve Twins (93 - 04)	♦ 3466
BMW R1200 (04 - 06)	♦ 4598
BSA Bantam (48 - 71)	0117
BSA Unit Singles (58 - 72)	0127
BSA Pre-unit Singles (54 - 61)	0326
BSA A7 & A10 Twins (47 - 62)	0121
BSA A50 & A65 Twins (62 - 73)	0155
DUCATI 600, 620, 750 and 900 2-valve V-Twins (91 - 05)	♦ 3290
Ducati MK III & Desmo Singles (69 - 76)	◊ 0445
Ducati 748, 916 & 996 4-valve V-Twins (94 - 01)	♦ 3756
GILERA Runner, DNA, Ice & SKP/Stalker (97 - 07)	4163
HARLEY-DAVIDSON Sportsters (70 - 03)	♦ 2534
Harley-Davidson Shovelhead and Evolution Big Twins (70 - 99)	♦ 2536
Harley-Davidson Twin Cam 88 (99 - 03)	♦ 2478
HONDA NB, ND, NP & NS50 Melody (81 - 85)	◊ 0622
Honda NE/NB50 Vision & SA50 Vision Met-in (85 - 95)	◊ 1278
Honda MB, MBX, MT & MTX50 (80 - 93)	0731
Honda C50, C70 & C90 (67 - 03)	0324
Honda XR80/100R & CRF80/100F (85 - 04)	2218
Honda XL/XR 80, 100, 125, 185 & 200 2-valve Models (78 - 87)	0566
Honda H100 & H100S Singles (80 - 92)	◊ 0734
Honda CB/CD125T & CM125C Twins (77 - 88)	◊ 0571
Honda CG125 (76 - 07)	◊ 0433
Honda NS125 (86 - 93)	◊ 3056
Honda CBR125R (04 - 07)	4620
Honda MBX/MTX125 & MTX200 (83 - 93)	◊ 1132
Honda CD/CM185 200T & CM250C 2-valve Twins (77 - 85)	0572
Honda XL/XR 250 & 500 (78 - 84)	0567
Honda XR250L, XR250R & XR400R (86 - 03)	2219
Honda CB250 & CB400N Super Dreams (78 - 84)	◊ 0540
Honda CR Motocross Bikes (86 - 01)	2222
Honda CRF250 & CRF450 (02 - 06)	2630
Honda CBR400RR Fours (88 - 99)	◊ ♦ 3552
Honda VFR400 (NC30) & RVF400 (NC35) V-Fours (89 - 98)	◊ ♦ 3496
Honda CB500 (93 - 01)	◊ 3753
Honda CB400 & CB550 Fours (73 - 77)	0262
Honda CX/GL500 & 650 V-Twins (78 - 86)	0442
Honda CBX550 Four (82 - 86)	◊ 0940
Honda XL600R & XR600R (83 - 00)	2183
Honda XL600/650V Transalp & XRV750 Africa Twin (87 to 07)	♦ 3919
Honda CBR600F1 & 1000F Fours (87 - 96)	♦ 1730
Honda CBR600F2 & F3 Fours (91 - 98)	♦ 2070
Honda CBR600F4 (99 - 06)	♦ 3911
Honda CB600F Hornet & CBF600 (98 - 06)	◊ ♦ 3915
Honda CBR600RR (03 - 06)	♦ 4590
Honda CB650 sohc Fours (78 - 84)	0665
Honda NTV600 Revere, NTV650 and NT650V Deauville (88 - 05)	◊ ♦ 3243
Honda Shadow VT600 & 750 (USA) (88 - 03)	2312
Honda CB750 sohc Four (69 - 79)	0131
Honda V45/65 Sabre & Magna (82 - 88)	0820
Honda VFR750 & 700 V-Fours (86 - 97)	♦ 2101
Honda VFR800 V-Fours (97 - 01)	♦ 3703
Honda VFR800 V-Tec V-Fours (02 - 05)	♦ 4196
Honda CB750 & CB900 dohc Fours (78 - 84)	0535
Honda VTR1000 (FireStorm, Super Hawk) & XL1000V (Varadero) (97 - 05)	♦ 3744
Honda CBR900RR FireBlade (92 - 99)	♦ 2161
Honda CBR900RR FireBlade (00 - 03)	♦ 4060
Honda CBR1000RR Fireblade (04 - 07)	♦ 4604
Honda CBR1100XX Super Blackbird (97 - 07)	♦ 3901
Honda ST1100 Pan European V-Fours (90 - 02)	♦ 3384
Honda Shadow VT1100 (USA) (85 - 98)	2313
Honda GL1000 Gold Wing (75 - 79)	0309
Honda GL1100 Gold Wing (79 - 81)	0669

Title	Book No
Honda Gold Wing 1200 (USA) (84 - 87)	2199
Honda Gold Wing 1500 (USA) (88 - 00)	2225
KAWASAKI AE/AR 50 & 80 (81 - 95)	1007
Kawasaki KC, KE & KH100 (75 - 99)	1371
Kawasaki KMX125 & 200 (86 - 02)	◊ 3046
Kawasaki 250, 350 & 400 Triples (72 - 79)	0134
Kawasaki 400 & 440 Twins (74 - 81)	0281
Kawasaki 400, 500 & 550 Fours (79 - 91)	0910
Kawasaki EN450 & 500 Twins (Ltd/Vulcan) (85 - 04)	2053
Kawasaki EX500 (GPZ500S) & ER500 (ER-5) (87 - 05)	♦ 2052
Kawasaki ZX600 (ZZ-R600 & Ninja ZX-6) (90 - 06)	♦ 2146
Kawasaki ZX-6R Ninja Fours (95 - 02)	♦ 3541
Kawasaki ZX-6R (03 - 06)	♦ 4742
Kawasaki ZX600 (GPZ600R, GPX600R, Ninja 600R & RX) & ZX750 (GPX750R, Ninja 750R)	♦ 1780
Kawasaki 650 Four (76 - 78)	0373
Kawasaki Vulcan 700/750 & 800 (85 - 04)	♦ 2457
Kawasaki 750 Air-cooled Fours (80 - 91)	0574
Kawasaki ZR550 & 750 Zephyr Fours (90 - 97)	♦ 3382
Kawasaki Z750 & Z1000 (03 - 08)	♦ 4762
Kawasaki ZX750 (Ninja ZX-7 & ZXR750) Fours (89 - 96)	♦ 2054
Kawasaki Ninja ZX-7R & ZX-9R (94 - 04)	♦ 3721
Kawasaki 900 & 1000 Fours (73 - 77)	0222
Kawasaki ZX900, 1000 & 1100 Liquid-cooled Fours (83 - 97)	♦ 1681
KTM EXC Enduro & SX Motocross (00 - 07)	♦ 4629
MOTO GUZZI 750, 850 & 1000 V-Twins (74 - 78)	0339
MZ ETZ Models (81 - 95)	◊ 1680
NORTON 500, 600, 650 & 750 Twins (57 - 70)	0187
Norton Commando (68 - 77)	0125
PEUGEOT Speedfight, Trekker & Vivacity Scooters (96 - 05)	◊ 3920
PIAGGIO (Vespa) Scooters (91 - 06)	◊ 3492
SUZUKI GT, ZR & TS50 (77 - 90)	◊ 0799
Suzuki TS50X (84 - 00)	◊ 1599
Suzuki 100, 125, 185 & 250 Air-cooled Trail bikes (79 - 89)	◊ 0797
Suzuki GP100 & 125 Singles (78 - 93)	◊ 0576
Suzuki GS, GN, GZ & DR125 Singles (82 - 05)	◊ 0888
Suzuki 250 & 350 Twins (68 - 78)	0120
Suzuki GT250X7, GT200X5 & SB200 Twins (78 - 83)	◊ 0469
Suzuki GS/GSX250, 400 & 450 Twins (79 - 85)	0736
Suzuki GS500 Twin (89 - 06)	♦ 3238
Suzuki GS550 (77 - 82) & GS750 Fours (76 - 79)	0363
Suzuki GS/GSX550 4-valve Fours (83 - 88)	1133
Suzuki SV650 & SV650S (99 - 05)	♦ 3912
Suzuki GSX-R600 & 750 (96 - 00)	♦ 3553
Suzuki GSX-R600 (01 - 03), GSX-R750 (00 - 03) & GSX-R1000 (01 - 02)	♦ 3986
Suzuki GSX-R600/750 (04 - 05) & GSX-R1000 (03 - 06)	♦ 4382
Suzuki GSF600, 650 & 1200 Bandit Fours (95 - 06)	♦ 3367
Suzuki Intruder, Marauder, Volusia & Boulevard (85 - 06)	♦ 2618
Suzuki GS850 Fours (78 - 88)	0536
Suzuki GS1000 Four (77 - 79)	0484
Suzuki GSX-R750, GSX-R1100 (85 - 92), GSX600F, GSX750F, GSX1100F (Katana) Fours	♦ 2055
Suzuki GSX600/750F & GSX750 (98 - 02)	♦ 3987
Suzuki GS/GSX1000, 1100 & 1150 4-valve Fours (79 - 88)	0737
Suzuki TL1000S/R & DL1000 V-Strom (97 - 04)	♦ 4083
Suzuki GSX1300R Hayabusa (99 - 04)	♦ 4184
Suzuki GSX1400 (02 - 07)	♦ 4758
TRIUMPH Tiger Cub & Terrier (52 - 68)	0414
Triumph 350 & 500 Unit Twins (58 - 73)	0137
Triumph Pre-Unit Twins (47 - 62)	0251
Triumph 650 & 750 2-valve Unit Twins (63 - 83)	0122
Triumph Trident & BSA Rocket 3 (69 - 75)	0136
Triumph Bonneville (01 - 05)	♦ 4364
Triumph Daytona, Speed Triple, Sprint & Tiger (97 - 05)	♦ 3755
Triumph Triples and Fours (carburettor engines) (91 - 04)	♦ 2162
VESPA P/PX125, 150 & 200 Scooters (78 - 06)	0707
Vespa Scooters (59 - 78)	0126
YAMAHA DT50 & 80 Trail Bikes (78 - 95)	◊ 0800
Yamaha T50 & 80 Townmate (83 - 95)	◊ 1247
Yamaha YB100 Singles (73 - 91)	◊ 0474

Title	Book No
Yamaha RS/RXS100 & 125 Singles (74 - 95)	0331
Yamaha RD & DT125LC (82 - 87)	◊ 0887
Yamaha TZR125 (87 - 93) & DT125R (88 - 02)	◊ 1655
Yamaha TY50, 80, 125 & 175 (74 - 84)	◊ 0464
Yamaha XT & SR125 (82 - 03)	◊ 1021
Yamaha Trail Bikes (81 - 00)	2350
Yamaha 2-stroke Motocross Bikes 1986 - 2006	2662
Yamaha YZ & WR 4-stroke Motocross Bikes (98 - 07)	2689
Yamaha 250 & 350 Twins (70 - 79)	0040
Yamaha XS250, 360 & 400 sohc Twins (75 - 84)	0378
Yamaha RD250 & 350LC Twins (80 - 82)	0803
Yamaha RD350 YPVS Twins (83 - 95)	1158
Yamaha RD400 Twin (75 - 79)	0333
Yamaha XT, TT & SR500 Singles (75 - 83)	0342
Yamaha XZ550 Vision V-Twins (82 - 85)	0821
Yamaha FJ, FZ, XJ & YX600 Radian (84 - 92)	2100
Yamaha XJ600S (Diversion, Seca II) & XJ600N Fours (92 - 03)	♦ 2145
Yamaha YZF600R Thundercat & FZS600 Fazer (96 - 03)	♦ 3702
Yamaha FZ-6 Fazer (04 - 07)	♦ 4751
Yamaha YZF-R6 (99 - 02)	♦ 3900
Yamaha YZF-R6 (03 - 05)	♦ 4601
Yamaha 650 Twins (70 - 83)	0341
Yamaha XJ650 & 750 Fours (80 - 84)	0738
Yamaha XS750 & 850 Triples (76 - 85)	0340
Yamaha TDM850, TRX850 & XTZ750 (89 - 99)	◊ ♦ 3540
Yamaha YZF750R & YZF1000R Thunderace (93 - 00)	♦ 3720
Yamaha FZR600, 750 & 1000 Fours (87 - 96)	♦ 2056
Yamaha XV (Virago) V-Twins (81 - 03)	♦ 0802
Yamaha XVS650 & 1100 Drag Star/V-Star (97 - 05)	♦ 4195
Yamaha XJ900F Fours (83 - 94)	♦ 3239
Yamaha XJ900S Diversion (94 - 01)	♦ 3739
Yamaha YZF-R1 (98 - 03)	♦ 3754
Yamaha YZF-R1 (04 - 06)	♦ 4605
Yamaha FZS1000 Fazer (01 - 05)	♦ 4287
Yamaha FJ1100 & 1200 Fours (84 - 96)	♦ 2057
Yamaha XJR1200 & 1300 (95 - 06)	♦ 3981
Yamaha V-Max (85 - 03)	♦ 4072

ATVs

Title	Book No
Honda ATC70, 90, 110, 185 & 200 (71 - 85)	0565
Honda Rancher, Recon & TRX250EX ATVs	2553
Honda TRX300 Shaft Drive ATVs (88 - 00)	2125
Honda TRX300EX, TRX400EX & TRX450R/ER ATVs (93 - 06)	2318
Kawasaki Bayou 220/250/300 & Prairie 300 ATVs (86 - 03)	2351
Polaris ATVs (85 - 97)	2302
Polaris ATVs (98 - 06)	2508
Yamaha YFS200 Blaster ATV (88 - 02)	2317
Yamaha YFB250 Timberwolf ATVs (92 - 00)	2217
Yamaha YFM350 & YFM400 (ER and Big Bear) ATVs (87 - 03)	2126
Yamaha Banshee and Warrior ATVs (87 - 03)	2314
Yamaha Kodiak and Grizzly ATVs (93 - 05)	2567
ATV Basics	10450

TECHBOOK SERIES

Title	Book No
Twist and Go (automatic transmission) Scooters Service and Repair Manual	4082
Motorcycle Basics TechBook (2nd Edition)	3515
Motorcycle Electrical TechBook (3rd Edition)	3471
Motorcycle Fuel Systems TechBook	3514
Motorcycle Maintenance TechBook	4071
Motorcycle Modifying	4272
Motorcycle Workshop Practice TechBook (2nd Edition)	3470

◊ = not available in the USA   ♦ = Superbike

The manuals on this page are available through good motorcycle dealers and accessory shops.
In case of difficulty, contact: **Haynes Publishing**
(UK) +44 1963 442030   (USA) +1 805 498 6703
(SV) +46 18 124016
(Australia/New Zealand) +61 3 9763 8100

Preserving Our Motoring Heritage

< *The Model J Duesenberg Derham Tourster. Only eight of these magnificent cars were ever built – this is the only example to be found outside the United States of America*

Almost every car you've ever loved, loathed or desired is gathered under one roof at the Haynes Motor Museum. Over 300 immaculately presented cars and motorbikes represent every aspect of our motoring heritage, from elegant reminders of bygone days, such as the superb Model J Duesenberg to curiosities like the bug-eyed BMW Isetta. There are also many old friends and flames. Perhaps you remember the 1959 Ford Popular that you did your courting in? The magnificent 'Red Collection' is a spectacle of classic sports cars including AC, Alfa Romeo, Austin Healey, Ferrari, Lamborghini, Maserati, MG, Riley, Porsche and Triumph.

A Perfect Day Out

Each and every vehicle at the Haynes Motor Museum has played its part in the history and culture of Motoring. Today, they make a wonderful spectacle and a great day out for all the family. Bring the kids, bring Mum and Dad, but above all bring your camera to capture those golden memories for ever. You will also find an impressive array of motoring memorabilia, a comfortable 70 seat video cinema and one of the most extensive transport book shops in Britain. The Pit Stop Cafe serves everything from a cup of tea to wholesome, home-made meals or, if you prefer, you can enjoy the large picnic area nestled in the beautiful rural surroundings of Somerset.

> *John Haynes O.B.E., Founder and Chairman of the museum at the wheel of a Haynes Light 12.*

< *The 1936 490cc sohc-engined International Norton – well known for its racing success*

The Museum is situated on the A359 Yeovil to Frome road at Sparkford, just off the A303 in Somerset. It is about 40 miles south of Bristol, and 25 minutes drive from the M5 intersection at Taunton.
Open 9.30am - 5.30pm (10.00am - 4.00pm Winter) 7 days a week, *except Christmas Day, Boxing Day and New Years Day*
Special rates available for schools, coach parties and outings Charitable Trust No. 292048